AQUINAS AND THE
NICOMACHEAN ETHICS

Aristotle's *Nicomachean Ethics* is the text that had the single greatest influence on Aquinas's ethical writings, and the historical and philosophical value of Aquinas's appropriation of this text provokes lively debate. In this volume of new essays, 13 distinguished scholars explore how Aquinas receives, expands on, and transforms Aristotle's insights about the attainability of happiness, the scope of moral virtue, the foundation of morality, and the nature of pleasure. They examine Aquinas's commentary on the *Ethics* and his theological writings, above all the *Summa theologiae*. Their essays show Aquinas to be a highly perceptive interpreter, but one who also brings certain presuppositions to the *Ethics* and alters key Aristotelian notions for his own purposes. The result is a rich and nuanced picture of Aquinas's relation to Aristotle that will be of interest to readers in moral philosophy, Aquinas studies, the history of theology and the history of philosophy.

Tobias Hoffmann is Associate Professor of Philosophy at The Catholic University of America, Washington, DC. His most recent book is *Creatura intellecta* (2002) and he has edited several anthologies, including *A Companion to Angels in Medieval Philosophy* (2012).

Jörn Müller is Professor of the History of Philosophy at the University of Würzburg. His most recent book is *Willensschwäche in Antike und Mittelalter* (2009) and he has edited several anthologies, including a collection of commentaries on Plato's *Phaedo* (2011).

Matthias Perkams is Lecturer in Ancient and Medieval Philosophy at the University of Jena. His most recent book is *Selbstbewusstsein in der Spätantike* (2008). He has edited several anthologies and Latin-German text editions, most recently *Peter Abaelard, Theologia Scholarium* (2010).

AQUINAS AND THE
NICOMACHEAN ETHICS

EDITED BY

TOBIAS HOFFMANN, JÖRN MÜLLER, AND
MATTHIAS PERKAMS

CAMBRIDGE
UNIVERSITY PRESS

CAMBRIDGE
UNIVERSITY PRESS

University Printing House, Cambridge CB2 8BS, United Kingdom

Cambridge University Press is part of the University of Cambridge.

It furthers the University's mission by disseminating knowledge in the pursuit of
education, learning and research at the highest international levels of excellence.

www.cambridge.org
Information on this title: www.cambridge.org/9781107576407

© Cambridge University Press 2013

First published 2013
First paperback edition 2015

A catalogue record for this publication is available from the British Library

Library of Congress Cataloguing in Publication data
Aquinas and the Nicomachean ethics / edited by Tobias Hoffmann,
Jorn Muller, and Matthias Perkams.
pages   cm
Includes bibliographical references and index.
ISBN 978-1-107-00267-8 (hardback)
1. Thomas, Aquinas, Saint, 1225?–1274.   2. Aristotle. Nicomachean ethics.
I. Hoffmann, Tobias, 1967– editor of compilation.
B765.T54A683   2013
171'.3 – dc23   2013011403

ISBN 978-1-107-00267-8 Hardback
ISBN 978-1-107-57640-7 Paperback

Additional resources for this publication at www.cambridge.org/hoffmann

Contents

Contributors

KEVIN FLANNERY, S. J. is Professor of the History of Ancient Philosophy at the Gregorian University in Rome.

MARKO FUCHS is Research Associate in Philosophy at the University of Bamberg.

JEFFREY HAUSE is Associate Professor of Philosophy and of Classical and Near Eastern Studies at Creighton University.

JENNIFER A. HERDT is Professor of Christian Ethics at Yale University.

TOBIAS HOFFMANN is Associate Professor of Medieval Philosophy at The Catholic University of America.

T. H. IRWIN is Professor of Ancient Philosophy in the University of Oxford.

BONNIE KENT is Professor of Philosophy at the University of California, Irvine.

JÖRN MÜLLER is Professor of the History of Philosophy at the University of Würzburg.

MICHAEL PAKALUK is Professor of Philosophy and Chair of the Department of Philosophy at Ave Maria University.

MATTHIAS PERKAMS is Lecturer in Ancient and Medieval Philosophy at the University of Jena.

MARTIN PICKAVÉ is Canada Research Chair in Medieval Philosophy at the University of Toronto.

CANDACE VOGLER is the David B. and Clara E. Stern Professor of Philosophy at the University of Chicago.

KEVIN WHITE is Associate Professor of Medieval Philosophy at The Catholic University of America.

Acknowledgements

We are grateful above all to the authors for their excellent contributions to this volume. Our thanks are also due to Hilary Gaskin for her valuable suggestions, as well as to her staff at Cambridge University Press. Additionally, we would like to express our gratitude to Francis Feingold, who undertook linguistic revisions, proofread the manuscript, and compiled the index, and to Elena Marchetti for her advice in finding a suitable cover image. Finally, we would like to thank the Alexander von Humboldt Foundation and The Catholic University of America for their support of this project.

Abbreviations

Aristotle

An.	*De anima*
Cael.	*De caelo*
Cat.	*Categoriae*
EE	*Ethica Eudemica*
EN	*Ethica Nicomachea*
Int.	*De interpretatione*
Phys.	*Physica*
Pol.	*Politica*
Rhet.	*Rhetorica*
Top.	*Topica*

Aquinas

In BDT	*Super Boethium De trinitate*
In Sent.	*Scriptum super libros Sententiarum*
QDA	*Quaestiones disputatae De anima*
QDC	*Quaestio disputata De caritate*
QDM	*Quaestiones disputatae De malo*
QDV	*Quaestiones disputatae De veritate*
QDVCard	*Quaestio disputata De virtutibus cardinalibus*
QDVCom	*Quaestio disputata De virtutibus in communi*
Quodl.	*Quodlibet*
SCG	*Summa contra Gentiles*
SLA	*Sententia libri De anima*
SLDCM	*Sententia super librum De caelo et mundo*
SLE	*Sententia libri Ethicorum*
SSM	*Sententia super Metaphysicam*
ST	*Summa theologiae*
ST 1	*Prima pars*
ST 1–2	*Prima Secundae*
ST 2–2	*Secunda Secundae*
ST 3	*Tertia pars*

Other abbreviations

a.	articulus
arg.	argumentum
pr.	prooemium
q.	quaestio
qc.	quaestiuncula
resp.	responsio (i.e., corpus articuli)
s.c.	sed contra

CHAPTER ONE

Introduction

Tobias Hoffmann, Jörn Müller, and Matthias Perkams

The ethics of Thomas Aquinas should be counted among the most fruitful and influential approaches to moral philosophy. It is often seen as the medieval counterpart to the towering achievements of ancient and modern ethics produced by thinkers like Aristotle and Immanuel Kant.[1] But its impact cannot be measured solely in terms of its contribution to the history of philosophy. Leading proponents of contemporary virtue ethics have drawn heavily on Aquinas's ethics in their seminal works on the topic. To mention just one famous example: Alasdair MacIntyre's attempt to revitalize virtue ethics as a rival ethical paradigm to modern deontology and consequentialism culminates in his extensive treatment of Aquinas.[2] MacIntyre argues that the main achievement of Aquinas's approach is grounded in his successful blending of two traditions that might at first glance seem incompatible: on the one hand, Aristotle's moral philosophy, which centers on earthly happiness and its achievement by way of naturally acquired virtues like wisdom, prudence, justice, temperance, and courage; on the other hand, Augustine's moral theology, which stresses that complete happiness exists only in the afterlife and is attained by the divinely infused virtues of faith, hope and charity.

MacIntyre's claims may certainly be disputed in several respects, but at its core his thesis stands unchallenged: it is generally agreed that Aquinas developed his ethics thanks largely to a close reading of Aristotle's *Nicomachean Ethics* (*EN*). To date, the scholarship in this area has provided no clear picture of how Aquinas deals with and depends on Aristotle's ethics. The question of how to assess his attitude toward Aristotle's moral philosophy is still highly controversial and largely influenced by preconceived ideas about the relationship between ancient and Christian ethics. For some scholars, Aquinas's use and interpretation of the *EN* is merely a

[1] To mention just one recent example: Irwin 2007 devotes nine chapters (about 220 pages) to Aquinas in his reconstruction of the historical development of ethics from Antiquity up to the Reformation.
[2] See MacIntyre 2007 (1st edn. 1981), chs. 12–13; 1988, chs. 6–11; 1990, chs. 5–6.

piece of theology that has no value as an interpretation of Aristotle. For others, Aquinas's reading of the *EN* is a highly successful elucidation of Aristotle's own intention. Efforts to mediate between the two positions have not been able to bring the issue to rest. Thus the question remains open: Did Aquinas distort and obscure Aristotelian ethics, or did he draw out more clearly some of its deeper implications?

The present volume intends to make some progress on these issues by offering a more systematic approach than has yet been done. By way of introduction, we will now map out the major issues involved in answering the question about Aquinas's relation to Aristotle's *Ethics*. First, we will provide a rough sketch of Aristotle's influence on Aquinas's ethics, which will be refined by the essays contained in this book. Here we will devote some space to Aquinas's commentary on the *EN*, the *Sententia libri Ethicorum*; for though – as we will argue below – this work is not necessarily the best source from which to study the relation between Aquinas and the *EN*, it nevertheless has been the subject of some scholarly debate, and here is the best place to present an overview of it (Section 1.1). This section will also enumerate various problems, questions, and issues surrounding Aquinas's handling of the *EN* in his whole œuvre, which will be addressed in our volume. The second task of this introduction is to state the specific aims and the overall structure of the project as it is instantiated in the individual contributions to the volume (Section 1.2). Lastly, we will take a glance at some key conclusions that will result from the investigations in this volume (Section 1.3).

1.1   A sketch of Aristotle's influence on Aquinas's *Ethics*

Aristotle's enormous influence on Aquinas's own moral thinking is well attested by the fact that the *EN* is by far the most frequently cited single work in his major systematic writings on ethics, the *Sentences* commentary (*In Sent.*) and the *Secunda Pars* of the *Summa theologiae* (*ST*).[3] Furthermore, the definitive account of his ethics in the *ST* (especially in the *Prima Secundae*) shows significant structural parallels with Aristotle's treatment; this is most noticeable in the way he structures the whole subject matter of moral philosophy but is also evident in his treatment of some individual topics. Aquinas was well acquainted with Aristotle's ethics from the earliest stages of his academic career. As a student in Paris in 1246–47, he

---

[3] For a detailed analysis of these quotations and the different uses to which Aquinas puts them throughout his career, see Jordan 1992. For some statistics, see Chapter 3, Section 3.4, in this volume.

probably had already become familiar with the early commentaries on the first three books of the *EN*, written by different masters in the faculty of arts.[4] But the quantum leap was achieved by the Latin translation of all ten books of the *EN* carried out by Robert Grosseteste, bishop of Lincoln – the so-called *translatio Lincolniensis* – at approximately this time.[5] When, shortly afterward, Aquinas became a student of and secretary to Albert the Great at Cologne during the years 1248–52, he was given responsibility for the editing of his teacher's course, *Super Ethica*, the first Latin commentary on the whole of the *EN*. His intense editorial work deeply influenced Aquinas's own view of Aristotle's ethics, and it meant that he knew both texts, the Aristotelian source as well as Albert's commentary on it, virtually by heart from early on.[6]

Aquinas composed his own commentary on the *EN*, the *Sententia libri Ethicorum*, rather late in his life, approximately 1271–72, while he was teaching at Paris for the second time in his academic career.[7] Aquinas must have accorded considerable importance to commenting on the *EN*, for, as a professor of theology, he had many other obligations, and commenting on philosophical texts would not have been high on the list. Therefore, the *SLE* would seem to be the natural place to look for the way in which Aquinas understood and then adopted, criticized, and/or transformed Aristotle's ethics. But in order to see whether it actually is the best basis for assessing Aquinas's Aristotelianism, it is important to be clear about the interest Aquinas was pursuing in composing this commentary.

A recent debate between Mark Jordan and Christopher Kaczor illustrates well one of the major hermeneutic difficulties concerning the *SLE*. Does Aquinas intend to offer his own views on the matters investigated in this commentary (as Kaczor supposes), or does he merely want to offer an adequate interpretation of Aristotle's text (as Jordan thinks)? Put differently: Does the commentator speak in his own voice throughout, even when he

---

[4] Gauthier 1971, xv–xvii, argues for this because of the way Aquinas, even late in his career, deliberately uses earlier translations of the *EN* and reproduces some of the arts masters' mistaken interpretations. The earlier translations are the *Ethica vetus*, i.e., the "older" translation of books 2 and 3, and the *Ethica nova*, which covered book 1; together they formed the *Liber Ethicorum*. For a good overview of the impact of the *EN* on medieval ethics see Wieland 1982, which was supplemented by recent contributions to the topic in Bejczy 2008.

[5] The critical edition is found in fascicles 3 and 4 of Aristoteles Latinus 26/1–3. The revised text used by Aquinas is printed at the beginning of each *lectio* in the Leonine edition of the *SLE*.

[6] For a detailed account of the sources of Aquinas's study and use of the *EN* and for many other philological details relevant to our topic, see Gauthier 1969 and 1971.

[7] The critical edition of the *SLE* was provided by Gauthier in 1969 as volume 47 of the Editio Leonina. Bourke 1974 defends an earlier dating of the *SLE* against Gauthier (and many others). He thinks that Aquinas developed it as a draft for a course of lectures for young beginners in the Dominican order around 1261–64, but only completed the editing and had it copied later in Paris, after 1270.

is not explicitly contradicting Aristotle?[8] This problem is mainly caused by the literary form of the *SLE*: it is a literal commentary that sticks very closely to the Aristotelian text, only occasionally raising difficulties or entertaining digressions in order to illuminate the subject further. (Albert, by contrast, offers much more discussion of the text, adding *quaestiones* in his first commentary and many digressions in his second one.) The controversy between Jordan and Kaczor hinges mainly on their different understandings of various "disclaimers" in the *SLE* by which Aquinas seems to distance himself from Aristotle, at least in some areas.[9] But on a deeper level the *SLE*'s literary form indicates a general problem concerning its nature. Three different approaches have been tried:

(1)   The *SLE* as a (crypto-)theological work: arguably still the most influential scholarly treatment of the *SLE* was presented 60 years ago by Henry Jaffa, a student of Leo Strauss, in his *Thomism and Aristotelianism*. The main thrust of his argument is that in his commentary Aquinas imputes at least six non-Aristotelian principles of revealed theology (e.g., personal immortality and divine providence) to the *EN* in an unwarranted manner and thus turns the *SLE* into a statement of his own Christian convictions.[10] Although there has been much criticism of Jaffa's work, in detail as well as in general, there are still some scholars who follow his general approach.[11] The main difference between them and Jaffa himself concerns their respective evaluations of this model: while most of them applaud Aquinas's approach in the *SLE* as a fruitful development of Aristotle's moral philosophy (see, e.g., Jenkins 1996) and as a long-standing contribution to the project of a theological *ethica perennis*, Jaffa mainly views it as a deliberate distortion of Aristotle's work.

(2)   The *SLE* as a philosophical work: James Doig, who has written the most comprehensive treatment of the commentary to date, defends

---

[8] As Chenu 1950, 177 thinks. For Aquinas's philosophical commentaries on Aristotle in general, see Grabmann 1926, Owens 1974, Elders 1987, and Jenkins 1996.

[9] While Jordan 1991 thinks that these disclaimers show that Aquinas does not identify with what Aristotle writes, Kaczor 2004 argues to the contrary: exactly because Aquinas clearly indicates where he diverges from Aristotle, he subscribes to the rest of the text. In reply, Jordan emphasized that their discussion is not a purely exegetical one, but rather a dispute "about whether Thomas can be drafted into the service of certain modern projects" (Jordan 2004, 379).

[10] See Jaffa 1952, especially 186–8 for the six principles.

[11] For a powerful criticism of Jaffa's whole project, see the short but venomous review by Gauthier 1954, 56, who considers Jaffa's study an "amateur work" ("non pas . . . un livre de science, mais . . . les réflexions d'un amateur," 159). As a matter of fact, Jaffa's book offers more of an essay in intellectual history than a thorough philosophical analysis of Aquinas's texts. Furthermore, it is clearly outdated in scholarly terms.

Aquinas against Jaffa's accusations and claims that Aquinas in his commentary elaborated and adopted precisely what he views as the basic philosophical content of the *EN*, without any illicit importation of theological doctrine. Doig emphasizes the crucial junctures where Aquinas tacitly or overtly departs from previous philosophical readings of the *EN* in the commentaries of Averroes, Albert the Great, and the Arts Masters. The focus here is mainly on historical points and therefore bypasses some crucial philosophical issues. Nonetheless Doig considers the *SLE* to be "philosophical in nature" (Doig 2001, xvi) and sees it as the most important contribution to Aquinas's statement of his own moral philosophy, somehow independent from the ideas worked out in the *Secunda Pars* and elsewhere in his theological works (which Doig takes into account only occasionally).[12]

(3) The *SLE* as a "mere" commentary: apart from these diametrically opposed interpretations by Jaffa and Doig (which are at the same time contributions to the long-standing debate of whether there is an "autonomous" philosophical ethics in Aquinas at all),[13] there is a kind of "deflationary" reading that stays clear of both Scylla and Charybdis. As Ralph McInerny put it in his foreword to the reprint of C. I. Litzinger's English translation of the *SLE*, "Thomas took his first and primary task to be getting the Aristotelian text right. Far from baptizing Aristotle, Thomas as a commentator is intent on rescuing Thomas [*recte*: Aristotle] from the misreadings of Averroes and others."[14] In this approach, which dates back at least to the great medievalist Martin Grabmann (1926, 283), the *SLE* is regarded as a basically exegetical project in which Aquinas tries to come as close as possible to Aristotle's intention (*intentio Aristotelis*) without venturing into the perilous dichotomy of "philosophy versus theology."[15] This reading sensibly avoids some of the very thorny issues of the general debate in favor of concentrating on concrete analysis, but it seems to neglect what Aquinas states unequivocally in one of his commentaries on Aristotle, namely that "the study of philosophy is

[12] See Doig 2001, esp. ch. 6, where he offers a systematic reconstruction of the contents of the *SLE*.

[13] See Bradley 1997, who argues against the attempt by Kluxen 1964 (3rd edn. 1998) to extract a philosophical ethics from the theological synthesis in Aquinas. For this controversy with regard to the *SLE* in particular, see Doig 2001, ch. 4.

[14] McInerny 1993, x. A drawback of this reprint is the fact that the translation published by Litzinger in 1964 has not been adjusted to the critical text by Gauthier, which appeared in 1969.

[15] See, e.g., Bourke 1974, Elders 1987, 77–123, Jordan 1992, and Kenny 1999.

not for the sake of knowing what people have said but to attain to the truth."[16]

These three interpretations are to a certain extent tied to another difficulty that besets the interpretation of the *SLE*: what motivated Aquinas to write this commentary? Since it most certainly did not grow out of his ordinary academic teaching at the time of its composition – it is not based on an actual course given in Paris between 1269 and 1272 – it must have been undertaken for other reasons. Was it perhaps intended as a kind of basic textbook for students in order to introduce them to the central issues of moral philosophy? One plausible and widespread assumption is that Aquinas composed this commentary, along with the simultaneous *Tabula libri Ethicorum*, as a preparation for the comprehensive account of ethics he gives in the *Secunda Pars*. This reading is mostly favored by authors who see the *SLE* as a kind of theological work, or at least as a part of a larger theological project. But Doig (2001, ch. 5) has offered some evidence that the *SLE* might postdate large portions of the *Secunda Pars*. This fact would point rather in the opposite direction; namely that the *SLE*, rather than being instrumentally subordinated to theological purposes, was instead composed as an independent contribution to philosophical ethics. This issue certainly does not affect the *SLE* alone but rather would in principle affect every philosophical commentary written by Aquinas; nevertheless, it bears further witness to the complexities at work here.

While the character of the *SLE* is the subject of lively debate, this debate takes place for the most part in journal articles and book chapters, each of which have a rather limited scope and which exemplify a tendency to unjustified generalizations. The only book-length studies available in English are by Jaffa and Doig.[17] The reluctance on the part of scholars to deal with the *SLE* in adequate detail may have been partly caused by the hermeneutic difficulties mentioned above. It was probably also caused by the fact that – of all people – René Antoine Gauthier, who spent a considerable amount of time on his truly outstanding edition of the *SLE*, belittled it as an "œuvre manquée," a failed work, especially when

---

[16] Aquinas, *Sententia super librum De caelo et mundo* 1.22 n. 8, Editio Leonina 3:91a: "studium philosophiae non est ad hoc quod sciatur quid homines senserint, sed qualiter se habeat veritas." That Aquinas is interested in the "truth of the matter" (*veritas rei*) and not only in the opinions of others is also attested in the *SLE* (e.g., 10.13 lines 116–22).

[17] There are two books available in German that focus directly on the reception of the *EN* in Aquinas's ethics with particular emphasis on the *SLE*: Papadis 1980, which offers less of an analysis than a paraphrase of the *SLE*; Rhonheimer 1994, which is more ambitious and more thorough, but tends to read Aristotle as well as Aquinas in an idiosyncratic manner. For an excellent Italian monograph that studies the notions of practical reason, moral science, and prudence in the *SLE*, see Melina 1987.

compared with his teacher Albert the Great's first commentary on the *EN*.[18] To be sure, the *SLE* has also been defended by some scholars as a serious contribution to our understanding of Aquinas's ethical views and as an insightful commentary on the *EN*,[19] but the overall tendency is still not in its favor: it is thought that it does not really help us to understand the Aristotelian text properly, or else that it lacks originality, especially when compared to the treatment of ethical topics in the *ST*.

1.2   Issues, aims, and structure of this volume

Notwithstanding the hermeneutic problems outlined above, any genuine attempt to consider the influence of Aristotle's *EN* on the formation of Aquinas's ethics will have to take the *SLE* and the interpretations offered in it seriously. But a purely internal analysis of this work runs the risk of losing the overall perspective which is needed in order properly to evaluate Aquinas's achievements. So far, not enough attention has been given to Aquinas's Aristotelianism or lack thereof in his non-commentary writings on ethics. Yet a comparison between the *SLE* and his major theological works like *In Sent.* and *ST* is especially crucial for illuminating Aquinas's appropriation of Aristotle, for in the *SLE* he is engaged specifically with commenting on Aristotle, whereas in the theological works he incorporates Aristotle's ethics more freely into his own ethical theory. The single-minded concentration on the *SLE* is a major shortcoming of both Jaffa's and Doig's treatments of the issue, and this shortcoming must be mended, especially in those topics where Aristotelian ethics seems to clash with a Christian outlook. To give just one prominent example: How does Aquinas deal with the fact that Aristotle praises magnanimity as the crowning achievement of virtue while the opposite attitude (i.e., humility) is praised in Christianity (see Gauthier 1951 and Hoffmann 2008)? Or to put it more generally: How is it possible for a Christian author like Aquinas to incorporate a catalog of pre-Christian virtues into his religious world view? The analysis of issues like these also promises to offer valuable insights into Aquinas's understanding of the relationship between reason and faith.

Consequently, Aquinas's commentary has to be compared with his systematic investigation of the corresponding ethical matters in his major

---

[18] See Gauthier and Jolif 1970, I,1:131. See also Gauthier 1971, where he calls the *SLE* in a slightly less derogatory manner an "œuvre de sagesse."

[19] The *SLE* was hailed by Shorey (1938, 90) as the most useful commentary on the *EN* ever written. Anthony Kenny (1999, 16) praises it as follows: "On the topic of happiness in particular he often grasps Aristotle's meaning where twentieth-century commentators have missed it."

theological works (not only the *Secunda Pars*, though this should remain a key focal point, but also, for instance, his disputed questions on the virtues, on evil, etc.). Given the controversial views sketched above, the following questions have to be addressed in the course of a more comprehensive investigation of Aquinas's appropriation of the *EN*:

(1)   What are Aquinas's goals in commenting on the *EN*? Does he simply want to offer an adequate reading of the text or is he after the "truth of the matter"? Is the *SLE* philosophical or theological in nature – or neither?

(2)   How good an interpreter of the *EN* is Aquinas – that is, how Aristotelian are his interpretations in terms of historical accuracy? Does he try to integrate Aristotle's views into a different theological or philosophical framework (e.g., Stoicism or Neoplatonism)?

(3)   How does he fare in comparison with earlier medieval interpreters of the *EN*, especially with Albert the Great's *Super Ethica*?

(4)   How does his treatment of the *EN* in the *SLE* differ from his treatment of the *EN* in his systematic theological writings? What accounts for these differences?

(5)   In which areas does Aquinas develop insights from Aristotle's ethics in a new direction? Does he do so intentionally or not?

(6)   Does he offer convincing and fruitful clarifications of key issues from the *EN*? Does he offer persuasive solutions to problems the *EN* raises?

(7)   To what extent does the topic under discussion contribute to a Thomistic "moral philosophy" that might be of interest to contemporary virtue ethicists?

Focusing on these questions will help to refine the nature of the relationship between Aristotle's and Aquinas's ethics. Furthermore, the originality of Aquinas in his appropriation of Aristotle's *Ethics* may be measured on two different levels: first, on a historical level, especially in comparing his understanding of Aristotle with earlier interpretations of the *EN* by his contemporaries; second, on a philosophical level, that is, regarding the cogency and fruitfulness of his treatment of ethical matters.

The overall structure of this volume is designed to capture and mirror the relationship between Aquinas's and Aristotle's ethics as closely as possible by concentrating mainly on the treatment of the major topics which Aquinas inherits from the *EN*: happiness (Jörn Müller); voluntary action (Matthias Perkams); the moral virtues in general (Bonnie Kent); some of the moral virtues in particular: courage (Jennifer Herdt), truthfulness (Kevin Flannery), and justice (Jeffrey Hause); prudence (Tobias

Hoffmann); incontinence (Martin Pickavé); friendship (Marko Fuchs); and pleasure (Kevin White).

In order to provide the volume with a unitary outlook, these authors were encouraged to pay special attention to the list of questions raised above and to structure their essays in the following way:

(1) A summary of Aristotle's position, corroborated by contemporary Aristotelian scholarship, emphasizing aporiai and unsolved problems of interpretation;

(2) Treatment of the relevant issue(s) by Aquinas, with attention both to the formal commentary in the *SLE* and the systematic treatments in *In Sent./ST* (and possibly elsewhere), highlighting any divergences from Aristotle (possibly including also a comparison with Albert's reading in his first *Ethics* commentary, *Super Ethica*, if this were to prove helpful for a refined understanding of Aquinas's position);

(3) Assessment of the philosophical implications of Aquinas's account.

In addition to these contributions to specific issues, the volume is framed at both ends by chapters focusing more generally on the historical accuracy of Aquinas as a commentator on the *EN* (Terence Irwin), on the original method and structure employed in his ethics (Michael Pakaluk), and on the reception of Aquinas's approach in contemporary virtue ethics (Candace Vogler).

1.3 A glance at the results

It is not our intention to provide an exhaustive summary of all the results presented in the individual contributions to this volume. The issues are too complex and the contributors' inquiries are too nuanced to allow for sweeping generalizations. But it is worth highlighting some key points that emerge from the essays in this volume.

(1) In his *SLE*, Aquinas mostly offers a charitable reading of Aristotle's text. He does not distort the text and does not try to introduce a hidden theological agenda as Jaffa suggested (Herdt, Irwin, White). Occasionally, he criticizes Aristotle and signals the need for further clarification, for example with regard to lying (Flannery), but he does not simply smuggle extraneous theological positions into his commentary under the guise of Aristotelianism. In some cases, he tries to improve on the *EN* by adding philosophical considerations that are not openly professed by Aristotle but that Aquinas takes to be implied in Aristotle's statements. A striking example is the

difference between perfect and imperfect happiness, which, according to Aquinas, follows from the Aristotelian criteria of happiness but is not clearly stated by Aristotle himself (Müller). Thus, the *SLE* is more than just a literal exposition of Aristotle's text.

(2) On some points, Aquinas clarifies, expands, or even corrects Aristotle's views (Flannery, Fuchs, Hause, Herdt, Pakaluk). Thus in the *SLE* Aquinas explains the structure of Aristotle's text, addresses its key aporiai and from time to time adds insights from other philosophical traditions. His most conspicuous and conscious deviations from Aristotle, however, were not introduced into his commentary but should rather be sought in his theological writings.

In Aquinas's theological writings we find what are at least in some respects elaborations of Aristotelian themes. His account of truthfulness in the *ST* contains many non-Aristotelian ideas, even though he never loses sight there of Aristotle's treatment in the *EN* (Flannery). Regarding his theory of justice, many of Aquinas's shifts are quite subtle, but Aquinas's treatment of the topic in the *ST* focuses much more on general justice than Aristotle's does (Hause). Aquinas's account of practical principles is highly indebted to Aristotle, but, in addition to "particular practical principles" that he envisions in Aristotelian fashion, he also introduces self-evident "universal practical principles" that are at most only implicit in Aristotle (Hoffmann).

His deviations from Aristotle become more radical when he replaces the Aristotelian notion of friendship with an account of love that is only in certain respects informed by Aristotle (Fuchs). Aquinas furthermore argues that true courage has to be directed by grace toward the heavenly good, as is clear from his treatment of Christian martyrdom (Herdt).

(3) The way in which Aquinas handles Aristotle's ethics varies considerably with each topic discussed in the *EN*. Generally speaking, these variations may be due to at least two different factors. First, there is the influence of other philosophical traditions (like Stoicism and Neoplatonism) on his discussion of the issues, for instance, the significant Stoic contribution to Aquinas's understanding of willing and willed actions (Perkams). Although Aquinas sees Aristotle's *EN* as Antiquity's most valuable contribution to ethics, this does not mean that he simply dismisses other contributions from that period.

Second, there is his interaction with his contemporaries. As a university teacher Aquinas participated in several contemporary debates, which provide the background and sometimes even the framework for his discussions of particular issues. To mention just one example: his emphasis on the imperfect nature of worldly happiness in both the *SLE* and his theological works can be understood as a reaction to "Averroistic" readings, inspired by Albert's commentaries, of Aristotle's doctrine of happiness in the arts faculty (Müller). Awareness of these particular debates may sometimes be more helpful in contextualizing and understanding Aquinas's ethics than general considerations concerning the literary genre. Quite often, Aquinas's goal is simply to contribute to current debates rather than to build up his own complete system of thought.

(4) One crucial notion deserves special mention: the will. Some contributors to this volume (Irwin, Kent, Perkams, and Pickavé) point to the peculiarity of the interpretation Aquinas gives of the will as a power of the soul, to be distinguished from both the practical intellect and from non-rational inclinations, in comparison with the views of both Aristotle himself and of Aquinas's teacher Albert the Great. As a matter of fact, Aquinas's views on the will imply that the systematic structure of his action theory and ethics differs from Aristotle's in an important respect.

Aquinas does not merely assume that the will, as a rational appetite, is a distinct power of the soul. He also takes the further step of claiming that *prohairesis* (Lat. *electio*), i.e., the mental act by which, according to Aristotle, human beings make decisions, has to be ascribed primarily to the will (Irwin). Here he deviates consciously from both Aristotle and Albert, who had defined *prohairesis/electio* as an act that is common to practical reason and appetite, or will, for that matter.

Aquinas thinks, however, that *electio* has to be understood as a true choice by which somebody opts for one of several possible courses of action. Thus the will depends upon the possibilities presented to it by the practical intellect, which guides it to its decisions. Practical reason itself, however, is not determined to one concrete object, for there is a great variety of goods one may pursue. Consequently, for Aquinas, any rational apprehension of a good has to be completed by the will if an act is to take place.

This leads to at least two important differences from Aristotle. First, for Aquinas, the most fundamental action of a human being is the "internal act" of the will, which is completed when the will accepts one course of action proposed by reason (Perkams). The "external act" is in Aquinas's eyes a secondary phenomenon, while it is the only action considered in Aristotle's theory.

Second, Aquinas does not think that someone's choices can be completely determined by the dispositions of his or her character (Kent). At any given moment, reason can focus its attention on objects to which the person is not inclined by his or her already existing dispositions. Consequently, the will can choose differently from what an individual's dispositions would suggest. Thus Aquinas ascribes to virtue a much less determining role than Aristotle did.

It is our hope that this volume will elicit further discussion on the influence of Aristotle's *EN* on the development of Aquinas's ethical thought, and that it will provide the debate with a broadened and refined scholarly basis for its fruitful continuation.

CHAPTER TWO

Historical accuracy in Aquinas's commentary on the Ethics

T. H. Irwin

2.1 Aquinas as historian

Aquinas does some things that a good historian should do. He reads the text closely and sometimes tries to work out Aristotle's intention, from the context and from other works (*ST* 1.79.7 ad 1; 1–2.50.1).[1] But a historian can soon identify serious faults in his approach to Aristotle, and these faults may convince us that he is a bad historian.

An obvious and significant limitation is his failure to refer to the Greek text.[2] His comments do not rest on detailed knowledge of the Greek. He sometimes refers to the sense of a Greek word,[3] but he does not discuss the senses of important terms in the *Ethics*. He relies on a Latin translation that is sometimes misleading. In some significant and familiar cases he is misled. He sometimes takes a point for granted that he would not have taken for granted if he had referred to the Greek rather than the Latin. I will discuss some cases later.

Apart from these recurrent opportunities for misunderstanding and mis-interpretation, Aquinas sometimes interprets the Latin version so as to reach a false rendering of the Greek. When Aristotle says of the incontinent "σῴζεται γὰρ τὸ βέλτιστον, ἡ ἀρχή" (*EN* 7.8.1151a25–6), the Latin has "optimum principium," which Aquinas takes to mean "the best principle is preserved." He takes "optimum" to be an adjective agreeing with "principium." This is an impossible rendering of the Greek, where "τὸ βέλτιστον" is neuter and "ἡ ἀρχή" is feminine. The Greek means "the best

---

[1] Chenu 1964, 153n57, cites evidence of Aquinas's interest in the "intentio" of Aristotle and other authors.

[2] Chenu 1964, 152, 216, maintains that Aquinas "neither effectively knew nor handled the Greek original," though he may sometimes have had information about it. He cites Durantel 1919, 39–49. See also Pelzer 1964, ch. 6, at 185.

[3] See *ST* 1.29.2 resp.; 1.29.3 arg. 3. In this passage, Aquinas relies on Boethius for information on the Greek terms. See also n. 21 below.

thing is preserved, the principle"; it says nothing about a best principle as opposed to other principles.

But a more serious objection to Aquinas, from a historian's point of view, arises from his aims and methods. He does not study Aristotle in order to understand Aristotle, but in order to discover the truth. In his view, "the study of philosophy does not aim at knowledge of what people have thought, but at knowledge of how the truth of things is" (*Sententia super librum De caelo et mundo* 1.22 n. 8). We should therefore expect that his interpretation of Aristotle will be unhistorically influenced by his views about the truth.[4]

Aquinas does not say he tries to fit Aristotle into this general philosophical outlook. His explicit aim is exposition. But he agrees with Scotus's aim of ascribing to Aristotle the most reasonable position that is consistent with the text.[5] Since his philosophical outlook forms his conception of what is most reasonable, he is bound to intrude this outlook into his account of Aristotle. Some have argued that his commentary on the *Ethics* is theological rather than philosophical.[6]

These features of Aquinas's approach to Aristotle help us to understand what contemporary critics mean when they assert that Aquinas is not looking for a genuinely "historical" understanding of Aristotle. One critic speaks of a "tension between the Christian tradition and a historical reading of the *Ethics*" (Kent 1995, 74). Though a philosopher who is sympathetic to the Christian tradition might gain something from Aquinas's treatment of Aristotle, the historian should not, on this view, listen to Aquinas. In particular, his commentaries on Aristotle should be read as aids to the understanding of Aquinas, but not as aids to the historical understanding of Aristotle.[7]

---

[4] "[Aquinas's] effort was, indeed, foredoomed to failure, since it attempted the impossible task of framing a coherent system out of the heterogeneous data furnished by Scripture, the Fathers, the Church, and 'the Philosopher'; and whatever philosophic quality is to be found in the work of Thomas belongs to it in spite of, not in consequence of, its method" (Sidgwick 1886, 145–6). Similarly, Kent 1995, 93 comments on distortions by alleged "Augustinians": "Modern scholars might justifiably fault them for distorting Aristotle's thought, for papering over genuine conflicts between Aristotle's ethics and psychology, on the one hand, and the teachings of Augustine and other Christian authorities, on the other. But if we do fault them, let us bear in mind that Thomas Aquinas and other quasi-'Aristotelian' masters of theology engaged in similar distortions."

[5] Wolter 1990, 165, cites a comment by Scotus on his attitude to Aristotle: "Regarding the meaning [*intentio*] of these philosophers, Aristotle and Avicenna, I do not want to attribute more absurd things to them than the things they themselves say, or the things that necessarily follow from the things they say. And from the things they say I want to take the most reasonable understanding [*intellectus*] I can." (*Ordinatio* 1.8.2.1 n. 250, Editio Vaticana, IV:294)

[6] Doig 2001, Introduction, discusses this question, giving references to different views.

[7] Gauthier maintains this estimate of the historical value of the commentary on the *Ethics*; see Gauthier and Jolif 1970, I,1:130–2.

Before we look more closely at Aquinas, it will be useful to pause on a more general question. What should we look for in an accurate "historical" understanding of Aristotle, and how do we know that Aquinas lacks such an understanding?

2.2   A strict historical view

If contemporary philosophers or classical scholars who undertake to write a line-by-line commentary on a work of Aristotle were to ask themselves what they are trying to achieve, they might claim that they aim at historical accuracy. For a start, they might want to distinguish their task from the tasks that other readers of Aristotle might set themselves. Sometimes a philosopher finds some of Aristotle's remarks suggestive and wants to appropriate them. Sometimes a philosopher thinks Aristotle is broadly right on some question, and so wants to expound an Aristotelian position sympathetically. Neither of these aims is the aim of the commentator.

If philosophers simply claim to be inspired by Aristotle, we need not hold them to an accurate exposition of the text. But if they want to defend or to attack Aristotle, we can reasonably expect a greater degree of accuracy. If someone defends or attacks some view that cannot reasonably be attributed to Aristotle, we learn nothing about the strengths and weaknesses of his view. Still, the demand for accuracy should not be too exacting. If we want to show that Aristotle is on to something, we need not undertake to defend everything he says. Nor need we confine ourselves to a paraphrase of his actual words, or of their logical consequences. We may also appropriately fill gaps in his theory, or apply it to questions that he does not consider.

In contrast to these philosophical approaches to Aristotle, a historical approach aims at a higher degree of accuracy. We study grammar, syntax, and vocabulary in order to grasp the meaning of a given sentence. We read Greek literature, history, and philosophy in order to fit Aristotle into the right historical sequence. We do not confine ourselves to the aspects of Aristotle that seem philosophically plausible or interesting, but we try to understand everything he says, whether we think he is on the right or the wrong track.

These are commonplace remarks about a historical approach. Some add that a genuinely historical approach to Aristotle should avoid philosophical evaluation and should describe his position only in terms that were available to him. According to this strict historical view, we should try to do no more than reconstruct Aristotle's intentions, or the interaction between his intentions and the expectations of his original readers. In these respects our approach should be purely descriptive and should refrain from evaluation.

One might argue that this strict historical view is impossible because its crucial demands are in principle impossible to satisfy. One might maintain, for instance, that the author's intention is unknowable, or that we cannot separate historical description from philosophical evaluation. These "post-positivist" doubts about a strict historical approach are worth discussing, but I do not rely on them. I assume, for present purposes, that a strict historical view can be coherently stated, and that it could guide the practice of historians of philosophy.

From this strict historical view one might infer that Aquinas is not a good historian and that his account of Aristotle is historically inaccurate. In this spirit one might contrast Aquinas and other medieval commentators with "the erudite who contentedly goes about the historical reconstruction of an obsolete system" (Chenu 1964, 207). Whereas the historian is concerned to describe the errors as well as the truths in Aristotle, Aquinas looks for the truth.[8] As Cajetan says, Aquinas often glosses Aristotle in favor of the truth.[9]

2.3   Historical accuracy and philosophical judgment

But is the strict historical view correct? Some doubts arise about whether it accurately captures everything that a historian might seek to discover, and especially about whether the historian's task is purely descriptive without involving philosophical evaluation.

Even if historians should confine themselves to the author's intentions, philosophical questions are relevant to a historical interpretation. According to Aristotle, his discussion of prudence and virtue of character makes it clear that we cannot have either without the other, and that we cannot have one virtue without all the others (6.13.1144b32–1145a2). He does not say in detail why his discussion supports these conclusions. But since he affirms them, and he probably does not affirm them for no reason, it is up to us to find his reasons. We need to think about the most plausible connection

---

[8] See the passage from Gilson quoted with approval by Chenu 1964, 213–14.

[9] Cajetan on *ST* 2–2.174.4, quoted by Chenu 1964, 207. Cajetan observes that Aquinas's purported gloss on Aristotle is not really a gloss on him at all, or else "non glossa textus illius inquantum est Aristotelis, sed inquantum est philosophi. Quoniam philosophia non est nisi verorum, et constat verum non esse vero contrarium."

between what he says about prudence and virtue and what he says about these mutual implications. Our reflections may lead us to reinterpret our initial views of what he says about prudence and virtue. Since he does not set out his case, we have to reconstruct it with the help of philosophical judgment.

Our reconstruction will result in a hypothesis about Aristotle's intentions. It may be wrong; Aristotle may have thought hastily and superficially about the connection that he affirms, and the argument he would have offered if he had been asked might have been laughably inadequate. To evaluate this possibility, we need to ask whether he reveals a tendency to offer laughably inadequate arguments for major claims in his ethical theory, and again we need philosophical judgment to decide which arguments are laughably inadequate. If he does not normally offer laughably inadequate arguments in such cases, we are more likely to capture his intention through a reasonably plausible argument than through a laughably inadequate one. And so, if we are to reconstruct Aristotle's intentions, we may, and indeed we must, appeal to philosophical plausibility.

But in any case historical accuracy does not require us to restrict ourselves to the intentions of the author, or to the interaction between the author and his original readers. If history is about what Alcibiades did and what happened to him, historians need to look at the various aspects of what he did. We can say what he did by describing his actions not only through his intentions but also through their effects; in the latter case, what he did is what he achieved. Even if he did not intend to make Sparta the strongest power in Greece, that was what he achieved, if it was the effect of his actions. If historians of philosophy were to confine themselves to reconstruction of intentions, they would be accepting a restriction that historians in general do not accept. The reconstruction of intentions, therefore, is not the historian's only legitimate aim.

One reason to stick strictly to intentions may be the fear of anachronism. An account is historically inaccurate if it attributes to a philosopher some concept that he clearly did not possess, or if it makes sense only in the context of a debate in which he clearly did not participate. Though it may sometimes be difficult to find a non-circular argument to show that a philosopher did not possess a given concept or did not participate in a particular debate, anachronism of this sort would indeed undermine a claim to have grasped the philosopher's intentions, or to have described how he saw a problem.

Nonetheless, historical accuracy may require us to describe a philosopher's achievements in terms that were not available to him or to his contemporaries. If we were to claim that Aristotle's account of the soul disproves both materialism and dualism, our claim would not be refuted by the mere fact that Aristotle was unaware of materialism and dualism, as we conceive them. No anachronism is involved in this claim, because it does not set out to describe Aristotle's intentions and does not ascribe to him any concepts that he lacks. Similarly, it is not anachronistic to claim that Aristotle offers a plausible alternative to deontological moral theories that he had never heard of.

Whether these claims about materialism, dualism, or deontology are true or false depends on the logical connections between Aristotle's theory and theories that we (as opposed to Aristotle) describe in these terms. By "logical connections" I mean not only the conclusions that deductively follow from Aristotle's theory, but those that it is reasonable to accept in the light of his theory. If we understand "logical connections" in this sense, the exploration of logical connections between Aristotle's views and views he never heard of may help us to understand Aristotle's historical achievement. Hence logical connections deserve the attention of the historian.

We can ask these questions about Aristotle because he offers arguments, and arguments have unnoticed and unintended consequences. Aristotle did not ask about the logical connections between his theories and theories he had never heard of; but the relevant questions can nonetheless be asked and answered. We need not ask ourselves what Aristotle would have said if he had been asked these questions. The structure of his views allows us to answer questions about logical connections without idle speculation about what he would say in some historically absurd circumstances.

On this point the historian's assessment of philosophical achievement is different from the social or political historian's assessment. The social or political historian considers achievement by looking at the causal consequences, intended or unintended, of intentional actions. Historians of philosophy do not consider the causal consequences of a philosopher's views (unless they are tracing influences), but they do consider the logical connections. Social and political history evaluates achievements beyond intentional action because actions have causal consequences. Historians of philosophy evaluate achievements because philosophical views have logical connections.

For these reasons, historians of philosophy who ask these questions about logical connections do not cease to be historians. They are not engaged in philosophy with a special technique as opposed to history with a special subject matter (in Jonathan Bennett's phrase; 1974, 6). They are engaged in history with a special subject matter, because its subject matter is philosophical theories with logical connections. This special subject matter is, however, properly studied by philosophy with a special technique. Without the special subject matter, we would not have a suitable object for a special technique of philosophy. The special technique consists in the exploration of the logical connections between a given philosopher's views and other views; the technique is possible because philosophical views have logical connections.

This conception of a historical inquiry explains why philosophical works of the past are appropriate objects of philosophical study and appropriate starting points for philosophical reflection. We have no reason to concede that history of philosophy, understood as the philosophical study of past philosophers, is not a genuinely historical study. If questions about Alexander's or Caesar's or Leonardo's achievements are proper questions for a historian, questions about Aristotle's achievements are proper questions for a historian too. But insofar as Aristotle's works are philosophical, the appropriate historical examination of this aspect of his achievement is a philosophical examination.

I would not be at all displeased if some readers of these remarks took them to be trite and obvious. I have certainly not tried to say anything original or surprising about what historians of philosophy can or should do. But I believe these points are worth bearing in mind when we are told that a particular interpretation is or is not historically accurate. If what I have said is true, the strict historical view provides the wrong standard for judgments about historical accuracy. We should not expect accurate historians to describe without philosophical evaluation, or to confine themselves to reconstruction of a philosopher's intentions, or to avoid the use of concepts and arguments that are not available to the philosopher himself. If a judgment of inaccuracy is based simply on the fact that an interpreter uses concepts or standards that go beyond the intentions of the philosopher being studied, the judgment is to that extent unjustified.

If, therefore, Aquinas uses Aristotle to answer questions that are asked by, say, Augustine or by the Scriptures, it does not follow that he commits an anachronism, or that he distorts Aristotle. If the answer is not Aristotelian at all but simply relies on a particular theological outlook with no support from the text, Aquinas gives a historically inaccurate account. But if the non-Aristotelian question and the Aristotelian answer have the right logical connection, and the Aristotelian answer can reasonably be derived from Aristotle, then Aristotle answers the question, even though he does not intend to, and the answer is part of a full and accurate historical account of Aristotle's achievement. To decide whether Aquinas contributes to the historical understanding of Aristotle, we need to ask not whether he asks questions that Aristotle asks, or expresses them in Aristotelian terms, but whether his answers are appropriately related to Aristotle.[10]

I am not trying to argue that Aquinas's answers never distort Aristotle for philosophical or theological reasons that are alien to Aristotle. This universal conclusion would be justified only in the light of a complete examination of the *Ethics* commentary. I am arguing for the more modest conclusion that his answers sometimes deserve the attention of the historian. If a plausible case can be made to show that he has grasped some of the logical connections of Aristotle's remarks, his views help us to form a historically accurate account of Aristotle. To see whether his claims about Aristotle are correct or plausible, we cannot simply look at his general statements about his aims. We have to examine his treatment of individual passages.

2.4   The desiring part and the non-rational part

In *EN* 1.13 Aristotle introduces his division of virtues into virtues of character and of thought. To explain this division he divides the soul into two parts. One part of the soul "has reason fully and within itself" (1103a2). Another part is "non-rational, but shares in a way in reason" (1102b13–14). This second part is "appetitive, and in general desiring" (ἐπιθυμητικὸν καὶ ὅλως ὀρεκτικόν, 1102b30).

Aristotle seems to say that one part is characterized by reason and the other by desire. If, therefore, we attribute any sort of reasoning to agents, we are describing their rational part, and if we attribute any sort of desire to them, we are describing their non-rational part that shares in reason. When Aristotle calls this non-rational part "appetitive," he refers to appetite (ἐπιθυμία), one of the three types of desire that he ascribes, following Plato, to the tripartite soul. The other two types are spirit (θυμός) and wish (βούλησις). It is plausible to suppose that the phrase "appetitive and in general desiring" covers all these three types of desire. If this is what Aristotle means, he implies that all types of desire belong to the non-rational part.

---

[10] Some of Gauthier's reasons (see n. 7 above) rest on Aquinas's use of philosophical views and assumptions that he takes to be alien to Aristotle. He rejects, e.g., Aquinas's insertion of his views on the will into his discussion of Aristotle. I consider some of the questions about the will in Section 2.4 below.

This interpretation allows us to treat the passage as simply saying what it initially appears to say. Aquinas is one of the commentators who have accepted it.[11] He asserts that Aristotle puts the will (*voluntas*, the rendering of "βούλησις" that he found in Grosseteste's version) in the non-rational part, and that the phrase "in general desiring" (*universaliter appetibile*, *SLE* 1.20 line 30) includes all desire (*omnis vis appetitiva, sicut irascibilis et voluntas*, line 143).

But though this interpretation is initially plausible, it raises difficulties that ought to be especially clear to Aquinas, given his views about other Aristotelian doctrines. The most general difficulty arises from Aristotle's normal view about *boulēsis*. In *De anima* 3 he treats it as an essentially rational desire (3.10.433a21–4), and he describes incontinence as the overcoming of *boulēsis* by non-rational desire (3.11.434a11–14). Aquinas is well aware of these remarks in the *De anima*. Indeed, they are his ground for attributing a belief in essentially rational desire, and therefore a belief in the will (*voluntas*), to Aristotle (*SLA* 3.8 lines 99–130; *ST* 1.80.2; 1.82.1 arg. 3; 1.87.4; *QDV* 22.4 s.c. 1).

If Aristotle believes in essentially rational desire, the initially plausible interpretation of his remark on the rational and the non-rational part becomes less plausible. For if it is right, Aristotle includes all the desires mentioned in *De anima* 3.9, including *boulēsis*, within the non-rational part. This conception of desire is difficult to reconcile with the *De anima*. But this phrase is the basis for Aquinas's frequent claim that the will is rational "by participation" just as non-rational desire is.[12] At the same time he maintains that the will belongs to reason, as the *De anima* says (*SLE* 1.20 lines 167–8). It depends on rational beliefs and judgments, which are rational "per essentiam" (*ST* 1–2.61.2). The will shares the non-material character of reason (*SLE* 3.12 lines 22–38).

Aquinas's efforts to reconcile his interpretation of our chapter of the *EN* with his other views about Aristotle requires us to understand "rational by participation" in two ways: (1) The will is rational by participation insofar as it is not identical to reason but essentially responds to reason as such. This sort of rationality by participation requires the will to be essentially rational desire. (2) Non-rational desire is rational by participation insofar as it does not essentially respond to reason as such, but can be guided by it in the way young children can be guided by their parents. Our chapter, however, says nothing about two ways of being rational by participation.

---

[11] See Stewart 1892, Burnet 1900, and Gauthier and Jolif 1970, ad loc.
[12] *SLE* 1.20 lines 142–6; *ST* 1–2.56.6 ad 2; 1–2.59.4 ad 2; 1–2.61.2 resp. and ad 2; 2–2.58.4 ad 3.

The only sort of participation in reason that Aristotle allows to the desiring part is the second kind mentioned by Aquinas.

Further difficulties arise from the description, in the same chapter, of continence and incontinence. Both of these display a conflict between the non-rational and the rational part, in which the rational part is correct (1102b14–25). According to Aristotle, both continent and incontinent agents suffer a conflict between their non-rational desire and their correct decision (προαίρεσις). If this is a conflict between the non-rational part and the rational part, decision belongs to the rational part. This is also Aquinas's view of Aristotle's position. Unlike Aristotle in this particular passage, Aquinas observes that the continent and incontinent form decisions (SLE 1.20 lines 83–4: "uterque . . . eligit abstinere"; lines 103–4: "quae ratio eligit"). But Aristotle takes decision to be a type of desire (ὄρεξις), and so he must attribute desire to the rational part. And so, if the initially plausible interpretation of "appetitive and in general desiring" is correct, Aristotle contradicts himself within this one chapter.

But a reasonable alternative is available. "In general desiring" may indicate not that all desire is included in the non-rational part, but rather that the non-rational part is simply a desiring part, in contrast to the rational part, which does not simply desire but rather has distinctively rational desires. If this is what Aristotle means, he does not assign all desire to the non-rational part.[13]

The choice between the two interpretations of "in general desiring" raises a question that often faces an interpreter. If the first interpretation is initially more straightforward and plausible, and the second gives a better sense, we have to decide whether the sacrifice of initial plausibility is justified by the better sense. In this particular sense, the sacrifice of initial plausibility is small and the improvement of sense is great. And so we ought to prefer the second interpretation.

Moreover, this second interpretation is far more attractive than the first if we agree with Aquinas's interpretation of Aristotle's moral psychology. As we have seen, Aquinas treats the will as essentially rational desire, and he maintains that Aristotle recognizes precisely this sort of desire in the De anima. If he had allowed his view about the will and his view about Aristotle's recognition of the will in the De anima to form his view of our passage in the Ethics, he would have had very strong reasons to maintain the second interpretation. He would also have found the right interpretation.

---

[13] See Heliodorus, Commentaria in Aristotelem Graeca, 19.24.20; Aspasius, 35.22, 36.2 (τὸ ὀρεκτικὸν καὶ παθητικόν); Eustratius, Commentaria, 20.118.33–5.

Now perhaps I have exaggerated the costs of the first interpretation and the benefits of the second. I have not pursued the relevant exegetical questions in enough detail to justify a firm decision. But if what I have said is right, it shows something about Aquinas as an interpreter. We might suppose that he most often goes wrong in his interpretation of Aristotle because he does not stick to the plain sense of the text in front of him. He deviates from the plain sense of the text, we might suppose, because of "extraneous" considerations – his views about what Aristotle must mean, either given what Aristotle seems to say elsewhere, or given what Aquinas thinks Aristotle should mean. This diagnosis of Aquinas's errors is completely wrong in the present case. Had he relied on the "extraneous" considerations, he would have given the right account of this passage. His errors result from acceptance of the initially plausible view of the text and inattention to the "extraneous" considerations. Though he could easily have found the right interpretation, and though he gives the grounds for preferring the right interpretation, he does not offer it, because he sticks too scrupulously to the apparently plain sense of the text.

This conclusion is reasonable even if we stick to the strictly historical questions about Aristotle's intentions. The second interpretation relies on the assumptions that Aristotle probably did not intend to contradict what he says in the *De anima* and probably did not intend to contradict himself in the space of a few lines. Some readers may object that these assumptions are excessively charitable, because they overlook Aristotle's frequent tendency to contradict what he says in other works, or even what he says within the space of a few lines.[14] Such an objection is worth considering; but in itself it is not guaranteed to be any more historically accurate than the minimal claim about consistency that I have mentioned.

Moreover, if we understand historical questions, as I have argued we should, to be broader than questions about an author's intentions, it is even more reasonable to find the second interpretation attractive. It is a historical question about the Aristotelian texts whether they express a consistent position, either within the space of twenty lines or within the Corpus as a whole. Even if Aristotle is inconsistent, or not clearly consistent, a particular inconsistency might or might not be easily removed. If it is easily removed, it is historically more accurate to attribute a consistent overall position to Aristotle than to attribute an inconsistent position.

---

[14] David Bostock's commentary on *Metaphysics* 7–8 (Bostock 1994) is marked by extreme opposition to allegedly over-charitable assumptions about Aristotle's tendency towards consistency.

In this case, therefore, Aquinas's error results from reliance on principles that many historical interpreters would applaud. He tries to do justice to the text of Aristotle in front of him, and does not try to impose an interpretation that would fit more easily into the moral psychology of Aristotle or of Aquinas. His choice is mistaken, but not unreasonable.

2.5 Happiness as complete

Some questions about the character and composition of happiness arise in the translation and interpretation of a passage in *EN* 1.7 about the completeness and self-sufficiency of the good.

> Moreover, we think it is most choiceworthy [Lat. *eligibilem*] of all goods, not being counted together [*connumeratam*]. Counted together, then, clearly, we think it more choiceworthy with the smallest of goods; for the good that is added becomes an extra quantity of goods, and the larger of two goods is always more choiceworthy. (1097b16–20)

Aquinas's Latin version is close enough to the Greek to raise the same questions of interpretation. Two paraphrases of this passage have been proposed:

(1)   The good is most choiceworthy if it is chosen without being counted together, but not most choiceworthy if it is counted together. It is the greatest single good, but it is also part of a greater good when it is counted with the goods that are not included in it.

(2)   The good is most choiceworthy because it is not counted together with other goods, but would not be most choiceworthy if it were counted together with other goods. Since it is the compound of all goods, it cannot be part of a greater good that results from counting it together with the goods that lie outside it.

These two interpretations differ in their account of the supposition contained in "counted together." The first interpretation takes this to be a correct supposition, insofar as the good can properly be added to goods that lie outside it. The second interpretation takes the supposition to be impossible. The Greek of this passage, taken by itself, allows both interpretations. So does the Latin version.[15]

---

[15] This is true of the *translatio antiqua*, printed in the Parma, Marietti, and Leonine editions. (The Parma and Marietti texts contain several errors in nn. 65–6.) The *translatio recens* (printed in the Parma edition, vol. 21:19b, and taken from the Didot edition of Aristotle; see preface to vol. 18)

According to the second interpretation, Aristotle takes happiness to be comprehensive, because no other non-instrumental goods can be added to it to produce a greater good than happiness. If happiness is comprehensive, it is more difficult to see how it could consist wholly in contemplation. If it did, contemplation would be the only non-instrumental good. But Aristotle does not seem to believe this exclusive claim about contemplation, because of his remarks on the virtues of character. Hence the second interpretation is preferable.[16]

But this second interpretation faces a difficulty in the light of Aristotle's claims about happiness and good fortune. We might suppose that if happiness is comprehensive, and someone is happy, he cannot become happier; for if he became happier, would some further good not be added to happiness, so that the addition would result in a greater good than happiness? Aristotle, however, believes that happiness can both be improved by addition of further external goods and be lost because of misfortune (1.10.1100b22–30).

Aquinas takes this to be a good reason to favor the first interpretation over the second. He explains the passage on counting together by referring back to Aristotle's previous claim that happiness is self-sufficient (1.7.1097b14–16). A self-sufficient good makes life choiceworthy and lacking nothing (*nullo indigentem*).[17] But we might understand "lacking nothing" in two ways: (1) lacks no necessary good; (2) lacks no good that can belong to human life.[18] These two ways to understand self-sufficiency match the two interpretations of the passage on counting. Once we see that we can take self-sufficiency the first way, we can also endorse the first interpretation of counting (*SLE* 1.9 lines 198–213). Hence we can understand how Aristotle takes happiness to be complete and self-sufficient, but still capable of improvement. The passage on counting, according to the first interpretation, fits the first understanding of self-sufficiency. Since Aristotle does not take happiness to be complete in such a way that nothing can be added to it, he does not intend the second claim about self-sufficiency and adding (*SLE* 1.16 lines 110–25).

prefers the first interpretation, since it renders the first sentence by "aliquid maximum omnium optandum, etiam solum absque bono alio omni."

[16] I will not try to support this judgment in favor of the second interpretation any further on this occasion. The numerous discussions of this passage include: Crisp 1994, Heinaman 1986, Price 1980, Lear 2004, Kenny 1992, and Irwin 2012.

[17] This is the Leonine text. Marietti and Parma have "nullo exteriori indigentem," which fits Aquinas's paraphrase in *SLE* 1.9 line 175. We might also render the Latin, and the underlying Greek, as "needing nothing added," but this rendering would not make it clear why Aquinas thinks two interpretations of the phrase are possible.

[18] Kenny 1999, esp. 18, discusses Aquinas's account of self-sufficiency.

Aquinas, however, does not entirely reject the second interpretation of self-sufficiency and counting. On the contrary, he believes that Aristotle sometimes takes the good to meet these conditions. God as the "total good" meets these conditions (*SLE* 1.9 lines 181–98). Since the happiness we can achieve in this life does not meet these conditions, it is not complete happiness (*SLE* 1.16 lines 205–22). Both views about the self-sufficiency of happiness have to be accepted, in the appropriate contexts, in order to understand Aristotle's whole account of the good.

This interpretation relies on the less plausible interpretation of the passages on self-sufficiency and counting. Moreover, we might object that Aquinas's description of the two grades of self-sufficiency, and therefore of two grades of completeness, rests on his un-Aristotelian concern to prove that happiness in the afterlife is superior to happiness in this life.

These objections underestimate the plausibility of Aquinas's suggestion about self-sufficiency. Aristotle has to recognize something like two grades of happiness and two grades of completeness in order to explain how we can be happy even though good fortune might make us happier. His remarks about the completeness and self-sufficiency of happiness do not make it clear how he intends to make room for added good fortune. But it is reasonable, if we confine ourselves to his intentions, to suppose that he intends his different remarks to make a consistent position. And even if he had no determinate intention about how to make them consistent, we have a reasonable question about whether and how his views are in fact consistent, once we spell out their logical consequences. Aquinas offers reasonable answers to these historical questions.

2.6   The role of the will

I have already commented on Aquinas's introduction of his concept of the will into his comments on Aristotle. I argued that he has a good reason to suppose that Aristotle's remarks on *boulēsis* describe the will; both he and Aristotle recognize this essentially rational desire. But though they both acknowledge the will, it does not follow that they attribute just the same role or roles to it. The Latin versions may give a misleading impression of the role that Aristotle assigns to the will. For they render "*hekousion*" by "*voluntarium*," and the obvious verbal connection between "*voluntarium*" and "*voluntas*" suggests that agents are candidates for praise and blame insofar as they have wills. Since Aquinas believes that we are responsible for our actions insofar as we have wills, the Latin rendering suggests to him that Aristotle agrees with him. Alternatively, we might say that his knowledge of the Latin Aristotle encourages him to accept this view about responsibility and the will. In either case, the apparent support that results from "*voluntarium*" in the Latin version disappears when we find "*hekousion*" in the Greek text; for it is not cognate with "*boulēsis*" and does not by itself suggest that *boulēsis* makes us candidates for praise and blame.

Aquinas, therefore, would probably have argued more carefully and taken less for granted if he had known what we know about the Greek text. But would he have had to abandon his claim that Aristotle agrees with him about responsibility and the will? His case does not rest entirely on the verbal connection that is present in the Latin but absent from the Greek. For in some places where "*voluntarium*" does not appear in the Latin version, he argues on different grounds that Aristotle is talking about the will.

Aristotle believes that actions we are praised or blamed for are "up to us" (ἐφ' ἡμῖν). An action is up to us if the origin is in us (1110a15–18), and when we do an action voluntarily, we are in control (κύριοι) of that action (1113b30–1114a3). But what sort of internal origin makes an action up to us? A minimal answer would say that an action is up to us just in case it is voluntary, and it is voluntary just in case we know that we are doing it. This answer has an unwelcome consequence that Aristotle points out not in his discussion of the voluntary in Book 3, but in Book 5; we know that we are growing old and dying, but neither of these things is voluntary, because neither is up to us (5.8.1135a33–b2; *SLE* 5.13 lines 75–80). Book 5 probably originates in the *Eudemian Ethics*, which argues that an action is voluntary only if we know that we are doing it and it is up to us not to do it (*EE* 2.9.1225b8–10). The Nicomachean discussion of the voluntary does not mention this Eudemian qualification, but unless Aristotle assumes something like it, his account of what is up to us is obviously unsatisfactory.

What further mental state, then, will satisfy the Eudemian qualification? We might think that we need only add that actions that are up to us are caused by our desire. It is puzzling that the Nicomachean account has so little to say about desire. The Eudemian discussion examines it more fully (2.9.1225a36–b1). It suggests that the addition of desire to knowledge does not yet make an action up to us; for some desires may be strong and compelling enough to force us to act, and if our action is forced, it is not up to us, even though it results from our desire (2.8.1225a30–3). To find what makes an action up to us, we need to mention more than knowledge and desire. The Nicomachean account of the voluntary neither asks nor answers this Eudemian question.

It may seem perverse to mention the *Eudemian Ethics* in a discussion of Aquinas; for he had no access to *EE* 2, and he knew nothing about the Eudemian origin of *EN* 5. But the Eudemian discussion is relevant because it presents an objection to the Nicomachean discussion. The objection cannot be anachronistic: it actually occurred to Aristotle. How, then, does the Nicomachean discussion deal with the Eudemian objection? Some possible answers are: (1) The Eudemian objection has not yet occurred to Aristotle. (2) He chooses to ignore it. (3) He believes that it is somehow misguided. (4) He implicitly answers it, because he does not suppose that knowledge and desire ensure that an action is up to us. Aquinas's views on the will defend the fourth answer.

We can evaluate this defense if we consider excuses that are offered for bad action or bad character. Aristotle mentions pleas that rely on the Eudemian conception of desire that is powerful enough to compel us. These pleas claim that all actions aiming at the pleasant or the fine should be treated as forced actions (*EN* 3.1.1110b9–11). Aristotle answers that we should not hold pleasant or fine things responsible for our actions, but we should regard ourselves as the causes, as being "an easy prey" (εὐθήρατον, *venabilem*) to such things (1110b13–14).

What sort of causal relation makes us an "easy prey"? We might suppose that Aristotle simply means that we pursue pleasant and fine things because we want to. But this answer does not address the Eudemian objection that some desires can be sources of compelled action that is not up to us. If Aristotle is to address that objection, he needs to argue that the relevant causal relation excludes this plea of compulsion. Aquinas offers an argument of this sort, since he maintains that in such cases we permit ourselves to be overcome, and that our permission is needed because our will is capable both of accepting and of rejecting these objects of desire (*SLE* 3.2 lines 142–50).

These remarks about permission and the will have no explicit source in Aristotle. But Aquinas may still be right to introduce them into his exposition. Unless Aristotle takes for granted something that he does not say, his answer is open to serious objection. The Eudemian discussion shows that Aristotle at some point recognizes that the objection is serious. It is not unreasonable for an expositor to suggest an answer to the objection. Since Aquinas's answer is available to Aristotle, it deserves consideration as a plausible exposition of the passage. If it is unlikely that Aristotle simply ignores or overlooks the Eudemian objection, Aquinas's answer may capture Aristotle's intention. But even if it does not capture Aristotle's intention, it answers a question about the logical character of his theory; for it shows that the distinctions drawn in the Nicomachean discussion may avoid the Eudemian objections. This is an answer to a historical question about Aristotle's achievement.

We can say something similar about Aristotle's claim in *EN* 3.5 that sometimes we can fairly blame people who act wrongly because they are drunk and people who behave carelessly, even though they cannot help what they do when they are drunk and cannot help their careless behavior. These people cannot plead that their inability to avoid doing what they did exempts them from blame; for they were in control (κύριος, *dominus*) of not getting drunk and not becoming careless (1113b30–1114a7). But what does this control consist in? We have similar options to those that we considered in the passage on being an easy prey. Aquinas offers the same sort of answer; in his view, the relevant sort of control is exercised by the will (*SLE* 3.12 lines 22–38). Aristotle does not say that this is what he intends, but the context supports Aquinas. For Aristotle has just said that since *boulēsis* is for the end, and deliberation is about means to ends, actions about means to ends are in accordance with decision and voluntary.[19] Since the activities of the virtues are about means to ends, virtue and vice are up to us (1113b3–7). In this case our control over whether we are virtuous or vicious is derived from the role of wish, deliberation, and decision in virtue and in acting virtuously.

Whether or not Aquinas is right to introduce the will into his account of Aristotle on praise and blame, we ought to take him seriously as a historically accurate interpreter. The mere fact that Aristotle does not mention *boulēsis* in every place where Aquinas mentions the will does not show that Aquinas's exposition is historically inaccurate. For if we want to understand what Aristotle means by saying that someone leaves himself an easy prey to pleasure, and that someone is in control of taking care, we have to add something to what Aristotle actually says. Similarly, if we want to know what Aristotle achieves in his account of the *hekousion*, we can legitimately ask whether he has a coherent or plausible account of reasonable conditions for being a candidate for praise and blame. We need to ask these questions if we seek historical accuracy. Aquinas asks these questions and gives reasonable answers to them. He therefore advances the historical interpretation of Aristotle. In his treatment of responsibility

---

[19] Aquinas takes Aristotle to mean that the activities of the virtues are voluntary *because* they are in accordance with decision (*SLE* 3.11 lines 14–20).

he does what he should have done, but did not do, in his treatment of the division of the soul: he uses philosophical argument both to clarify Aristotle's meaning and to clarify the philosophical implications of Aristotle's view.

2.7 The *kalon*

It may appear especially implausible to cite Aquinas's treatment of the *kalon* as a contribution to the historically accurate understanding of Aristotle. For in almost all the places in the *Ethics* where Aristotle uses "*kalon*," the medieval Latin translators translate it as "*bonum*."[20] Aquinas does not know when "*bonum*" renders "*kalon*." Aristotle's use of "*kalon*" rather than "*agathon*" in particular contexts ought to attract the notice of a translator and an interpreter. Since Aquinas is unaware of the fact, he can neither record nor explain it, and therefore his exposition is sometimes inaccurate and misleading.[21]

Nonetheless, he often takes Aristotle to be talking about the *honestum* in passages where Aristotle uses "*kalon*," but the Latin has "*bonum*." Aquinas's remarks about the *honestum* at these places in his commentary result from his philosophical judgment that Aristotle is in fact (whatever words he uses) talking about the *honestum*. He believes it is appropriate in contexts

---

[20] See, e.g., 1094b15, 1099a27, 1100b27, 30, 1104b31, 1110b15, 1114b6, 1115a30, b23, 1116a11, b3, 1117a8, 1120a27, 1122b6, 1168a33, 1169a6 ff. At 1099a22 and 1123b8 the translation used by Aquinas has "pulchrum," which he uses in *SLE* 4.7 lines 152–60. "*Bonum*" is used to render "καλόν" at *Met.* 12.7.1072a28, and at 1078a31. In the last passage Moerbeke's version has "Quoniam autem bonum et malum (Greek: τὸ ἀγαθὸν καὶ τὸ καλόν) alterum, hoc quidem enim semper in operatione, bonum autem et in immobilibus." One manuscript reads "*optimum*" for "*malum*." Vuillemin-Diem (Aristoteles Latinus 25/3.2 ad loc.) suggests that Moerbeke might have conjectured "κακόν" for the "καλόν" that he read in the text. The Translation Anonyma (Aristoteles Latinus 25/2) has "Sed quoniam agathon, id est valde bonum, et bonum diversum," where the same editor suggests that "id est . . ." might be a gloss.

[21] See Pelzer 1964, ch. 6. Grosseteste supplies "notulae" to his translation, which often comment on the sense of Greek words or sentences. But he introduces "*bonum*" for "καλόν" without comment, and I cannot find any comment throughout his translation. At the beginning of *EN* 3.5 he remarks that one might use "*turpe*" instead of "*malum*" to render "αἰσχρόν" (Aristoteles Latinus 26/1–3, p. 183), but he makes no parallel comment about "*bonum*" (p. 187). He does the same with bravery (p. 191).

See also Franceschini 1933. At pp. 85–124 he quotes many of Grosseteste's careful observations on Greek terms. In *Commentarius in angelicam hierarchiam* ch. 2 (Franceschini, 106–7) Grosseteste comments on the translation of "καλόν," and suggests that "*pulchrum*" rather than "*bonum*" is sometimes suitable. He connects these different terms with alternative etymologies of "καλόν." If we derive it from "κάλλος," then "*pulchrum*" is a good rendering. If we derive it from "καλεῖν," then "*bonum*" is suitable, "quia bonum suapte natura omnia vocat in sui appetitionem." He does not comment on "*honestum*" as a possible rendering. (It is not relevant to his immediate purposes in this commentary.)

where he finds (i) a contrast between good and pleasant, (ii) claims about praiseworthiness, and (iii) claims about disinterestedness. When he detects a mention of the *honestum*, he normally has at least one of these features in mind. He identifies the specifically moral good with the *honestum*. He relies on St. Ambrose and Cicero, and hence indirectly on Stoic sources, for the view that the relevant features (rationality, non-instrumental goodness, praiseworthiness, unselfishness) are features of the *honestum*.[22] But he also believes that this conception of the *honestum* is part of an Aristotelian moral theory.

Is Aquinas right to attribute views about the *honestum* to Aristotle? Here we raise a larger interpretative question about the character of the *kalon* in Aristotle, and about similarities or differences between his conception of the *kalon* and the Stoic conception that Cicero and others render by "*honestum*." But before we reject Aquinas's view, we ought to be impressed by his success in identifying places where Aristotle actually uses "*kalon*." Since this judgment leads to the identification of instances of "*kalon*," we may reasonably suppose that Aquinas is on to something about Aristotle.

2.8 Conclusion

I have discussed four examples to illustrate some features of Aquinas's method. In the first example I noticed that Aquinas avoids reliance on "extraneous" considerations – Aristotle's other views, Aquinas's moral psychology – and sticks to the passage in front of him. In the first example he gets Aristotle wrong. In the other examples he relies on these "extraneous" considerations, and either gets Aristotle right or comes closer to getting him right.

In the last three examples Aquinas's comments introduce his philosophical views without any explicit warrant from the text. From the strict historical point of view, this admission proves that Aquinas's comments cannot be historically accurate. I have argued against any inference of this sort. Once we think more carefully about what historical accuracy might properly involve, we can see why it would be unreasonable to avoid philosophical judgments, and why it might be quite appropriate to rely on one's own philosophical judgment in the exposition of Aristotle. The question should not be about whether interpreters argue on the basis of their

---

[22] See *SLE* 2.3 lines 153–60, *SLE* 4.4 lines 105–18, *SLE* 4.6 lines 139–44, *SLE* 8.3 lines 20–38, *SLE* 9.7 lines 110–25, *SLE* 9.8 lines 24–33 and lines 114–26, *SLE* 10.9 lines 85–99. The Stoic sources of Aquinas's conception of the *honestum* are made clear in Albert's *Super Ethica*.

T. H. Irwin

philosophical judgment, but about whether their judgment contributes to the understanding of Aristotle's intentions or of his achievement. I have picked a few cases where interpreters can reasonably discuss whether Aquinas's exposition gets Aristotle right. But whatever we eventually decide on this question, he suggests attractive lines of interpretation. If we want to reach a historically accurate account of Aristotle, we ought not to ignore Aquinas's contributions to this goal.

CHAPTER THREE

Structure and method in Aquinas's appropriation of Aristotelian ethical theory

Michael Pakaluk

I wish to address questions of structure and of method in the general appropriation of Aristotelian ethical theory by Aquinas. Under the heading of "structure" I wish to consider principally the scheme of the cardinal virtues in *ST* 2–2, which Aquinas develops in order to organize comprehensively the subject matter of ethics, or, as he says in the Prologue to that part, "so that nothing pertaining to ethics will be overlooked." How much of this scheme is present already in Aristotle? Is the scheme motivated by difficulties in Aristotle? Can it count as a plausible development of Aristotelian ethics? To address these questions properly, we must attend to some key differences in ethical method between Aristotle and Aquinas. Accordingly I will in closing offer a few observations concerning this potentially vast topic.

3.1 Some problems in Aristotle's ethics

Aristotle's treatment of the virtues raises various questions about the nature, number, individuation and relationship of the virtues, which, it is natural to suppose, Aristotle would have been prepared to answer at least tentatively, yet which he never explicitly addresses, for example: What is a virtue anyway? Are some virtues more basic than others? If so, how are less basic virtues related to more basic ones? How should virtues be identified and distinguished from one another? How many virtues are there altogether? Aquinas's scheme of the cardinal virtues provides elegant answers to all of these questions.

(1) What is a virtue? Aristotle gives a famous definition of *moral* virtue ("a state issuing in choices in accordance with a mean relative to us, as a person of practical wisdom would define it," *EN* 2.6.1106b36–1107a2, cf. 2.6.1106b16); yet he regards moral virtues as only one class of human virtues, and human virtues as only one instance of virtue generally, since horses and eyes, as he says, also have virtues (2.6.1106a17–21). Given the

definiteness of his assertions about virtue in *EN* 1 and 2, Aristotle looks to be working with some concept of virtue in general: for example, he says that honor is supposed to be given on account of virtue (1.5.1095b29); virtue is a kind of potential, and not the highest good, because it can lie dormant, unexercised (1.5.1095b33, also 1.8); a virtue is a good in the category of quality (1.6.1096b25); virtue is worth choosing for its own sake, even if nothing were to follow (1.7.1097b2); the addition of virtue does not alter the characteristic work (ἔργον) of a thing or the kind of action that is done (1.7.1098a10–12); activity in accordance with virtue is inherently pleasant, and its pleasures are never at odds with one another (1.8.1099a11–21); happiness seems a prize awarded to virtue (1.9.1099b15); virtue can be perfect or imperfect (1.7.1098a17, 1.9.1100a4, 1.11.1101a14, 1.13.1102a6); and virtue is analogous to physical strength (1.12.1101b16, b33; 2.2.1104a11–18, a30–3). Aristotle could hardly have asserted these things if he lacked a definite notion of what a virtue is. And yet he never purports to offer a general account of virtue, even though, in giving that sort of general account of moral virtue, he apparently concedes that a general account would be desirable.

(2) Are some virtues more basic than others, and, if so, what makes them so? Aristotle evidently does regard some virtues as more basic, as revealed in how he refers to virtues in those passages in the *EN* in which, as if in passing, he gives lists of virtues, or refers to virtues (or persons as having the virtues) by way of example. There are over two dozen such passages,[1] but to give a few representative instances:

> Thus in doing just actions we become *just*, in doing moderate actions we become *moderate*, and in doing courageous actions we become *courageous*. (2.1.1103a34–b2)

> For indeed we are *just*, *moderate*, and *courageous*, and we have the other [states of character] right from birth. (6.13.1144b5–6)

> The same consideration applies also to justice and the other virtues: . . . a person will be more *just* or more *courageous*, and he will do *just* and *moderate* actions to a greater or lesser degree. (10.3.1173a17–22)

> A *wise* person or a *just* person, and the rest, will need necessities for living, but, once someone is sufficiently equipped with these, the just person needs others towards whom and with whom he can do just actions; likewise also

---

[1] There are similar lists and examples, of course, in such works as the *Topics*, yet there Aristotle may simply be referring to virtues which he takes others to regard as obvious or more basic. But compare *Pol.* 7.1.1323a27–9, where he singles out courage, moderation, justice, and practical wisdom.

the *moderate* person and the *courageous* person, and each of the others. (10.7.1177a28–32)[2]

In these passages moderation is given as an example some 20 times; courage, 16; justice, 14; and then other virtues are mentioned once or twice at most. Either courage or moderation is included in every passage. Courage and moderation are paired together 14 times, and when paired together, justice is included half the time as well. So *prima facie* there are three paradigmatic virtues for Aristotle: moderation, courage, and justice. (He tends to use "courage and moderation" when the context involves virtues that moderate passions, which is a narrower scope, and "justice" along with either "courage" or "moderation" in contexts in which a reference to the moral virtues in general is needed, a broader scope.) Moreover, each of these paradigmatic virtues is used at times by Aristotle as a label for the virtuous person simply speaking. This point is obvious as regards justice, since Aristotle says that "justice" in one sense refers to all of the virtues together (5.1.1130a8–9), and Aristotle frequently uses "equitable" (ἐπιεικής), his term for a person who has a refined type of justice, as a term signifying virtue in general (see, e.g., 1.13.1102b10). "Moderate" too, however, can also be used to mean "virtuous" (4.3.1123b5, 4.4.1125b13, 10.8.1179a12, perhaps also 1.13.1103a8, 10.9.1179b33), and apparently so can "courageous" (9.5.1167a20).

In short, it turns out that Aristotle almost never refers to the virtues of Book 4 as examples or in lists of virtues, instead preferring to mention the virtues of Books 3 and 5.

(3) If some virtues can be more basic, how are those less basic virtues related to them? I do not mean merely the question of how the Book 4 virtues relate to the Book 3 and 5 virtues but also, for instance: Aristotle mentions a variety of traits related to practical wisdom (φρόνησις) in Book 6 – insight (σύνεσις), understanding (συγγνώμη), sound deliberation (εὐβουλία) – but how they are related to that apparently more basic virtue is unclear. Similarly, are statecraft (πολιτική) and estate administration (οἰκονομία) species of practical wisdom, or something else? Again, the virtue of justice is grouped with "equitability" (ἐπιείκεια), yet apparently there are also species of justice – distributive, commutative, retributive, and reciprocal. Even among the paradigmatic virtues similar questions arise: although Aristotle groups pleasures of touch together as though they

---

[2] Other such passages in *EN* are: 1101b14–16; 1102b27–8; 1103a5–7; 1103b13–21; 1103b34–1104a12; 1104a18–19; 1104a25–7; 1104a33–b3; 1104b4–8; 1105a15–17; 1105a28–31, b2–12; 1168b25–8; 1172b23–5; 1178a10–11; 1178a28–33.

constitute a single domain, surely the virtues that deal with pleasures of the table are different from those that deal with pleasures of the bed. Gluttony is different from lust.

(4) And then how are virtues to be distinguished from one another? Even among the apparently paradigmatic virtues it is unclear what should serve as the paradigmatic instances of these. Aristotle notoriously defines courage in relation to a relatively uncommon activity – remaining steadfast on the frontline of battle in the face of an attacking enemy – which raises a host of difficulties: How can this virtue be acquired, since the occasions to practice it are rare (see, indeed, 3.12.1119a26–7)? Why should the virtue's activity be defined in so restrictive a way, when courage or something like it seems necessary in nearly all human domains? Similarly, he defines moderation with respect to the narrow class of pleasures of touch, while acknowledging (throughout Book 7) that weakness of will (ἀκρασία), and then apparently some kind of moderation, is exhibited in some qualified way toward other objects of pleasure and attraction.

(5) Finally, one wants to know whether Aristotle's list of virtues is proposed by him as exhaustive, and on what grounds. Apparently he believed that it was, and that those grounds would be apparent from his discussions, since he says: "Resuming the discussion of each virtue, let us state: what each virtue is; what matters it deals with; and how it does so. At the same time it will become clear as well how many virtues there are" (3.5.1115a4–6). So here our difficulty is not even implicit, yet it is difficult to see how the question is to be answered.[3]

3.2 The Aristotelian solutions of Aquinas

As mentioned, Aquinas answers all of these difficulties through his theory of the "cardinal" or "principal" virtues. Obviously a theory of the principal virtues must do two things. First, it must have some basis for picking out certain virtues as most basic; second, it must stipulate the manner in which other, less basic virtues may be counted as related to those most basic virtues. As Aquinas's theory of the principal virtues depends upon a definition he gives of the "essence" of virtue in general, it may be seen that it offers answers to all five questions raised above. He constructs the theory entirely out of ideas and distinctions in Aristotle; nonetheless, in the SLE he does not attribute this theory to Aristotle: rather, at best, the commentary interprets Aristotle's ethics in such a way that it is

[3] For an attempt at an answer on grounds implicit in the EN, see Pakaluk (2011).

consistent with and, as it were, can naturally take the form of his own theory.

3.2.1 Basic virtues

Of the two tasks mentioned, the first is the more important for Aquinas, since he thinks that a principal virtue may be shown to be such antecedently to any attempt to attribute all other virtues to them. The identification of certain virtues as truly principal would establish that other virtues are *somehow* derivative, even if it is not immediately clear *exactly how*, just as, once we identified the main branches coming from the trunk of a tree, we would know that every other branch had to be an offshoot of one of these, even if we did not yet know which.[4]

In outline, Aquinas's theory of the principal virtues is the following. A virtue generally speaking is "the perfection of a power" (*potentiae perfectio*), which makes a power (or a kind of thing insofar as it has that power) such that it achieves its full functioning unless somehow impeded (*ST* 1–2.55.2 resp., 1–2.55.3 ad 2, *QDVCom* 2 resp.). As will be explained further below, Aquinas takes Aristotle to have affirmed this definition in *De Caelo* 1 and *Physics* 7. A virtue *of a human being*, then, would be a perfection of the distinctively human power of rational action, which makes a human being such that he achieves his full functioning unless he is somehow impeded. Some perfections of a distinctively human power only make a human being *apt* to achieve full functioning: such a perfection would not be a human virtue in the strict sense. Aquinas maintains that the so-called intellectual virtues are like that. They equip someone to live a good and happy life, but, since they do not involve motivation, they do not actually make someone such that he will indeed live such a life provided he is not somehow impeded. Aquinas takes this to be reflected in our language (*ST* 1–2.56.3 resp., *QDVCom* 7 ad 2), as we do not call someone who has acquired a skill "good simply," a "good man," but rather good *at something* or *in some respect*, for instance a "good *doctor*."

Only a moral virtue can be a virtue in the strict sense, then, and so the principal virtues would have to be among the moral virtues. In the literature on Aristotle's ethics, it is common to describe a virtue as a trait that *disposes* someone to do good actions or act reasonably in some

---

[4] In *QDVCom*, for instance, Aquinas mentions the possibility of relating other virtues to the cardinal virtues almost as an afterthought (*QDVCom* 12 ad 26). Similarly, Aquinas hardly ever says that principal virtues can be called "cardinal" because all other virtues "hinge" upon them (but see *QDVCard* 1 ad 12 for one such case).

domain.[5] Yet on Aquinas's view, such a description wrongly characterizes a moral virtue as if it were merely an intellectual virtue. Alternatively, one could say that the description is acceptable only if one understands that someone's being suitably "disposed" to act reasonably also includes his so resolutely wanting to act reasonably in that domain that he predictably will do so, apart from his being somehow impeded.

Aquinas next applies the definition of virtue in the following way. A power is a potentiality, and any potentiality is correlated with the actualization (*actus*) which that potentiality is for – a truism of Aristotelian metaphysics. Hence virtues may be considered either, so to speak, from the side of potentiality or from the side of actuality. That is to say, if a virtue is a perfection of a power, and a power exists to be actualized in some kind of activity (*operatio*) or achievement, then the most basic virtues may be identified by looking either to the most basic relevant powers, or to the most basic relevant sorts of activities. Aquinas believes that both of these approaches imply that the same four virtues are principal: practical wisdom, justice, moderation, and courage (*ST* 1–2.61.2 resp., *QDVCard* 1 resp.).

Adopting Aristotle's psychology in *An.* and *EN*, Aquinas holds that the basic human motivations are (a) the power that is the locus of sense desire (ἐπιθυμία, *appetitus concupiscibilis*); (b) the power that is the locus of strivings to prevail against obstacles (θυμός, *appetitus irascibilis*); and (c) the power of rational desire (βούλησις, *voluntas*). The virtue that perfects sense desire – in the sense of making someone such that he has sense desire only as consistent with what is reasonable – is moderation; that which similarly perfects the others are courage and justice. Practical wisdom gets included as a fourth because practical reason presupposes motivation and is at least in that respect distinguished from theoretical reason (*EN* 6.2.1139a35–b1; *ST* 1–2.57.4 resp.). If a virtue in the strict sense is a trait that does not merely make someone *apt* to act reasonably but also makes him *want*, fixedly and resolutely, to act reasonably, then practical wisdom looks to be a virtue in that sense too, insofar as one can claim that someone with practical wisdom does not merely "know how to" figure out, for instance, what is the courageous or moderate thing to do under the circumstances, but also *wants* to figure this out effectively: he *wants* to reason well, and to do so practically, that is, not as remaining on the level of thought, but as actually executing what was thought out.[6] So from

---

[5] See for instance Kraut (2012), according to whom an ethical virtue is "a tendency or disposition."
[6] Hence the puzzle as to whether a prudent person can display weakness of will: *EN* 7.1.1145b17–19.

the point of view of a virtue's perfecting a motivational power, Aquinas identifies four such basic virtues on the basis of a specific interpretation and elaboration of Aristotelian psychology. The result is consistent with the view of the *EN* and its language of "parts" of the soul: practical wisdom is the virtue of the part of the soul having *logos* (1.13.1102a28–b28) insofar as it is oriented to practice; justice is the virtue of the part of the soul which does not have *logos* but hearkens to *logos*, i.e., of specifically rational desire (Aristotle's characterization of justice mentions acts of willing specifically, as Aquinas points out [*EN* 5.1.1129a9; *ST* 2–2.58.4 resp.]);[7] and Aristotle certainly seems to agree with the view that courage and moderation are virtues in the non-rational parts of the soul (3.10.1117b23–4).

From the point of view of a virtue's causing the full actualization of a power, Aquinas arrives at the same result, reasoning in the following way. A virtue is a trait that, again, makes someone such that his activity – what he does, what he is responsible for – is reasonable. But there are four basic types of such activity: his thinking itself, as practical and directed at action; his actions ordinarily so-called, that is, his external actions (*actiones*), including those that order or confer external goods; and how he is affected (*passiones*). This last category splits into two, Aquinas thinks, on the grounds that acting reasonably in the realm of the passions involves regulating both the passions by which we are drawn to something and the passions by which we are repulsed from something. These two sorts of passions imply two sorts of tasks or achievements, if one is to act reasonably in spite of them – being reasonable when a passion might otherwise deflect us by drawing us to something else, and being reasonable when a passion might otherwise deflect us by impelling us away[8] – which the ordinary distinction between the virtues of moderation and courage confirms (*ST* 1–2.61.2 resp.). The language of the *EN* is clearly broadly consistent with this division: practical wisdom's activity, as an intellectual virtue, consists of thinking; justice, Aristotle says, involves the assignment of goods to persons in such a way as to achieve an equality (5.3.1131a15–18); and courage and moderation are described by Aristotle as intermediate conditions concerned with different sorts of passions.

So Aquinas picks out four virtues as principal, thus carrying out the first task of formulating a theory of cardinal or principal virtues, on the basis of a

---

[7] But see Perkams (2008a, 135–9) for reasonable concerns about whether Aquinas, in giving this specific interpretation of Aristotelian particular justice, is in fact relying upon notions of the will found in other philosophical sources.

[8] We would refer to these differently as "restraint" versus "steadfastness."

definition of virtue in general that he finds in Aristotle (*Cael.*, *Phys.*);
an account of appetitive movement in the human soul that he also
takes from Aristotle (*An.*, *EN*); and a distinction among types of actualization that is in a general way supported by Aristotle's language in
the *EN*.

3.2.2   How secondary virtues relate to basic virtues

Aquinas's execution of the task of showing how secondary virtues can be
attributed to basic virtues also depends on Aristotelian materials. Here
a distinction is helpful. Aquinas will often construct a theory and then,
having done so, devote himself to showing that the theory is harmonious
with, and indeed accounts for, the views of respected authorities.[9] Let us
call these two aspects "construction" and "harmonization," respectively.
Now, although Aquinas is intent to harmonize his theory of the cardinal
virtues with various authorities, he takes his materials for the construction
of that theory from Aristotle. In particular, although he makes it clear
that the language of "parts," which he wishes to preserve, comes from
the Stoics (his main referent is Cicero, *De Inventione* 2.159–164), he uses
Aristotelian ideas to explain how one virtue may be considered a "part" of
another.[10]

   The main idea is that the virtue of anything is a whole, and hence any
distinction among virtues, involves a kind of analysis of the parts of a
whole.[11] That virtue is a whole is guaranteed by the nature of a thing: each
kind of thing has a unified nature that aims at and sets a thing of that kind on
the pursuit of a unified end, but since a virtue is a perfection of a power, then
the virtue distinctive of that kind of thing would be a trait that makes it such
that it will achieve that unified end (unless it is somehow impeded). This
is true for human beings as much as any other kind of thing, and so even
the distinction of intellectual from moral virtues, and of principal virtues
from derivative ones, involves an analysis of what in reality is a functioning
whole.

---

[9] In *SLE* 1.12 he clearly regards *EN* 1.7–8 as a paradigm of this sort of approach.

[10] Aquinas is aware that the label "cardinal" for the principal virtues does not derive from Aristotle (it
derives from Ambrose of Milan), and also that Aristotle does not explicitly pick out four virtues as
basic. See the careful language at *SLE* 1.16 lines 96–100; Aquinas says there that to take Aristotle's
language of "foursquare" (τετράγωνος) at *EN* 1.10.1100b21 to refer to the four cardinal virtues is
unwarranted, as it "seems not to correspond to the meaning of Aristotle, who is nowhere found to
make that sort of enumeration."

[11] This is a presupposition of *EN* 1.7 and 1.13, but compare Cicero, *De Inventione* 2.159: "Est igitur in
eo genere omnes res una vi atque uno nomine amplexa virtus."

If the identification of individual virtues involves a kind of analysis, then if there are various ways that a whole can be analyzed into parts, there are various ways in which one virtue may be identified as a part of another. For types of analysis of a whole into parts, Aquinas draws upon Aristotle, *Met.* 5.25–26, *An.* 2.3, and *EN* 1.13, although he systematizes and clarifies Aristotle's distinctions in an interesting way. There are three basic types of relationship of part to whole, Aquinas claims: integral, subjective, and potential. An integral part is an element without which the whole would not exist, such as the walls and roof of a house; such a part is "integral" insofar as it serves to compose the unified whole of which it is a part. A subjective part is a species, such as the way in which "horse" and "dog" serve to divide up "animal": if all of the species were accounted for, then so would the whole, which is the genus. It is called a "subjective" part because each species can serve as the subject of which the genus term is predicated, as in "a horse is an animal" and "a dog is an animal." A potential part of some power is a capacity to act or be acted upon, which can be accounted *part* of what that power is capable of. Admittedly the language can mislead: a potential part is not something which is potentially a part, but rather an actual part of what the power does as a whole.[12] The schema by which Aquinas settles on just these three part–whole relationships is the application of the distinction Aristotle commonly draws among univocal, equivocal, and analogous predication (*Cat.* 1, *EN* 1.6, and *Met.* 4.2, 7.1). The predicate for the whole can be predicated *univocally* of a subjective part; the predicate for the whole can be predicated only *equivocally* of an integral part; and the predicate for the whole is predicated, Aquinas claims, only *analogously* of a potential part (*ST* 1.77.1 ad 1).

Although Aquinas in the *SLE* does not ascribe a theory of "parts" of principal virtues to Aristotle, he does interpret the *EN* as drawing a distinction between principal and subsidiary virtues. For example, *EN* 6.9–10 deals, he says, with certain virtues *connected with* prudence (*adiunctis prudentiae*, *SLE* 6.8 line 4); again, the virtues discussed in *EN* 4 are presumably secondary insofar as they consider certain goods that are secondary in comparison with the good of maintaining life, with which courage and temperance are concerned (*SLE* 4.1 lines 2–4). However, Aquinas does not attribute to Aristotle any assignments of secondary virtues to primary ones,

---

[12] It is important to observe that for Aquinas a "part" of a power in this sense includes not simply direct or natural applications of a power but also indirect or, so to speak, transferred applications. An analogy would be what is called the "off-label" use of a drug in medicine, where a drug developed and approved as safe for one purpose, is by chance found to have application for some other purpose – a discovered and transferred application of the drug's "power."

even when we might expect him to do so. For instance, in the *ST* he follows Cicero and regards magnificence as a part of courage, and liberality as a part of justice – a view that would help to underwrite Aristotle's claim that these virtues differ in kind, and not merely as regards the quantity of the sums of wealth expended – and yet in the *SLE* Aquinas does not suggest that Aristotle held any such view.[13]

3.3   Defining virtue

As regards the first three of the difficulties stated above, involving the proper way of identifying the virtues and distinguishing virtues from one another, we have seen that Aquinas walks a fine line, employing Aristotelian materials to develop a theory that seems a plausible and even natural development of Aristotle's views, yet taking care in the *SLE* not to attribute every element of that theory to Aristotle. The fourth difficulty deserves separate attention, because Aquinas's resolution seems fairly open to the charge that he interprets Aristotle inexpertly. That difficulty, again, is that Aristotle seems to define some virtues too restrictively, in defining courage as fearlessness on the battlefield, and moderation as the rational regulation of pleasures of touch.

As explained above, Aquinas regards a virtue as, so to speak, the fortification of a power. From this it would apparently follow that a virtue can be picked out in as many ways as a power. The power of eyesight, for example, can be picked out by its subject, that is, by what it is in (the eye); or by what objects actualize it (colors); or by what actions count as its actualizations (seeings); or even by its relation to other powers ("the most informative sense," etc.). Likewise, Aquinas holds that courage can be picked out by its subject (the irascible appetite); by what objects serve to actualize it (fearful ones); what actions count as its actualizations (the rational regulation of passions of fear and confidence) – but also, inasmuch as a virtue is a fortification of an active power, by reference to its fullest realization, that is, to the most extreme exertion of its "strength" (*SLE* 3.14 lines 115–24). The idea is commonsensical, especially when identifying a strength in relation to a group of persons who each have it in some degree: "one must climb Class 5 routes to be considered a true rock climber;" "skill in the French horn at the professional level implies mastery of the Strauss concerti;" and so on. Identifications like this are relative to a class of

---

[13] Aquinas seems diffident in some assignments of "parts" of virtues to principal virtues, for example, "liberality is *reckoned by some* a part of justice" (*ST* 2–2.117.5 resp.; cf. 2–2.129.5 resp.).

persons at a particular time and place (rock climbers; professional hornists). Similarly, a "strength" of a fundamental human power would presumably have to be picked out in relation to all human beings in general. Thus, for example: What is the ultimate "feat of strength" for a human being, of steadfastness as regards feelings of fear and confidence when facing fearful threats? This would not be identified appropriately, Aristotle insists, as, say, standing firm in the face of earthquakes or tidal waves, since these terrifying objects fall outside the typical human range (3.7.1115b7–11, b26–8). It would be as absurd to expect a human being to stand firm when facing them as to expect a skilled rock climber to scale glass surfaces that only flies can ascend. Rather, it would mean something like: facing the terror of a murderous enemy, when spontaneous action is called for (which calls upon and reveals character), for the sake of the most noble cause, one's fatherland (9.8.1169a19, 1.2.1094b8). That, or presumably anything equivalent, would be the human ultimate as regards the rational regulation of emotions of fear and confidence.

Obviously such a specification leaves it open for courage of a lesser degree to be displayed in many other circumstances, just as someone who plays the Mozart concerti is still a good hornist. Also, it leaves open the possibility that the same "strength" picked out by its extreme accomplishment will end up strengthening activity in other domains. For example, an accomplished runner will have an endurance that will aid him in any sport or physical activity; an engineer's skill at painstaking and clear analysis will prove valuable in a wide range of practical deliberations. In much the same way, Aquinas holds, the four principal virtues play a role in any virtuous action whatsoever. He ingeniously argues for this (*QDVCard* 1 resp.) in relation to the three "conditions of virtuous action" in *EN* 2.4.1105b31–3. Aristotle says there that the difference between, on the one hand, doing an action that is merely like the action that would be done by a virtuous person in the same circumstances – but that even a non-virtuous person might do, say, through following instructions or in response to the threat of someone else – and, on the other hand, an action that externally is like that but that is actually a virtuous action, is that in the latter case the agent (i) knows what he is doing; (ii) chooses the action for its own sake; and (iii) acts from a firm and stable character. Aquinas then says that, in any virtuous action whatsoever, the principal virtue of courage serves to strengthen dimension (iii), by providing steadfastness and determination; that of justice serves to strengthen (ii), by lending clarity about the right way to order one's actions, that is, about how virtuous actions should not be done instrumentally, merely for some ulterior motive; prudence serves to strengthen (i), for obvious reasons; and then moderation serves to strengthen refinement in the execution of the action – that is, for hitting the mean precisely as regards object, time, manner, degree, and so on – because moderation as a strength of character is distinctive for achieving propriety and fittingness in one's actions.[14]

We said that the procedure of picking out a strength through its greatest "feat of strength," relative to a class of persons having a certain ability, is a commonsensical idea, and that Aquinas understands Aristotle to be doing just this in the way courage and other virtues are specified in the *EN*. Aquinas in the *SLE* (3.14 lines 119–20), *QDVCom* (1 resp.), and *ST* (1–2.55.1 arg. 1) refers for support to a passage from the *De Caelo*, where this idea seems to be found in a general form: "If something has the power to move, or to lift weights, we always denominate it relative to its utmost capacity, for example, 'the power to lift a hundred talents' or 'the power to walk a hundred stadia,' even though it is also a power to do anything within that . . . we do so on the supposition that a power should be defined relative to its goal and its utmost extreme (ὡς δέον ὁρίζεσθαι πρὸς τὸ τέλος καὶ τὴν ὑπεροχὴν τὴν δύναμιν)" (*Cael.* 1.11.281a7–12). Aquinas glosses the passage as "The power of each sort of thing is denominated with respect to its end, that is, through the utmost and through the maximum which it is capable of, and by virtue of its own excellence" (*SLDCM* 1.25 n. 4), which he regards as a very general principle, which has correct but non-obvious applications in a variety of domains. For example, he says, we say that "the length" of a thing is its maximum measurement, although it certainly has all the lengths short of that maximum; or again we define a human being as a "rational animal," even though human beings also have the power of sensation, because, Aquinas says, "that which is utmost and maximum is perfective and gives the species of a thing" (*ibid.*). That is why "virtue is assigned to a thing on no other basis than its excellence, that is, only insofar as that which is most excellent, out of everything of which it is capable, is found in it. And another translation puts it: 'Virtue is the utmost of a power' (*virtus est ultimum potentiae*), because, that is, the virtue of a thing is marked out by reference to the utmost of which it is capable (*virtus rei determinatur secundum ultimum in quod potest*). This holds even for the virtues of the soul, since we refer to something as a 'human virtue' if it is that through which a human being is capable of what is most excellent

---

[14] Aquinas gives several explanations on Aristotelian grounds of what he takes to be the Stoic view of the principal virtues as equally operative in every action (for example, *ST* 1–2.61.3 resp.), yet he says plainly that Aristotle's approach of first specifying the principal virtues in relation to their ultimate realization in distinctive "matter" is more sound (*melius*, ibid.).

in human actions, that is, in action which is in accordance with reason" (*ibid.*). In the *SLE* commentary on the virtue of courage, repeating the same words, and echoing fairly precisely Aristotle's own language, Aquinas says that "a virtue is marked out by reference to the utmost of a power, as is said in *De Caelo* 1, and it is for this reason that the virtue of courage is concerned with those things that are the most frightening – so that it does not turn out that anyone endures dangers more than does a courageous man" (*SLE* 3.14 lines 119–23).

Harry Jaffa, in *Thomism and Aristotelianism* (1952), famously raised objections precisely to Aquinas's interpretation of Aristotle on this point. Jaffa claimed that (i) the *De Caelo* passage articulates "a perfectly mechanical conception, or, rather, an explanation of the 'maximum' applied to mechanical power," which Aquinas wrongly applies to interpreting Aristotle's discussion of the moral "power" of courage (Jaffa 1952, 72); that (ii) on account of this wrongheaded application of a mechanical concept to ethics, because mechanical powers admit of a more precise specification than moral powers (witness Aristotle's examples of "hundred talents" and "hundred stadia"), Aquinas is misled into presuming that ethical matters admit of a greater degree of accuracy than Aristotle would allow; and, finally, that (iii) in particular, Aquinas's pretensions to accuracy mislead him in the present instance to ascribe limits to human action and human powers that Aristotle did not accept, since Aquinas failed to see that what he had wrongly interpreted as the "utmost of a power" for courage is in fact not the utmost, because human beings who possess courage to the heroic degree described at the beginning of Book 7 can presumably transcend any putative ultimate achievable by the ordinary virtue of courage. "The possibility that there is a higher kind of courage than that here described [viz. in Book 3] is thus precluded by the very principle used to explain the present definition of courage," Jaffa complains (p. 73).

But these objections are clearly misguided. As regards objection (i), there is no indication that Aristotle in the *De Caelo* intends to be explaining "power" and "virtue" in any restricted, putatively "mechanical" sense. Indeed, a comparable discussion in *Phys.* 7.3.246a10–247a15, also cited by Aquinas in *QDVCom* (1 resp.),[15] is revealing in this regard, for there Aristotle distinguishes and discusses a series of cases, first applying "power" and "virtue" to inanimate objects, then to living non-rational

---

[15] Note that the Marietti edition and Ralph McInerny's translation give the reference incorrectly as *Met.* 7 rather than *Phys.* 7. For Aquinas's discussion in his *Physics* commentary, see 7.5 n. 6.

beings, and finally to the human soul. So Aristotle's own example licenses Aquinas's application of the definition to human virtues. Not that it would even be possible for Aristotle's discussion to confine itself to a "purely mechanical" conception of power in natural substances, as the notion of a "purely mechanical" power is post-Cartesian and anachronistic: indeed, in the *De Caelo* Aristotle is presuming that the heavens are living and even divine. As regards (ii), Aquinas's commentary on the *De Caelo* and *Physics* passages show that he is well aware that, following Aristotle, "power" and "virtue" need to be specified in a manner suited to each particular domain: they are general metaphysical notions that, like "matter" and "form," need to be specified appropriately in various domains, in the manner of an analogy. In any case, there is clearly nothing overly precise, and no exaggerated pretension to accuracy, in holding simply that courage is to be defined with reference to steadfastness on the battlefield. As regards (iii), Aristotle says explicitly that the heroic virtue he mentions briefly at the beginning of Book 7 is "beyond us" (ὑπὲρ ἡμᾶς) and even "divine" (θείαν) (7.1.1145a19–20); whereas in Books 3–5 he is obviously discussing virtues which are not "beyond us," that is, traits which are virtues relative to the class "human beings," and hence steadfastness in the midst of battle would represent the "utmost of power" for a human being qua human being (ὡς ἄνθρωπος, 3.7.1115b11), facing objects not so frightening as to overtax human nature (cf. 3.1.1110a25–6).

3.4 The difference in method between Aquinas's ethical theory and Aristotle's

Although Jaffa is obviously incorrect in objecting that Aquinas, in his discussion of courage, ineptly applies "mechanical" notions to moral philosophy, still one may wonder about the appropriateness of Aquinas's reliance, in his ethical theory, on Aristotelian natural philosophy and metaphysics, both for explaining Aristotle's ethics and for developing his own Aristotelian account of ethics. Is such a procedure consistent with Aristotle's strictures on method? It would seem that Aristotle's method, by his own account (7.1.1145b2–7), involves first gathering together the relevant trustworthy views for the particular topic at hand, the *phainomena* (or *endoxa*), and then resolving apparent difficulties in such a way as to vindicate or "save" these *phainomena*, to the greatest extent possible. Such a method would apparently neither introduce nor require the introduction of highly general principles of natural philosophy or metaphysics. Moreover, Aristotle regards ethics as falling within the discipline of statecraft (πολιτική) and written mainly for the benefit of legislators.[16] Accordingly, Aristotle's own rule seems to be that he will introduce ideas from areas of philosophy other than ethics only to the extent that these notions are necessary for the discipline of statecraft and will be illuminating to legislators. Indeed, at various points in the *EN*, Aristotle dismisses issues in metaphysics or natural philosophy as irrelevant to his investigation.[17] But the principles that Aquinas relies on seem to offend against this rule. Finally, Aristotle clearly regards ethics and statecraft as an exercise of practical reasoning. But practical reasoning, he holds, differs from theoretical reasoning in having starting points that are not general truths but rather goals to be achieved. A "principle" in practical reasoning is like an objective: practical reasoning then proceeds by working backward from that objective until it arrives at something to be done here and now, for the purpose of achieving that objective. But if to give a principle in ethics is to give or clarify a goal, then principles from metaphysics or natural philosophy seem to have no place: that is, Aquinas seems to confuse practical reasoning with theoretical reasoning (see 3.3.1112b11–31 and 6.2.1139a20–31).

Aquinas takes a different view of Aristotle's method, and in any case understands himself to be engaging in a very different kind of project. The former point is signaled in Aquinas's treatment of the aforementioned passage in *EN* 7.1, which is typically the starting point of recent discussions of Aristotle's method (see Barnes 1981, and Nussbaum 1986, chs. 8–9). Aquinas in the *SLE* in effect ignores the passage. He merely gives a paraphrase commentary restating the passage, and the only comment he contributes by way of explication is deflationary: after stating that "if in any subject matter the difficulties are solved and the plausible views are left standing as if true (*derelinquantur quasi vera*), then it has been adequately dealt with," he says, "and if thus we establish all of those views which are most plausible about the things that have been said, and if not all – because it is not in our capacity as human beings to omit nothing from consideration – most of them, or the most fundamental of them."[18] Aquinas does not interpret the passage as offering any important or privileged account of Aristotle's method. He evidently views it as playing the role merely of a bridge paragraph, introducing the discussion that follows, but adding nothing to what is evident in that discussion.

---

[16] See, e.g., *EN* 1.2.1094b7–11; 1.13.1102a12–27; 3.1.1109b33–5; and 7.11.1152b1–4.

[17] See *EN* 1.6.1096b30–1; 1.7.1098a29–34; 1.9.1099b13–14; 1.12.1101b34–5; 1.13.1102a23–6; 8.1.1155b8–10; and 8.8.1159b23–4.

[18] What Aristotle calls *phainomena*, Aquinas refers to as *probabilia*, that is, plausible or *prima facie* tenable views. (Elsewhere, following Boethius, Aquinas uses *probabilia* for Aristotle's *endoxa*.)

Aquinas's comments on what might be regarded as an analogous method-
ological passage in *Met.* 3.1 are highly interesting in this regard, because
in discussing there (*SSM* 3.1 nn. 6–7) why Aristotle puts all of the difficulties that he will consider in the *Metaphysics* at the beginning of that
work, Aquinas in effect reveals his view as to why Aristotle raises difficulties generally. There are three reasons, he says, why Aristotle put all of the
difficulties at the start of his investigation in the *Metaphysics*: (i) because
metaphysics considers reality in general and most basically; (ii) because
Aristotle's predecessors followed the wrong order of inquiry in metaphysics,
beginning from abstractions and trying to draw inferences about sensible
things, rather than the reverse, and so all of the difficulties arising from
this improper method had to be stated immediately by Aristotle, before he
began his own investigation of metaphysics according to what he regarded
as the appropriate method; and finally (iii) because metaphysics has a special affinity with logic, and thus metaphysics is appropriately preceded by
a dialectical exercise that gives rise to the main issues for study. From these
considerations it would hardly be surprising if the dialectical examination
of difficulties were unimportant in *EN*: there would not be any need in
ethics for a propaedeutic exercise in dialectics, as ethics is not especially
related to logic; confusions arising from Aristotle's predecessors' having
employed the wrong method will be infrequent and will need to be only
occasionally addressed (as perhaps in *EN* 1.6 and 8.1); and, otherwise, one
should expect that in ethics, as in any other particular science, difficulties
will be addressed on an as-needed basis (as presumably in *EN* 1.9–12 and
9.5–12), but not, it seems, as inseparably related to the inquiry in general
or in any of its parts.

On this view, it would be expected that the systematic statement of
difficulties and the investigation into their resolution, in the manner of
EN 7.1–2, would be relatively uncommon in the *EN*. Indeed, Aquinas's
tendency is apparently to downplay the role of difficulties, even in those
sections in which some difficulties are stated. For example, a natural way
of reading Book 1 is as leading up to a definition of happiness and then,
in *EN* 1.9–12, dealing with certain difficulties arising from this definition;
and yet Aquinas in the *SLE* describes only one of these chapters as raising a
difficulty.[19] Again, as regards *EN* 9, we find that Aquinas indeed describes
some of the later chapters as raising doubts, but for him this begins with
Chapter 8, not Chapters 5–7, as one might have thought. Outside the

---

[19] For instance, he describes *EN* 1.9, rather, as being about "the cause of happiness" (*SLE* 1.14 lines
3–4).

handful of chapters like this, where difficulties are discussed as the occasion requires, Aquinas seems to regard difficulties as playing only a slight role in Aristotle's exposition.[20]

So Aquinas differs from recent scholars of Aristotle, negatively, in interpreting the exposition of *EN* as only occasionally taking its start dialectically from difficulties. But he also differs, positively, in understanding Aristotle as engaged in a more constructive and more systematic "science" of ethics than scholars typically wish to attribute to Aristotle. That Aquinas discerns much system and structure in Aristotle's exposition is evident from the *SLE*. But what deserves special emphasis is how Aquinas regards that exposition as based upon and governed by fundamental insights or, as we might call them, "principles," which are frequently metaphysical in character, or related to important ideas in Aristotelian natural philosophy. Aquinas regards these principles as exerting a pervasive force in *EN*, even if they are stated only once by Aristotle. That this is so is evident if, for instance, one looks at the nature of the references to the *EN* in Aquinas's systematic works, such as in the *ST*, as these references can be used as a kind of guide to the significance of the passages Aquinas refers to. It is widely appreciated that Aristotle is a prominent authority in the *ST*: Aristotle is referred to in explicit citations almost as often as Augustine.[21] Of references to Aristotle, about two-thirds are to the *EN* (about 1200 out of 1800). Yet it is perhaps not appreciated that the bulk of these references are to a relatively small number of sentences in *EN*. For example, considering *EN* 2 only, of some 174 explicit references to that book in *ST*, 123 are to passages that are referred to at least three times. Some passages are cited with remarkable frequency, such that four of these make up about one-third of all references to Book 2: the three conditions of virtue (2.4.1105a31–3) are referred to 13 times (e.g., *ST* 1–2.56.2 arg. 2); that virtue makes that which has it good and renders its work good (2.6.1106a15–16) is referred to 14 times (e.g., *ST* 1–2.20.3 arg. 2); the definition of moral virtue (2.6.1106b36–1107a2) is referred to 14 times (e.g., *ST* 1–2.58.1 arg. 2); and the claim that virtue concerns what is difficult and good (2.6.1106b28–33) is referred to 11 times (e.g., *ST* 1.95.4 arg. 2).

A reasonable interpretation of this and similar evidence is that Aquinas *already* understands the *EN* as affirming "principles," frequently

---

[20] Bostock's (2000) careful examination of Aristotle's method in *EN*, concluding that "there is very little of the Ethics that can be explained simply as an application of the method set out in VII.1" (219), is broadly supportive of Aquinas's view.

[21] I do not consider here the many implicit references to Aristotle, that is, the places where Aquinas uses a phrase taken from Aristotle to invoke an Aristotelian idea, but without explicitly giving its provenance.

metaphysical in nature, which he himself embraces and employs in various ways in his own systematic work, combining them with other "principles" to arrive at interesting results. We have already seen some of the uses to which Aquinas puts what he takes to be Aristotle's definition of virtue. Additionally, by looking to those places in general in the *ST* where Aquinas cites this principle,[22] one may observe the various uses to which it is put: for instance, Aquinas also uses it to give a justification for the analogy between virtue and health or strength (*ST* 1–2.55.2 resp.); to argue that a virtue must be in a power as in a subject (*ST* 1–2.56.1 resp.); in support of the claim that it cannot but be the intention of the law and of lawgivers to make citizens good (*ST* 1–2.92.1 resp.); and even to give a kind of anti-consequentialist argument that the only consequences to be taken into account in estimating the goodness or badness of an action are those that follow naturally and directly from the action itself (*ST* 1–2.20.5 arg. 1 and ad 1).

So Aquinas might say with some plausibility that to rely on principles from Aristotle's natural philosophy or metaphysics in order to resolve a difficulty arising within Aristotle's ethical philosophy is consistent with Aristotle's own procedure. Yet he would deny in any case that his project is the same as Aristotle's. In none of his works, except perhaps the *De Regno*, does he take himself to be engaged in anything like political prudence (πολιτική), but rather "sacred doctrine" (*sacra doctrina*), which he regards as transcending the difference between speculative and practical reason: "Although among philosophical disciplines," he says, "some are speculative and some are practical, sacred doctrine comprises both . . . although it is speculative more than practical, because it is more concerned with divine things than with human actions; it is concerned with human actions only insofar as through them human beings are directed to a perfect knowledge of God" (*ST* 1.1.4 resp.).

3.5   Conclusion

In the matters we have considered, Aquinas develops Aristotle's ethical theory in the *EN* by resolving difficulties inherent in the *EN*, drawing on principles taken from Aristotle to do so. He does so as part of a project that he regards as primarily speculative, accounting for the truth of things, and not merely practical, aiming at the good. Ironically, it was precisely

---

[22] Through either the phrase "utmost of a power" or the formula "makes that which has it good and renders its work good."

because Aquinas aimed to see ethics *sub specie aeternitatis*, i.e., within sacred doctrine as he understood it, that he strove to develop Aristotelian ethics in such a way as to rationalize it thoroughly and embed it in the best natural philosophy and philosophical framework of his time.

The result is that in comparison with Aristotle's ethics, Aquinas's has both strengths and weaknesses. Aristotle's ethics is more catholic: because it is proposed as an exhibition of practical reasoning in the service of legislators with practical interests, it prescinds from unnecessary commitments in natural philosophy or metaphysics, even at the cost, apparently, of leaving certain nagging difficulties unresolved. Precisely because of this approach, it has proved to be attractive to interpreters with very different metaphysical commitments. It has seemed that Aristotelian ethics can retain its plausibility even when detached from any "metaphysical biology" (see MacIntyre 2007, xi and 196) that might be taken to undergird it.

And yet we want an ethical system to be true. We presume that an ethical theory, if it is true, must have a formal structure, consistent with the best contemporary accounts of the world, and that admits of being more deeply articulated as investigation proceeds and deepens. Consequentialist and deontological theories have been attractive from these considerations, and virtue ethics has seemed weaker in comparison. Aquinas's virtue ethics, through its broad reliance on Aristotelian philosophy, has a clever, deep, and compelling rational structure, which we have only touched upon here. Yet its claim to truth depends crucially on the claims to truth of Aristotelian natural philosophy and metaphysics.

CHAPTER FOUR

Duplex beatitudo
Aristotle's legacy and Aquinas's conception of human happiness

Jörn Müller

Without doubt happiness (εὐδαιμονία) is the central concept on which ancient moral philosophy was founded. It would even be justifiable not only to describe the ethics of antiquity as "eudaimonistic" – as Immanuel Kant did in a rather derogatory fashion – but to apply this label to the whole of ancient philosophy. As Augustine remarks (*De civitate Dei* 19.1), the main reason for doing philosophy is that it strives for and ultimately promises the achievement of the highest good, i.e., happiness. Thus, the notion of *eudaimonia* lies at the heart of philosophy itself, when it is understood not as a purely theoretical inquiry but as a certain form of life.

Consequently, Christian authors' approach to philosophy is very much shaped by their understanding of happiness. It has, for instance, been argued that Aquinas's moral theology is itself a kind of "eudaimonistic" project heavily indebted to Aristotle;[1] some even see Aquinas as advocating a genuine "moral philosophy" revolving around the concept of happiness, which he supposedly develops mainly from his reception of the *EN*.[2] But these claims are highly controversial. How one evaluates them should depend mainly on how Aquinas actually deals with Aristotle's notion of *eudaimonia*. In this chapter I will first sketch out the basic characteristics of Aristotelian happiness (Section 4.1). Afterwards, I will briefly examine Albert the Great's two commentaries on the *EN* (Section 4.2); as will become apparent later, Aquinas's interpretation of Aristotelian happiness in his own commentary, the *Sententia libri Ethicorum* (*SLE*), can be understood at least partly as a critical reaction to the highly influential reading of his teacher. In Sections 4.3–4.5, I will outline Aquinas's understanding of happiness, starting from his commentary and proceeding to the theological works. This will enable us, finally, (a) to evaluate the way in which Aquinas's

---

[1] See Guindon 1956. For a criticism of a eudaimonistic reading of Aquinas see Leonhardt 1998.
[2] See Kleber 1988; Kluxen 1998; Doig 2001.

theological background shaped his reading of Aristotelian *eudaimonia* and (b) to provide a balanced assessment of the influence that the *EN* had on Aquinas's development of his own account of happiness (Section 4.6).

4.1 *Eudaimonia* in Aristotle's *Nicomachean Ethics*

Aristotle develops his account of happiness in Books 1 and 10 of his *Nicomachean Ethics*. His starting point is provided by the observation that human practices always aim at achieving certain ends; therefore, "good," when predicated of what such practices seek after, mainly conveys this idea of goal-directed finality. Now, goods are not always completely final, since we regularly pursue certain ends in order to achieve other goals by means of them. There is, thus, a hierarchy of ends inherent in human practices, which prompts Aristotle to make the following observation:

> If then there is some end in our practical projects that we wish for because of itself and we do not choose everything because of something else, . . . it is clear that this will be the good, i.e., the highest good. (*EN* 1.2.1094a18–22)

Now, there seems to be a unanimous agreement: "Happiness" (εὐδαιμονία) is what all men profess to be ultimately looking for. But this is obviously only a verbal agreement since there seems to be universal disagreement about what exactly *eudaimonia* consists in: is the highest good we all seek wealth, pleasure, honor, or knowledge? This disagreement motivates Aristotle to develop his own account of happiness. This is done in two steps.

(1) First, he delineates two formal conditions that have to be met by every possible candidate for the role of the highest good.

(a) The "criterion of ultimate finality": the candidate has to be a "most final end" (τέλος τελειότατον), i.e., something which in the hierarchical order of our pursuits is always at the top of the pyramid. It is always chosen for its own sake and never for the sake of something else (*EN* 1.7.1097a25–b6).

(b) The "criterion of self-sufficiency": the candidate has to be self-sufficient in the sense that it makes life desirable on its own, i.e., without any further addition, and is in no way lacking or deficient (*EN* 1.7.1097b14–20).

(2) But since Aristotle wants a more determinate picture of happiness, he turns to his famous "function argument" (*EN* 1.7.1097b22–1098a20), which relies on the idea that what is good for man fundamentally depends on what man is and does. Now, what sets man apart from all other living beings in this world is rationality. The distinctive human function is therefore to be located in rational activity, which should be performed on the highest

possible level. The quality of this performance is tied to the notion of "excellence" or "virtue" (ἀρετή), since virtue in general is what makes a man good and causes him to perform his function well (see *EN* 2.6.1106a22–4). Aristotle sums up these considerations on the nature of happiness in the following definition:

> The good for man is an activity of soul in accordance with virtue, or if there is more virtue than one, in accordance with the best and most perfect one [κατὰ τὴν ἀρίστην καὶ τελειοτάτην]... in a complete lifetime. (*EN* 1.7.1098a16–18)

But this is still, as Aristotle readily admits, only an outline or sketch of the highest good, which does not explicitly state in which good(s) happiness truly consists. Especially at stake is the question of what is meant here by the "most perfect virtue." The basic issue is the exact meaning of "τελειοτάτη." Some interpreters take Aristotle to be saying that a happy man achieves "complete" virtue in life by performing various intellectual and moral activities in a rationally structured life. This view is called "inclusivism"; it implies that the quality of human life is not solely dependent on the performance of one single virtue but rather on a complete set of them, and is completed by various other intrinsically valuable goods (see, e.g., Crisp 1994). But if one takes "τελειοτάτη" to designate exactly one virtue, namely "the most final one" that ranks above all the others, its activity would be the single worthwhile good. This monolithic intrinsic goodness would "exclude" all other virtues from the definition and the essence of happiness; consequently this reading is called the "exclusivist" view (see, e.g., Kraut 1989). By arguing that Aristotle seems to waver between these two conceptions of the single end, W. F. R. Hardie (1965) opened up a long-standing debate in Aristotelian scholarship about whether the *Nicomachean Ethics* favors an "inclusivist" or "exclusivist" picture of happiness.

The problem of these rival readings of the Aristotelian definition is not alleviated by looking at the final account of happiness in *EN* 10 but rather deepened in its scope. Since Book 1 had provided only a formal sketch of happiness, Aristotle now obviously intends to give a material account of the form(s) of life that satisfy the conditions as well as the definition outlined above. But his "final" answer is again highly ambiguous. First, he praises the "theoretical life" (βίος θεωρητικός) of the philosopher as "perfect happiness" (τελεία εὐδαιμονία, 10.8.1178b7) for several reasons: most importantly because the highest philosophical knowledge is always sought for its own sake (thus meeting the criterion of ultimate finality) and because the philosopher is supremely independent of external circumstances and goods (thus fulfilling the criterion of self-sufficiency). But even as he extols the contemplative life as man's supreme happiness in an exclusivist manner, Aristotle reminds the reader that this life somehow transcends human nature and is more adequate for the solitary gods than for us as corporeal beings living in a social world. Consequently, he introduces a second[ary] (δευτέρα) form of happiness, the civic life, which consists in the activity of the various moral virtues and thus very much fits the "inclusivist" bill.

To summarize, in the end Aristotle offers not one unified account of happiness but rather a "twofold happiness." This leaves the reader puzzled in several respects:

(1) How does Aristotle conceive of the relationship between these two sorts of happiness? Are they really two different forms of life between that one can choose, or are they parts of a single mixed form of human life? Does the philosopher really need moral virtues in order to lead a perfect life, or could he do without even them?

(2) Since happiness is the good for and of man, these issues fundamentally involve the anthropological basis of the *EN*. While Aristotle's description of man as (i) a composite being made up of soul and body in his natural philosophy and (ii) as a naturally political animal (φύσει πολιτικὸν ζῷον) in his *Politics* (1.2.1253a2–3) seems to favor the more "down-to-earth" inclusivist view, *EN* 10 also contains a more "celestial" vision of man, which lends credit to the exclusivist reading. This exclusivist view then raises the question: is the Aristotelian man ultimately identical with his immaterial intellect?

4.2 Philosophical happiness in the two Ethics commentaries by Albert the Great

Albert wrote two commentaries on the *EN*: *Super Ethica* (1250–52) and *Ethica* (around 1262). *Super Ethica* is the first Latin commentary on the whole *EN* after its translation by Robert Grosseteste in 1246–47, predated only by partial commentaries on the first three books of the *EN*.

Those earlier commentaries contained a rather confused theological reading of Aristotle's notions of human happiness and virtue (see Wieland 1981; Celano 1986). According to them, Aristotle thinks that happiness is achieved after death through a heavenly union with God that is to be achieved in by the gift of supernatural virtues. This idiosyncratic reading was based on a curious variation in the pre-Grosseteste translation they had at hand. At 1.10.1101a20–1, the *Ethica nova* (the older translation of *EN* 1) contains the statement that we can be "happy like angels" (*beatos ut angelos*); this would fit the biblical promise (Mt 22:30) that in heaven we will become "like angels" through the beatific union with God. The original Greek actually reads "μακαρίους δ' ἀνθρώπους," later correctly translated as "*beatos ut homines*" by Grosseteste. This crucial passage is to be kept in mind because it provides a key to Aquinas's understanding of Aristotelian happiness (see Section 4.3).

Albert is certainly keen on correcting these fundamental misunderstandings, especially regarding the nature of Aristotelian happiness.[3] First of all, he stresses that Aristotle is talking about worldly happiness and not about heavenly bliss because the latter is outside the scope of philosophical inquiry (*Super Ethica* 1.3 n. 19, Editio Coloniensis 14:17 lines 50–5). In his two commentaries, Albert generally tries to keep philosophy and theology apart as neatly as possible in order to reconstruct a genuinely philosophical ethics (see Müller 2001). Consequently, he declares that God is certainly the first principle of everything but that "civil or contemplative happiness, about which philosophers argue, is in our power because it is acquired by our operations" (*Super Ethica* 3.6 n. 190, p. 170 lines 65–8). Worldly happiness is not immediately dependent on God's grace and is certainly not caused by divinely infused virtues, but rather by acquired ones.

By this strategic separation of philosophical and theological discourse about happiness, Albert has overcome the grossly harmonizing theological readings of the *EN* in the earlier commentaries and created room for an independent philosophical understanding of Aristotelian *eudaimonia*. His own reading of it has the following distinctive features.

(1) Albert thinks that the twofold form of human happiness, *felicitas civilis* and *contemplativa*, is mirrored by the structure of the *EN*: while Book 1 is about civil happiness, Book 10 is concerned with the theoretical life; these are the two orders of happiness. The definition of happiness outlined by Aristotle in *EN* 1 refers primarily to the moral life. According to Albert, the "most perfect" virtue that causes (civil) happiness is prudence, assisted by the other moral virtues.[4] This reading seems at first glance to favor an inclusivist view of Aristotelian civil *eudaimonia*, in which all the virtues as well as external goods would be included. But Albert is very clear that only prudence constitutes the essence of the beatific activity (*operatio felicitatis*) in the civil order; the moral virtues simply provide for and complete its activity, while external goods are merely valuable in an instrumental sense. He is therefore exclusivist with regard to the civil order.

---

[3] In his *Sentences* commentary (4.49B.6, ed. Borgnet 30:675a), Albert bursts out that these commentaries "corrupted rather than explained" the *EN*.

[4] *Super Ethica* 6.17 n. 579, Editio Coloniensis 14:499 lines 35–9; *Ethica* 1.9.1, ed. Borgnet 7:139b.

But the civil order is not truly independent from the contemplative one. Albert actually tends to a single-order exclusivist interpretation of overall happiness rather than a two-order one, as becomes most apparent in his reading of *EN* 10 (see Müller 2009a): there is only one final, monolithic end to which all virtues and activities (whether practical or theoretical) aim, namely the fulfillment of the human intellect in contemplation. Thus, contemplative happiness provides the supreme and overarching order. Civil happiness is not an independent form of life apart from theoretical happiness, but it is ultimately ordered toward it in a hierarchically integrated form of life. Thus, prudence is merely a dispositional prerequisite for securing the internal and external conditions necessary for bringing to maximal fruition what is truly best in us, namely our intellect, via contemplation. As a consequence, the moral and political life is conspicuously "downgraded" in Albert's understanding of Aristotelian happiness.

(2) This exclusivist reading of *eudaimonia* in the *EN* is based on an anthropology that seems to owe more to the (Neo-)Platonic identification of man with intellect than to Aristotle's picture of man as a composite being made up of body and soul. The human soul is created "in the shadow of intelligence," as Albert approvingly quotes Isaac Israeli (*Super Ethica* 1.7 n. 35, p. 32 lines 85–6). He takes Aristotle in *EN* 10 to mean that the intellect is "the whole man" (*totus homo*; see *Ethica* 10.2.3, ed. Borgnet 7:628a) and accordingly states in *De intellectu et intelligibili* (1.1.1, ed. Borgnet 9:478b) that "man is solely intellect."

(3) The main thrust of Albert's interpretation becomes clear when he discusses the objects of beatific contemplation. While Aristotle is rather sketchy here, Albert identifies the "divine" objects with the "separate substances" (*Super Ethica* 10.9 n. 887, p. 742 lines 7–9), i.e., the highest immaterial and intelligible forms. The final twist of this conception surfaces in his second *Ethics* commentary, where Albert explicitly ascribes knowledge of the separate substances to the human "acquired intellect" (*intellectus adeptus*).[5] This concept goes back to the Graeco-Arabic interpretation of Aristotle's notoriously unclear theory of intellect (νοῦς) as presented in his *De anima* 3.4–5. Albert elucidates the idea behind the "acquired intellect" in several of his writings (Müller 2006). The acquired intellect is the final perfection of the human mind, reached by continuous philosophical studies. Scientific inquiry enables us to grasp all the forms and principles of the sensible world; through the repeated process of abstraction by which the

---

[5] As I have argued in Müller 2006 and 2009a, in the background here is a development in Albert's thought between his composition of *Super Ethica* and, about ten years later, of *Ethica*.

"active intellect" (*intellectus agens*) effectually produces these forms as intelligible beings in the "possible intellect" (*intellectus possibilis*), the human
mind moves gradually closer to its own immaterial substance and finally
transcends the barrier of the sensible world completely:

> Then the active intellect adheres to the possible intellect as form to matter.
> This composition is called acquired and divine intellect by the Peripatetics,
> and in this state man is made perfect in order to perform his peculiar
> function . . . which is to contemplate perfectly through himself and to know
> the separate [substances]. The manner and the operation of this conjunction
> [of the active and possible intellect] fits Aristotle's account in the tenth book
> of the *Ethics*, where he almost says this. (Albert, *De anima* 3.3.11, Editio
> Coloniensis 7/1:222 lines 4–11)

Thus, in his understanding of contemplative happiness Albert closely links
EN 10 and the noetic account of *De anima* 3.[6] Although he is heavily
indebted to Arab thinkers, especially Alfarabi, Avicenna and Averroes,
he does not subscribe to the idea that the agent intellect itself must be
a separate substance identical for all human beings (this is the notorious
"Averroistic" idea of the "unicity of the intellect"). For Albert the active and
the passive intellect are parts of the human soul, not transcendent entities.
But he sticks to the underlying idea that the "acquired intellect," as a formal
conjunction (*coniunctio*) of *intellectus agens* and *possibilis*, assimilates our
cognition to the higher spheres of being in the Peripatetic cosmology:
through the acquired intellect we can grasp the essence of immaterial
beings directly and intuitively, no longer relying on sense-perceptions. In
his reading, Albert is obviously taking his cue from Aristotle's remark in *EN*
10.7.1177b33 that contemplation allows us to "immortalize" (ἀθανατίζειν)
ourselves as far as humanly possible when he identifies the *intellectus adeptus*
as the "root of immortality" (*radix immortalitatis*; see, e.g., *Ethica* 9.2.1, ed.
Borgnet 7:570a). This is one more indication of the supreme quality that
Albert ascribes to philosophical happiness in its highest form. Nowhere
in his *Ethics* commentaries does he describe it as deficient or somehow
lacking. Contrary to what the late Augustine maintains in *De civitate Dei*
9.5 – that everyone is bound to be miserable in this life – Albert seems
ready to recognize a genuine worldly happiness, a *felicitas in via*, to be
realized by man's own intellectual achievements. By so doing, he reinstates
philosophy as a distinct way of life and a road toward true happiness.
Thus, his transformation of Aristotle's *bios theōrētikos* from *EN* 10 with
the help of a Neoplatonic theory of the intellect created an ethical ideal

---

[6] This central link is also forged explicitly by Albert in *De anima* 3.3.6, Editio Coloniensis 7/1:215 lines
19–28; 3.3.11, p. 222 lines 9–11.

of philosophical felicity; this was taken up forcefully by later "Averroists" like Siger of Brabant and other masters in the arts faculty and officially condemned in 1277 (see Piché 1999, articles 40 and 176). But it had already received the earlier disapproval of his own disciple, Thomas Aquinas.

4.3   Imperfect happiness in Aquinas's *Sententia libri Ethicorum*

Right from the start, Aquinas constructs a kind of metaphysical framework for Aristotelian happiness. He takes up the first sentence of the *EN*, the statement that the good is what is universally desired – which Aristotle only applies explicitly to human practices – and applies it to the whole world: even non-intelligent beings strive for what is good without comprehending it, and they do this "under the direction of the divine intellect" (*ex ordinatione divini intellectus*, *SLE* 1.1 line 171). Everything has a natural desire (*desiderium naturale*) for goodness (*SLE* 1.2 lines 44–6) which aims at the realization of its ultimate perfection by its operation (1.2 lines 184–9). Thus, man's striving for goodness is not a peculiar feature of intelligent human beings and their actions but only a special case of a principle that pervades the whole of nature: man has a natural desire for happiness because his existence is ordered toward his perfection in action by a divine intellect. Aristotle's analysis of human practices in terms of means and ends is thus integrated from the outset into a kind of metaphysical and speculative framework, as is also done in the systematic treatise on happiness in the first five questions of *ST* 1–2.

The specific operations toward which creatures naturally aim are certainly not identical; nevertheless they all aim somehow at one good, because every form of goodness is ultimately rooted in a similitude to and participation of the highest good (*SLE* 1.1 lines 178–83). This comes very close to the idea developed in *SCG* 3 that everything naturally acts and strives for the sake of its ultimate good, i.e., its own perfection (chs. 2–3 and 16), and that this is ultimately realized by the creature's being assimilated to God, the highest good (chs. 17–24). Thus, Aquinas seems to leave the back door open for the distinction between God as the single end of all creatures (the "*finis cuius*") and the variety of different species' forms of striving for him (the "*finis quo*"), on which his treatment of human happiness in *ST* 1–2 is based;[7] we will come back to this later (in Section 4.5).

Aquinas's view of the structure of the whole *EN*, which underlies his understanding of Aristotelian happiness, is significantly different from

---

[7] The basic idea of this distinction is visible in *SLE* 1.10 lines 22–45, but Aquinas does not introduce the terminology of the *ST* in his commentary.

Albert's. For Aquinas, Book 1 contains an outline treatment of happiness in general which only receives its final specification in Book 10. What goes on between these two books is mainly prompted by the definition of happiness reached in *EN* 1.7, as "an operation of the soul according to perfect virtue": Books 2–9 are intended to examine the meaning of the second part of the definition by discussing the virtues and related phenomena. The role of Book 10 is to discuss the "perfect virtue" in whose operation happiness consists. Albert had simply identified this virtue with prudence in his commentary on Book 1, based on his conviction that this definition was only of civil happiness, while Book 10 was devoted strictly to contemplative happiness. Since Aquinas, unlike Albert, does not dissociate these two books of the *EN* but sees them as essentially linked, he comes to a different conclusion: the "perfect virtue" that Aristotle hints at in his definition in *EN* 1 can only be wisdom (*sapientia*) as it is discussed in *EN* 6, and in Aquinas's view the purpose of Book 10 is to justify this identification and spell it out more completely (see *SLE* 10.10 lines 57–78).

Now, in the end Albert somewhat attenuates his disruptive view of the *EN*'s structure by unifying the two forms of happiness into a single "mixed life" that is hierarchically ordered toward contemplation. This tends to an exclusivist reading of the whole *EN*, which in the end marginalizes moral activity. Aquinas sees the value of the social and political life differently; he does not reduce Aristotelian happiness to contemplation but states only that happiness consists "more" (*magis*) or "more principally" (*principalius*) in the contemplative than in the active life.[8] He also stresses that the wise man deliberately chooses (*eligit*) the moral virtues and the social life (*SLE* 10.12 lines 115–20) – not as instruments for enabling contemplation, but rather because of their own intrinsic value. Thus, the two forms of happy life are still recognizable as distinct forms of human perfection[9] – albeit of different quality – in Aquinas's *SLE*, which gives support to the thesis that he offers an overall inclusivist interpretation of the *EN*.[10]

Aquinas generally pays close attention to the two criteria offered by Aristotle for identifying true happiness: "ultimate finality" and "self-sufficiency." When discussing the second one he introduces an important distinction:[11] to be self-sufficient may mean – in a strict sense – to be

---

[8] See *SLE* 1.10 lines 114–21 and *ST* 1–2.3.5 resp. Very telling is the extensive use of the arguments drawn from *EN* 10 in Aquinas's treatment of the superiority of the *vita contemplativa* over the *vita activa* in *ST* 2–2.182.1.

[9] This is also mirrored in *ST* 2–2.179–82; see esp. 179.1–2.

[10] See Bradley 1997, 377–87, and Bossi de Kirchner 1986; while Kenny (1999, 19) interprets Aquinas's account as exclusivist.

[11] *SLE* 1.9 lines 181–217. For a discussion of this reading see Chapter 2, Section 2.5, in this volume.

absolutely complete in goodness so that virtually nothing good can be added to augment it. According to Aquinas, this is not the nature of human happiness as Aristotle describes it because such a form of self-sufficiency can only be attributed to God as the highest good *simpliciter*. The weaker sense of self-sufficiency that is appropriate to human happiness is only to lack nothing of what man naturally desires – which does not preclude the addition of further goodness. This difference points to an important insight that Aquinas thinks is pervasively present throughout the *EN*: if we take the Aristotelian criteria for happiness literally, human activities will always somehow fall short of it.

Aquinas here picks up a thread from the (usually neglected) second part of *EN* I, where Aristotle tries to reconcile his definition of happiness with common convictions about *eudaimonia*, especially concerning the influence of misfortune. In his discussion, Aristotle generally sticks to the idea that virtuous activity is the essential and constitutive part of happiness, but he is also ready to admit what Martha Nussbaum (1986) has aptly termed "the fragility of goodness." There are circumstances so severe that even the virtuous man cannot be called truly happy any longer (see also Gauthier 1951, 65–75 and 88–90). Aquinas basically agrees: the moral life partially depends on exterior goods that may be lost against one's will, and philosophical contemplation can be disturbed or even completely extinguished, by, e.g., mental illness (*SLE* 1.16 lines 148–52).

Furthermore, Aquinas points to the Aristotelian definition of happiness which closes with the formula that the virtuous activity has to last for "a complete life" (ἐν βίῳ τελείῳ) in order for somebody to be called really happy. From this, Aquinas gleans a third criterion for happiness in addition to "ultimate finality" and "self-sufficiency": stability of virtuous activity (encompassing its continuity and even its perpetuity) is also a hallmark of ultimate happiness in the full sense,[12] and Aquinas recognizes that fulfillment of this condition is naturally limited in human life. With this in mind he formulates an obvious conclusion that nevertheless has far-reaching consequences for his understanding of the scope of Aristotelian happiness:

> Thus continuity and perpetuity, which are not found in the present life, belong to the nature of perfect happiness. Hence perfect happiness [*perfecta felicitas*] cannot be had in this life. (*SLE* 1.10 lines 165–7; see also 1.14 lines 177–83)

---

[12] Aquinas regularly emphasizes that true happiness has to be stable, permanent, or even immutable; see, e.g., *ST* 1–2.2.3 ad 2.

To put it the other way around: The kind of happiness that Aristotle describes with his two forms of life in *EN* 10 is only an "imperfect happiness," which can be had in this life. Aquinas thinks that this is even stated by Aristotle himself, at the end of his discussion of the "Solonic problem" regarding whether somebody can be called happy during his life or only in retrospect (*EN* 1.10). In Aquinas's understanding this passage brings into focus the fundamental question of whether human beings can be perfectly happy in this world at all. When Aristotle finishes his discussion by stating that we may describe someone "who is active in accordance with perfect virtue . . . throughout a complete life" as happy and adds "but happy as human beings" (*EN* 1101a20–1), Aquinas virtually jumps at this qualification (see *SLE* 10.13 lines 141–4; 10.16 lines 218–22): to be happy "in a human way" means to be imperfectly happy because it cannot be compared to the ultimate form of happiness enjoyed by higher beings like angels and God. Aquinas regularly uses the catchphrase "*beati ut homines*" in his theological works to corroborate his view that Aristotle speaks about only the *beatitudo imperfecta* in this life, while perfect happiness is reserved for the afterlife.[13]

But this reading seems to brazenly ignore the fact that Aristotle himself explicitly speaks of the contemplative life as "perfect happiness" (τελεία εὐδαιμονία) in *EN* 10.7.1177b24. Aquinas has to show that even the philosophical life does not really meet the Aristotelian criteria of ultimate finality and self-sufficiency but is somehow radically deficient.

4.4 Aquinas's critique of an "Averroistic" reading of human happiness

In general, only on rare occasions does Aquinas explicitly comment on earlier interpretations of the *EN* in his *SLE*; therefore, it is remarkable how comparatively often he strikes out against Averroes or "Averroistic" readings of the text. This is most conspicuous when he defends his reading of Aristotelian happiness:

> From this it is clear that Aristotle places the ultimate human happiness in the activity of wisdom – which he treated above in Book 6 – and not in a conjunction with the active intelligence, as some pretend. (*SLE* 10.13 lines 137–41; see also *ST* 1.88.1 resp.; *SCG* 3.44)

The "Averroistic" idea of a conjunction (*continuatio*) with the separate "agent intellect" (*intellectus agens*) as the basis of the beatific operation, i.e.,

---

[13] See *In Sent.* 3.27.2.2 resp.; 4.49.1.1 qc. 4 resp.; *SCG* 3.48; *ST* 1–2.3.2 ad 4; *ST* 1–2.5.4 resp.

of the intuitive knowledge of the higher immaterial substances, is already known to us from Albert's commentary on *De anima* 3 and his interpretation of philosophical happiness in his *Ethica* 10. Aquinas rejects this reading for several reasons, which come to the surface at various points in his *SLE*:[14]

(1) He attacks the idea put forward by Averroes that the active intellect is itself a separate substance and argues that Aristotle himself understood it as a part of the human soul (see *SLE* 10.10 lines 40–50). So far he is still in substantial agreement with Albert.

(2) But he also explicitly argues against the possibility of man's intuitively knowing the intelligible forms of separate substances at all. Aquinas sticks to the basic idea that all our knowledge in this life is ultimately derived from our sense perceptions and the imaginative representations (*phantasmata*) stemming from them. Even in our highest intellectual cognition we always have to turn back to these perceptions ('*conversio ad phantasmata*'). As Carlos Steel (2001) has shown, this is exactly the point where Aquinas parts company with his teacher: Albert thinks that the "acquired intellect" enables us to have intuitive knowledge of the separate substances the way they themselves have it, while Aquinas stresses throughout his writings that intellectual knowledge of this sort is not available to us, at least not in our lifetime (see *SLE* 1.10 lines 22–35).

This is not a purely epistemological dispute. It goes to the heart of an anthropological divergence between them: Albert has a more Neoplatonic vision of man, as an intellect that is able to overcome the borders of the sensible world and accomplish a kind of divinization by means of philosophy, while Aquinas sees human existence and cognition in this world as tied to the fact that man is a natural composite of body and soul.

(3) Aquinas also thinks that the ideal of philosophical happiness that Albert and some of his followers favored simply does not fit the Aristotelian text. Albert's reading of contemplative happiness in *EN* 10 turns out to be a very elitist way of life: it can be realized only by the chosen few who have devoted their whole life to philosophy in order to reach this final stage of the "acquired intellect." Aquinas notes somewhat ironically that only a few, or perhaps no one at all, could claim in this life to be in a formal conjunction with the active intellect and thus know all things (*SLE* 1.14 lines 91–5; *SCG* 3.42). But this elitist vision of human happiness flies in the face of the Aristotelian dictum from *EN* 1.9.1099b18 that every man

[14] See also *In Sent.* 2.18.2.2; *ST* 1.88.1; *SCG* 3.42; *QDV* 18.5; *QDA* 16.

who is not incapacitated is able to attain happiness (*ST* 1.88.1 resp.; *SCG* 3.44). Therefore, it cannot be what Aristotle had in mind.

Thus, it is certainly part of Aquinas's overall intention in the *SLE* to correct an "Averroistic" misreading of *EN* 10 that may have been invited by Albert's understanding of this text.[15] But this is not only a battle about the correct interpretation of Aristotle: Aquinas is equally skeptical about the philosophical ideal of perfect happiness encapsulated in the Albertinian interpretation of *EN* 10. Since our natural knowledge of immaterial things remains necessarily limited, philosophical happiness in this life simply cannot be termed "perfect" but rather remains fundamentally "imperfect." In the end, it is not even "self-sufficient" in the weaker sense of the Aristotelian criterion because it does not fully satisfy our natural desire. Aquinas argues for this on the basis of the famous first sentence of Aristotle's *Metaphysics* (1.1.980a21), according to which "all men by nature desire to know." This human *desiderium naturale* can be fulfilled only by the full knowledge of the first cause of everything, i.e., of God's essence; all knowledge that falls short of this supreme object is deficient and ultimately does not quench our thirst for knowledge. Therefore, Aquinas repeatedly argues against the thesis that knowledge of the separate substances already constitutes perfect happiness. Our intellect's general aim is to attain truth, as Aristotle professes in *EN* 6.2.1139b12, and thus it can come to rest only in truth itself – God (*ST* 1–2.3.7, resp.). But the highest knowledge of something is achieved only by grasping its essence. Since philosophical contemplation cannot reach this in the case of God, it does not really fulfill our natural desire and therefore ultimately falls short, simply speaking (although its imperfection remains proportionate to our finite nature). Therefore, according to Aquinas's understanding of the *EN*, perfect human happiness as described by Aristotle himself cannot be attained in this life. This is also stressed consistently in his theological writings (*SCG* 3.48; *ST* 1–2.5.3), to which we now turn.

[15] Here I am in substantial agreement with Doig 2001, who maintains that it is one of the central purposes of the *SLE* to correct earlier commentaries on the *EN*, especially Averroes's middle commentary and Albert's *Super Ethica*. But it has to be noted that the explicit link between contemplative happiness and the Averroistic idea of conjunction is neither made in Averroes's commentary on the *EN* nor in Albert's *Super Ethica*, but only in Albert's later *Ethica*, which Doig does not take into consideration. The possible influence of *Ethica* on *SLE* is still unclear. Most scholars ignore it or deliberately play it down (e.g., Bourke 1974, 245 and 247), usually without detailed argument. But Gauthier has already hinted at an influence (Praefatio, p. 256*), and the indirect evidence offered above by the marked contrast between Aquinas's presentation of Aristotelian happiness and Albert's "importation" of the *intellectus adeptus* into *EN* 10 may prove significant, if one is inclined to dig deeper than is possible here.

4.5   Perfect happiness in Aquinas's theological writings

But does not all this imply that our natural desire for knowledge and our longing for perfect happiness may be finally frustrated altogether? Aquinas argues along the following lines: since our desire for perfect happiness is natural and "God and nature do nothing in vain" (see Aristotle, *De caelo* 1.4.277a32), it will not be frustrated; hence in the end we will reach perfect happiness. Aquinas adds another argument that follows from what we already know: since perfect happiness cannot be attained in this earthly life, our natural desire for it should be fulfilled after death. This insight can be derived from Aristotle's considerations on the nature of happiness:

> But because all this does not seem to meet the above conditions required for happiness [scil. ultimate finality, self-sufficiency, and stability], he adds that we call "happy as men" those who are subject to change and cannot attain perfect happiness. Since a natural desire is not in vain, we can correctly judge that perfect happiness is reserved for man after this life. (*SLE* 1.6 lines 218–22)

Note that Aquinas marks his view on the necessity of reserving perfect happiness for the afterlife not as an Aristotelian teaching but as a conclusion that "we" can draw from his treatment. What this perfect life after death consists in can be gathered from Sacred Scripture: it must be a relationship with God in heaven by which we become "like angels" (Mt 22:30). In this "angelic happiness" – note the contrast to "*beati ut homines*" – man will not only see God *in* his essence but also *through* his essence: God will not be known through any intermediate cognition and intelligible forms, but will be directly joined to man in a heavenly union; thus, God finally becomes the form of the human intellect.[16] Only heavenly beatitude satisfies all the criteria for perfect happiness that Aquinas emphasizes so much in the *SLE*:

(1) *Ultimate finality*: Only God as the highest good can be the final goal of the universal striving for goodness which Aquinas finds in the beginning of the *EN* (see above, Section 4.3). Beyond God and his all-encompassing goodness nothing can be sought as a further good. Since the human will has the good as its natural object, it will come to rest in this universal goodness of God (*ST* 1–2.2.8–9).

(2) *Self-sufficiency*: The natural desire for knowledge and truth that is implanted in our intellect is also satisfied to the highest degree imaginable

---

[16] See *ST* 3.92.1. It is quite interesting that the wording concerning the union with God used here by Aquinas comes very close to the Averroistic model of conjunction with the separate intellect.

by the essential knowledge of God as the first cause of all things (*ST* 1–2.3.8).

(3) *Stability*: Since in heaven this operation is completely unhindered by any external or internal impediments, it is permanent and immutable. The full satisfaction of this criterion is granted to man by the eternal life (*vita aeterna*) enjoyed in the union with God (see *SCG* 3.62).

Since only the essential vision of God fully meets all three criteria for perfect happiness, it is no wonder that Aquinas also defends its attainability against possible doubts that man might not be able to reach it even in the afterlife (see *SCG* 3.25 and 3.57). A denial of this possibility would not only contradict the biblical promises but would also render the natural desire of human beings vain, thus putting the providential character of creation in doubt. In Aquinas's view, the vision of God as the essence of perfect human happiness and its attainability in the afterlife is therefore required by theological as well as philosophical considerations.

In drawing this picture, Aquinas's treatise on happiness in *ST* 1–2.1– 5 relies heavily on a distinction that comes to the fore when he inquires if there is one final goal (*finis ultimus*) for all beings (*ST* 1–2.1.8). In some sense, there is: God as the final cause at which all creatures aim is the single end (*finis cuius*) of everything. On the other hand, all creatures have their specific *finis quo*, their proper mode of attaining their end or perfection: they participate in the similitude of God in different manners. In the case of rational creatures like human beings this specific *finis quo* is to have knowledge of God. The *finis cuius* thus is the "external" end or good, while the *finis quo* is its "internal" acquisition (see *In Sent.* 4.49.1.1 qc. 2 resp.).

This distinction allows for some subtle points concerning the conceptualization of happiness. Aquinas can regard happiness as uncreated (*ST* 1–2.2.8) as well as created (*ST* 1–2.3.1) without contradiction, depending on the scope of "*summum bonum.*" Happiness is uncreated if the notion of the highest good refers to God as the external *finis cuius* of human striving; it is created when it designates the internal realization of the vision of God in the human soul. Aquinas makes use here of the Platonic idea of participation: ultimately, only God *is* happiness in its essential form, while the intellectual creatures take part in it via a certain operation, the beatific vision. This difference between uncreated happiness in God and the created happiness that is a kind of participation in it is another form of *duplex beatitudo*, one which conceptually precedes the distinction between perfect and imperfect human happiness (*In Sent.* 4.49.1.2 qc. 1 ad 1). The connection just outlined between *beatitudo creata* and *increata*, between *finis cuius* and *finis quo*, highlights the overall ontological or theocentric basis of Aquinas's understanding of human happiness: the highest good for human beings is dependent on the highest good for the world. Our natural striving for perfect happiness turns out, in the end, to be an implicit desire to see God (Bradley 1997, 459).

This fundamental dependence of the *summum bonum hominis* on the *summum bonum simpliciter* is not restricted to the level of final causality. God is not only the ultimate object but also the intrinsic formal cause of the beatific vision, and as such he effects it immediately.[17] According to Aquinas, "happiness is something exceeding the limits of created nature" (*ST* 1–2.5.6. resp.), which means that it can never be realized by mere natural means but only with the aid of supernatural grace (*ST* 1–2.5.5 resp.; *SCG* 3.52). This leads to a seemingly paradoxical position: our natural desire for happiness can be fulfilled only by a supernatural end (God) and with supernatural assistance (grace).[18]

Now where does this vision of perfect heavenly happiness leave the imperfect happiness of earthly human life? Aquinas is certainly engaged in countering the impression, created by Albert and some "Averroistic" commentaries on the *EN*, that philosophical happiness in this life can be legitimately called "perfect." But this does not come down to a whole-hearted denigration of it in the style of Augustine. Aquinas sees some kind of continuity between imperfect and perfect happiness because the contemplative happiness possible in this life is "a kind of participation in [perfect] happiness" (*aliqualis participatio beatitudinis*: *ST* 1–2.5.3 resp.; 3.6 resp.), for it shares, albeit imperfectly, the object of the *visio Dei*:

> Now the contemplation of divine truth is accessible to us in an imperfect manner, "through a mirror and enigmatically." Thus, it provides us with a kind of beginning of happiness [*inchoatio beatitudinis*] which begins here so that it may be completed in the future. Therefore, Aristotle too states in *EN* 10 that supreme happiness consists in the contemplation of the highest intelligible. (*ST* 2–2.180.4 resp.)

Worldly beatitude is an anticipation of what is still to come: in heaven we will see God no longer in a mirror but directly, face to face (1 Cor 13:12). Philosophical contemplation cannot provide us with this ultimate form

---

[17] I owe this observation to Katja Krause, whom I would like to thank for an attentive reading of this text.

[18] See esp. *QDV* 27.2 resp.; *In BDT* 6.4 ad 5. This raises a lot of difficult theological questions, e.g., whether the concept of a natural desire ultimately compromises the supernatural character of man's end. For detailed discussions see Bradley 1997, ch. 9, and Feingold 2010.

of knowledge, and requires supernatural assistance for the fulfillment of
man's natural desire for happiness. As so often in Aquinas's thought, grace
does not destroy nature but perfects it.

4.6 Aquinas and Aristotelian happiness

In the final analysis, Aquinas's overall view of happiness is theological and
eschatological rather than philosophical (see Leonhardt 1998 contra Kleber
1988). This imposes some limits on what philosophy can contribute to
understanding it; as Aquinas explicitly states in the *SLE* (1.9 lines 164–
5), the happiness of the afterlife ultimately exceeds rational investigation.
The aim of life which the philosophers take into consideration does not
transcend the framework of nature (*QDV* 14.3 ad 9) and consequently
does not pertain to the gracious gift of heavenly happiness. Therefore,
the philosophers simply cannot have "full knowledge" (*plena notitia*) of
happiness, which is the major reason why they posit a happiness consisting
in the contemplation of the separate substances that may be had in this life
(*SCG* 3.63; *ST* 3.92.1).

But this does not mean that philosophy's contribution in this area is
marginal or even entirely superseded. Aquinas leaves no doubt that Aristotle's *EN* provides the best available philosophical account of happiness
in this life, an account worthy of being reconstructed in detail. He credits
it with some important insights related to the nature of perfect happiness,
especially concerning the "formal" criteria pertaining to it like finality, self-
sufficiency, and stability, which would have to be fully met in order for the
natural human desire for ultimate perfection to be completely fulfilled. If
these conditions are taken strictly, it is possible to detect the fundamental
deficiency inherent in every worldly form of happiness, including the civil
and the contemplative life that Aristotle describes. According to Aquinas,
the philosophical inquiry into the nature of happiness in the *EN* ends up
with a kind of aporetic result: the perfect happiness that is sought after by
all men and that is at the center of philosophy itself cannot be had in this
life.

Based on this philosophical insight regarding "imperfect happiness," one
has to transcend the borders of rational investigation toward the reflection
on man's ultimate perfection possible in an afterlife. This shift from earthly
beatitudo imperfecta to heavenly *beatitudo perfecta* is certainly the crucial
element in Aquinas's attitude toward Aristotelian happiness (see Celano
1987). Some scholars suppose that it is exactly at this point that Aquinas
transforms the Aristotelian notion to match his own theological convictions

concerning the immortality of the soul and divine providence.[19] Does Aquinas ultimately "baptize" Aristotle's concept of happiness?

A detailed investigation into this issue would involve a close reading of several disputed passages in the *SLE*, which is not possible here.[20] But my general impression is that Aquinas did not intentionally distort Aristotelian happiness in the *SLE* in order to adjust it to his own theological purposes (Adams 1991, 98–9); he primarily wants to get to the meaning of the text and the essential doctrines contained in it (Bourke 1974, 258; Elders 1987, 87). Most importantly, nowhere in the *SLE* does he introduce the idea of a happy afterlife as an explicit Aristotelian teaching; rather, this idea is presented as something hidden in his writings, which can be brought to light by a careful reading. Explicitly, Aristotle deals only with the happiness of this life. Aquinas's overall reading of the *EN* seems to match his earlier judgment that Aristotle offers no explicit position toward the *beatitudo in patria*, neither confirming nor denying it in the *EN* (*In Sent.* 4.49.1.1 qc. 4 resp.: "*nec asserens nec negans*").

There is certainly no "double truth" at work here that would juxtapose the *EN* and the biblical teaching on happiness. In Aquinas's view, Aristotle is rather in a kind of "pre-established harmony" with the eschatological view of perfect happiness championed by theology. But Aquinas does not look for a crude reconciliation or short-circuit between these two conceptions, i.e., he does not return to the naive identification of the Aristotelian notion of happiness with heavenly beatitude maintained by the earlier theological commentaries on the *EN*, which had already been decisively dismissed by Albert. The main difference between Aquinas and his teacher seems to be as follows: while Albert deliberately separates philosophy and theology in his two commentaries and thus seals off Aristotelian happiness from the religious outlook, Aquinas uses the *EN* as a kind of starting point for a broader theological inquiry into the nature of perfect happiness – an inquiry that, unlike Aristotle's ethical enterprise, is not limited by the bounds of natural reason.

---

[19] See Jaffa 1952, 187–8, who identifies six "non-Aristotelian" principles as theological imports to the *SLE*, among them the beliefs that perfect happiness is impossible in this life and that its attainment in the afterlife is bound up with personal immortality. Doig 2001, 109–93, argues against Jaffa that his six principles are not theological imports, but rather that Aquinas believed them to be philosophical and proper to Aristotle. For a detailed critique of Jaffa see also Kleber 1988, 66–72.

[20] See esp. *SLE* 1.17 lines 142–53, where Aquinas cuts off a possible discussion of the afterlife with the remark that "we have discussed this elsewhere." See Jaffa 1952, 146–8, who accuses Aquinas of identifying Aristotle with himself qua theologian, and the criticism of this reading by Leonhardt 1998, 149–52.

Now, to what extent did the *EN* have an influence on Aquinas's view of happiness in his theological writings? Since philosophy is not competent in matters of eschatological beatitude, Aquinas usually looks to Aristotle only for analysis of earthly happiness. But he also frequently has recourse to the *EN* in the context of strictly religious discussions, e.g., in his treatment of the evangelical beatitudes promised by Christ in the Sermon on the Mount (Mt 5:3–11).[21] In my opinion, there is one basic Aristotelian idea from the *EN* that pervades Aquinas's treatment of *beatitudo* right from the start, namely that it is essentially an intellectual activity. To think of happiness as an activity (ἐνέργεια) and neither as a kind of external good nor an internal state or habit of the person is a kind of trademark of Aristotelian ethics, and Aquinas defends it from the very beginning in his theological works (*In Sent.* 1.1.1.1 resp., *ST* 1–2.3.2). The "intellectualist" character of Aristotelian happiness with its emphasis on the supreme value of contemplation is mirrored in Aquinas's repeated arguments for the preponderance of the intellect over the will in human happiness (see, e.g., *ST* 1–2.3.4). Our final perfection is first and foremost a kind of supreme intellection, upon which the ultimate love of God follows, as Aquinas stresses with an eye to the rival Franciscan view on this subject. Certainly, there are significant biblical passages which mention the vision of God as our ultimate goal (Mt 5:8; Jn 17:3; 1 Cor 13:12), but none of them is specific enough to provide Aquinas with convincing arguments for an intellectualist understanding of happiness – which is exactly what the *EN* (especially in Book 10) does.

But it has to be noted that this intellectualist vein in Aquinas's own understanding of perfect happiness does not sidetrack his overall inclusivist interpretation of Aristotle's *EN*. Against Albert's exclusivist interpretation of happiness in Neoplatonic terms, Aquinas sticks to the basic Aristotelian idea that worldly happiness can have two distinct forms, i.e., action and contemplation. There truly is a *duplex beatitudo imperfecta* and not only one "perfect philosophical happiness," as in Albert's reading. Therefore, the virtues and actions of the civil life are worth considering even if they are not directly ordered toward contemplation. Viewed from a purely exegetical level, Aquinas's interpretation of Aristotelian *eudaimonia* in terms of an "imperfect happiness" does sometimes stretch the text of the *Nicomachean Ethics* to its limits. But the considerable intellectual maneuvering space

---

[21] See Guindon 1956, 199–201, and Kenny 1999, 19–21, who stresses "that the Christian texts are distorted to fit the Aristotelian context, rather than the other way round."

which Aquinas gains by this hermeneutical move for his own account of a twofold happiness certainly gives some justification to his approach to the text. As happens quite frequently in the history of philosophy, a rather dubious reading of other texts provides a thinker with the basis for a theory that is cogent and challenging in its own right.

CHAPTER FIVE

Aquinas on choice, will, and voluntary action

Matthias Perkams

In the 1950s René Antoine Gauthier laid out the main points of divergence between Aristotle's ethics and his medieval interpreters Albert and Aquinas. Two of the most essential points he made have to do with action theory: First, that the notion of will was lacking in Aristotle (1958; 2nd edition with new introduction 1970, I, 1:255–66). Second, that Aristotle did not yet see the difficulties with freedom between alternative possibilities, with the result that he simply presupposed it even though his general philosophical outlook should have excluded it (1970, II,1:217–20).

If we look at the recent scholarship on those points, we find a rather curious situation. On the one hand, many contemporary scholars agree with Gauthier that the ancient philosophers, including Aristotle, had neither a word nor even the notion corresponding to the medieval (and modern) concept of will. It is only authors from Augustine on who are credited with attaching substantial weight to the notion of the will in the discussion of human action (Dihle 1982).

Modern interpretations of Aquinas, on the other hand, do not give the impression that the will was a crucial notion for his theory of action. Denis Bradley represents a widespread opinion when he says that "the volitional act follows upon and is thus subordinate to the intellectual act . . . As long as the agent's practical judgment is free, his or her choice is free" (1997, 342 and 346). Indeed, many authors label Aquinas an "intellectualist."[1] Some of them infer from this that Aquinas is interpreting Aristotle correctly because he has basically the same concept of practical reason as Aristotle (Westberg 1994a, 38–9 and 120; Pasnau 2002, 225) or because Aristotle "implicitly" has the same theory of will as Aquinas (Irwin 1992; Rhonheimer 1994, 187).[2] Thus, contemporary scholarship might suggest that Gauthier need not have warned us after all not to try "to find the

---

[1] For a good definition of "intellectualism" and a more complex overview of the debate concerning Aquinas's theory of action, see Eardley 2003, 837–9.

[2] T. H. Irwin also advocates a similar position in Chapter 2, in this volume.

complete saint Thomas in Aristotle" by reading the will into Aristotle's theory of action (1970, II,1:220). There are still some scholars, however, who give the will more influence in their accounts of Aquinas's action theory.[3]

Regarding freedom or the "free will problem," we encounter a no less confusing situation. While it is still controversial whether Aristotle accepted freedom between alternative possibilities (Sorabji 1980; Jedan 2000), it seems obvious that Aquinas did. Recent discussions on this point, however, have been controversial as well. Authors who take Aquinas to be an intellectualist part ways about whether his account is libertarian (Mac-Donald 1998; McCluskey 2002) or compatibilist (Hause 1997, Pasnau 2002). "Voluntarist" interpretations, not surprisingly, tend to be libertarian, but even a libertarian interpreter may claim, as Eleonore Stump does, that Aquinas's explicit theory of *liberum arbitrium* and choice does not actually extend to all human acts (Stump 2003, 278–87). This would give the impression that Aquinas has no clear account of human freedom.

In order to evaluate Aquinas's understanding of *EN* 3.1–5, all these points have to be borne in mind. In my eyes, a close reading of Aquinas reveals that between his views and Aristotle's there is a remarkable difference which has left its traces even in the *SLE*. This difference is due, first, to Aquinas's conviction that choice (*electio*, προαίρεσις) is primarily an interior act of the will, which is guided by practical reason but does not follow its commands automatically. While Aquinas uses largely Aristotelian vocabulary to describe this, his starting point is Augustine's explanation of human freedom in terms of acts of the will, which are entirely in man's power. In this respect, his account is far from anything one could reasonably ascribe to Aristotle. Second, Aquinas's conception of a particular practical reason, which is crucial for understanding both his libertarian account of freedom and the role he assigns to the will, seems to be largely his own achievement, though this aspect of the theory is influenced more heavily by Aristotle.

To support my argument, I will first study Aquinas's explanation of *EN* 3.1–5 in the *SLE*. Then I will turn to Aquinas's systematic writings for the theoretical background behind those comments. For the sake of brevity I will neglect the complex question of whether Aquinas's views on these points developed within his career; my personal impression is that such changes are at best marginal (cf. Westberg 1994b).

---

[3] See, e.g., Kent 1995, 155–75, and Hoffmann 2007; see also Chapter 6 in this volume, esp. pp. 97–100.

5.1   Aquinas's interpretation of *EN* 3.1–5 in the *SLE*

5.1.1   The overall structure of Aquinas's interpretation

Aquinas's interpretation of *EN* 3.1–5 reveals from the outset a special interest in "choice." He states explicitly that Aristotle's definition of virtue as a "habit issuing in choices" (*habitus electivus*, ἕξις προαιρετική, 2.6.1106b36) requires a special treatment of that topic.[4] The other main concepts discussed in 3.1–5, "the voluntary" (*voluntarium*, ἑκών) and "the will" (*voluntas*, βούλησις), are in Aquinas's view connected with choice: the voluntary embraces all acts that are done "of one's own accord" (*sponte*), while the will looks to the end envisaged by the action, thus determining what one wants to reach by one's choices (*SLE* 3.1 lines 7–11). Furthermore, "the genus of choice" is the voluntary; the specific difference of choice is "resulting from deliberation" (*SLE* 3.5 lines 34–9; 3.6 lines 116–20).[5] This fits well with Aquinas's statement that the subject of *EN* 3.1–5 is not those actions that cause our virtuous or vicious habits, but rather those that are brought about by "the virtue, which works by way of choice" (*SLE* 3.1 line 5).

Aquinas's interpretation of *EN* 3.1 does not indicate that he thought this subject was particularly problematic. The problems which this text presented for medieval readers had been discussed by Albert the Great in the questions of his *Super Ethica*, e.g., the relationship between sin (*peccatum*) and the voluntary (*Super Ethica* 3.2 n. 160, Editio Coloniensis 14:144). Aquinas for his part concentrates mostly on explaining Aristotle's text; often he points out systematic structures in the text that he thinks Aristotle deliberately intended. For example, he says that the reason Aristotle divides his treatment of the involuntary according to whether it is caused by force or ignorance is to take account of the appetitive and the cognitive aspects of action (*SLE* 3.1 lines 68–78).

Regarding ignorance and its consequences, Aquinas, interpreting 3.1.1110b18–24, emphasizes that an action done out of ignorance is only "against someone's willing" (*contra suam voluntatem*), such that it cannot be ascribed to this person, if he regrets it once his ignorance is dispelled (*SLE* 3.3 lines 10–43). Aristotle's ignorance "within choice" (*in electione*, ἐν τῇ προαιρέσει, 1110b31) pertains, in Aquinas's view, to a particular judgment

---

[4] Aquinas explains the formulation that virtue is a habit "issuing in choices" by a cross-reference to *EN* 8.13.1163a22–3, where Aristotle states that "the determinant of virtue and character lies in decision." This formulation is repeated quasi verbatim and without further qualifications in Aquinas's commentary (*SLE* 8.13 lines 215–16).

[5] On Aquinas's interpretation of the voluntary, see Bonnie Kent's observations at pp. 100–2.

occurring in the context of a concrete action (his example is of somebody thinking that it is good to sin "now"); it is distinguished from ignorance "at the level of the universal" (1110b32), i.e., ignorance of what should be done and avoided in general. Gauthier contested Aquinas's interpretation; in his view, in 1110b31 ignorance "within choice" concerns universals, such as the universal premise in a practical syllogism (Gauthier and Jolif 1970, II,1:183). While the correct interpretation of Aristotle is hard to decide, it is useful to highlight the close link Aquinas establishes between choices and particular actions.

Furthermore, Aquinas separates ignorance of an action's essential features from ignorance of its so-called circumstances, which is how he interprets the subsequent list of conditions the ignorance of which will make an action involuntary (1111a2–6). He spends an unusual amount of space explaining and categorizing these circumstances into those that concern the causes of an action (its efficient, principal, and instrumental causes) and those that concern the action itself, i.e., its genus, its subject matter, and the way it is carried out (*SLE* 3.3 lines 123–60). In doing so he is following Albert, who had detected in this passage the "circumstances" of Cicero's *De inventione* (1.34–41) and had argued that "they increase an action's blameworthiness or praiseworthiness" (*Super Ethica* 3.2 nn. 166–8, pp. 148–51). The long treatment Aquinas devotes to the circumstances in the *SLE* indicates that he too considered them an important topic of ethical theory. For Aquinas, moral knowledge must cover not only universal rules but also circumstances, that is, the specific features of the agents and their actions.

5.1.2   Aquinas's treatment of choice in the SLE

Let us now take a closer look at Aquinas's discussion of that concept that we have identified as the core term of *EN* 3.1–5: choice. Already for many medieval authors before Aquinas, *electio* is the core concept for the explanation of "free agency" (*liberum arbitrium*).[6] Albert declares in his *Super Ethica* that "choice is an act of one power, which is called free agency, which is a power different from both reason and will, but taking part in both of them" (*Super Ethica* 3.4 n. 173, p. 154 lines 53–6). In linking *liberum arbitrium* and choice[7] Albert is following Philip the Chancellor,

---

[6] Albert's use of *electio* is explained well in Hoffmann 2006, 81–8. My reason for rendering *liberum arbitrium* as "free agency" will become clear later on; see below, p. 79.

[7] The same doctrine can be found in Albert's systematic works, e.g., *De homine*, Editio Coloniensis 27/2:517–18. Cf. Westberg 1994a, 106–10.

who had made this connection in his *Summa de bono*, written around 1220 (ed. Wicki, 1:160 and 1:173). Here Albert would also have read that free agency is a faculty of both reason and will; this opinion, which had been discussed by numerous twelfth-century theologians, can be found also in the *Sentences* of Peter Lombard.[8] The position that the act of this faculty is choice or consists in choosing was apparently put forward in only the thirteenth century.[9]

In contrast to Albert, Aquinas does not mention *liberum arbitrium* – a term that he consistently links with choice in his systematic works – in his interpretation of *EN* 3.1–5 (see Hoffmann 2006, 88). While thus being careful not to introduce concepts alien to the *EN* into his explanation, he makes some noteworthy points that are not to be found directly in either Albert or Aristotle. One of these is the connection he draws between choice and virtue at the beginning of his exegesis of *EN* 3.3: the immediate result of virtue is the agent's interior choice, and not his exterior operation. In fact, a virtuous agent may be hindered from performing virtuous acts and still remain virtuous, and a vicious agent may perform apparently good acts because of a bad choice, e.g., when he chooses to strive for vainglory. Thus, it is strictly speaking the choice and not the outward action that is blameworthy or praiseworthy (*SLE* 3.5 lines 18–28). There are good reasons for questioning whether Aristotle shared this opinion. To be sure, the fact that some choices are not carried out may be explained by distinguishing between choice and the exterior action, as Aquinas does. For Aristotle, however, to ask whether a choice has been carried out is equivalent to asking whether any action has been performed *at all*. For Aquinas, in contrast, the interior choice is *in itself* an action.[10]

A further point should arouse our interest: the relation between choice and will. Aquinas does not exploit the translation of *boulēsis* as *voluntas* for ascribing to Aristotle a general notion of will. Rather, he understands the Latin Aristotle's *voluntas* in *EN* 3.4 as the primary act of the faculty of will, which is directed to its proper object, i.e., the good, in the same way that the primary act of the intellect is directed to the intellect's proper objects, i.e., self-evident first principles (*SLE* 3.10 lines 9–19).

This becomes clearer in Aquinas's explanation of *EN* 3.2. Here, he takes Aristotle to be discussing all four principles of human acts: reason, will,

---

[8] As can be seen from the material collected by Lottin 1957, 12–74.

[9] Lottin 1957, 81–127. See especially the anonymous *Summa* quoted at p. 84 line 20: "Liberum arbitrium est principium electionis," and the remarks concerning Albert's *Super Ethica* at pp. 126–7.

[10] Aquinas's concept of action is analogous, and thus the term can be applied to quite different mental or bodily activities; see Brock 1998, 7–48.

desire, and spirit (*SLE* 3.5 lines 70–6). While accepting the way Aristotle distinguishes choice from both desire and spirit, he emphasizes that "it appears closely related to" will (*voluntas*; βούλησις, 3.2.1111b19–20). Will and choice, Aquinas continues,

> both belong to the same power, i.e., to the rational appetite, which is called will. But will [βούλησις] refers to the act of this power by which it tends to the good unconditionally [*absolute*], whereas choice refers to the act of that same power which is related to the good insofar as it pertains to human action, in which we are directed towards a particular good. (*SLE* 3.5 lines 147–54)

Thus, he ascribes to the faculty called will not only Aristotle's *boulēsis*, but also his *prohairesis*, i.e., choice. He qualifies this move in his interpretation of Aristotle's paradoxical statements that choice is "deliberate desire" (*consiliabile desiderium*, 3.3.1113a11) or "intelligence qualified by desire or desire qualified by thought" (*appetitivus intellectus vel appetitus intellectivus*; 6.2.1139b4–5). In the first case, Aquinas calls choice "an act of the rational appetite which is called will" (*SLE* 3.9 lines 56–7); in the second case, he states that the formulation "desire qualified by thought" is "truer" (*verius*), because the objects of choice are good or bad, not true or false (*SLE* 6.2 lines 213–16). Thus, while not denying that in one respect "choice is essentially an act of the intellect, insofar as the intellect orders the appetite" (*SLE* 6.2 lines 209–10), he displays a clear preference for ascribing choice primarily to the will.

The main reason for this preference seems to be his conviction that only by performing an act of will are we really *acting* well or badly; the right cognition of an object as good or bad only means that we have *the power* to act so. In this way Aquinas explains at some length Aristotle's short remark that it is "choosing that makes us people of a certain quality" (3.2.1112a1–3). He calls it the first of five arguments by which Aristotle proves that choice is different from opinion, but it is not unfair to say that it is the only one of these five arguments that is not taken directly from Aristotle's text (*SLE* 3.6 lines 35–60). Aquinas's interpretation thus reveals an underlying moral psychology that assigns quite different roles to reason and will in the causation and explanation of actions, but which, however, focuses especially on the role of the will.

At this point, it is worthwhile to return to the difference between Aquinas's ascription of choice to the will and Albert's understanding of *liberum arbitrium* as a third power different from will and reason, but having a share in both of them. Albert's reading, even if it simply repeats a traditional medieval explanation of *liberum arbitrium*, may have correctly grasped Aristotle's own intention here: many contemporary Aristotelian scholars likewise do not think that Aristotle posited a special faculty called "will," distinct from rational cognition, to explain human actions. Aquinas, on the contrary, does find a will, defined as a form of appetite that depends upon reason's judgments, in Aristotle's text. This interpretation is closely connected with his own account of the respective roles of reason and will in bringing about an action. Thus, in order to understand the philosophical theory that Aquinas finds in *EN* 3.1–5, we have to investigate the way he describes human action in his systematic works.

5.2   Aquinas's own theory of choice, will, and voluntary action

Aquinas frequently points out the importance of choice or *electio* as "the distinguishing mark of free agency"; statements like this can be found in all of his treatments of *liberum arbitrium*, both in his earlier and his later writings (*In Sent.* 2.24.1.2 resp.; *QDV* 24.1 ad 1; *ST* 1.83.3 resp. [see the quotation above]; *QDM* 6 arg. 1 lines 1–3).

The philosophical implications of this focus on choice, however, are not totally clear. As I said earlier, Eleonore Stump has pointed out that not everything Aquinas treats as belonging to freedom of agency seems to be covered by *electio*. She draws attention especially to *ST* 1–2.6–17, Aquinas's most detailed account of the stages leading to a human action. Here Aquinas describes several acts of intellect and will, most of which he seems to distinguish from choice.[11] The structure of this section broadly follows the order of *EN* 3.1–5, such that it can be read as a "commentary by questions" on Aristotle's text[12]: voluntariness (q. 6), circumstances (q. 7), will (qq. 8–10), choice (q. 13), and deliberation (q. 14). It adds in, however, treatments of fruition (q. 11), intention (q. 12), consent (q. 15), employment of means (q. 16), and command (q. 17).

Out of this list, the most striking example of an act of the will that does not seem to be a choice is consent, which is defined by Aquinas as an act of will which follows upon a deliberation (*consilium*) indicating that there is only one possible chain of action suited for reaching a proposed end. Consequently, a consent of this kind is not a choice between alternative possibilities (*ST* 1–2.15.3 ad 3). Even more fundamentally, rational deliberation in general is obviously a human action, but not a choice, if choice

---

[11]   An earlier, less complete parallel is *QDV* 22.13–15.

[12]   Gauthier calls the *Secunda pars* of the *Summa theologiae* "le commentaire par *questiones* qui devait normalement compléter l'*exposicio littere*" (Gauthier and Jolif 1970, I, 1:131).

is, as in the *SLE*, principally an act of the will. Apparently, then, many human acts have to be excluded from being choices between alternative possibilities; consequently, the role of acts of the will in Aquinas seems to be rather restricted (Stump 2003, 294–7).

Such a position, however, fails to explain why Aquinas himself stresses so often that free agency is exercised chiefly in making choices, and why he ascribes them principally to the will. Indeed, in his systematic writings as well as in the *SLE*, he frequently repeats his preference for the expression "desire qualified by thought" over "intelligence qualified by desire" (*In Sent.* 2.24.1.3 resp.; *QDV* 24.6 resp.; *ST* 1.83.3 resp.; *ST* 1–2.14.1 resp. and ad 1). It should be clear that a correct evaluation of Aquinas's theory of action has to grasp *why* these points are so important for him. In order to elucidate this, I will focus first on the rationality of choice; then I will attempt to explain the will's role in choice; and finally I will look at the interaction of reason and will.

5.2.1 Choice as the rational human act par excellence

To start with, it is useful to remember the method Aquinas uses to address questions concerning faculties of the human soul. The basic principle, which is formulated in *De anima* 1.1.402b9–16 and widely accepted in the Aristotelian tradition, is that faculties are to be defined by their acts, which in turn are to be distinguished by their objects (*ST* 1.77.3 s.c. and resp.).

Now, *liberum arbitrium* for Aquinas is the "faculty" of reason and will to bring about "human acts" (*actiones humanae*).[13] The human acts of *liberum arbitrium* are distinguished from mere "acts of a man" (*actiones hominis*), because human acts "are of his own deliberate willing" (*ex voluntate deliberata procedunt*) (*ST* 1–2.1.1 resp.). Furthermore, Aquinas describes *liberum arbitrium* as a sort of "free agency," insofar as it is defined by actions rather than, e.g., by omissions – though they, too, can be voluntary (*ST* 1–2.6.3 resp.; 1–2.71.5 ad 2). In short, the specifically human act is choice, because choices are acts of will, which are always informed by reason.

The role of reason within choice is closely connected to a salient feature of *liberum arbitrium*, namely the ability to act otherwise (*ST* 1.83.3 resp.). This ability is explained by an implied prior act of reason, because only reason – the root of freedom (*radix libertatis*) – is able to take alternative

---

[13] He calls *liberum arbitrium* a *potentia*; see *In Sent.* 2.24.1.1; *QDV* 24.4 resp.; *ST* 1.83.2 resp.

ways of acting into account (*ST* 1.83.1 resp.). By pointing to the necessity of rationality for human agency, Aquinas takes up Aristotle's point in *EN* 3.3 that "choice presupposes deliberation" (*ST* 1–2.14.4 ad 1; *ST* 2–2.47.1 ad 2; cf. *ST* 1.83.3 resp. and ad 2). For Aquinas, deliberation is the *collatio*, i.e., the comparison of different courses of action suitable for reaching a certain end, which is required for choice (*ST* 1.83.3 ad 3; *ST* 1–2.14.3 resp.). This leads us to a further respect in which reason is essential for human freedom: human beings must be able to act independently from sensuality (*ST* 1–2.13.6 resp.; 1–2.75.3 resp.; 1–2.77.1 resp., at the end). This point, too, has to do with the comparative aspect of rational judgment, because this aspect constitutes the main difference between rational judgment and the "natural judgment" that guides the behavior of animals, which always follows a "natural instinct" (*ST* 1.83.1 resp.; *QDV* 24.1 resp.).

Thus, the nature of rational judgment implies that the objects of choice can be weighed against each other, or, in other words, that they are good only from a certain perspective. Aquinas explains this by saying that the objects of human actions are "particular contingent things," which include many "conditions or circumstances" (*ST* 1–2.14.3 resp.). He takes this to be Aristotelian doctrine: "The particular conditions of an individual thing are its individuating accidents. Aristotle refers to particulars as circumstances" (*ST* 1–2.7.1 s.c.; cf. *EN* 3.1.1110b33 and 1111a24; *SLE* 3.4 lines 17–20). It has been argued that only his fidelity to Aristotle impelled Aquinas to insert the treatment of circumstances in *ST* 1–2.7, immediately after discussing the voluntary (Gründel 1963, 612–15). However, given the importance that he assigns to particularity, it seems more correct to say that his scrupulously following the Aristotelian order of treatment is evidence of his desire to demonstrate the Aristotelian character of a view that was very much his own:

> Man is capable of directing his acts . . . in an individual way, because he has intellect and reason. By them he can perceive the different ways in which something is good or bad, depending upon its fittingness for different individuals, times, and places. (*SCG* 3.113, Editio Leonina 14:360a–b)

Thus, the object of a human being's deliberated acts always depends upon the way the individual agent perceives his particular situation. Any single act of this kind is either good or bad, even if its exterior performance might indeed be morally indifferent (*ST* 1–2.18.9 resp.).

It is clear, then, that no act of choice can be separated from rational deliberation: its freedom resides in the agent's being capable of embracing different possible courses of particular action, which are available only because they are investigated and presented by reason.

5.2.2   *Choice as the only free act of will*

Now we are ready to ask what role the will itself has to play within this scheme. This is rendered especially difficult by Aquinas's frequent statements saying that choice seems to follow automatically, at least in normal cases, on the final conclusion of reason (*sententia vel iudicium*) (cf. *QDV* 22.15 resp.; *ST* 1.83.3 ad 2; *ST* 1–2.13.1 ad 2; 1–2.13.3 resp.). Thus the will seems to lack any clear function, which is the main motive for the widespread intellectualist readings of Aquinas.

For a start, I would like to point to Aquinas's distinction between "the choice of actions, which is always in a man's power (*electionem operum, et haec semper in hominis potestate existit*), and the performance or execution of actions, which is not always within man's power" (*QDV* 24.1 ad 1). This remark is important, because Aquinas ascribes the interior act primarily to the will and calls it "the elicited act of the will," while he says that the exterior act is formed by reason (*ST* 1–2.18.6 resp.; 1–2.19.1 resp.). The interior act is qualified as good or bad by its end (*ST* 1–2.19.1–2), if it does not include the intention to perform an exterior act that is already bad in itself (*ST* 1–2.19.2 ad 2). Given the passage we just quoted, all these points seem to serve the purpose of excluding every act that is not always within human power from the definition of choice, within which free agency resides. This can be seen from Aquinas's discussion of the relationship between the will and constraint. Both "volition itself" (*ipsum velle*) and "the act which is commanded by the will and executed through some other power" are voluntary actions. Constraint, however, can impede us from carrying out our exterior act; thus these acts are not always voluntary (*ST* 1–2.6.4 resp.; 1–2.6.5 ad 2). The requirement that man be in undiminished control of his free actions, then, is crucial for restricting free actions in the strictest sense to interior ones.

At this point one should take into account an important source for medieval doctrines of freedom: Augustine's discussion of necessity and freedom in Book 5 of *De civitate Dei*, chs. 8–11, which Aquinas quotes frequently (e.g., *ST* 1–2.6.4 s.c.; *QDV* 22.5 resp.; 24.1 ad 20; 24.12 ad 10; *ST* 1.82 arg. 1 and ad 1). This text presents a doctrine of freedom that is largely inspired by Stoic ideas, because Augustine presupposes that the Stoic notion of fate and the Christian concept of God are quite similar to each other (5.8, CCSL 48:201 lines 15–20).[14] Augustine's solution likewise reveals Stoic influence: he distinguishes between two types of necessity, one "which lies outside our power and does what it may even when we are unwilling, such as the necessity of death," and another "according to which we say that it is necessary for something to be as it is or to happen as it does." The first of these two necessities does not limit man's willing, while the second does (5.10, p. 208 lines 14–21). However, this second necessity applies also to certain attributes of God, e.g., his life or his foreknowledge, but without diminishing their intrinsic dignity. Why then, Augustine asks, should it diminish human freedom? Indeed, God's knowledge that certain human acts are free guarantees that they are what they appear to be, i.e., acts regarding which man could have chosen otherwise (5.10, p. 208 line 20–p. 210 line 8). Furthermore, human wills are free to act because, though God did indeed give all beings their power to act, yet He did not give individual persons their occurrent acts of will (*omnium potestatum dator, non voluntatum*; 5.9 p. 207). If all this is right, we can be confident that any act that appears evidently within our power must be free in reality. And indeed we know that there are acts "that we would certainly not do if we were unwilling. This is primarily true of volition itself" (*quo primitus pertinet ipsum velle*; 5.10 p. 208 line 18). Here, the Stoic concept of an interior consent is replaced by an act of will, the freedom of which cannot be doubted.

Aquinas was obviously very impressed by this text. He understood Augustine to be saying that "something can be both necessary and yet voluntary" (*QDV* 24.12 ad 10; *ST* 1.82.1 arg. 1), which influenced his own understanding of voluntariness, as we will see below.[15] Regarding acts about which we are free to choose otherwise, Aquinas adopts two of Augustine's points: first, that free acts must be in our power (*in potestate nostra*), and second, that "volition itself" (*ipsum velle*) is the most obvious example of such an act. Both points are reflected in the definition of choice quoted from *QDV* 24.1 ad 1: the text can be interpreted as saying that choice is an act of will that somehow changes the world just by being chosen.

---

[14] The interpretation of this text proposed here has been explained at greater length in Perkams 2008c, where some alternative interpretations are also described.

[15] Indeed, it was probably crucial for his understanding of the causal effectiveness of God, but it would require another study to show this in detail.

Further observations about acts of this sort can be found in the *Summa theologiae*. Augustine's formula *ipsum velle* appears already in the first article of the *Prima Secundae*:

> An act can be willed in two ways: first, as being commanded by the will, for example speaking or walking; second, as being elicited by the will, as in the case of volition itself [*ipsum velle*]. But it is impossible that the elicited act itself should be the ultimate end, since the end is the objective of the will ... And consequently even there some human act, at least the volition itself [*aliqua actio hominis, ad minus ipsum velle*], will be on account of the end [*propter finem*]. Therefore it is true to say that man always acts for an end, even in the doing of the act which is the ultimate end. (*ST* 1–2.1.1 ad 2)

In Aquinas's terminology, then, Augustine's "volition itself" is the "act elicited by the will," i.e., the interior act of will that we are discussing. Thus freedom, in Aquinas's own treatment of the subject, resides basically in Augustine's interior acts of will. The text just quoted shows how he links this idea with Aristotle's theory of action: by defining every elicited act of the will as an act that advances an end, he interprets it as an Aristotelian choice, for choice in his view is the act by which "the will becomes fully proportioned [to the end] by willing what is for the sake of the end completely," even if it has not yet executed this act in the outward world (*ST* 1–2.16.4 resp.). Aquinas clarifies his concept of choice further by adopting Aristotle's distinction between *prohairesis* or *electio* and *boulēsis* or *voluntas*: the former act is confined to what serves the end, while the latter – in the strict sense – is concerned with the end itself (*QDV* 22.5 resp.; *ST* 1–2.8.2 resp. and ad 1; 1–2.12.1 resp.; 1–2.13.3 resp.).

Aquinas also introduces ideas from *EN* 3.1 and *De civitate Dei* 5 into his conception of voluntariness (ἑκών or *voluntarium*). In *ST* 1–2.6, his only systematic treatment of the subject, Aquinas defines the voluntary as every action that is directed by an interior principle toward an end that is known (*ST* 1–2.6.1 resp.). According to him, this is Aristotle's definition, as expounded in *SLE* 3.4 lines 13–20.

On the other hand, the fact that this definition of voluntariness does not include the possibility of acting otherwise, which is crucial for *liberum arbitrium* (*QDV* 24.1 ad 20; *ST* 1.82.1 resp.), reflects Augustine's theory: Aquinas explains this fact by having recourse to Augustine's distinction between "two forms of necessity, i.e., the necessity of coercion, which never befalls the will, and the necessity of natural inclination," which allows in a certain sense for voluntary actions that are not free (*QDV* 22.5 resp.).

The expression "natural inclination" reveals the reason for Aquinas's interest in this doctrine. For him – in contrast to later authors such as John Duns Scotus – every voluntary act stems from a natural principle, because it corresponds somehow to the natural ends a creature is striving for (*ST* 1–2.6.5 resp.; 10.1 resp.). Consequently, the human will includes the natural tendencies humans either share with other animals or possess in virtue of their own rational nature, which are directed to objects "like beatitude and what is implied by it, like being, cognition of truth, etc." (*QDV* 22.5 resp. lines 199–201; cf. *ST* 1.82.1 resp.; *ST* 1–2.10.1 resp.; 1–2.94.2 resp.), because the ultimate end is, at least in its formal structure, necessarily the same for all human beings (*ST* 1.82.2 resp.; *ST* 1–2.1.6 resp.). In other words, the ability to act otherwise (*liberum arbitrium*) presupposes a will, which is necessitated in the sense of being subject to a natural inclination toward the ultimate end.

For Aquinas, what Aristotle is speaking about in *EN* 3.4 is an act of will taken in this sense, as aimed directly at the end (cf. *ST* 1–2.8.2 resp. and ad 1). This first act of will is necessary to provide the motive force for any further act that serves to reach this end (*ST* 1.82.1 ad 3; *ST* 1–2.13.3 resp.), i.e., for the realm of choices where free agency is possible (*ST* 1.83.4 resp.). It is brought about by God as a natural instinct toward himself (*QDM* 6 resp. lines 407–17; *ST* 1.83.1 ad 3; *ST* 1–2.9.4 resp.). Thus, one cannot decide to strive for the end qua end; one simply does so. In other words, an individual performs further acts by his or her deliberate will, by which he or she intends to reach the end for which he or she has this (non-deliberate) instinct. Those further acts are choices, i.e., moral or human acts of will that are in our power and that are the basis of exterior actions.

With this basic distinction between the two acts of "will" and choice in mind, we can conclude that every interior act of the will that is not exclusively seeking the ultimate end is a choice, i.e., an act of the will that is concerned with what promotes the end and that is guided by practical reason.[16] That this holds true for any of the acts mentioned in *ST* 1–2.12–17 is clear if one pays attention to the following statement of Aquinas:

> Since acts of will are self-reflective, one may say that in each of them there is consent, choice, and employment, so that, as it were, the will consents to choose, and consents to consent, and effectively employs itself to consent and to choose. (*ST* 1–2.16.4 ad 3; cf. 1.16.4 ad 1)

---

[16] I omit here the act of fruition (*ST* 1–2.11), which poses special problems. See Westberg 1994a, 132.

In other words, the different stages of action name certain steps that are denominated primarily from the perspective of the action-causing process. However, the identification of the individual steps as "consents," "choices," or "intentions" is not absolute; rather, each of them is an act of the will that can be named differently if taken from a different perspective. Similarly, the same act of will can be regarded as being aimed both at an end and at a step toward that end (*ST* 1–2.13.3 resp.), and the same act can be called both a "command" (*imperium*) and a "commanded act" (*actus imperatus*), both of which can in turn be regarded either as an act of reason or an act of will (*ST* 1–2.17.4–6). In the end, any act of will can be interpreted as a choice, with one exception: the act of will in the narrow sense that is directed exclusively to the final end.

5.2.3 *The respective roles of reason and will*

Having emphasized the importance that Aquinas assigns to the fact that choices are acts of the will, we can now return to the question of how this dependence upon reason shapes those acts of will, and, given this influence of reason, what role remains to the will. This analysis will help us to understand in what sense Aquinas's concept of human freedom is libertarian.

Aquinas's understanding of the interaction between deliberation and will within choice is a special instance of his general teaching regarding the distinction between acts of appetite and acts of cognition (cf. Brock 1998, 137–86). Principally, he distinguishes willing and knowing as belonging to different genera of causes (*QDV* 22.10 resp.). However, reason and will are not disjunctive, mutually exclusive contraries but are rather mutually directed and informed (*QDV* 22.12 lines 98–117); one could say that their complex interaction constitutes human behavior.

Generally speaking, the function of reason is to "determine or specify the object" of action, or to give it its form; in this sense, it is the *formal* cause of the action, which "determines" its concrete content (*ST* 1.80.1 resp.; *ST* 1–2.9.1 resp.; 1–2.10.2 resp.; *QDM* 6 resp. lines 408–23). The will for its part is the *efficient* or agent cause, i.e., it produces the action itself (*ST* 1.82.4 resp.) – where "action" includes the elicited act of will as well as the "exterior" action resulting from it. Consequently statements like "with respect to the determination of the act, which concerns the object, the intellect moves the will" (*ST* 1–2.9.1 ad 3) are not making a claim about efficient causality. The practical intellect "causes movement not by carrying it out, but by, as it were, guiding to movement" (*ST* 1.79.11 ad 1).

Aquinas sometimes says that the intellect provides the *final* cause of the action, too, because the subsequent act of will receives from the intellect the end which it aims at (*ST* 1.82.4 resp.). This way of speaking presupposes, however, that the will is – due to its inherent natural instinct – already striving for something good, i.e., "the good and the end in general" (*ST* 1.82.3 resp.; *ST* 1–2.9.1 resp.; cf. *SLE* 3.5 lines 150–1). However, due to the universality of the general good and end, "the inclination of the will is open to many" courses of action (*ST* 1.82.2 ad 2; *ST* 1–2.10.1 resp., ad 2, and ad 3; *QDM* 6 resp. lines 288–92 and 410–17). Furthermore, a universal object as such is not suited to produce an action at all, because any operation is concerned with particulars (*QDM* 6 resp. lines 418–49; *ST* 1.80.2 ad 3). Every human being, then, must use his particular reason to find out which apparent particular goods are truly good and which are not (cf. *ST* 1–2.19.1 ad 1). Even particular reason, however, cannot by itself produce an act subject to differentiation into good or bad; rather, all intellectual acts are differentiable only according to truth and falsity, and thus do not have any moral quality in and of themselves (*ST* 1–2.19.1 resp.). Thus, the intellect gives an action its final cause insofar as it specifies a possible good as an object of human willing, which only the will can carry out (cf. *ST* 1.82.3 resp.).

One has to distinguish the acts described here from those other acts, mentioned above, which for Aquinas are both voluntary and necessary. His point about the latter is as follows: if some good is presented to the will as including all perfection, it will move the will necessarily in the sense that it would not be possible for the will to want something else instead. Acts of the will that are necessary in this sense include the striving for beatitude and for the goods that are perceived as necessarily required for beatitude (*ST* 1–2.10.2 resp. and ad 3).

Now, Aquinas qualifies this statement by saying it applies only to the will-act's specification, not to its production by the will's own efficient or agent causality. Such a necessary determination, then, would affect the will only "if one wills anything at all" (*ST* 1–2.10.2 resp.). Similar statements can be found in other works of Aquinas: "Regarding its act, insofar as [the will] can perform an act of will or not perform it..., the will possesses freedom in any state of its nature vis-à-vis any object" (*QDV* 22.6 resp. lines 141–2 and 146–8); or again, "the will does not follow reason necessarily" (*QDV* 22.15 resp. lines 55–6). In *QDM* 6 he explains that the will is free either to want beatitude or not, "because one is capable of not wanting, at this moment, to think about beatitude, since even the very acts of intellect and will are particulars" (*QDM* 6 resp. lines 437–40; cf. *ST* 1–2.10.2 resp.).

These statements concerning the willing of the final end qualify Aquinas's opinion, quoted above, that the will always follows a judgment of reason. They show that his view does not mean that a choice of the will automatically follows any judgment of reason: rather, it remains possible for the will to act or not to act (cf. *QDV* 22.6 resp.; 22.15 resp.; *ST* 1–2.9.1 resp.; 1–2.13.6 resp.), and to act more or less intensely (*melius vel debilius agatur*, *QDM* 6 resp. lines 316–17). In order to elucidate this point, Aquinas in *QDM* 6 gives a list of reasons why someone considering a certain particular good can nonetheless choose to strive for another particular good instead. This is possible, first, because one might, by a rational judgment, prefer goods of one kind over those of another kind; second, because one's attention might be directed more to one aspect of a given situation than to another; and third, because one's will might be disposed to react to certain situations differently than another's might, as can be seen by comparing a quiet man with an ill-tempered one (lines 450–67). Aquinas illustrates this last point, which concerns the will's action directly, by quoting *EN* 3.5.1114a32–b1: "Such as a person's character is, so the end will appear to him." If we take the well-known context of this statement into account, we see that the will's interaction with reason rests in large part upon the habits it has acquired. Virtuous or vicious habits, however, are still "subject to the will," inasmuch as one can remove and change one's dispositions (lines 466–81).[17] The will, then, reacts to the particular possibilities proposed by reason according to its virtues or vices: these habits make the will more or less prone to act according to certain descriptions of what is good (see also *ST* 1–2.58.5 resp., at the end).

All this is due, for Aquinas, to the incompleteness of practical reason itself. He mentions cases where a rational judgment "fluctuates between alternatives and makes no decisive ruling" upon the will (*ST* 1–2.17.5 ad 1); it seems reasonable to extend the range of such situations widely, to the point of ascribing to Aquinas an "indeterminacy inherent in every decision to act" (Westberg 1994b, 53). Given the emphasis he places on the infinity of circumstances that make a reason-based action good or bad (*ST* 1–2.19.10 resp.), it is hard to see how Aquinas could understand human practical reason as regularly issuing all-things-considered judgments that do not leave any leeway for the will. Rather, his point seems to be that no

---

[17] Cf. Bonnie Kent's explanation of this point in this volume, Chapter 6, pp. 106–9.

single act of practical reason can ever grasp a situation completely, because such judgments mirror the ever-changing relationship between a concrete, particular human being and his no less particular surroundings.

Given this indeterminacy of practical reason, one can describe the interaction of reason and will in bringing about actions along the following lines. First, for the reasons discussed in Section 2.1, the will can never act without being guided by reason, at least under natural circumstances. Second, however, this does not mean that any act of practical reason is already an action or itself brings about an act of will: "Choice . . . demands, as regards appetite, that what counsel determines be accepted by the appetite" (*ST* 1.83.3 resp., cf. ad 3; *ST* 1–2.58.2 resp.; 1–2.58.4 resp.). In other words, an action takes place only when somebody accepts or wills one of reason's proposals; this acceptance is itself the action in question, since it is an interior act of will that is a good or bad action in the strictest sense (*ST* 1–2.74.1 resp.; 74.2 ad 2). We can conclude, then, that no action is performed when one simply fails to react to this or that proposal by consenting to it or choosing it. Instead, we may suppose, he or she can for the moment simply leave the on-going, possibly infinite process of thought or deliberation unattended (cf. *ST* 1–2.14.6), probably because his or her will is lacking the habits necessary for reacting adequately to certain proposals offered by practical reason. The intellect, then, is a necessary, but in itself not sufficient, condition for human action, which always consists primarily in an act of the will.

Before concluding, one may note that this is true also for the formation of human higher-order convictions, by which, according to some interpreters, practical reason molds the will's habits in such a way as to render them necessary. One could think, e.g., of decisions about the relative importance that somebody wishes to accord to certain natural ends within his own life, such as in the case of somebody thinking about whether to become a monk or a politician. For example, Scott MacDonald bases his case for interpreting Aquinas as an intellectualist libertarian on the assumption that such "meta-judgments" themselves are in fact free.[18] However, according to the account proposed here, higher-order decisions are free only for the exact same reason that every *electio* is free (cf. *ST* 1–2.13.6 resp.): because practical reason's object, the universal good that includes every particular good, can never of itself determine practical reason to any of the goods that may be included in it. Rather, any (relatively) universal judgment about

---

[18] MacDonald 1998, 322–8. Pasnau 2002, 221–7 arrives at a compatibilist reading of Aristotle by similar considerations; cf. Hause 1997.

which of those concrete goods was to be pursued would still have to be completed by an act of the will. In Aquinas's own words, to the will "corresponds...one common good...This universal good embraces many particular goods, toward none of which is there a determinism within the will" (*ST* 1–2.10.1 ad 3). Even regarding the most universal goals one wishes to pursue, then, choices still have to be performed (cf. *ST* 1–2.10.1 resp.; 94.2 resp.).[19]

5.3 Conclusion

Let us now summarize our findings, elaborating on the thesis proposed at the beginning. Like many of his contemporaries, Aquinas used *electio* (choice), the Latin word translating *prohairesis*, to describe the acts produced by man's faculty of free agency, called *liberum arbitrium*. Aquinas ascribes to choice the full measure of freedom available within his system:

(1) In one sense, choice is free because it results from the natural inclination toward beatitude. Thus, it is voluntary in the sense of being caused by the individual agent himself in a conscious way. Aquinas takes this to be the opinion of both Aristotle and Augustine.

(2) In another sense, choice is free because it is the act of the human will, which has alternative possibilities open to it. This is due to its objects' being the many and diverse particular goods that are apprehended by reason as leading toward the final end. The willing of the end itself, however, is both voluntary and necessary, according to the Augustinian doctrine in Book 5 of *De civitate Dei*. Aquinas identifies this choice-capable will with the Aristotelian *boulēsis* from *EN* 3.4.

(3) Finally, since choice is an interior act of the will, it is free in the sense of not being necessitated by any factor outside human reason, and cannot be impeded from taking place. It is thus the act about whose freedom there can never be any doubt.

This last point is crucial for determining the relationship between Aquinas's concept of will and Aristotle's corresponding notion, because it reveals Aquinas's commitment to the belief that acts of the will are a necessary condition for free agency. His concept of will is not confined to simply positing a "rational appetite," which, according to some authors, is at least implicitly present in Aristotle too. Rather, his view is that this faculty also produces internal acts, the human actions that are free par excellence and which, since they give the whole action its form, are first

---

[19] Some ideas regarding this point can be found in Perkams 2005 and Perkams 2008b.

and foremost the objects of moral evaluation. I cannot see any parallel to this view, which is primarily inspired by Augustine's explanation of human freedom, within Aristotle's theory. To be sure, Aquinas's explanation of such acts as choices of a "deliberated will," informed by a rationality concerned with particulars, is Aristotelian in many respects, but this only confirms the intermingling of Aristotelian, Christian, and Neoplatonic elements, which is characteristic of Aquinas's whole theology and philosophy.

It would not be right to pass over the merits of this approach in silence. By integrating an Augustinian concept of interior freedom and an Aristotelian philosophy of nature, Aquinas is able not only to affirm that the will is open to alternative courses of action but also to interpret this as a natural phenomenon. In order to realize the importance of this fact one need only compare it with Duns Scotus's sharp distinction between reason as a deterministic natural agent on the one hand and will as a free agent on the other: by this latter view, agency ceases to be a common notion (*Quaestiones super libros Metaphysicorum Aristotelis* 9.15 nn. 22–4, Opera Philosophica 4:680–1). In contrast to this view, which deeply influenced modern philosophy, Aquinas's standpoint leaves much more room to develop an overarching theory of nature and freedom, even if it makes stronger assumptions about the possibility of alternatives than modern compatibilists would like to allow for.[20]

---

[20] For further ideas on this point I refer to Stump 2003, 305–6.

CHAPTER SIX

Losable virtue
Aquinas on character and will

Bonnie Kent

Can virtuous people lose their virtue through moral backsliding? According to Aristotle, they cannot. Virtuous people never act from weakness or impulsiveness, contrary to their own better judgment. They have no base appetites for physical pleasures that they must work to control. In this they differ not only from persons with *akrasia* but also from those with mere continence (*EN* 7.1.1145b1–2, 7.9.1151b34–1152a3). Virtuous people are not prone to slacking off, either. They cannot lose their virtue by declining to exercise it, as someone might gradually lose his physical strength. On Aristotle's view, they will "always, or by preference to everything else," do and reflect on what is virtuous (*EN* 1.10.1100b18–22).[1] The surest sign of their character comes in combat, when they face the prospect of wounds and death. Virtuous people do not deliberate about whether to fight honorably or to save their own skins. Even when they have no time to deliberate, their courage ensures that they act well (*EN* 3.8.1117a15–22, 3.9.1117a35–b15).

There is no controversy among contemporary interpreters about whether this is Aristotle's understanding of virtuous character.[2] Debates for the last decade have centered on its philosophical merits. Should we reject Aristotle's account of virtue as elitist? Should we develop an account more consistent with empirical psychology? Should we abandon the notion of moral character entirely?[3]

Aquinas's ethics does not invite the same challenges as Aristotle's, in part because his conception of virtuous character seems more realistic.[4] In

I owe a debt of gratitude to Tobias Hoffmann, Jörn Müller, and Matthias Perkams for their informed and insightful comments on drafts of this article.

[1] Quotations from the *Nicomachean Ethics* have been adapted from Aristotle 1980. Modifications are made mainly for the sake of terminological consistency and to eliminate gendered terms not in the Greek text. All other translations in this essay are my own.

[2] Many scholars think that Aristotle considers vicious character equally fixed, though occasionally some (e.g., Di Muzio 2000 and Destrée 2011) still oppose this interpretation.

[3] For critiques of both Aristotle's psychology and his moral elitism see Doris 2002 and Adams 2006.

[4] My remarks in this essay concern naturally acquired virtues, not virtues given by grace, unless otherwise indicated.

q. 53 of the *Prima Secundae* he argues that virtue can be destroyed in three
ways: "through ignorance, through passion, or even through choice" (*ST* 1–
2.53.2). These three ways correspond to three kinds of sin (or wrongdoing:
peccatum), which Aquinas later explores in detail (*ST* 1–2.76–78). As he
explains it, the tripartite division considers sin in terms of its different
psychological sources: reason, sense appetite, and will, respectively. In all
three cases, though, the will is the "first mover" (*ST* 1–2.74.2 ad 1). Hence
sins from ignorance are ones resulting from a lack of knowledge that the
agent could have and should have had. It was her own fault she did not, as
when a driver drinks too much to decipher traffic signs and ends up causing
an accident. By the same token, sins from passion are ones resulting from
emotions that the agent could have and should have controlled. Only if
someone has entirely lost the use of reason does Aquinas consider behavior
driven by the passions involuntary (*ST* 1–2.77.7 resp.).

Aquinas's argument in q. 53 clearly concerns the kind of virtues Aristotle discusses, not virtues supernaturally infused by God's grace, because
both this question and the preceding one focus on dispositions gradually
acquired through human learning and practice, then gradually weakened
and lost. Infused virtues, as Aquinas understands them, are not acquired
in the same way, nor do they deteriorate in the same way. (They are lost all
at once, through a single act of mortal sin.) Equally important, Aquinas's
argument that virtuous dispositions can be destroyed appears in a broader
discussion of dispositions in general. By presenting it at this point in the
Summa theologiae, before his overall focus shifts to virtues, he makes it
look like a relatively uncontroversial point about human psychology. As
a person's actions, over time, can produce dispositions, so too can they
destroy them.

Now one might think that Aquinas's conflict with Aristotle reflects a
normative difference: he has less exacting standards for what counts as
a virtuous person. This is true, though a difference in psychology is at
least equally important. Aquinas does not think that a virtuous disposition
ever determines the agent to choose virtuous acts. So even if someone
did acquire the constellation of dispositions constituting virtuous character as Aristotle understands it, Aquinas would still believe her at risk
of losing her virtue. The danger is not that a naturally acquired virtuous
character might be destroyed all at once but that it might be lost little
by little. One reason Aquinas regards this as a real possibility lies in his
conception of the will as a capacity for free choice. Another lies in his own
conception of a disposition as something used by the will (*QDM* 6 resp.,
ST 1–2.71.4 resp.).

The startling aspect of Aquinas's argument that virtue can be lost is that Aristotle, of all people, is the sole authority he cites on behalf of his own position:

> The Philosopher says that forgetfulness and deception are the destruction of knowledge. By sinning someone even loses a virtuous disposition. And virtues are generated and destroyed by contrary actions, as it is said in Book 2 of the *Ethics*. (*ST* 1–2.53.1 s.c.)

The dictum Aquinas attributes to Book 2 of the *Ethics* cannot be dismissed as some slip made only in a single question of the *Prima Secundae*. For he cites the same saying earlier, in his commentary on the *Sentences*, in a later section of the *Prima Secundae*, as well as in the *Secunda Secundae* and disputed questions thought to be contemporary with the *Secunda Secundae*.[5] The saying makes it look like Aristotle himself thought that virtuous people can lose their virtue.

We get the same impression from a second dictum, which Aquinas attributes to Book 6 of the *Ethics*: "[Physical] pleasure destroys the appraisal of prudence (*delectatio corrumpit existimationem prudentiae*)." He cites this three times in his commentary on the *Sentences*, twice in the *Prima Secundae*, and twice in the *Secunda Secundae*.[6] Aquinas invokes the saying as support for his view that "prudence is not taken away directly by forgetfulness but is more destroyed by the passions" (*ST* 2–2.47.16 resp.). Does Aristotle actually make the remark attributed to him? It would be strange if he did, for this would indicate that virtuous people, like akratics, have appetites for pleasure that can warp their practical judgment.

Of course, the *Summa theologiae* is a theology textbook, not a guide to the history of philosophy. Readers cannot take it for granted that the sayings it attributes to Aristotle represent Aristotle's views or even that Aquinas believed that they do. Did he actually believe Aristotle considered virtuous people at risk of moral backsliding? To answer the question one must consult his commentary on the *Ethics*. But does the commentary itself present his interpretation of the historical Aristotle, or is the account given there of Aristotle's teachings scarcely different from the one given in Aquinas's theological works?

---

[5] *In Sent.* 4.1.1.2 qc. 1 ad 2, *ST* 1–2.71.4 s.c., *ST* 2–2.47.16 arg. 2, *QDC* 6 arg. 3. The exact wording of the dictum varies a bit, but the sense is always the same, and Aquinas always attributes it to Book 2 of the *Nicomachean Ethics*.

[6] *In Sent.* 2.5.1.1 resp., 2.22.2.2 resp., 3.33.2.5 ad 1; *ST* 1–2.33.3 s.c., resp., 1–2.59.3 arg. 3, 2–2.47.16 resp., 2–2.53.6 resp.

In this chapter I argue that the account of Aristotle's teachings given in the *Ethics* commentary differs significantly from the one given in his theological works. Although the commentary includes much more than Aquinas's exposition of Aristotle, there is enough straight exposition to suggest that he consciously disagreed with Aristotle about the losability of virtue.

The remainder of the chapter proceeds as follows: First, I show that Aquinas's commentary interprets Aristotle's remark about the destruction of virtue correctly. Aquinas also interprets Aristotle's remark about pleasure correctly, although the very last line of his *lectio* – quite surprisingly, considering what precedes it – suggests that prudence *can* be lost through appetites for pleasure contrary to reason. This leads me to address some general problems that Aquinas's *Ethics* commentary poses for interpreters.

Second, I discuss Aquinas's concept of the will as a capacity for free choice: a notion central to his conviction that people can lose their virtue. My remarks here will be brief, partly because of the enormous complexity of the topic, partly because Aquinas has nothing to say about freedom in the psychological sense in his commentary on Aristotle's *Ethics*.

Finally, I consider two parts of his *Ethics* commentary where Aquinas clearly injects his own opinion: that virtues divide into principal and merely secondary virtues, and that a disposition is something we exercise when we *will*. I argue that both help to support Aquinas's thesis that people can lose their virtue through moral backsliding. In his commentary, however, they offer little more than tantalizing glimpses of the ethics and psychology Aquinas himself develops in his theological works.

6.1   Strengths and pitfalls of Aquinas's *Ethics* commentary

Aquinas's commentary on the *Nicomachean Ethics* has one indisputable strength: it sometimes enables us to tell how he interpreted the historical Aristotle. Considering how often Aquinas quotes snippets from the *Ethics* out of context in other works, readers might well wonder: is he deliberately turning them to his own purposes, or did he simply misunderstand what Aristotle meant? When it comes to the losability of virtue, I think Aquinas's commentary shows that he did understand what Aristotle meant. Let's begin with the saying about the destruction of virtue quoted above, then consider what Aristotle's *Ethics* actually says and how Aquinas interprets the text.

The saying that "virtues are generated and destroyed by contrary actions" derives from Book 2, ch. 1, where Aristotle argues that we acquire virtues, as

we do skills, by performing similar activities. On its own, the line suggests
that a person might lose his virtues by behaving badly, but taken in context,
it shows at most that Aristotle failed to choose his words with sufficient
care. He does not mean that virtues, once acquired, can be destroyed by
contrary actions. Aristotle means that the wrong kind of upbringing can
ruin one's capacity for virtue:

> Again, it is from the same causes and by the same means that every virtue
> is both produced and destroyed, and similarly every art [or skill: τέχνη];
> for it is from playing the lyre that both good and bad lyre-players are
> produced. And the corresponding statement is true of builders and all the
> rest; people will be good or bad builders as a result of building badly . . . This
> is why the activities we exhibit must be of a certain kind: it is because the
> dispositions [ἕξεις] correspond to the differences between these. It makes no
> small difference, then, whether we form habits of one kind or of another
> from our very youth; it makes a very great difference, or rather *all* the
> difference. (*EN* 2.1.1103b7–11, b21–5)

Aquinas's commentary on this passage interprets Aristotle's remark about
the destruction of virtue as Aristotle intended it. He does not take Aristotle
to mean that virtuous people are at risk of moral backsliding:

> [Aristotle] says first that it is from the same causes, in different ways, that
> virtue is both produced and destroyed; and likewise with regard to any art.
> He shows this first with regard to the arts . . . And as it is with the arts, so it
> is with the virtues. People who act well in their dealings with others become
> just; people who act badly become unjust; and likewise, people who act in
> dangerous situations and become accustomed to fear and confidence, if they
> do this well, become brave; yet if they do it badly, they become cowards.
> And the same holds for temperance and mildness regarding appetites and
> feelings of anger, so that it may be said universally that similar dispositions
> are produced by similar actions . . . Hence [Aristotle] further concludes that
> it makes a great difference, not a small one, that someone is habituated from
> youth to acting well or badly – indeed, everything depends on this – for we
> retain more firmly things impressed upon us from childhood. (*SLE* 2.1 lines
> 145–9, 158–67, 172–6)

Some other passages show Aquinas diluting strong statements by Aristotle
but without grossly distorting their meaning. Take, for example, Aristotle's
assertion that his paragon will "always, or by preference to everything
else . . . do and reflect on what is virtuous, and he will bear the fortunes of
life most nobly and altogether decorously" (*EN* 1.10.1100b18–22). Aquinas
presents Aristotle's claim about what such a person *will* do as a claim about
what he *can* do (*SLE* 1.16 line 85). In the same vein, where Aristotle declares

that the virtuous person "will never do acts that are hateful and mean-spirited," Aquinas inserts the qualifier *probabiliter* (*EN* 1.10.1100b34; *SLE* 1.16 line 167). In neither passage does he do more than to weaken a strong thesis.

In contrast, the saying "[physical] pleasure destroys the appraisal of prudence," which the *Summa* attributes to Book 6 of the *Ethics*, misrepresents what Aristotle says in ch. 5. The relevant passage shows Aristotle making a point about moral development very much like the one made in the passage from Book 2. He does not argue that pleasure can ruin the judgment of someone with the virtue of prudence. Aristotle suggests that pleasure can destroy people's practical judgment, so that those with disordered appetites fail to acquire prudence:

> The remaining alternative, then, is that [prudence] is a true and reasoned disposition to act with regard to the things that are good or bad for a human being. For while making has an end other than itself, action cannot; for good action itself is its end. It is for this reason that we think Pericles and men like him have prudence, namely, because they can see what is good for themselves and what is good for people in general . . . (This is why we call temperance [σωφροσύνην] by this name, as something that preserves prudence [ὡς σῴζουσαν τὴν φρόνησιν].) Now what it preserves is a judgment of the kind we have described. For it is not any and every judgment that pleasant and painful objects destroy and pervert, e.g., the judgment that the triangle has or has not its angles equal to two right angles, but only judgments about what is to be done. For the originating causes of the things that are done consist in the end at which they are aimed; but the person who has been ruined by pleasure or pain forthwith fails to see any such originating cause. (*EN* 6.5.1140b4–18)

In commenting on this passage Aquinas again interprets Aristotle correctly. Aquinas takes him to mean that physical pleasure destroys *practical* judgment, not "the appraisal of prudence":

> [Aristotle] says that, because prudence concerns good and bad things to be done, for this reason temperance is called *sōphrosunē* in Greek, as if it preserves the mind, from which prudence gets the name *phronēsis*. But temperance, insofar as it moderates the pleasures and pains of touch, preserves an appraisal of this kind, namely one concerning things to be done which are good or bad for a human being. And this is clear from the contrary, because the pleasure and pain which are moderated by temperance do not totally destroy or distort every appraisal, producing a contrary one, such as the theoretical judgment that a triangle does or does not have three angles equal to two right angles; rather, pleasure and pain destroy and distort appraisals concerning judgments about what is to be done. (*SLE* 6.4 lines 112–26)

Aquinas's commentary on this chapter continues smoothly, faithfully explaining Aristotle's thinking, until the very last line of his *lectio*. Aristotle concludes by observing that prudence, unlike intellectual dispositions having no connection to appetite, cannot be forgotten (*EN* 6.5.1140b29–30). Aquinas reports Aristotle's conclusion, then adds that prudence *can* be lost in a different way:

> Prudence is not consigned to oblivion through disuse; *it is destroyed through the cessation of right appetite* which, as long as it remains, causes reason to be continually engaged with things belonging to prudence, so that oblivion cannot come unnoticed. (*SLE* 6.4 lines 190–6, emphasis added)

Aquinas's remark about how prudence can be destroyed fits nicely with the *Summa*, where he argues that even a virtuous person can sin from passion, and then proceeds to cast incontinence as a temporary condition anyone on earth might experience. It does not fit so comfortably into his commentary on the *Ethics*. There is nothing in the preceding passages of the *lectio* laying the ground for this remark, nor does Aquinas explain it in the next *lectio*, where he returns to arguments given in the text of the *Ethics*.

Aquinas's commentary on Book 7, ch. 10 of the *Ethics* presents a similar problem. In this chapter Aristotle marshals a series of arguments to establish that the same person cannot be both prudent and incontinent simultaneously. Aquinas begins with a faithful account of Aristotle's arguments and continues for some time in the same vein, then injects a view with no foundation in the *Ethics*:

> From these things that have been said we can grasp what the subject of continence and incontinence is. The concupiscible [appetite] cannot be said to be the subject of both, because the continent and the incontinent do not differ according to base appetites, which both have; nor is the subject of both reason, because both have right reason. *It remains, therefore, that the will is the subject of both*, because the incontinent sins willingly, as was said, whereas the continent willingly holds to reason. (*SLE* 7.10 422–3 lines 87–97; emphasis added)

We should not take this passage as a conscious departure from Aristotle just because Aquinas introduces the will (*voluntas*). Although contemporary translations of the *Ethics* never use the word "will" to denote a power of the soul, the medieval Latin edition does use the word *voluntas* to translate the Greek *boulēsis* (a word for rational appetite now commonly translated into English as "wish"). So Aquinas has ample justification for discussing the will in his commentary. On the other hand, there is nothing in the text of the *Ethics* to suggest that continence and incontinence belong to the will. For Aristotle the paradigm of incontinence is a normally rational person so affected by his appetite for physical pleasure that he behaves irrationally. The incontinent does not *choose* to act as he does.[7] Aquinas has better grounds for attributing continence to the will, though here we see some development in his own works. In the *Prima Secundae* he attributes continence to "the rational part" of the soul, a vague term, since it includes both intellect and will. Only later, in the *Secunda Secundae*, does he attribute continence specifically to the will (*ST* 1–2.58.3 ad 2, *ST* 2–2.155.3 resp.)

When Aquinas's *Ethics* commentary attributes continence and incontinence to the will, is he spelling out a conclusion he believes implicit in Aristotle? Or is he simply presenting his own view, based largely on a psychology Aristotle does not share? I see no way to judge from the passage itself. Although it does not begin "The Philosopher implies that," Aquinas quite often gives straight exposition of Aristotle without explicit attribution. Although the passage does begin by referring to what *we* can grasp, Aquinas's use of the first-person plural cannot be taken to flag some shift in perspective. The commentary includes many instances of the first-person plural where it means only "we human beings," or "we who think like Aristotle," not "we Christians" or some other group that excludes Aristotle.

I myself interpret both of the passages quoted above as places where Aquinas consciously moves beyond explaining the historical Aristotle. This judgment, however, rests only in part on the striking shift from remarks with a clear textual basis to remarks with none whatsoever. It also rests on my view of the commentary as a whole as a hybrid document. Vernon Bourke has already argued that the commentary reflects lectures Aquinas originally composed at Orvieto in 1261–64, then edited many years later, during his second regency at Paris (Bourke 1974, 255). I shall not devote space to detailing Bourke's arguments here. Suffice it to say that this understanding of the commentary both helps to explain its striking unevenness and avoids a general objection to the now-entrenched dating of Aquinas's works: how could any mere mortal have had time to compose all the works attributed to his second regency? Evidence that some parts of the commentary date from 1271–72 do nothing to establish that the entire commentary, or even most of it, was composed then.

---

[7] *EN* 7.8.1151a5–7; see also Chapter 11 in this volume.

For many years scholars have battled about the character of Aquinas's *Ethics* commentary as a whole and his purpose in writing it. Is it a philosophical work or a theological work? Did he write it to improve his understanding of Aristotle, as a mature expression of his own moral philosophy, or for some other reason?[8] Much of the controversy seems predicated on the assumption that Aquinas's commentary has some hidden unity of approach, reflecting some single overall purpose. If it reflects instead a hybrid of work done at different times, possibly for somewhat different purposes, the very assumption fueling the controversy is suspect.

6.2 The will as a capacity for free choice

In question 6 of his *Disputed Questions on Evil* Aquinas argues vehemently against the thesis that the human will is necessarily moved to choose, albeit by causes internal to the agent rather than external forces. Not only does he reject this thesis as contrary to the Christian faith, he declares that it "subverts all the principles of moral philosophy" (*QDM* 6 resp. lines 248–56). Aquinas follows with a long, detailed account of free choice (*libera electio*). A key element of it is the denial that an individual's disposition (*habitus*) determines him to will what he does. According to Aquinas, the will moves itself and all other powers regarding the performance of an act:

> Indeed, I understand because I will, and likewise I use all powers and dispositions because I will. Hence the Commentator [Averroes] defines a disposition in [his commentary on] Book 3 of the *De anima*: "A disposition is that which someone uses when he wills." (*QDM* 6 resp. lines 351–4)

Aquinas does not consider moral dispositions an exception to the rule. As a person might not will to exercise her skill when she has the opportunity to do so, so she might not will to exercise her moral virtue.

This particular question of the *De malo* is thought to date from around December 1270, only a year or two before Aquinas put his commentary on the *Ethics* in its final form (Torrell 2005, 336, 343). If scholars are right about the dating, Aquinas had an opportunity to insert remarks about "free choice" or "free decision" (*liberum arbitrium*) into his commentary. Yet there are none to be found. When Aquinas uses forms of the word "free" in his *Ethics* commentary, he gives it the same political meaning

---

[8] Some recent contributions to this long-running controversy include Doig 2001, Kaczor 2004, and Jordan 2006, ch. 4. See also the Introduction to this volume.

Aristotle himself does. He never describes either the will or the mental act of choice as free.

To be sure, Aquinas's commentary includes various remarks giving the will a more expansive role than Aristotle himself gives rational appetite. We might take these either as cases where Aquinas injects his own views or as cases where he interprets Aristotle with extreme charity. Either way, one could put together all such remarks in the commentary and they would still fall well short of explaining Aquinas's own conception of the will. Two examples must suffice.

(1) On Aristotle's view, the notion of the voluntary (ἑκούσιον) has no necessary connection with rational appetite. He expressly claims that children and even animals act voluntarily (*EN* 3.1.1111b8–9). Even if one thinks, as some scholars do, that Aristotle has another thicker concept of the voluntary, his analysis of *akrasia* makes it clear that he counts as voluntary actions that human adults do from non-rational appetite. Aristotle does not think it necessary to trace all actions eligible for praise or blame to a single power of the soul.

Aquinas's commentary on *EN* 3.1 begins by explaining what he thinks Aristotle means by the voluntary. The term applies to children and animals, signifying only that they act of their own accord (*sponte*), not that they have the use of reason or that they are moved to act by the will (*SLE* 3.4 lines 40–55). Yet when Aquinas turns to Aristotle's next argument – against the Socratic thesis that nobody does wrong voluntarily – his commentary takes a surprising turn. Aristotle observes that the Socratic thesis makes noble acts voluntary while treating acts done from anger or non-rational appetite as involuntary. He declares this idea "absurd" because "one and the same thing is the cause" (*EN* 3.1.1111a27–9). Aquinas presents this single cause not as the same living organism or its soul but as the power of will:

> This second supposition [the Socratic thesis] seems to be absurd, since there is <one> cause of everything a human does, whether good or evil – namely, the will. Indeed, however much anger or non-rational appetite may intensify, a human rushes into acting only with the consent of the rational appetite. (*SLE* 3.4 lines 64–9)

Nowhere in Aristotle's works can one find the concept of consent that Aquinas invokes. When forms of the word "consent" appear elsewhere in his commentary on the *Ethics*, they simply mean to agree. In this one passage, though, Aquinas uses "consent" with the quasi-technical meaning given it in scholastic psychology. When he explains in the *Summa* how the mental act of consent differs from other mental acts, he certainly does not appeal to Aristotle. He draws instead on John Damascene and Augustine.

(2) In *EN* 3.5 Aristotle argues that actions and moral dispositions are not voluntary in the same way. We always have control over our actions; we control only the beginning of our moral dispositions. Hence Aristotle compares acquiring a moral disposition to developing an illness. It was once in the agent's power not to be ill, but it is no longer in her power (*EN* 3.5.1114b26–1115a3). The chapter suggests that Aristotle considers the effects of bad upbringing irreversible – a depressing view, though one supported by his repeated references to vicious people as "incurable."

Aquinas's commentary takes "voluntary" to mean subject to the will, then interprets Aristotle's thesis as a weak one: that dispositions, once acquired, are not *entirely* subject to the agent's will, so that people with bad moral dispositions cannot improve *right away*:

> [Aristotle] shows that bad dispositions [*habitus*], after they are produced, are not entirely subject to the will. For this reason he says it does not follow from the fact that someone becomes unjust voluntarily that he can at any time stop being unjust and become just. And he proves this by a comparison with physical conditions [*dispositiones*] . . . So too for vicious dispositions: because at the beginning it was in a person's power not to become unjust or incontinent, we say that people are willingly unjust and incontinent, although after they become people of this kind, it is no longer in their power to stop being unjust or incontinent right away; rather, great effort and practice is required. (*SLE* 3.12 lines 108–14, 125–32)

Despite the view presented in this passage, Aquinas reports most of Aristotle's references to vicious people as "incurable" without amendment (*SLE* 4.4, 5.15, 7.8, 9.4). He does not suggest that they can improve their characters.

In contrast, Aquinas argues in his theological works that nobody in this life is truly "obstinate in evil," as evil angels are. He rejects the idea that anyone is incurable partly on theological grounds (we can be cured by God's grace), and partly on psychological grounds. Even the psychological grounds, though, should not be considered apart from God as the creator of human nature. Aquinas makes this clear in his youthful commentary on the *Sentences*, when elaborating on Augustine's remark, "It is indeed in a human being's power to change his will for the better, but there is no power unless it be given by God" (*Retractationes* 22.4). Aquinas explains that the

change of one's will for the better can be understood either with reference
to the civic good or the good of grace. In the first case all human beings
receive from God the natural power to change. In the second our natural
power is insufficient: someone can change only with the power bestowed
by God's grace (*In Sent.* 2.28 expositio textus). In another early work,
his *Disputed Questions on Truth*, Aquinas asserts that even a bad moral
disposition never corrupts the soul so completely that the agent cannot be
led away from vice by argument.[9] In his *Disputed Questions on Evil* he adds
that vice is called incurable not because the agent's will completely adheres
to sin but only because of the subject's condition. In the present life, which
tends to be deficient in temporal goods, people seeking relief have a steady
incitement to sin (*QDM* 13.3 ad 8; *EN* 4.1.1121b12–16).

6.3   Two key conceptual changes

We come at last to two conceptual differences between Aquinas and
Aristotle, which do much to explain why Aquinas regards virtue as los-
able. In his view, a virtuous person must have the four principal virtues but
may lack many other secondary virtues. She need not have the long list of
moral virtues discussed by Aristotle. Equally important, Aquinas defines
a disposition as a capacity used by the will. Even a virtuous disposition
only inclines the agent to choose virtuous acts; it does not determine her
to do so. Since people can act out of character, their characters can change
over time. Aquinas includes in his commentary on the *Ethics* both his
division between principal and secondary virtues and his conception of a
disposition as something used by the will. In his commentary, though, we
get only a glimpse of positions that his theological works develop in great
detail.

6.3.1   Principal virtues

The notion of four "cardinal" or "principal" virtues, terms Aquinas uses
interchangeably, can be found in works by the Stoics, the Church Fathers,

---

[9] *QDV* 24.11 resp. Both here and in his commentary on the *Sentences* Aquinas adduces as support
a passage from Aristotle's *Categories* claiming that a bad person, if led into better ways of living,
might make really great progress or even change completely (*Cat.* 10.13a20–31; *In Sent.* 2.28 expositio
textus). Few scholars give much weight to this passage, not only because it conflicts with many
other parts of the Aristotelian corpus, but also because it belongs to the controversial section of the
Categories known as the *Post-praedicamenta*. Aquinas himself cites the passage only in his theological
works, never in his commentaries on Aristotle.

and Cicero. The big four are always prudence, justice, temperance, and courage (or fortitude: *fortitudo*). Aquinas was quite aware that Aristotle did not group these four virtues together for special treatment. In his commentary on Book 1 of the *Ethics* he even faults contemporaries for suggesting otherwise. Some claimed that Aristotle's description of the virtuous person as "foursquare (τετράγωνος) beyond reproach" – an expression taken from the poet Simonides – refers to the four principal virtues. Aquinas objects that "this does not seem to be according to the meaning of Aristotle, who is never found to make such an enumeration" (*SLE* 1.16 lines 98–100). Nevertheless, Aquinas himself introduces the topic of principal virtues in his commentary on Book 2.

Aquinas distinguishes between two ways of understanding the principal virtues. On one view, these virtues are taken in a very general sense, so that all other virtues become species of the big four. On the view Aquinas attributes to Aristotle, which he himself supports, the big four have a far more restricted scope. Courage, for example, concerns constancy in situations involving fear of death, not constancy in all situations that a virtuous person encounters. According to the second view, principal virtues are so-called because of their importance, not their generality. Secondary virtues are not species of the big four, although they can be traced back to the principal virtues (*SLE* 2.8 lines 64–98).

Since Aquinas does little in his *Ethics* commentary to illuminate the relation between principal and secondary virtues, one must turn to his theological works to see how it figures in his own ethical theory. He uses the distinction to demote many virtues praised by Aristotle to "potential parts" of the principal virtues that might be "annexed" to them.[10] The distinction has no small importance, because it enables him to restrict Aristotle's thesis about the reciprocity of the virtues and thus to bring the highly idealized ethics of antiquity down to earth.

Aristotle argues in Book 6 of his *Ethics* that nobody can have a moral virtue without prudence, nor can someone have prudence without *all* of

---

[10] According to Aquinas's distinction between "integral," "subjective," and "potential" parts of a principal virtue, integral parts are constitutive features of the principal virtue, on a par with the roof of a house. Subjective parts are related to the principal virtue in the way that different biological species are to the genus. Potential parts are secondary virtues that might be joined to the principal virtue because they "participate" in it in a limited way, but since the principal virtue can clearly exist without any secondary virtue, I think it fair to interpret Aquinas's decision to classify some virtue as merely a potential part of a principal virtue as a significant demotion. While Aquinas's use of this tripartite distinction between different kinds of parts of a principal virtue is strictly his own, Jörn Müller finds that the distinction itself comes from Albert the Great's *De bono* (Müller 2008, 86–8; Albert, *De bono* 2.2.10, Editio Coloniensis 28:112).

the moral virtues.[11] When Aquinas reports this argument in the *Prima Secundae*, he appears to agree. Look closely, though, and one finds a more modest conclusion: that prudence cannot exist without *some* dispositions (*aliquos habitus*) regarding particular principles of action (*ST* 1–2.58.5 resp.). Why does Aquinas not say that prudence requires all the moral virtues? One reason is that he wants to resolve a puzzle about Aristotle's *Ethics*: is it necessary that the virtuous person have a large-scale virtue like magnificence, or would the ordinary virtue of liberality suffice? Aquinas declares that the virtuous person need not have such large-scale virtues. Their ordinary counterparts suffice (*ST* 1–2.65.1 ad 1). Yet this cannot be Aquinas's chief concern, for in the very next question liberality itself becomes marginal, not essential, as the virtue of justice is. Aquinas argues that someone can have justice without liberality but not vice versa (*ST* 1–2.66.4 ad 1).

The four principal virtues are integrated in such a way that they cannot be separated. An individual cannot acquire any of them without acquiring them all, and they form the indispensable foundation for all other moral virtues. It would be a mistake, though, to assume that Aquinas grants them special status only on psychological grounds. The special status of the big four also reflects a normative judgment: that they are "principal in *worth*" (*ST* 1–2.66.4 resp.).

In the *Secunda Secundae*, where Aquinas presents his theory of virtue in detail, we find a long list of virtues cast as secondary virtues that are only potentially parts of the big four. For example, friendliness and truthfulness join liberality as secondary virtues that might be annexed to the principal virtue of justice (*ST* 2–2.80.1 resp.). "Good temper" (πραότης, *mansuetudo*) becomes a secondary virtue that might be annexed to the principal virtue of temperance (*ST* 2–2.143.4 resp.). If Aquinas demotes most of the moral virtues discussed by Aristotle to the status of secondary, adjunct virtues, he does the same with many of the virtues discussed by Cicero and Macrobius. He grants other virtues higher status, either as integral parts of some principal virtue or as "subjective parts," meaning species of some principal virtue. For example, Aquinas treats as species of temperance the virtues of abstinence (regarding pleasures of eating), sobriety (regarding pleasures of drinking), and chastity (regarding sexual pleasures). Chastity itself might take either the form of conjugal continence or the more extreme form of virginity. Aquinas follows Augustine in insisting that the difference

---

[11] *EN* 6.13.1144b32–1145a2. In his *Ethics* commentary Aquinas follows Aristotle closely, explaining that all the moral virtues are connected by prudence. The sole modification he suggests concerns a large-scale virtue like magnificence (*SLE* 6.11 lines 159–70).

between the two lies in a person's soul, not the condition of his or her body (*ST* 2–2.143 resp., 2–2.152.3 ad 2, 2–2.152.4 resp.).

This enormously complex theory of virtue reflects Aquinas's concern to recognize many different kinds of people as virtuous: women as well as men, the poor as well as the rich, celibate religious people as well as married lay people. He refuses to exclude someone from the ranks of the virtuous just because (say) she lacks the money she would need to acquire liberality or the opportunity and experience she would need to acquire the military form of courage. Aquinas's treatment of courage shows him making the virtue broad enough to encompass different kinds of mortal dangers, such as the risk of catching a fatal disease when ministering to the sick, while still keeping courage more specific than the Stoics do (*ST* 2–2.123.5 resp.).

Although an individual can become more virtuous by acquiring secondary, adjunct virtues, she qualifies as a virtuous person without them. Hence the vast majority of people Aquinas considers virtuous are less all around experienced in practical terms and less all around integrated in emotional terms than Aristotle's paragon. Aquinas refuses to make virtue a lofty ideal that very few, if any, real people can attain. He accordingly warns virtuous people about the risk of moral backsliding.

Imagine that someone has lived his entire life in extreme poverty but still managed, admirably, to acquire the four principal virtues. Thanks to a winning lottery ticket, he suddenly becomes a multimillionaire. If all goes well, he will at least acquire the virtue of liberality. Ideally, he will acquire the large-scale virtue of magnificence as well. Regrettably, real people sometimes fail to develop as they should. Our lottery winner might be so habituated to frugality that he fails to help even the most worthy causes. He might remain merely just even when his newfound wealth makes it possible for him to be liberal. His wealth might also place him in the company of people who acquired their fortunes by defrauding others and using bankruptcy laws to avoid paying their debts. Should our lottery winner begin emulating his newfound "friends," he could even end up losing, over time, the virtue of justice. And if he loses the virtue of justice, he will lose the other principal virtues too.

Now someone might object that I am misreading Aquinas: when he uses the division between principal and merely secondary, adjunct virtues to widen and diversify the ranks of virtuous people, he means this division to apply only to the moral virtues infused by God's grace, not naturally acquired moral with the same names. So Aquinas only widens and diversifies the ranks of virtuous Christians. There is indeed some basis for this objection – namely, that his most detailed discussion of secondary, adjunct virtues appears in the *Secunda Secundae*, a text focused overwhelmingly on infused virtues. Against this, though, is the fact that he also presents the distinction between principal and secondary virtues in his commentary on Aristotle's *Ethics* and his *Disputed Questions on the Virtues in General* (*QDVCom* 12 ad 26, ad 27). Aquinas has more to say about the distinction in the *Secunda Secundae* not because it applies exclusively to infused virtues but because he himself cares much more about infused virtues, so that his account of them is in many respects more detailed than his account of naturally acquired virtues. For him naturally acquired virtues are intrinsically imperfect and virtues only in a relative sense by comparison with God-given virtues (*ST* 2–2.23.7 resp.; *QDVCard* 2 resp.).

6.3.2   *Dispositions, including virtues*

Aquinas's commentary on *EN* 3.2 includes one of those passages where he segues from explaining Aristotle to introducing a view with no basis in Aristotle, leaving readers puzzled over whether he misunderstood Aristotle's thinking. The passage begins with the indisputably Aristotelian thesis that decision or choice – *prohairesis* in Greek, *electio* in Latin – is not the same as opinion; but it proceeds to invoke an eyebrow-raising dictum from Averroes and concludes with the un-Aristotelian thesis that people are called good *simpliciter* because they have a good will:

> Aristotle shows that choice is not the same as a certain kind of opinion, namely about those things it is in our power to do. And he shows this by five arguments, the first of which is this. From the fact that we choose good or bad things we are called certain kinds of people, namely, good or bad ones; we are not called good or bad from the fact that we have an opinion about good or bad things, whether true or false … The reason for this difference is that someone is called good or bad not on the basis of capacity but on the basis of action, as it says in Book 9 of the *Metaphysics*, that is, not from the fact that someone is able to act well but from the fact that he does act well. It follows from the fact that a person is perfect in understanding that the person is able to act well, but not that he does act well, as it follows from the fact that someone has the disposition of grammar that he is able to speak correctly; but to speak correctly it is requisite that he will this – for *a disposition is that whereby one acts when one wills*, as the Commentator [Averroes] says [in his commentary] on Book 3 of *De anima*. Thus it is evident that a good will makes a person act well according to every capacity or disposition obedient to reason; and so from the fact that someone has a

good will he is called a good person without qualification. From the fact that he has good understanding a person is not called good without qualification, but only good in a relative sense, for example a good grammarian or a good musician. (*SLE* 3.6 lines 31–8, 40–58; *Met.* 9.9.1051a4–15)

In effect, the definition of a disposition (*habitus*) attributed to Averroes marks a transition from Aristotle's thought to Aquinas's own psychology and ethics. Dispositions are a topic of great concern to Aquinas. He treats them in enormous detail in the *Prima Secundae* (qq. 49–54). Aristotle has much to say about dispositions (ἕξεις) too, though not in his *Ethics*, where he defines moral virtue as a disposition but largely takes the general concept of a disposition for granted. Aquinas's commentary on the *Ethics* mirrors that approach. Although he works in his central thesis, about the relation between dispositions and the will, he does not expatiate on his own conception of a disposition.

The saying attributed to Averroes appears again and again in Aquinas's theological works: "A disposition is that whereby one acts when one wills (*habitus est quo quis agit cum voluerit*)." Never does Aquinas attribute this conception of a disposition to Aristotle himself. Sometimes the saying attributed to Averroes appears in conjunction with one attributed to Augustine: either "a disposition is that whereby one acts when there is a need (*cum opus est*)," or "a disposition is that whereby one acts when it is time to do so (*cum tempus affuerit*)."[12]

What Averroes actually says differs significantly from the dictum Aquinas repeatedly invokes. According to Averroes,

> This is indeed the definition of a disposition, namely, that someone having a disposition understands by virtue of it what is proper to himself in his own right and when he wishes [*quando voluerit*], without needing something external for this.[13]

One might perhaps take "*voluerit*" to mean *wills* rather than *wishes*; but the passage cannot reasonably be taken to mean that a disposition is that whereby one *acts* when one wills, as opposed to *understands* when one wills. For in this section of his commentary on *De anima* Averroes is discussing the intellect, not discoursing on dispositions in general. More specifically,

---

[12] For the conjunction of Averroes and Augustine see *In Sent.* 3.3.1.1 s.c., *ST* 1–2.49.3 s.c., *QDVCom* 1 resp. For Augustine's definition of a *habitus* see *De bono coniugali* 21.25. Albert the Great attributes the same saying to Averroes that Aquinas does: "Habitus est quo quis agit cum voluerit" (e.g., *Super Ethica* 5.1 n. 363, Editio Coloniensis 14:307 lines 60–1). In one place, though, Albert misattributes the saying to Augustine (*In Sent.* 1.3.10.39 resp., ed. Borgnet 25:150).

[13] *Commentarium Magnum in Aristotelis De anima* 3.18, ed. F. S. Crawford, 438 lines 26–9.

Averroes is trying to make sense of Aristotle's puzzling remark that the active intellect is a *hexis* like light, which makes potential colors into actual colors (*An.* 3.5.430a14–17).

Aquinas knew what Averroes actually said by the time he wrote the *Contra Gentiles*, because in this work, albeit in no other, he quotes the line correctly: a *habitus* is that whereby one understands when one wills. Ironically, neither in the *Contra Gentiles* nor in his own commentary on *De anima* does Aquinas endorse Averroes's interpretation of Aristotle's puzzling remark. Aquinas thinks that when Aristotle declares the active intellect a *habitus* like light, he is only using *habitus* in the broad sense, to mean something one possesses, not in the more narrow, technical sense of disposition (*SCG* 2.78, *SLA* 3.4 lines 36–40).

Aquinas's misquotation of Averroes lends support to the conception of a disposition Aquinas himself develops in the *Prima Secundae*. At first his notion of a disposition looks Aristotelian. It looks much less so as his account of dispositions proceeds.

Like Aristotle, Aquinas emphasizes the normativity of dispositions: they are states that make something good or bad, either in its own right or in relation to something else (*ST* 1–2.49.1–2). Like Aristotle, Aquinas claims that dispositions are resistant to change, though he infers from this that no disposition in the strict sense can belong primarily to the body. By their very nature, he argues, physical conditions are liable to change (*ST* 1–2.50 resp. and ad 2). While Aquinas seems to endorse Aristotle's thesis that dispositions are connected with actions, not mere movements or changes, he uses the saying from Averroes to interpret the connection with action in a decidedly un-Aristotelian way. Not only does Aquinas deny that animals can have any dispositions in the strict sense (because they lack the power of will), he weakens Aristotle's distinction between moral dispositions on the one hand, and skills and other rational capacities on the other.

Aristotle highlights the role of desire or choice only in discussing the exercise of rational capacities. The individual must choose whether to exercise them, and if so, for what purpose (*Met.* 9.5.1047b31–1048a16). The choice is external to the capacity. Thus it is no evidence against someone's possession of a skill that she chooses to take a break from exercising it or sometimes uses it to produce the opposite of its characteristic result. Aristotle denies that the same holds for moral virtues, partly because there are no breaks from the moral life and partly because moral virtues are one-sided, with choice built into them. Since virtues are by their very nature stable, active dispositions to make good choices, it *is* evidence against someone's possession of a virtue that she fails to choose correctly or, worse, chooses badly (*EN* 6.5.1140b22–4). For Aristotle the virtuous person's constellation of dispositions constitute the self. There is no independent "I" capable of choosing.

For Aquinas there is indeed an independent "I." By their very nature, all dispositions are principally related to the will. We use the disposition or not, as we will (*ST* 1–2.50.5 resp.). Although people may be strongly inclined to act in accordance with their dispositions, they are never determined to act in accordance with them. In earthly life, even the moral character of virtuous people remains a work in progress. If they act well, they will strengthen their virtuous character, perhaps even adding secondary virtues to the principal ones they already have. If they act badly, they will weaken and perhaps ultimately lose their virtuous character.

Does Aquinas simply eliminate the distinction between moral virtues and mere rational capacities or skills? On the contrary, he insists that a virtue, unlike a skill, cannot be put to bad use. This belongs to the very definition of virtue suggested by Peter Lombard's *Sentences* and endorsed by Aquinas (*ST* 1–2.55.4 resp.). But here the "no bad use" doctrine should be interpreted along Augustinian lines. Virtues cannot be put to bad use because they are dispositions always directed to morally good ends. The agent nevertheless remains free not to use his virtues, even to act contrary to them. This is why Augustine treats virtues as greater goods than powers of the soul, such as free choice. Unlike virtues, powers of the soul can be badly used (*De libero arbitrio* 2.19).

Aquinas's conviction that virtuous people can lose their virtue through moral backsliding carries with it a more cheering corollary: with enough time and effort, vicious people can improve. In both cases the individual's power of free choice gives her the capacity to change her character. Now it might well be far more likely than not that she will continue making the kind of choices she has in the past, so that the virtuous person remains virtuous and the vicious one vicious. This probabilist account, however, still diverges significantly from Aristotle's. As Aquinas's ethical theory denies that anyone on earth is infallibly virtuous, so it denies that anyone on earth is incurably vicious.

CHAPTER SEVEN

Aquinas's Aristotelian defense of martyr courage

Jennifer A. Herdt

The virtue of courage has long been central to debates over the relationship between Aristotle and Aquinas. This is due in large part to its centrality to Harry Jaffa's argument that Aquinas fundamentally misconstrued Aristotle. Aquinas, Jaffa charged, wrongly regarded Aristotle's Book 3 account of courage as definitive, missing the developmental character of Aristotle's ethics and the fact that a fresh start is made at the beginning of Book 7.[1] Jaffa's claims have been hotly disputed for six decades, in the context of a broader debate that reaches back to the early twentieth century and beyond (Jenkins 1996, 39). The aim of this chapter, however, is neither to retrace these debates nor scrutinize Jaffa's idiosyncratic reading, but rather to take a fresh look at Aquinas's relationship to the *Nicomachean Ethics* by returning to the core primary texts on courage that bear on Aquinas's appropriation of Aristotle: the *Nicomachean Ethics* itself, Albert the Great's first commentary on the *EN*, Aquinas's commentary on Peter Lombard's *Sentences* (*Scriptum super libros Sententiarum*), his commentary on the *EN* (*Sententia libri Ethicorum*), and the *Summa theologiae*. Some recent commentators have made much of the fact that Aquinas parts ways with Aristotle dramatically in regarding martyrdom, rather than battlefield valor, as the principal act of fortitude (De Young 2003, 147–80). And it is undeniable that Aquinas's full understanding of fortitude is in this and other respects thoroughly theological in character. Yet when Aquinas's account of courage is held up against the broader theological tradition, what is most striking is not the departures from Aristotle as such, but the way in which Aquinas goes beyond Aristotle in affirming the exemplarity of martyr courage in a way

I am grateful to Jordan Wales for his creative initiative as research assistant for the initial stages of this project, and to the editors of this volume for their attentive editorial work on the manuscript.

[1] Jaffa argued that Aquinas in his discussion of courage in the commentary on the *Nicomachean Ethics* creates a "principle of the ultimate" that wrongly transfers an Aristotelian account of physical motion to the virtues, and so ends up with a "perfectly mechanical conception" of virtue incapable of degree or development (Jaffa 1952, 72–3).

that builds on, rather than repudiating, Aristotle's analysis of battlefield courage.

7.1   Bravery in the *Nicomachean Ethics*

In Book 3 of the *Nicomachean Ethics*, Aristotle turns from a discussion of the virtues in general to accounts of the individual virtues. He begins with bravery. He had earlier offered a brief account of how each virtue can be grasped as a mean. There, too, he began with bravery, calling it the mean in feelings of fear and confidence (*EN* 2.7.1107a33–b1). In neither book does he show any interest in offering a systematic account of their number or a justification of the order of presentation.[2] Plato, in contrast, had in Book 4 of the *Republic* developed a carefully structured account, according to which the virtues of wisdom, courage, and temperance correspond to the structure of both the soul and the city, while justice is constituted by the proper order of the constituent parts. Courage was for Plato the virtue of the warrior class, governing spirit (θυμός) and overcoming obstacles to the good. In the hierarchy of the city, warriors are placed between the governing and business classes, reflecting Plato's conviction that the rational and spirited parts of the soul properly govern the appetitive part. For Plato there existed a functional unity of the virtues; they can be (partially) independently gained and lost, but in order perfectly to have one of them one must have the others, since only then is an ordered pursuit of the good secured.

Aristotle accepts the notion that courage has to do with *thumos* and with overcoming obstacles to the pursuit of the good. Setting aside his predecessor's speculative psychology, however, Aristotle understands the moral virtues as craft-like habits that allow their possessor to live well. Instead of seeking to correlate the moral virtues to different powers of the soul, Aristotle multiplies them into an array of specific virtues, each limited to a precise arena of the moral life and consisting of a mean in feeling or action. Thus in Book 2 his primary concern is with showing how each individual virtue constitutes a mean in feeling or action. In the discussion of bravery in Book 3, meanwhile, he is concerned to specify its proper sphere of operation and the sense in which it is a mean. Only gradually does it emerge that bravery consists not simply in a mean in feelings of fear and confidence, but rather in the fact that despite the fact that he

---

[2] Michael Pakaluk does, though, plausibly suggest that Aristotle's order of exposition follows Plato in identifying bravery and temperance as virtues of the non-rational parts of the soul (2005, 159).

fears certain things, including the most terrifying things, the brave person nevertheless stands firm against these things, and does so for the sake of the end aimed at by virtue (*EN* 3.7.1115b11–13).

For Plato, there was an *analogy* between the warrior classes and spirit; these are potentially powerful forces for the good, able to overcome barriers that stand in the way, but only if this potentially unruly energy is governed and directed. Since each soul possesses spirit, as well as desire and reason, each soul is in need of the virtues of courage, temperance, and wisdom, working together in justice. For Aristotle, in contrast, courage proper is defined by reference to, and seems to be limited to, those who face death in battle (*EN* 3.6.1115a33–6).[3] Aristotle is concerned to carve out more specifically that courage consists in steadfastness in the face of terrifying conditions of a particular kind, the most terrifying, those associated with death. But the death that is being faced must also be a death in fine circumstances, and Aristotle judges that "such deaths are those in war, since they occur in the greatest and finest danger" (*EN* 3.6.1115a30–1). In contrast, to be steadfast in facing death in a storm at sea or through sickness is not courage. He is not particularly explicit about why, but the notion of a fine death, the death that is *to kalon*, is surely key. A death that is fine is one faced for the sake of defending some important good. Aristotle notes that honor is granted by both city-states and monarchs to those who die in battle. His point is not that soldiers accept the possibility of death for the sake of receiving honor, but rather that they rightly receive honor because of their willingness to accept the possibility of their own extinction for the sake of some good that transcends their lives and is thus honored by the community. Beyond the requirement of a fine death, Aristotle also notes that courage is exemplified "on occasions when we can use our strength" (*EN* 3.6.1115b5). That is, courage is something active, in which strength is employed, not a matter of passive endurance, as in sickness.

In line with his understanding of the craft-like character of practical wisdom, Aristotle begins with commonly accepted beliefs and seeks to articulate the reasons that undergird these, preserving the truth embodied in communal practices and opinions while clearing up confusion and internal contradiction. So in his discussion of courage Aristotle is concerned to exclude much of what typically goes by that name – the so-called courage of those who face dangers for the sake of winning honor, rather than for the sake of what is fine, or of those compelled to face dangers. He likewise strips

---

[3] Quotations from the *EN* are from Aristotle 1999.

of the right to be deemed courageous those who trust that their experience and skill will win out (and thus do not really accept the possibility of death), of those impelled by mere adrenaline rather than a decision to stand firm for the sake of what is fine, and those who are simply temperamentally hopeful (*EN* 3.8.1116a15–1117a28). All of these counterfeit forms of courage fail to instantiate one or more of the features seen in the truly courageous person, who "stands firm against the right things and fears the right things, for the right end, in the right way, at the right time" (*EN* 3.7.1115b17). Aristotle does not, though, reflect on whether one can be truly courageous if fighting in an unjust war or unjust battle, i.e., if one is fighting only for the sake of some apparent good. He seems to assume that warriors are always fighting to defend some genuine good, or at least sees no need to add this stipulation.

Students of Aristotle have had a number of puzzles with which to wrestle (Young 2009, 442–56; Pears 1980, 171–88). First, courage is described as being concerned with two things, fear and confidence, not simply with one, as in the usual model, i.e., the way temperance is concerned with sensual pleasure and liberality with wealth. This doubling seems to suggest that courage should split into two virtues, each with its own mean. Second, Aristotle names not two vices between which courage is the mean, but three: an excess of fearlessness, an excess of confidence, and an excess of fear, so there is a further question about how courage is to be understood as a unified virtue. Third, since the courageous person seems to feel fear, and fear involves the desire to avoid what one fears, courage seems to be an instance of self-control (ἐγκράτεια) and therefore to fall short of genuine Aristotelian virtue.

In response to these *aporiai*, contemporary scholars have moved in a variety of directions. So W. D. Ross argued that Aristotle's triad should be replaced by two dyads and hence two virtues, that of caution (opposed to rashness) and that of courage (opposed to cowardice), arguing further that Aristotle's account of courage points to the fact that all the virtues are actually forms of self-control (1923, 205–7). J. O. Urmson suggested that courage should rather be understood in terms of two triads, one a mean between overcaution and rashness, the other a mean between cowardice and insensitive fearlessness. Urmson thus preserves the doctrine of the mean but divides courage into two (1980, 169–70). David Pears and Charles Young have both argued that something like these two triads must be distinguished, but at the same time seen as intrinsically related to one another, preserving the unity of the virtue of courage as well as the doctrine of the mean (Pears 1980, 182–4; Young 2009, 451). Courage concerns both fear of loss of life and the cheering prospect of success in battle, but these are connected; fears must be confronted if success is to be achieved. Moreover, Young argues, courage properly understood does not amount to an instance of self-control, since the desire to avoid loss of life is not directly contrary to the desire to preserve life while acting courageously; self-control implies a victory over a directly contrary desire, as if a desire to stand firm were to control a desire to flee (2009, 446–7).

Closely related to the question of whether courage is reduced to mere self-control is a puzzle surrounding the painfulness of courage. Despite his overall account of how good habituation trains our non-rational desires so as to make it possible for us to find enjoyment in virtuous actions, Aristotle says that bravery is painful (*EN* 3.9.1117a34). In fact, he suggests that the more virtuous the agent, the more painful the prospect of death, since such a person is aware of being deprived of the greatest goods (*EN* 3.9.1117b12). So he concludes that the exercise of virtue is pleasant only insofar as we attain the end (*EN* 3.9.1117b17). The analogy he offers is that of a boxer, who finds the punches painful, but the end of honors pleasant. What, then, constitutes the end, what is fine in war, for the brave person? If the end is standing firm against what is painful when that is fine, it would seem that the defeated brave warrior can nevertheless be spoken of as having attained the end and therefore of finding pleasure in acting bravely (Pakaluk 2005, 166). But if the end is victory, then the defeated brave warrior is left simply with the pain of being knowingly deprived of great goods.

Aquinas and other medieval interpreters of Aristotle recognized and wrestled with these interpretive puzzles. But they also faced other challenges, as they worked to understand Aristotle's account of virtue in a way that could be reconciled with their affirmation of Christ as perfect exemplar of all virtue. If perfect courage was displayed in Christ's meek submission to death on the cross, and emulated by the endurance of martyrs, how could Aristotle's account of active battlefield courage be correct? And more generally, how could an understanding of good human action as frustrated by sin and rooted necessarily in divine gift be harmonized with Aristotle's understanding of human moral achievement?

7.2 Fortitude in Albert the Great's *Super Ethica*

While Albert the Great's *Super Ethica* is a literal commentary on the *Nicomachean Ethics*, it imports a great deal from Albert's own intellectual inheritance, especially in the questions he adds to the exposition of the text.

Following theological tradition reaching back to Ambrose, fortitude is discussed as one of four Platonic virtues dubbed "cardinal," the number and interrelation of which are both treated as worthy of attention. A Ciceronian definition of fortitude as twofold, undertaking dangers and enduring hardships, is adopted, thereby opening conceptual space for a defense of martyr courage that can likewise be traced back to Patristic thought. Albert discusses the four Ciceronian parts of fortitude, which are foreign to the *Nicomachean Ethics*. He also takes up the question of whether fortitude is properly understood as a general or a specific virtue. In this and other respects his commentary shows the influence of Philip the Chancellor (Houser 2004, 4).

Drawing on the *Ethica vetus*, i.e., the early translation of *EN* 2–3, Philip had developed a synthesis of the Aristotelian and Ciceronian accounts of virtue. In one sense, he regarded the cardinal virtues as universal conditions for the existence of virtue, linking these to the four conditions for genuine virtue given by Aristotle in *EN* 2.4.[4] The last of these, requiring the agent to act "from a firm and unchanging state," Philip linked with courage, understood as a quality of all virtuous actions (*EN* 2.4.1105a33–4; Philip, *Summa de bono*, ed. Wicki, 2:754 lines 7–15; cf. Houser 2004, 47–8). As a general characteristic of virtue, courage has to do simply with confronting the difficult. But Philip also defended a strict sense of each cardinal virtue; he took courage in this sense to concern exterior passions inflicted on the body. He explicitly associated the general sense of courage with Cicero and the special sense with Aristotle. He was also able to make room for two of Cicero's four principal parts of courage (magnanimity and perseverance) by considering these as particular virtues associated with the two primary acts of courage: attacking (*fortitudo in aggrediendo*) and enduring difficulties (*fortitudo in sustinendo sive patiendo*; *Summa de bono*, ed. Wicki, 2:823–4 lines 11–30). R. E. Houser argues that "this distinction between two senses – general and specific – of the cardinal virtues was Philip's great break-through in virtue theory, for the range of virtues could now be expanded to include treatment of the totality of good (and bad) action, thereby offering a systematically complete moral framework" (2004, 50). As we shall see, it was not, however, a resolution that sat easily with Albert and Aquinas.

One of Albert's clear concerns is to defend fortitude as a specific virtue, distinguished by its principal act. In some sense, this involves siding with

---

[4] In this summary statement, Aristotle writes that the agent must know what he or she is doing, choose the action, choose it for its own sake, and act from a firm state of character (*EN* 2.4.1105a32–4).

Aristotle over against the Stoic reduction to wisdom and their strong thesis of the unity of the virtues, but because it required a response to the Stoic position, and because it absorbed the scheme of four cardinal virtues (now as the hinge on which the door to life hangs) and even the Ciceronian notion that these virtues have parts, it went beyond Aristotle in a number of respects. Fortitude can indeed be said to be a general virtue, but not in the sense of being a general condition of all virtue. Nor is it even the case that the parts of fortitude are species of it as of a general kind. Rather, the four parts of fortitude enumerated by Cicero and accepted by Albert are so-called potential parts; they are secondary virtues related to but distinct from the virtue of courage in that they have to do with facing less challenging or terrible evils. They are said to be parts of fortitude, and fortitude is said to be general with respect to them, because, Albert holds, one who is able to stand firm in the face of the most terrible evils can also stand firm with respect to less terrible evils. Thus fortitude proper is defined according to the principle of the maximum or ultimate; it is principal with respect to its adjunct virtues in that it faces the maximal challenge.[5]

In general, then, Albert can be seen to be offering a systematizing account of Aristotle's thought that seeks to take it on its own terms (i.e., as lacking access to revealed truths) but that does not hesitate to make Aristotle's account more explicit and complete and prepare the conceptual ground for showing its harmony with Christian truth. Philip the Chancellor had waffled on the question of whether the cardinal virtues were acquired or infused. Albert treats them as acquired, not simply in his commentary on the *Nicomachean Ethics*, but also in *De bono*, where he divided the moral good into the good of habit and the good of grace, with the cardinal and subordinate "political" virtues clearly falling into the former category (*De bono* 2.11–16, p. 28; Cunningham 2008, 116). This was a decisive break with the authority of the Lombard. At the same time, Albert also began to grapple with the question of how grace relates to the acquired virtues, arguing that grace is united to the acquired virtues rather than remaining simply side-by-side with them. Infused virtue makes the deed one of grace, while acquired virtue makes the action easier for the agent to perform (*De bono* 2.1.5, p. 241).

---

[5] *Super Ethica* 3.8 n. 200, Editio Coloniensis 14:180–1; 3.10 n. 210, p. 190; *De bono* 2.1.1 n. 128, Editio Coloniensis 28:85; 2.1.2 n. 131, p. 86. Jörn Müller's helpful discussion also considers Albert's second commentary on the *Nicomachean Ethics* (2008, 78–88).

7.3 Fortitude in Aquinas's commentary on the *Sentences*

The commentary on the *Sentences* (*Scriptum super libros Sententiarum*), written while Aquinas was still in his course of studies at Paris (1252–56), bears ample witness to his teacher Albert's influence. Like Albert, Aquinas attends carefully to how the cardinal virtues are to be differentiated, whether they are infused or acquired, whether they consist in a mean, why they are called cardinal, in what sense they are general, in which power of the soul they exist, and their various parts and how these are to be understood. The *Sentences* commentary makes no attempt to remain within the Lombard's frame of reference but rather brings to bear a set of questions arising out of the task of assimilating Aristotelian thought within the inherited theological framework of infused cardinal virtues reducible to love. More specifically, Aquinas follows Albert in arguing that fortitude is general only in a restricted sense (*In Sent.* 3.33.2.1). He also espouses the principle of the maximum, arguing that virtues are named according to what is complete and last and most manifest (*In Sent.* 3.33.2.4). Hence, the principal matter of virtues having to do with irascible passion must be that which exceeds by the mode of intensity other passions existing in that power (*In Sent.* 3.33.2.1). Therefore, fortitude must be about the greatest danger, that of death. Similarly, he argues that enduring attack is a greater act of virtue than attacking evils, getting Aristotle on board with this Ciceronian move by skillfully appropriating a comment Aristotle makes in the context of discussing the painfulness of courage: that it is more difficult to withstand something painful than to refrain from something pleasant (*In Sent.* 3.33.2.3, *EN* 3.9.1117a35).[6] While the virtue of fortitude deals only with the greatest difficulties of a human sort (i.e., death), fortitude as a gift of the Holy Spirit concerns difficulties that exceed human faculties (*In Sent.* 3.34.3.1 qc. 1 ad 1). Thus the scope of virtue and gift are differentiated in such a way as to preserve a meaningful range of activity for each.

7.4 Fortitude in the *Sententia libri Ethicorum,* compared with Albert's *Super Ethica*

Aquinas's commentary on the *Nicomachean Ethics* (*Sententia libri Ethicorum*) was composed at the same time as the corresponding parts of the *Summa theologiae* (1271–72). Like Albert, Aquinas divides the virtues into

---

[6] As did Albert, *Super Ethica* 3.11 n. 219, Editio Coloniensis 14:195.

those concerned with interior passions and those concerned with external actions. He does not go on, however, to distinguish passions elicited from within versus those elicited from without. Rather, he contrasts passions concerning those things that are destructive of human life (the sphere of fortitude) with passions preservative of human life (the sphere of temperance) (*SLE* 3.14 lines 15–20). The same commitment to systematizing Aristotle is present, together with variations that build on and improve Albert's systematizing commentary. Like Albert, Aquinas appeals to Aristotle's *De caelo* to argue that virtue must be determined according to the maximum of the faculty (*SLE* 3.14 lines 119–23; cf. Albert, *Super Ethica*, 3.8 n. 200, pp. 180–1; 3.10 n. 210, p. 190). Fortitude must deal then with the most terrifying thing, which is death, since it is the end of the present life, and visibly the loss of all goods, since "things that pertain to the state of the soul after death are not visible to us" (*SLE* 3.14 lines 28–9). Fortitude must moreover be concerned with death for the best of causes. Death undergone by someone fighting in defense of his country is an example of this, but Aquinas goes farther than Albert to underscore that this is simply an example and that the same quality belongs to the case of any other death undergone for the good of virtue (*SLE* 3.14 lines 146–7; cf. Albert, *Super Ethica* 3.10 n. 209, p. 188). Aristotle mentions death in battle, he suggests, simply because it is a particularly *frequent* example of people suffering death for the sake of the good. Thus the battlefield context is decisively relativized. Aquinas further specifies that such a death is undergone not simply for the good of virtue in general but in particular on account of the common good, which is the greatest good (*SLE* 3.14 lines 155–6). In this respect, too, Aquinas goes beyond Albert, who spoke merely of the good of dying for the republic (*Super Ethica* 3.8 n. 199, p. 180).

In comparison with Albert, who insists that Aristotle discusses four extremes, which can be reduced to two between which fortitude mediates, Aquinas sharpens the challenge posed by Aristotle, noting that he in fact considers three extremes: deficiency of fear, excess in daring, and excess in fearing. One can certainly affirm that the inordinately fearful person is lacking in daring, but that the *reason* for this lies in his or her fear (*SLE* 3.15 lines 157–61; cf. Albert, *Super Ethica* 3.10 n. 207, p. 186). The same cannot be said for the relationship between deficiency of fear and excess in daring. Here too, Aquinas hews more closely to Aristotle's account than did his teacher. He goes on to argue that fortitude establishes a mean in two distinct passions of the irascible power, both of which thus have to do with the arduous good. Daring is hope of attaining a difficult good, while fear is of the loss of a good under threat (*SLE* 3.15 lines 181–4;

cf. Albert, *Super Ethica* 3.10 n. 207, p. 186). In comparison with Albert, then, Aquinas seems less concerned here with establishing the unity of the virtue of fortitude than with building onto Aristotle's account of its complexity.

In discussing the issue of the pleasure in courageous action, Aquinas takes pains to point out the key disanalogy between the boxer and the courageous person, noting that because the good which boxer possess as an end is insignificant, the pleasure they otherwise take in the end for which they strive is "absorbed" by the stronger pain they experience due to their "sensible flesh" (*SLE* 3.18 lines 65–71). For the courageous, in contrast, some pleasure remains because the end for which they act is the good of fortitude itself (*SLE* 3.18 lines 76–7; cf. Albert, *Super Ethica* 3.11 n. 221, pp. 196–7). He suggests that Aristotle takes up the issue in order to refute the errors of the Stoics; the virtuous do feel pain, indeed, pain that is particularly intense given the great goods relinquished when the virtuous lose their lives. Unlike Albert, Aquinas makes no mention here of the martyrs, noting only circumspectly that some of the virtuous find death desirable due to the hope of a future life. "It did not, though, pertain to the Philosopher to speak of those things that pertain to the state of another life in this work" (*SLE* 3.18 lines 103–8; cf. Albert, *Super Ethica* 3.9 n. 203, p. 183).[7] Aquinas is thus content with the merest hint here of how Christian faith convictions would transform the picture; Aquinas is clearly committed to displaying the internal coherence of a perspective on which the goods of life are irrevocably lost with death and yet on which the courageous sacrifice of life for the sake of the goods of virtue remains meaningful. There is certainly no suggestion here, any more than in Albert, that giving up one's life is intelligible only for the martyr, who with hope and faith can "see" beyond the horizon of death.

Aquinas introduces greater intelligibility into his discussion of the similitudes of fortitude by building on Albert's efforts to show that the similitudes fail to incorporate essential features of virtuous action. Aquinas argues that these counterfeits of fortitude can be derived from Aristotle's general requirements for genuinely virtuous action: that the agent must know she is doing virtuous actions, that she must decide on them for their own sakes, and, third, that she do them from a firm and unchanging state (*EN* 2.4.1105a30). Distinct similitudes arise from acting without knowledge, from lacking choice and acting instead from passion, whether the

---

[7] Aquinas does refer in *SLE* 3.2 lines 52–3 to the patient suffering of St. Lawrence, but in the broader context of dying for the sake of virtue, not specifically in relation to Christian faith or martyrdom.

passion of anger or of hope, or from making a different choice than that made by the virtuous agent, i.e., by not choosing the difficult good, as the courageous do (perhaps because one does not regard it as difficult), or by choosing honors or avoidance of punishment rather than what is truly good (*SLE* 3.15; cf. Albert, *Super Ethica* 3.10 n. 209, p. 188; see Cunningham 2008, 189).

The *SLE*, then, is clearly influenced by Albert and, like Albert's *Super Ethica*, it introduces organizational structures and issues deriving from the theological tradition. But it works if anything more assiduously than the *Super Ethica* to hew closely to Aristotle's account and refrain from introducing truths dependent on revelation. At the same time, it succeeds more fully than Albert had in completing the logic and structure of Aristotle's thought in a manner that paves the way for its coherence with revealed truth.

7.5 Fortitude in the *Summa theologiae*

In the *Summa theologiae*, Aquinas has significantly more freedom to shape his discussion as he sees fit. His discussion of fortitude is largely consistent with the expositions offered in the *Sentences* commentary and the *SLE*, but what we find here is his own independent synthesis and one that is fully integrated into his overarching theological vision. Aquinas orders his overall discussion of the virtues according to the pattern established by Philip, first discussing virtues in general, then the theological virtues, followed by the cardinal virtues. Whether one distinguishes the virtues with respect to their formal principle or according to the subjects in which they exist, one arrives at the same four cardinal virtues. Virtue's formal principle is the good as defined by reason. Prudence is then the act of reason itself, justice is reason ordering operations, temperance curbs the passions that lead one to act against reason, while fortitude strengthens the agent when passions withdraw her from adhering to reason's dictates (*ST* 1–2.61.2; 2–2.123.1). Aquinas follows a broadly Aristotelian definition of the moral virtues as virtues of the powers that are rational by participation. He then goes on to define temperance as perfecting the concupiscible faculty and fortitude the irascible faculty. This contrasts with Albert's division, which proceeded first according to virtues concerned with actions versus those concerned with passions, and then, within the latter category, according to those concerned with passions elicited from within versus those elicited from without. It also departs from his own account in the *SLE*, which contrasts the sphere of temperance as the passions preservative of human life with that of fortitude as passions destructive of human life. The changes in the *Summa* bring him closer to Aristotle insofar as he now focuses neither on the source of the passions nor on their organic function but on fortitude's relation to fear and daring. It is at the same time more tightly connected with his own commitment to thinking of all virtue as ordering human agency according to the good of reason.

The ranking of the cardinal virtues in the *Summa* is likewise Aquinas's own: first prudence, then justice, fortitude, and finally temperance. Prudence is principal, since it actually possesses the good of reason, while justice follows because it effects the good, while the others moderate the passions lest they lead away from it. The order of fortitude and temperance is the least settled: in the *Prima Secundae* temperance precedes fortitude (*ST* 1–2.61.2), but in the *Secunda Secundae* Aquinas argues that fortitude precedes temperance because the fear of the dangers of death has greater power to make men recede from the good of reason than do the pleasures of touch (*ST* 2–2.123.12).

In his discussion of fortitude, Aquinas proceeds as he did with his discussion of prudence and justice, first considering fortitude itself, then its parts, followed by the corresponding gift of the Holy Spirit, and finally the precepts of divine law pertaining to it. Thus, Aquinas's discussion of the cardinal virtues (following the theological virtues), and fortitude in particular (culminating in a consideration of the corresponding gift of the Holy Spirit and precepts of divine law, as found in Dt 20:3–4), are set firmly within a theological context. At this point, he is not simply discussing the acquired or social virtues, which are virtues insofar as they are in a human person according to the condition of nature (*ST* 1–2.61.5 resp.). He had for the most part confined himself to this when first introducing the topic of virtue, and up to the introduction of the theological virtues in *ST* 1–2.62, but not thereafter.[8] In the *Secunda Secundae*, both acquired and infused cardinal virtues are in play. This becomes clear as Aquinas's discussion of fortitude unfolds.

In grappling with the issue of whether fortitude, and the cardinal virtues more generally, are to be understood as general or as specific, Aquinas notes that one can indeed speak of these as general conditions found in all virtues (*ST* 2–2.123.2 resp.). So, for instance, "it is fitting that every

---

[8] This is true only for the most part – he does defend an Augustinian definition of virtue with reference to infused virtue already in *ST* 1–2.55.4.

moral virtue... should be accompanied by a certain firmness so as not to be moved by its contrary: and this, we have said, belongs to fortitude" (*ST* 1–2.61.4 resp.).[9] When this route is taken, however, one is no longer speaking of distinct virtuous habits. Hence, other authorities, "with better reason," "take these four virtues according as they have their special determinate matter" (*ST* 1–2.61.4 resp.). As specific virtues, they are distinct habits, differentiated by diverse objects. They have a claim to being principal or cardinal either way; when considered as general conditions of virtue, they in some sense contain all the other virtues, while when considered as specific virtues, they are principal given the central importance of their special matter.

It is thus clearly important to Aquinas, as it was to Albert, to defend the cardinal virtues precisely as specific virtues and therefore as distinct virtuous habits. But Aquinas is more willing to incorporate the general sense of the cardinal virtues than was Albert.[10] He returns to the issue in the *Secunda Secundae* to note that fortitude's claim to being a cardinal virtue rests in its being a general condition of virtue (to act steadfastly). He then connects this back to fortitude's specific reference: those pains and dangers that are most feared are those leading to death, against which the brave are most properly said to stand firm (*ST* 2–2.123.11 resp.). He also appeals to the principle of the maximum, and to Aristotle's *De caelo* as its source, in order to suggest that there is something general about fortitude even when it is understood in a specific way: as a virtue is properly the extreme limit of a power, those who can stand firm in the most difficult things can stand firm in the face of less difficult challenges (*ST* 2–2.123.2 ad 1).[11] Thus we gain more profound purchase on steadfastness as a general condition of virtue by attending to the specific virtue of fortitude.

Aquinas hews close to Albert in his basic account of fortitude as the virtue that binds the will firmly to the good in the face of the greatest of evils, of which the most fearful of all on the bodily level is death (*ST* 2–2.123.4 resp.). Like Albert, Aquinas makes clear from the outset that fortitude must have to do not merely with facing dangers. Rather, what

---

[9] Quotations from the *ST* are from Aquinas 1947–48.

[10] Here I differ somewhat from the assessment offered by Müller (2008, 80), with whose interpretation and conclusions I am otherwise in substantial agreement.

[11] Regarding the "principle of the ultimate," James Doig (1993, 19; 2001, xvii) argues that Aquinas arrives at his mature position only in the *De virtutibus*, where he makes clear that a virtue is not an act but a habitus inclining a potency to the ultimate action of which that potency is capable. Hence, contra Jaffa, it is not the case that only the most perfect form of courage is "genuine courage." See also Chapter 3, Section 3.3, in this volume.

renders facing death a courageous act is the fact that one is encountering this possibility *just because of* one's pursuit of some good. But Aquinas displays more fully the significance of this move. For having seen this, he notes, we can appreciate that it may also be properly courageous to face sickness or shipwreck. The key is whether the danger is being encountered because of one's pursuit of the good. So tending a friend who is suffering from a deadly infectious disease, or undertaking a journey "with some godly object in view," rather than being held back by fear of shipwreck, or robbery, now count as properly courageous actions (*ST* 2–2.123.5 resp.). Aristotle's aristocratic courage begins to recede, and a virtue available to all comes into view (Bowlin 1999, 167–212). Christian thinkers had long worked to define martyrs as exemplary in courage. But Aquinas is not yet ready to unpack how martyrdom emerges as the principal act of courage, even if this argument already shows more fully than Albert how martyrdom can be reconciled with an Aristotelian account of courage. Aquinas's point at this stage is to show how even those living a humdrum ordinary existence can have opportunities for genuine courage.

Aquinas's account builds in this direction by expanding the concept of battle and relocating the requirement of activity from body to soul. An expanded notion of battle was implicit in Albert's treatment of martyrdom as an example of courage. But Aquinas offers a conceptual articulation of this expansion. In doing so, he dramatically expands the category "battle" by suggesting that courage may just as properly be exercised in private combat as on the battlefield.[12] His example of this is a judge who does not refrain from giving a just judgment through fear of some threat of death. This does not mean that Aquinas moves in the direction of a radical exclusion of military courage, however (Reichberg 2010, 338). The peace of the city is a real if proximate good, and it can be justly and courageously defended. But courage is displayed not just in any facing of death on the battlefield, but specifically in defending the common good "by a just fight." And facing death in battle is just one example of courage, even when courage is most specifically and strictly defined.

As noted earlier, Aristotle regarded courage as something necessarily active, something exemplified where we can "use our strength." Courage is a virtue of the strong, of those who can fight, not of the weak, or of those who suffer. Here Aquinas follows Albert, using Aristotle against

---

[12] Gregory Reichberg (2010, 343) notes that the concept of private war already existed in Aquinas's context, but normally involved a private resort to violence. Hence, Aquinas innovates in understanding it in terms of receiving violence.

himself; in the *sed contra*, it is Aristotle himself who serves as the source for the contrary opinion that "certain persons are said to be brave chiefly because they endure affliction" (*ST* 2–2 123.6 s.c.). This "common opinion" canvassed in passing by Aristotle offers Aquinas an entry point into arguing, in agreement with longstanding Christian appropriations of Cicero, that the principal act of fortitude is endurance.[13] The principal act must display the perfection of a virtue. Thus, it must exhibit a virtue under the most challenging conditions. One might well think that simply holding fast to the good in the face of attack is less of an achievement than oneself attacking the evil that threatens the good. But Aquinas inverts these assumptions, arguing that endurance may seem passive, but requires "an action of the soul cleaving most resolutely to the good" (*ST* 2–2 123.6 ad 2). Strength of soul is more ethically significant than bodily strength; it is more difficult and thus a greater achievement when a weaker person holds fast to the good in the presence of a stronger evil power than when a physically strong person relies on her strength in order to attack evil. One's steadfast adherence to the good is most fully and powerfully displayed in physical weakness. Again, while this move prepares the way for praising the courage of the martyrs, Aquinas seeks at this stage to make a more general point about enduring evils.

The account of delight experienced in the act of fortitude follows the lines established in the *Ethics* commentary, noting the various sources of bodily pain (in loss of life and limb), spiritual sorrow (in confronting the loss of the goods of a virtuous life), and spiritual pleasure (in clinging to the good) (*ST* 2–2.123.8 resp.). Fortitude prevents reason from being overcome despite pain, making it possible steadfastly to cling to the good, and delight in acting virtuously can overcome spiritual sorrow. But here Aquinas adds that the sensible pain of the body makes the agent insensible to the spiritual delight of virtue; only with the assistance of grace can any pleasure be felt in such action. Some pleasure remains to the brave, as he noted in the *Ethics* commentary, but here he adds – only with grace. We will return below to the question of the necessity of grace in connection with patience as one of the four parts of courage; as we shall see, even this is not intended to undermine the coherence of Aristotle's account.

Aquinas has now established the foundation for defending martyrdom as the principal act of fortitude in a way that harmonizes and builds

---

[13] Though he goes on to argue that martyrdom is the principal act of fortitude; cf. the introduction to q. 123.

on his Aristotelian account of courage. Martyrdom "consists essentially in standing firm in truth and justice against the assaults of persecution" (*ST* 2–2.124.1 resp.). The martyr cleaves to the good in the face of the threat of death, "the imminence of which is moreover due to a kind of particular contest with his persecutors" (*ST* 2–2.124.2 resp.). In other words, the martyr is properly said to be engaged in battle, though not on a battlefield, and so martyrdom is an act of fortitude in the most specific sense. Moreover, martyrdom exemplifies endurance, which has already been said to be the principal act of fortitude and properly active, not passive, even though it is not aggressive (*ST* 2–2.124.2 ad 3). The courage of martyrs is more praiseworthy than the courage of those who die in defense of their country not just because endurance is more proper to courage than attacking, but also because the Divine good to which martyrs cling exceeds not only the good of the individual but also the civic good (*ST* 2–2 124.5 ad 3): both its form and its end are greater. Since the good to which martyrs cling is specifically the Divine good, which cannot be grasped by natural reason, it should come as no surprise that we have to do here with gratuitous (infused) fortitude, rather than merely with civic (acquired) fortitude. This becomes clear in a reply to an objection that martyrdom is properly an act of charity, not fortitude. Aquinas responds that martyrdom is elicited by fortitude but commanded by charity; without charity it is not meritorious and "avails not" (*ST* 2–2.124.2 ad 2; see Knobel 2004, 125–41; Sherwin 2009, 29–52).

The *Summa theologiae* account of the vices opposed to fortitude closely follows the lines established in Aquinas's *Ethics* commentary. Aquinas deals in three successive questions with the vices of fear, fearlessness, and daring. The unity of courage is affirmed by calling it a mean between timidity and fearlessness, even if distinct vices related to fear and to daring must be distinguished in order to make clear that fortitude establishes the mean in these two distinct passions of the irascible power (*ST* 2–2.126 ad 3). There is no vice of deficient daring, seemingly the missing character, because nature inclines us to take the offensive against that which thwarts us except when fear restrains us (*ST* 2–2.27.2 ad 3).

Like Albert, Aquinas readily parts ways with Aristotle in accepting the four Ciceronian parts of fortitude, while substituting Aristotle's magnanimity for Cicero's confidence (*ST* 2–2.128). He considers them both quasi-integral and potential parts. They are quasi-integral as necessary to an act of fortitude (magnanimity and magnificence for aggression, and patience and perseverance for endurance). They are potential parts as secondary virtues annexed to fortitude in the sense that they deal with lesser hardships in the same way as fortitude deals with the greatest hardships. It is not possible to undertake a full discussion of the parts of fortitude in this context, important as it is to take stock of how Aquinas reinterprets magnanimity, that most troublesome of pagan virtues, in such a way as to reconcile it with humility (*ST* 2–2.129.3 ad 4; see Hoffmann 2008, Keys 2003, and Herdt 2008, 77–80).

Particularly nuanced is Aquinas's treatment of the question of whether it is possible to have patience without grace. We are capable of bearing painful evils only for the sake of attaining some good end. Corrupt human nature is more prone to bear evils for the sake of sensible goods than for the sake of the goods grasped by reason (*ST* 2–2.136.3 ad 1). Further, "the fact that a man prefers the good of grace to all natural goods . . . is to be referred to charity, which loves God above all things," and it is impossible to have charity without grace (*ST* 2–2.136.3 resp.). This parallels Aquinas's earlier comment about martyrdom as possible only given grace and is likewise linked to the fact that the Divine good can be grasped only through the infused virtues. But Aquinas does concede that there are heathens who have endured many bodily evils "rather than betray their country or commit some other misdeed" (*ST* 2–2.136.3). This is true patience, since it is a matter of enduring evils for the sake of goods grasped by reason. Such heathens display civic virtue, which is commensurate with human nature. Their action is oriented toward a natural human good, not the Divine good. Given the fall, they inevitably fall short of the good that would have been natural to them, but they can nevertheless work some particular good. Thus true, if not perfect and complete, patience is possible apart from grace. Of course, such acts, like all human actions, are possible only through the divine aid that makes all movement possible (*ST* 1–2.109.2). In this most generic sense one can affirm that patience, and thus fortitude, requires divine aid, but this is not supernatural grace and does not distinguish patient action from any other sort of action.

Aquinas concludes his treatise on fortitude with a question on fortitude as a gift of the Holy Spirit and on the precepts of law pertaining to fortitude and its annexed secondary virtues. The gift of fortitude lends confidence that all dangers will be finally overcome, not just that they may be endured (*ST* 2–2.139 ad 1). The Divine law meanwhile gives precepts of fortitude with a view to directing persons to God, thus complementing the infused virtues. While fortitude as gift is discussed more fully in the commentary on the *Sentences* than it is here, the point being made here is architectonic: in two distinct ways, by reference to gift and precept, these final questions on fortitude round out Aquinas's treatment of fortitude as intrinsically theological and fully integrated into his overarching account of the graced *reditus* of humankind to God.[14]

7.6   Conclusion

What, then, can we say about the relationship of Aquinas to Aristotle on the basis of the preceding discussion of courage? Jaffa's tendentious reading finds little support; his own reading of Aristotle is such a strong one that his dismissal of Aquinas's interpretation as unreliable seems an overly precipitate casting of the first stone. But neither does the claim made by Mark Jordan, that the *SLE* was a literal exposition of the text that sought only to offer a close reading of the text, seem persuasive (Jordan 2006, 69). Rather, we have found that Aquinas in his commentary on the *Nicomachean Ethics* sought to offer a reading that would (a) clarify the inner logic and implicit structure of Aristotle's thought, thereby addressing key *aporiai* recognized to this day by interpreters of Aristotle, and (b) indicate where Aristotle's understanding was limited by his lack of access to revealed truth. In doing so, Aquinas certainly does more than offer a close reading of the text, since he offers a reading structured and informed by the theological tradition (i.e., its acceptance of four cardinal virtues, of Cicero's definition of courage that paired attacking and enduring, its wrestling with general versus specific understandings of the virtues), even if he does not introduce theological authorities into the text. In doing so, he prepared the ground for his fuller account of fortitude in the *Summa theologiae*, one that took up the truth he found in Aristotle and showed how this could be incorporated with the truths of revelation and rational insights from the theological tradition into an understanding of how the virtues, acquired and infused, equip humankind as created in God's image, fallen, and capable through Christ of returning to their Creator. This lends support to Leo Elders's insistence that Aquinas sought what medieval commentators in general intended to do, "to make a text of an *auctoritas* useful for students in higher studies and to show the continuity of doctrinal development" (Elders 2009, 51–2). Hence, Aquinas aimed to locate the truth in Aristotle's text and bring it forward, developing it, often with the help of principles derived from Aristotle himself. John Jenkins, similarly, seems to be justified in his claim that where Aquinas's own views enter into the commentaries on Aristotle, they do so as a dialectical development of Aristotle's views that has itself

---

[14] Hence an appreciation of Christ as exemplar of courage, as of all virtue, is essential to a full understanding of Aquinas on courage, something I do not attempt to provide here. See Shanley 2008, 353 and De Young 2003, 150.

a claim to being termed an authentically Aristotelian approach to the text (Jenkins 1996, 41).[15] Courage on Aquinas's own account is most perfectly realized in the endurance of martyrdom, which clings to the Divine good by grace. Courage fully articulated is thus dramatically different from courage as understood by Aristotle. At the same time, Aquinas's purpose is not to subvert Aristotle, but rather to show how his partial truth points toward more complete truth.

---

[15] Jenkins helpfully distinguishes this stance from both appropriationist and historicist views (i.e., like those of Doig and Jordan, respectively), (1996, 40). Christopher Kaczor similarly argues that Aquinas treats Aristotle as offering a true, though not a full, account of reality, (2004, 373).

CHAPTER EIGHT

Being truthful with (or lying to) others about oneself

Kevin Flannery, S. J.

In *Summa theologiae* 2–2.109–113, Thomas Aquinas takes an idea with origins in *Nicomachean Ethics* 4.7 well beyond what Aristotle says there. As Kevin White puts it, Aquinas "extends Aristotle's relatively narrow concern with questions of truthfulness and falsehood about oneself to a more general consideration of truth and lies as such" (1993, 650). And yet, as I shall argue, the latter consideration is present in embryo in *EN* 4.7 as its core idea – a fact obscured for many by the very authority of the most important twentieth-century commentary on the *EN*, that of the Dominican René-Antoine Gauthier, which is deliberately non-Thomistic, including in its interpretation of *EN* 4.7 (Gauthier and Jolif 1970, I,1:275–6).

Section 8.1 situates *EN* 4.7 within the larger contexts of *EN* 4.6–8 and *EN* 4 itself; this gives us a good idea of what Aristotle himself regards as distinctive about the virtue (and corresponding vices) discussed in *EN* 4.7. Sections 8.2 and 8.3 are devoted to a detailed exegesis of the very finespun analysis conducted by Aristotle in *EN* 4.7. The detail is necessary in order to show more clearly the coherence of Aquinas's interpretation. Section 8.4 looks directly at this interpretation as set out in Aquinas's *Ethics* commentary. Section 8.5 examines the relationship between *ST* 2–2.109– 113 and *EN* 4.7, noting a surprising connection with Augustine.

8.1 Larger contexts

What have become known as the "homiletic virtues" are treated by Aristotle in *EN* 4.6–8. The first two virtues are said by Aristotle to be nameless, but we might call them "amiability" and "truthfulness"; the third Aristotle calls "wit" (εὐτραπελία; see Hoffmann 2011). That they are to be grouped together as homiletic virtues becomes apparent at the end of *EN* 4.8, where Aristotle remarks:

The means in life that have been described are, then, three in number; they
all have to do with community of certain words and actions. They differ,
however, in that one is concerned with truth, the other two with pleasure.
Of those concerned with pleasure, one has its place in jests, the other in
relations in the rest of life. (1128b4–9)

By far the most interesting, both philologically and philosophically, of these
virtues is truthfulness (treated in *EN* 4.7), but it is important also to know
something about the other two because they help us (1) to understand
what is distinctive about the homiletic virtues (within *EN* 4) and (2) to
understand what is distinctive about truthfulness among the homiletic
virtues.

Regarding (1), it is notable that in all three chapters (*EN* 4.6–8) Aristotle
is explicitly concerned with character: that is his emphasis. In previous
chapters of Book 4, his emphasis has been upon certain virtues as they
are connected to the exterior goods of wealth and honor. This includes
(although not obviously so) *EN* 4.5, which has to do with good temper,
as opposed to inordinate placidity (ἀοργησία) and ill-temper, for these
dispositions concern one's reaction to insults (1126a7–8), which constitute
a loss of glory. But in *EN* 4.6, Aristotle insists that he is talking about
what it is like to *be* an amiable man (1126b24–5); in *EN* 4.7, he focuses
in upon (as an indication of character) what someone does when nothing
is at stake; and in *EN* 4.8, he speaks of the ready-witted man as a law
unto himself – which in this context means only that determining what
is a proper witticism in a certain social context is a matter of having
the right subjective "feel" for things rather than following any set rule.
Put simply, the early chapters of Book 4 are concerned with wealth and
honor; the specified later chapters, with whether the *man* in question is
amiable, truthful, and/or properly witty.[1] As we shall see, wealth and honor
do come into the analysis of truthfulness; being truthful, however, is not
about wealth or honor but about being truthful.

Regarding (2), one of Aristotle's concerns over the course of *EN* 4.6–8 is
whether the field itself in which the virtue under consideration is situated
provides a standard by which that virtue might be measured. In *EN* 4.6,
which he says is concerned with pleasure (and pain), it seems that there is
none – or, at least, no fixed standard. The amiable man would prefer not
to cause pain in his relations with others, but he realizes too that that is

---

[1] *EN* 4.9, the last chapter in the book, is an outlier: in its first phrase, Aristotle acknowledges that its
subject (shame) is not really a virtue.

sometimes the best thing to do.[2] "In itself [καθ' αὑτό] he prefers giving pleasure (and is loathe to give pain); he will be guided, however, by the consequences, if these are greater: I mean the noble and the beneficial" (*EN* 4.6.1127a2–5). When (in *EN* 4.8) Aristotle discusses the well-bred man of wit, he at first suggests that, like the amiable man, he will never cause pain with his witticisms but then acknowledges that this would be a very indefinite standard since what causes pleasure or pain depends so much on the person listening (*EN* 4.8.1128a25–8). Aristotle does think that there are certain jokes that the properly witty man will never make, although in the end, as we have seen, he says that this man is "a law unto himself" (*EN* 4.8.1128a32). So, both amiableness and wit look to a rather subjective standard; truthfulness, on the other hand, as Aristotle says at the end of *EN* 4.8, looks to truth – and this provides an objective standard.

8.2 *EN* 4.7, Section 1: Falsehood as foul and blameworthy

Book 4 ch. 7, on the unnamed mean between impostery (ἀλαζονεία) and self-deprecation (εἰρωνεία) which we have called truthfulness, can be divided into two sections of roughly equal length: 1127a13–b9 and 1127b9–32.[3] Each section involves a major issue of interpretation, the first issue being Aristotle's statement that falsehood is per se foul and blameworthy, the second, his characterization of the non-truthful character types (the imposter and the self-deprecator). I shall go through the two sections in order.

EN 4.7 begins by setting truthfulness within the context of the homiletic virtues: it is "almost about the same things" as the previous chapter (on the amiable man and his foils) since to understand the truthful man as well as the character types with whom he is immediately contrasted is to understand how they deal with their own reputation, although in ways

---

[2] In this connection, it seems best not to accept the emendation suggested by Imelmann (1864, p. 18) (and accepted by the Revised Oxford Translation) at *EN* 4.6.1126b30; that is, it would be best to retain the words τοῦ μὴ λυπεῖν, found apparently in all the manuscripts, rather than changing the μὴ to ἤ. The emendation is unnecessary and rather weights the character of the amiable man toward being ready to inflict pain. Aristotle does say that the amiable man sometimes chooses to inflict pain (1126b33), but what especially characterizes him is a desire to minimize pain in his social dealings (1126b35, 1127a6). Rejecting Imelmann's emendation, therefore, the translation of the larger phrase would be: "it is by reference to what is noble and expedient that he will aim at not giving pain or at contributing pleasure."

[3] The word "impostery" is archaic. There is no other word, however, that so well represents the quality of being an imposter (ἀλαζών). The word ἀλαζονεία is sometimes translated "boastfulness," but that does not capture Aristotle's sense. As we shall see, Aristotle says that the man who boasts "for no reason" (1127b10) does not qualify as an imposter (an ἀλαζών); obviously, however, he would be a boaster.

that have a bearing upon truth and falsehood, whether in word or in deed. Employing an unusual word, Aristotle says that the truthful man is αὐθέκαστος, which means literally "each himself."[4] *Met.* 5.29 is useful in determining the precise meaning of the word as used in *EN* 4.7. In the *Metaphysics* passage, Aristotle discusses the liar (the ψευδής) and says that he, besides being fond of false statements, is like a false thing: inclined toward – or, at least, capable of – instilling false impressions in others (1025a4–6). So, the truthful man of *EN* 4.7 would be one who "comes across as he really is": if he is well-bred or accomplished, he will not hide that (although he will not flaunt it either [*EN* 4.4.1127b8–9]); if he is not, he will not come across – or, at least, deliberately come across – as someone who is.

Following these introductory remarks, Aristotle speaks directly about impostery, self-deprecation, and truthfulness. He says: "Each of these is done either for something or for nothing. Each person is such as are the things he says and does and so lives, if haply he does not act for something."[5] Like "impostery," the word "haply" is archaic, but it is necessary for representing accurately the sense of the remark. The idea is that those (for instance) who engage in impostery "for something" – for fame or gain, as he specifies later – are indeed imposters, although they do not constitute that character *insofar as* they have such ulterior reasons for so acting. Impostery itself has more to do with what they could conceivably – "haply" – do: act thus but not for fame or for gain. The man who behaves thus is the "typical" imposter in the literal sense: he constitutes the type, even if he might be more rare. Similarly, the truthful man may sometimes speak the truth for an ulterior reason, but such behavior is not what lies at the core of what it is to be a truthful person, which is rather speaking the truth for no such reason.

At this point, Aristotle turns his attention directly toward this core of the three character traits (impostery, self-deprecation, and truthfulness). "But in itself [καθ' αὑτό]," he says, "falsehood is foul and blameworthy, and truth is noble and praiseworthy." The idea here, it seems, is that foulness and nobility go from lying and truth-telling to the corresponding character types and not vice-versa. The imposter is blameworthy because he does not tell the truth; his impostery is not blameworthy simply because he is the

---

[4] The word also appears in *EE* 3.7.1233b39, where Aristotle discusses very briefly the "true" (ἀληθής) or "self-possessed" (πεπνυμένος) man (1234a2–3).

[5] "ἔστι δὲ τούτων ἕκαστα καὶ ἕνεκά τινος ποιεῖν καὶ μηδενός. ἕκαστος δ' οἷός ἐστι, τοιαῦτα λέγει καὶ πράττει καὶ οὕτω ζῇ, ἐὰν μή τινος ἕνεκα πράττῃ" (*EN* 4.7.1127a26–8). The translation "if haply" is given as the first option for ἐάν in Liddell and Scott's *Greek-English Lexicon*.

type of man he is. Similarly, the truthful man is praiseworthy because he tells the truth. It must be acknowledged that truth-telling is a genuinely virtuous act only if it is done as the truthful man would do it – that is, if it emerges from a virtuous person, but the virtue of truthfulness depends on acts of truth-telling and not vice-versa.[6] If there were no such thing as telling the truth, there would be no virtue of truthfulness. "And so," says Aristotle, "the truthful man is a mean and praiseworthy; and both the false men are blameworthy, but especially the imposter" (*EN* 4.7.1127a28–32). The one false man here is the self-deprecator, the other (obviously) the imposter. As Aristotle explains near the end of the chapter, the former can be quite attractive since he is often after neither gain nor reputation, but the latter is loathsome, no matter what his motivations.

Aristotle goes on then to say that in considering the truthful man he is interested not so much in conducting an external analysis of matters pertaining to injustice and justice in public agreements – to be true in these matters is to have another virtue, he says (presumably, particular justice [*EN* 5.1.1129a26–b1]) – as in understanding what it is to *be* a truthful man: what it is to have that character, given that character is revealed, as he has already said, in what a man does when nothing is at stake.

> Such a man would seem to *be* equitable [ἐπιεικής]. For he is a lover of the truth; and if, where it does not matter, he is true, he will also be true – indeed, more so – where it does matter, for he will avoid falsehood as shameful – which in any case he avoided in itself [καθ' αὑτό]. Such a man is praiseworthy. (1127b3–7)

Aristotle is clearly coming back here to his emphasis upon character rather than external acts – without, however, denying that character is affected by external acts, especially by those that are in themselves foul or noble. The truthful man does not just say true things: he is a lover of the truth (φιλαλήθης). This is demonstrated by his aversion to falsehood even when nothing is at stake. When something *is* at stake, this aversion will be even stronger precisely because he regarded falsehood as shameful (αἰσχρόν) even when nothing was at stake. In serious matters, it is even more important to shun all disgraceful behaviour.

Gauthier's commentary, first published in 1958 and slightly revised in 1970, represents these lines differently: indeed, in quite the opposite sense.[7]

---

[6] See *EN* 2.4.1105a26–b12. See also Aquinas, *ST* 2–2.109.1 resp.

[7] Jean Yves Jolif, who is listed with Gauthier as coauthor of their *Éthique à Nicomaque: Introduction, traduction et commentaire*, translated and commented on Books 2, 5, and 7.1.1145a15–7.10.1152a36. The rest of the work is by Gauthier; see the preface to the 1958 edition. The 1970 edition has a

"The liar lies and the truthful man tells the truth, at least when neither has a reason to act contrary to their inclination: in which case, the liar will tell the truth and the truthful man will lie."[8] This is difficult to square with Aristotle's remark that "where it does matter . . . he will avoid falsehood as shameful." How does Gauthier deal with the latter? His comment on that remark is as follows:

> Truthfulness is a sort of *refinement* which urges us to tell the truth even when we are not obliged; *a fortiori*, therefore, the truthful man tells the truth when it is obligatory in justice. But, as we have seen, the refinement of truthfulness does not extend as far as speaking the truth in situations in which, in order to perform a duty of justice (for example, in order to save the country), the sole means available to us is to tell a falsehood.[9]

Gauthier's back reference ("as we have seen") is to his own earlier argument on the remark that "In itself . . . falsehood is foul and blameworthy, but truth is noble and praiseworthy" (1127a28–30):

> The truthful man is he who, while absolutely nothing outside of it obliges him to do so, speaks the truth solely for love of the truth, as similarly the liar is he who, independently of every consideration of interest, speaks falsehood for the love of falsehood. It follows that the truthful man might utter falsehood, if the good of the country or of his friends or indeed his own good demands it (provided he harms no one, for then he would fall short of justice): this is not to offend truthfulness since he does not act *for love of falsehood*.[10]

Although Gauthier cites ancient commentators who share his interpretation and also mentions that "the justification of the useful lie" was common among the ancient Greeks (especially Plato), the primary support from

---

new introduction and makes only minor changes to the translation and commentary; see its preface, II,1:3n4.

[8] "Le menteur ment et le véridique dit vrai, à moins qu'il n'aient l'un et l'autre quelque motif d'agir contrairement à leur penchant: alors le menteur dira vrai et le véridique mentira" (Gauthier and Jolif 1970, II,1:309). This comment is specifically about 1127a28: "ἐὰν μή τινος ἕνεκα πράττῃ."

[9] Gauthier and Jolif 1970, II,1:310. Emphasis is Gauthier's.

[10] Gauthier and Jolif 1970, II,1:309. Emphasis is Gauthier's. Gauthier goes on in the same comment (p. 310) to call attention to the importance that Aristotle accords in his ethical theory to the subjective and to intention and then notes: "It matters little to him that speaking a falsehood should be *objectively* an offense against the truth: that which counts for him is that the *subject* does not have the intention to utter a falsehood but rather the intention to safeguard a legitimate good." He adds immediately: "Robert Grosseteste, once again, proves himself perspicacious in noting, in the margin of the Aristotelian text, his protestation: 'Secundum perfectionem vitae christinae nullo modo est mentiendum.'" The reference that Gauthier gives for the marginal note by Grosseteste is "Ms. Oxford All Souls Coll. 84, f. 51vb." Gauthier's interpretation is adopted by Zanatta 1986, 1:517–18. It is followed fairly closely also by Zembaty 1993; see especially p. 15.

within *EN* 4.7 for this interpretation is the phrase "ἐὰν μή τινος ἕνεκα πράττῃ" at 1127a28, which he translates as "à moins que ce ne soit pour un motif autre qu'elle même qu'il accomplisse son action" and I have translated as "if haply he does not act for something." (As we have seen, the phrase follows the remark, "Each person is such as are the things he says and does and so lives" [if haply . . .].) As suggested above, the expression "if haply" helps to make it clear that Aristotle is not excluding the possibility that, when something *is* at stake, a person's behavior will still issue from his character, but rather is pointing out that one perceives character best when *haply* – i.e., in a situation that could happen but is not necessary – nothing is at stake.

A secondary support for this (Gauthier's) interpretation from within *EN* 4.7 is the very remark that, if the truthful man is truthful where nothing is at stake, "he will also be true – indeed, more so – where it does matter" (1127b4–5). Gauthier argues that this latter phrase ("where it does matter" [ἐν οἷς διαφέρει]) pulls the relevant act out of the scope of truthfulness (the virtue discussed in *EN* 4.7) and places it within that of the virtue of justice, separated off from consideration at 1127a34–b1.[11] It would be irrelevant, therefore, to the analysis being conducted in *EN* 4.7. But this is unsustainable. In arguing that acts performed when nothing is at stake tell us how a person will react when something is at stake, Aristotle clearly has in mind the same virtue.[12]

8.3   *EN* 4.7, Section 2: Ways of being an imposter

The second section of *EN* 4.7 can be divided into two subsections: 1127b9–22 and 1127b22–32. The second subsection (on self-deprecation) is straightforward and need not be discussed further here. The first subsection does contain some textual difficulties, resolution of which provides insight into Aristotle's understanding of the virtue of truthfulness.

[11] I have in mind his comment, already quoted, upon 1127a28–30 to the effect that "the refinement of truthfulness does not extend as far as speaking the truth in situations in which, in order to perform a duty of justice (for example, in order to save the country), the sole means available to us is to tell a falsehood" (Gauthier and Jolif 1970, II,1:310). Gauthier's interpretation of Aristotle as recognizing a strict separation between truthfulness and justice leads him to say that Aristotle "does not even suspect that there might exist a *right to the truth* such that in any event there is a sort of obligation in justice to tell the truth" (Gauthier and Jolif 1970, II,1:310 ad 1127a34–b1). For a similar interpretation (that is, of Aristotle as separating truthfulness from justice), see Dirlmeier's commentary in Aristotle 1967, 389, n. 91,1.

[12] Gauthier's interpretation of the first section of *EN* 4.7 is a departure from what is found in the standard commentaries he was reading in the 1950s, which tend to interpret Aristotle as saying that the case in which nothing is at stake is simply a proving ground for moments of more critical import. See, for instance Stewart 1892, 1:358, and Grant 1885, 2:87.

Since these textual difficulties have to do with the structure of the argument, it will be good to begin with a translation of the relevant passage (the first subsection) in which its punctuation and articulation are made apparent:

> The man who (1), for no reason, pretends to more than in fact he is possessed of resembles the corrupt man (for otherwise he would not take pleasure in the falsehood) but he appears to be more silly than evil. When, however, (2) there is a motive, the man who acts thus (2a) for the sake of glory or fame is not greatly to be blamed – at least, *as* an imposter: the man who (2b) acts for the sake of money or for the things that lead to money is more disgraceful.[13] One postures, however, not in the capacity but in the choice (for it is in the habit and by being that sort of man that one postures – just as with the liar [ψεύστης]): there is the man (2c) who delights in falsehood itself and there is the man (2a/b) who desires either glory or gain. Those who (2a) posture for the sake of glory pretend to such things as will bring them praise or cause them to be accounted happy; those who (2b) posture for the sake of gain pretend to such things as are useful to their neighbors and the lack of which is easy to conceal: (the powers of) a diviner, for example, or a wise man or healer. For this reason, most imposters (2a/b) pretend to such things and pose as having them, for in them the above-mentioned things are found. (1127b9–22)[14]

It is clear from Aristotle's comments here that character type (1) is not, strictly speaking, an imposter (an ἀλαζών) at all. Such a man does posture but his posturing is more of a weakness than a deliberate vice: he makes no choice to deceive; he is simply vain.[15] That Aristotle sets this character type to one side suggests that Gauthier is on the wrong track in arguing that truthfulness – the central virtue discussed in this chapter – is a mere *raffinement*. As we have seen, Gauthier says: "The liar lies and the truthful man tells the truth, at least when neither has a reason to act contrary to their inclination: in which case, the liar will tell the truth and the truthful man will lie."[16] But if truthfulness had primarily to do with mere inclinations, the truthful man would be contrasted in a direct manner with this rather

---

[13] For the vocabulary used here, see above, n. 6.

[14] This way of punctuating the text is taken from Stewart 1892, 1:362; it is followed also by Zembaty (1993, 11) and by Irwin (Aristotle 1999, 64). In line 1127b12, I accept Imelmann's emendation ὡς γ᾽ ἀλαζών (Imelmann 1864, 11–12, reported in Susemihl and Apelt 1912). This is also the reading followed by the Revised Oxford Translation.

[15] By "choice" I mean προαίρεσις or "choice" in the strong sense, as described in *EN* 3.2.1111b4ff. See Flannery 2008, passim. The Latin translation used by Aquinas translates 1127b11 as "vanus autem videtur magis quam malum." This translates easily into modern English: this character type is not vicious but simply vain.

[16] Gauthier and Jolif 1970, II,1:309 (see above, n. 11).

silly "imposter" (who is not really an imposter at all). The truthful man is defined rather by Aristotle in contrast with the character types that follow – (2a), (2b), and especially (2c) – whose being the way they are has to do with habit and with choice.

Aristotle expounds these three related character types in a progressive manner, first drawing a distinction between (2a) impostery for the sake of glory (or public recognition) and (2b) impostery for the sake of gain, but then interjecting a remark – in effect, an allusion to *Met.* 5.29 – about the general characteristics of impostery as having to do with choice (προαίρεσις) and habit (ἕξις) and not with mere capacity (δύναμις). The sense of this interjected remark leads him to another character type, (2c), the man most directly opposed to the truthful man: this is the man who delights in falsehood (regarding reputation) itself (ὁ μὲν τῷ ψεύδει αὐτῷ χαίρων, 1127b16). Similarly, the liar (ψεύστης) of *Met.* 5.29 is a pure type, both wielding falsehood dexterously and choosing it for its own sake.[17] The central-case imposter (2c) must have *something* to do with either public reputation or gain (or both), for otherwise he would not be discussed in *EN* 4.7, but neither of these things is – or is any longer – the root cause of his actions. He has *chosen* impostery and now seeks it for its own sake; he has no respect for truthfulness, taking delight simply in deceit. This character type is rare – most (οἱ πλεῖστοι, 127b21) imposters, says Aristotle, pretend to qualities that bring glory and gain so that they might *have* glory and gain – but he is an identifiable type.

In *Met.* 5.29, Aristotle argues explicitly against ideas set out in Plato's *Hippias Minor*. In that dialogue, the character Socrates argues (although diffidently) that the truthful man is actually the best liar since he knows the truth and so knows best how to deceive (*Hp.Mi.* 368A8–369A2).[18] Socrates also argues that the man who tells lies voluntarily is better than the man who does so involuntarily (372D3–7) since he is the same as the man who tells the truth (367C7–D2) and to tell the truth voluntarily is better than to tell it involuntarily (366B7–C4). Socrates compares Achilles and Odysseus, maintaining that they were both liars, although Odysseus was the better man since he lied voluntarily. Odysseus is clearly portrayed by Homer as a liar, but so also (Socrates points out) is Achilles. Achilles at one

---

[17] "ἄνθρωπος δὲ ψευδὴς ὁ εὐχερὴς καὶ προαιρετικὸς τῶν τοιούτων λόγων" (*Met.* 5.29.1025a2–3): the discourses referred to (τῶν τοιούτων λόγων) are false discourses. The liar is mentioned here in *EN* 4.7 immediately before the words introducing type (3): "οὐκ ἐν τῇ δυνάμει δ᾽ ἐστὶν ὁ ἀλαζών, ἀλλ᾽ ἐν τῇ προαιρέσει (κατὰ τὴν ἕξιν γὰρ καὶ τῷ τοιόσδε εἶναι ἀλαζών ἐστιν, ὥσπερ καὶ ψεύστης), ὁ μὲν τῷ ψεύδει αὐτῷ χαίρων, ὁ δὲ δόξης ὀρεγόμενος ἢ κέρδους" (1127b14–16).

[18] The diffidence becomes apparent at *Hp. Mi.* 372D7ff. It is significant that, in *Met.* 5.29, Aristotle argues against "the argument in *Hippias*" (1025a6) and not against Plato (or even Socrates) explicitly.

point tells Odysseus that he will leave Troy by ship in the morning (*Iliad* 9.357–63) but a few lines later suggests to Ajax that he will not be leaving (9.650–5). Socrates's interlocutor, Hippias, defends Achilles, arguing first that he contradicted himself involuntarily, "forced by the misfortune of the army to remain and to help" (*Hp.Mi.* 370E5–9) but then arguing (after Socrates quotes Achilles's remarks to Ajax) that Achilles behaved thus out of simplicity (371D8–E3).[19] But Socrates rejects these arguments, for the reason mentioned: acting voluntarily is always better than acting involuntarily.

Aristotle responds to the earlier point (that the truthful man is actually the best liar) arguing that the character of the truthful man depends not upon any capacity also to lie but upon his choice to tell – and his delight in telling – the truth.[20] As for the idea that he who lies voluntarily is better than he who does so involuntarily, Aristotle attacks Socrates's supporting argument that it is better to limp voluntarily than to do so involuntarily (*Hp.Mi* 374C6–D2). Aristotle says that this argument illegitimately suggests that to limp voluntarily is to be lame. In fact, to limp voluntarily is not to be lame at all: it is to simulate being lame (1025a9–13).

All this is a help to understanding how Aristotle understands the truthful man in *EN* 4.7. He is the opposite of the liar of *Met.* 5.29 – or, more precisely, the opposite of such a liar who is also an imposter. His character depends not upon his capacity also to utter falsehoods but upon his choice to tell the truth regarding his own qualities and upon his settled practice of doing the same. He is as rare qua truth-teller as Odysseus is qua liar. That Aristotle alludes to *Met.* 5.29 at the crucial spot that he does (1127b14–15), just after introducing type (2c), also suggests that Aristotle is aware that truth-telling itself, which is at issue in *Met.* 5.29, is at the core of the analysis of the man who is truthful with others about himself.

---

[19] Reading in 371E1 "εὐηθείας" instead of "εὐνοίας" ("kindness"). If this reading (followed also in Cooper 1997) is correct, one can make a certain connection between Achilles and character type (1) in *EN* 4.7, who "appears to be more silly than evil" (μάταιος δὲ φαίνεται μᾶλλον ἢ κακός, 1127b11). The word "εὐήθεια" is also sometimes translated "silliness." Like character type (1), Achilles is supposed not to have made a choice to lie. It must be acknowledged, however, that Achilles has a motive for being false (to help the army). Aristotle's character type (1) acts without such a motive: he is just silly.

[20] At *Met.* 5.29.1025a2–3, Aristotle describes the liar as someone who inclines toward and chooses (εὐχερὴς καὶ προαιρετικός) false statements; at 1025a7–9, he notes that the truthful man (or, what amounts to the same thing in this context, the φρόνιμος) has the capacity to say what is false. We can presume that the truthful man inclines toward and chooses true utterances and that this is more important than any capacity to utter falsehoods.

But the connection with *Met.* 5.29 again means that Gauthier is wrong – in particular, in arguing that the truthfulness of the truthful man of *EN* 4.7 "does not extend as far as speaking the truth in situations in which, in order to perform a duty of justice (for example, in order to save the country)," lying becomes expedient (Gauthier and Jolif 1970, II,1:310). Such "refinement of truthfulness" characterizes not the truthful man of *EN* 4.7 but Achilles as portrayed by Hippias: "forced by the misfortune of the army to remain and to help." Achilles may not be the worst of character types, but he is certainly not Aristotle's truthful man.

8.4 Aquinas's commentary upon *EN* 4.7

In his commentary on the *Nicomachean Ethics*, Aquinas interprets *EN* 4.7 along the general lines just set out. Most importantly, he sees that, for Aristotle, the idea that lying is intrinsically evil is fundamentally determinative.[21] He adds to this assertion an explanation that he takes not from Aristotle but from Augustine: "Signs were instituted in order to represent things as they are; and so, if someone, lying, represents a thing otherwise than as it is, he acts inordinately and viciously."[22] Following this rather extraneous explanation, he adds another based on a remark in *EN* 4.7.1127a30–1 to the effect that telling the truth is a mean between two censurable (*vituperabiles*) extremes (*SLE* 4.15 lines 89–99); he apparently also has in mind *Met.* 4.7.1011b25–9.

Aquinas also gets right the remarks about the truthful man's being true where it does not much matter and *therefore* also when it does matter (1127a26–30, 1127b3–7). Says Aquinas, "For he loves the truth and tells the

---

[21] "Et [Philosophus] dicit quod mendacium secundum se est pravum et fugiendum" (*SLE* 4.15 lines 83–4). Aquinas's approach to lying is quite different from what he was taught by Albert the Great. In the latter's *Super Ethica*, which Aquinas compiled and edited for his teacher, Albert argues that, at least "with respect to the perfection of civil virtue," as opposed to a theological virtue, it is sometimes possible to lie "without detriment to virtue." Regarding Aristotle's saying at 1127a28–9 that a lie is "in itself... foul and blameworthy," Albert argues very implausibly that Aristotle does not mean that lying is evil "per se and essentially" but "per se" in the sense that, if nothing arises "for which sometimes, civilly, truth must be dispensed with," a lie is a bad thing (*Super Ethica* 4.14 n. 339, Editio Coloniensis 14:288 lines 64–85).

[22] *SLE* 4.15 lines 85–8. See White 1993, 646–7. At *ST* 2–2.110.3 resp., Aquinas uses this same sort of analysis ("voces [sunt] signa naturaliter intellectuum") and then immediately cites *EN* 4.7.1127a28–9, about falsehood or lying being foul and blameworthy. This reference is followed by a reference to Augustine's *Contra mendacium*. See also Aquinas's *In Sent.* 3.38.1–3, where both *EN* 4.7 and Augustine's *De mendacio* are cited constantly. In one text (*Quodl.* 8.6.4 resp., Editio Leonina 25:75b–76a), Aquinas mentions *EN* 2.6 and then associates with Aristotle's *Int.* 1.16a3–4 the analysis of lying in terms of *signa* that fail to correspond. In another text (*ST* 2–2.110.1 arg. 2 and ad 2), Aquinas associates *EN* 4.7 with Augustine's *De doctrina christiana* 2.3 (33–4). See also Augustine's *Enchiridion ad Laurentium de fide et spe et caritate* 7.22, and Aquinas's *QDV* 23.3 ad 2.

truth even in cases in which not much detriment or advantage is involved: and even more in those in which telling the truth or telling a falsehood does make a difference with respect to the detriment or benefit of another" (*SLE* 4.15 lines 129–33).[23] The second phrase here ("and even *more* in those") makes it apparent that he does not think that Aristotle's remark that this virtue is not about justice and injustice (1127a33–4) means that anything having to do with the detriment or benefit of others is excluded from consideration in the analysis of *EN* 4.7.

Aristotle's fuller remarks about the truthful man and public agreements run as follows:

> For we speak neither about the man who is truthful in public agreements, nor regarding such things as bear upon justice or injustice (for that would be to speak of another virtue); we speak rather of the man who, in cases in which such are not a consideration, both in his word and in his life is true by virtue of *being* the way he is by habit. (1127a33–b3)[24]

Aquinas regards none of this as denying that acts having a bearing upon justice and injustice do tell us something about whether a man is truthful (in the relevant sense) or not. Aristotle's remarks about prescinding from justice and injustice are in fact simply a way of setting aside the extraneous and identifying the character type who occupies – and defines – the center of the field: whom we might call the anti-Odysseus (regarding the way one handles oneself in society). Aquinas refers to *EN* 4.6 (on the amiable person).[25] Just as there, according to Aquinas, Aristotle is interested in the person who "wills to live pleasantly with others not because of love but because of an habitual disposition," so here he is interested in the person who is true on account of an habitual disposition. Neither Aristotle nor Aquinas excludes from the population studied in these two chapters the man who (respectively) acts out of love or the man who acts out of justice; the point is simply that such types, with their characteristic dispositions, are not the central (defining) character types of these chapters.

---

[23] Once again, Albert's interpretation of 1127b4–6 ("he will also be true – indeed, more so – where it does matter, for he will distance himself from falsehood as from a base thing") is quite different. The truthful man, he says, "flees lying as in itself base, when it is to no advantage, and is therefore laudable" (*Super Ethica* 4.14 n. 343, p. 291 lines 79–80).

[24] Following the translation available to him, Aquinas maintains that the sort of truth-telling excluded by Aristotle in the opening phrase of this quotation is truth-telling in "confessions," as when "someone, interrogated by a judge, confesses what is true" (*SLE* 4.15 lines 110–12). The translation of 1127a33–b1 that Aquinas was reading was: "Non enim de veridico in confessionibus dicimus, neque quaecumque ad iustitiam vel iniustitiam contendunt; alterius enim erunt haec virtutis" (Editio Leonina 47:250). He quotes the same text at *ST* 2–2.109.3 ad 3.

[25] *SLE* 4.15 lines 119–21; the back-reference is to *EN* 4.6.1226b22–5.

Aquinas also correctly identifies the three types of imposters spoken of by Aristotle in the first subsection (1127b9–22) of the second section of *EN* 4.7. Following Aristotle, he first – to use the labels employed above – excludes as an imposter character type (1): the "silly" (μάταιος) or vain man, who behaves as he does, says Aquinas, "out of a lack of order in the soul." This man, he says, "does not intend anything malicious, but is vain, inasmuch as he takes pleasure (*delectatur*) in something that in itself is neither good nor useful."[26] He speaks a bit later of imposters (2c) who "delight in impostery itself, indifferent with respect to whatever it is they pose for," then of imposters (2a) who pose for the sake of glory, and finally of imposters (2b) who pose for the sake of gain (*SLE* 4.15 lines 188–99).

That he considers (1) and (2c) different types becomes apparent when one compares the language employed. Aquinas's description of the (2c) imposter comes just after his consideration of what turns out to be Aristotle's allusion to *Met.* 5.29; there, at *EN* 4.7.1127b14, Aristotle says that the imposter exists as such "not in the capacity but in the choice." Aquinas remarks that this type "chooses [*eligit*] to lie . . . because he *delights* [*gaudet*] in the lie itself" (*SLE* 4.15 lines 184–5). Immediately afterwards, as we have just seen, he says similarly that representatives of type (2c) "*delight* [*gaudent*] in impostery itself" (*SLE* 4.15 line 189). Clearly this character type is different from character type (1) who intends nothing malicious but acts "out of a lack of order in the soul." Type (2c) chooses to pose, indifferent as to whether he achieves thereby fame or gain: it could be either or both or neither; type (1) "takes pleasure [*delectatur*] in something that in itself is neither good nor useful." In any case, Aquinas must have figured that, if Aristotle has said at 1127b11 that type (1) is not really bad, he could hardly go on to say that this same type (1) is identical to the confirmed and vicious liar introduced at 1127b16 (after the allusion to *Met.* 5.29).

The one evident lack in Aquinas's interpretation of *EN* 4.7 is his failure to note any connection with *Met.* 5.29, even though, as it seems, his commentary on *Met.* 5 was composed not long before his commentary on *EN*.[27] It is true that he does not include many cross references at all in the commentary on *EN*, but even in the passages of the *Summa theologiae* where he discusses matters proper to *EN* 4.7 (that is, in *ST* 2–2.109–113)

---

[26] *SLE* 4.15 lines 163–7. In lines 160–1, Aquinas says that this type acts for no other end than the "impostery" (or, more precisely, vanity) itself.

[27] Torrell says that the commentary on *Met.* 1–6 "may date from the academic year 1270–71"; he says, with more confidence, that the *SLE* "was composed in Paris, 1271–72" (Torrell 2005, 343–4). Weisheipl gives the same dates for the *SLE* and also notes that the *Sententia super Metaphysicam* 5.7–7.16 was composed before other parts of that commentary. His evidence for this is Aquinas's referring in *SSM* 5.7–7.16 to *Met.* 12 as *Met.* 11. See Weisheipl 1983, 379–80.

and where he makes many cross references (especially to *EN* 4.7 but also to the *Metaphysics*), he never refers to *Met.* 5.29.

Regarding the word "αὐθέκαστος" (*EN* 4.7.1127a23) ('each himself'), which, as suggested above, echoes ideas present in *Met.* 5.29, someone might want to argue that Aquinas was impeded from picking up the echo by the manuscripts of *EN* to which he had access (probably indirectly). He reports reading both *autochiastos* (*SLE* 4.15 line 60) and *autophastos* (*SLE* 4.15 line 63), neither of which is correct.[28] But he translates the first as "admirabilis," saying that Aristotle's idea is that the truthful man seeks no more admiration than is due to himself, and he translates the second as "per se manifestum," saying that the idea is that the same man manifests himself as he in fact is. Whatever the inadequacies of the transcriptions to which they correspond, these ideas are not far from what we do find in *Met.* 5.29, where Aristotle says that the liar is like a false thing, which gives a false impression of what it itself is (1025a4–6).

8.5   Truthfulness in *Summa theologiae* 2–2.109–113

In *ST* 2–2.109, Aquinas introduces what he speaks of as the virtue of truth (*virtus veritatis*), which he also calls veracity or truthfulness (*veracitas*). Although his account of this virtue goes beyond what Aristotle says in *EN* 4.7, there can be little doubt that he regards himself as speaking throughout this general section of the *Summa* of the virtue discussed in that chapter of the *Nicomachean Ethics*. In *ST* 2–2.109.1, where he enquires whether truth is a virtue, immediately after the objections, that is, in the *sed contra*, he says: "But, on the contrary, the Philosopher, in the second and the fourth book of the *Ethics*, places truth among the other virtues."[29] That he is discussing the *EN* 4.7 virtue remains his presupposition in all the relevant passages in *ST* 2–2.109–113.

It is not, however, as if he is unaware that he is expanding upon *EN* 4.7, for we find in this section a couple of passages that pertain to the relationship between *ST* 2–2.109–113 and *EN* 4.7. The first does not address this topic as an *issue* but considers rather what it means to be a particular virtue; the second, however, does address the issue directly. As to the first

---

[28] The word *autochiastos* comes apparently from the manuscript Gauthier designates as T and refers to as *Libri Ethicorum recogniti codex contaminatus quo Thomas usus est*. See Editio Leonina 47:214*. It is unclear where *autophastos* comes from. Neither word appears in Liddell and Scott's *Greek-English Lexicon*. But see Gauthier's remarks in Editio Leonina 47:264*–5*.

[29] The references are to *EN* 2.7.1108a19–23 and *EN* 4.7; see also the *sed contra* to *ST* 2–2.109.2. By the "other virtues," Aquinas apparently means the virtues besides the cardinal virtues, although he does regard truth as "annexed" to justice (*ST* 2–2.109.3).

passage, in *ST* 2–2.109.1 resp., Aquinas says that truth is the object of the virtue of truth. So, truth specifies (gives the species to) not only the act of telling the truth (*ST* 2–2.110.1 resp.) but also the virtue.[30] This, however, means that, even when the virtue is discussed in a limited context, such as in connection with the impression one deliberately instills in others, what is being discussed is the *virtue*, for the virtue as existing in that limited context gets its species (what it is) from no other source than its object and that object specifies the virtue itself, whole and entire. As we have seen, at the core of Aristotle's analysis in *EN* 4.7 of truthfulness and aberrations therefrom is the statement that "in itself (καθ' αὐτό) falsehood is foul and blameworthy, and truth is noble and praiseworthy" (1127a28–30). This statement is present in *EN* 4.7 because truth specifies not only the *act* of telling the truth but also the corresponding virtue, discussed in *EN* 4.7 in a limited context.

As to the second passage, in *ST* 2–2.109.2 ad 3, Aquinas says that "truth of life" is different from the virtue of truth, which he identifies simply as that virtue "according to which someone speaks the truth." Truth of life is much too general a consideration to constitute a special virtue, he says, and truthfulness (habitually speaking the truth) is a special virtue. This same thread is continued in *ST* 2–2.109.3 ad 3, where Aquinas again says that the virtue he is speaking about is neither truth of life, nor truth of justice (although in the body of the article he acknowledges some connection with justice), nor "truth of doctrine" (*veritas doctrinae*), which, he says, consists in the manifestation of truths such as pertains to science (*scientia*). But then he backs off this bald assertion:

> However, since truths that are knowable, insofar as they are known by us, are about us and pertain to us, in this respect the truth of doctrine can pertain to this virtue, and so can any other truth[31] by which one manifests, either in word or in deed, that one knows. (*ST* 2–2.109.3 ad 3)

The phrase "either in word or in deed" is a clear reference to *EN* 4.7.1127a20, which is referred to explicitly a few lines previously. The repeated emphasis on what is known by *us* and what pertains to *us* establishes the same connection: under discussion is the character trait opposed to impostery, both the trait and the associated aberrations having to do with the impression

---

[30] On the relationship between the species of the particular act and its object, besides *ST* 2–2.110.1, see *ST* 1–2.18.2. Aquinas establishes the connection between a virtue and its characteristic act at *ST* 1–2.55.2. The *sed contra* of *ST* 1–2.55.2 cites *EN* 2.6.1106a15–19.

[31] Aquinas means here "any other truthfulness." His language is dictated by the language of the objection.

we give of ourselves. But what is most interesting here is that Aquinas understands himself to be speaking in *ST* 2–2.109.2–3 – and, by implication, throughout *ST* 2–2.109–113 – about the virtue (and the corresponding act) at the core of *EN* 4.7, while at the same time acknowledging that one can apply the ideas found there to truth-telling more generally, since it all has to do ultimately with how we present ourselves.[32] It is true: someone who tells a lie is not necessarily an imposter in the full sense presented in *EN* 4.7, but he does represent himself falsely in his capacity as a knower.

A closely related passage appears in *ST* 2–2.111.3. In *ST* 2–2.109.2 ad 4, Aquinas acknowledges that simplicity, the opposite of duplicity, "by which one holds something in one's heart but manifests something else exteriorly," pertains to the virtue under discussion (truth or truthfulness). In *ST* 2–2.111.3 ad 2, he comes back to this issue and says that simplicity is the same as the virtue of truth:

> it differs only in the way it is conceived, for truth is spoken of according as signs correspond to things signified, but simplicity is spoken of according as one does not tend toward contraries, as when one intends one thing interiorly but pretends exteriorly to something different.[33]

So, truth-telling – which Aquinas presents here in purely semantic terms – and simplicity are the same thing, understood, however, from different perspectives. And both are in effect referred to the core virtue of *EN* 4.7: truthfulness, understood as habitually matching one's words and actions to one's beliefs and so not pretending to be something other than what one is – which would include pretending to believe something other than what one knows.

One final thing that very much merits mentioning regarding the treatment of truthfulness in the *Summa* is that in *ST* 2–2.110.2 Aquinas speaks of the man who lies "out of the sheer lust for lying, which proceeds from habit," citing not only the passage in the *Nicomachean Ethics* about what

---

[32] One's presentation of oneself as knowing enters at this point into the general argument of this section. See *ST* 2–2.109.4 resp., where Aquinas speaks of someone who downplays his own sanctity, his own knowledge, etc.

[33] "Et secundum hoc, ut supra dictum est [2–2.109.2 ad 4], virtus simplicitatis est eadem virtuti veritatis, sed differt sola ratione, quia veritas dicitur secundum quod signa concordant signatis; simplicitas autem dicitur secundum quod non *tendit* in diversa, ut scilicet aliud *intendat* interius, aliud *praetendat* exterius." In my translation, I have tried to maintain the very precisely expressive play on words (indicated here with emphases).

is called above character type (2c)[34] but also Augustine's *De mendacio*.[35] Indeed, the latter is his primary reference, for in this argument Aquinas is expounding Augustine's eight-part division of types of lying in *De mendacio* 14.25. Aquinas understands the first three types as adding gravity to the lying itself, as when a man lies in order to harm another. The last four types he understands as diminishing gravity, as when a man tells a lie in order to get a laugh or to save a life. It is the fourth type – tucked between the augmenting group and the diminishing group – that he connects with Aristotle's words in *EN* 4.7. He says that this type of lying "has its own quantity, without addition or diminution." It is described by Augustine as lying which "comes about out of the sheer lust for lying and deceiving – which is the naked lie."[36] It is extraordinary how closely Augustine's description of this central type of liar corresponds to the Odysseus-type character of *EN* 4.7 and *Met.* 5.29, who is addicted to lying itself.

In conclusion, there is no denying that, in *ST* 2–2.109–113, Aquinas says many things that are not found in *EN* 4.7, nor even easily derivable from things that are found there. And yet his presupposition throughout *ST* 2–2.109–113 that his expanded examination grows out of the same virtue presented in *EN* 4.7 is a well-founded one. A virtue receives its species not from the various things that might be said in expatiating upon it but from the object that gives the characteristic act of the virtue its species. This object – truth – is at the core of both *EN* 4.7 and *ST* 2–2.109–113.

---

[34] "And this is the lie that comes about out of the sheer lust for lying, which proceeds from habit, and thus also the Philosopher says in *EN* 4.7 that the liar, insofar as he is thus by habit, delights in the lie itself." The passage cited is *EN* 4.7.1127b14–17, where Aristotle speaks of choice, habit, and delight with regard to character type (2c). In *ST* 2–2.113.2, Aquinas discusses types (2a) and (2b). In *ST* 2–2.111.4, he refers to type (1). See also *ST* 2–2.112.2 ad 3, where he says that the behavior characteristic of type (1) can often be reduced to the jocose lie.

[35] Augustine, *De mendacio* 14.25, CSEL 41:444–6. In *ST* 2–2.110.2 arg. 2, the title referred to is *Contra mendacium*, but this should be *De mendacio*. Aquinas discusses the same passage at *In Sent.* 3.38.5, but without the interjected references to Aristotle.

[36] "Quartum, quod fit sola mentiendi fallendique libidine, quod merum mendacium est" (Augustine, *De mendacio* 14.25, CSEL 41:444).

CHAPTER NINE

Aquinas on Aristotelian justice
Defender, destroyer, subverter, or surveyor?

Jeffrey Hause

If the past sixty years' scholarship on Aquinas has proved anything, it is that Aquinas is an idiosyncratic thinker who is hard to categorize in any simple terms. This observation holds not just for his metaphysical and religious thought, but for his ethical thought as well, as we can see from the debates over Aquinas's use of Aristotle's ethics. No one doubts that Aquinas relies heavily on Aristotelian method, concepts, and distinctions, or that he subscribes to signature Aristotelian doctrines. At the same time, Aquinas obviously draws on post-Aristotelian, Biblical, and distinctively Christian sources, adding to his own ethical system features foreign to Aristotle (for instance, virtues unknown to Aristotle, the gifts and fruits of the Holy Spirit, and an account of natural law that is itself embedded in an account of eternal law). Some features of Aquinas's ethics mix Aristotelian with un-Aristotelian elements (for example, his account of the divinely infused virtues). Some scholars, such as Terence Irwin (2007), focus on Aquinas's defense and development of key Aristotelian ideas, illustrating the ways in which Aquinas, on philosophical grounds, remains Aristotelian in ethics. Others, such as Eleonore Stump (2011), stress Aquinas's Christian additions to and departures from Aristotle's ethics. It should come as no surprise, then, that scholars disagree about how to understand Aquinas's commentary on the *Nicomachean Ethics*. While some argue that it forms the basis of Aquinas's philosophical ethics,[1] others contend that it is a theological and not a philosophical work.[2] What these debates show is that any accurate answer to these questions must be both detailed and nuanced.

Since I cannot cover the whole of Aquinas's ethical writings, I can at best come to a provisional conclusion by looking at one small section

Many thanks are due to Thomas Brickhouse, who spoke with me at length about the thorniest issues in *EN* 5, and to Thomas Williams, who generously discussed his views on Aquinas's commentary with me. I would also like to thank participants in the 2011 Cornell Summer Colloquium in Medieval Philosophy. All translations are my own.

[1] See, for instance, Doig 2001.
[2] The most convincing example of this thesis is Bradley 1997.

of Aquinas's treatment of Aristotle: I will investigate the treatment of Aristotelian justice in his commentary on Book 5 of the *Nicomachean Ethics* and the way he incorporates this treatment into his systematic writings. This is a particularly interesting test case because in his commentary Aquinas undoubtedly misinterprets at least two of Aristotle's key contentions in ways that make Aristotle look more Thomistic: Aquinas asserts that universal justice is a particular virtue, and he holds that reciprocal and corrective justice constitute a single species of "commutative" justice. In addition, Aquinas clearly includes in his interpretation material that is foreign to Aristotle. He then uses his partly erroneous and expanded interpretation as the basis for his own treatment of justice in the *Summa theologiae*. So, if there is a case to be made that Aquinas is un-Aristotelian, anti-Aristotelian, or a subverter of Aristotelianism, we might expect to find it in his treatment of Aristotle on justice.[3]

However, most of what Aquinas offers in his commentary on Book 5 suggests a deep sympathy with Aristotle and a concern to interpret the text correctly yet charitably. Most of the commentary consists of Aquinas spelling out the organizing principles of Aristotle's treatment and a summary of Aristotle's views, generally in language very close to that of the Latin Aristotle (e.g., *SLE* 5.3 lines 1–15, 5.11 lines 1–26 and 160–84). Much of the rest consists of cross references (e.g., 5.3 lines 188–96), filling in details by appeal to claims made elsewhere in this work (e.g., 5.4 lines 160–8, 5.8 lines 102–17, 5.11 lines 91–113) or in other works (e.g., 5.2 lines 12–27, 5.13 lines 136–51), or illustrations (e.g., 5.4 lines 51–74, 5.6 lines 90–109). Some passages that might seem at first glance to be anachronistic or theological incursions are actually the thirteenth-century version of footnotes, in which Aquinas is clearly not explicating the text at all but adding notes so as not to leave the students of his day puzzled.[4]

The conscientious effort Aquinas makes to stick closely to Aristotle's language, to explicate the text by appeal to Aristotle's own views, and to uncover any hidden premises needed to show the soundness of the arguments makes it impossible to believe that getting Aristotle's philosophy

---

[3] I am generally in agreement with the conclusions Perkams 2008a reaches, in particular with his account of natural law in *SLE* 5. For this reason, I will focus on elements of Aquinas's discussion that Perkams does not treat.

[4] For instance, at *SLE* 5.11 lines 150–9 he assures his readers that princes who work on the people's behalf not only deserve honor and glory from the people, but also can look to reward from God; and at 5.12 lines 5–75 he attempts to map the juridical concept of *ius gentium* onto that of natural law. There is a strong case to be made that other putative theological intrusions in his commentary on the *Nicomachean Ethics* (I am not assuming the same is true for all of Aquinas's commentaries on Aristotle) function likewise as footnotes, including his remarks on the beatific vision in his treatment of Book 1.

right was not one of Aquinas's goals. In fact, as I hope will become clear, Aquinas arrives at his two major misinterpretations of *Nicomachean Ethics* 5 in his faulty attempt to interpret Aristotle accurately. Even so, Aquinas's well-known conviction that the purpose of investigations into philosophy should not be to know what people thought but to know what really is the case[5] implies that he must have some ulterior goal for striving to interpret Aristotle correctly, in particular, that he believes that such accuracy is conducive to discovering the truth.

On the other hand, what Aquinas adds to Aristotle shows that he does not merely want to *get* Aristotle right but also, in a sense, to *make* Aristotle right. It is crucial, however, to note the restraint Aquinas exercises in determining what elements he should add to his commentary. After all, when he covers the same issues in his systematic theological works, Aquinas makes hundreds upon hundreds of non-Aristotelian claims and distinctions, and even when he does adopt Aristotelian views, he often changes Aristotle's emphases or, as with the virtues, adapts them to a Christian conception of the good life and integrates them into his distinctive moral psychology. By comparison with what he says in his systematic works, Aquinas's additions in his commentary are few. The important question, then, is why he makes *these* additions rather than the hundreds of others he might have made but didn't. The answer, as I hope to show, is that Aquinas takes these particular additions to be needed to answer questions that Aristotle raises but leaves unanswered, to render Aristotle's claims consistent, and to ensure that the *Nicomachean Ethics* contains no theoretical gaps that could threaten the viability of the philosophical system. Aquinas is, in short, trying to establish through his commentary nothing less than a plausible, complete, and consistent Aristotelian philosophical ethics. What we cannot assume, however, is that Aquinas has any interest in this philosophical system for its own sake. In fact, as we will see, his extraordinary concern to spell out Aristotle's ethics has, in the end, an entirely theological purpose.

9.1   Universal justice

Aquinas's first misinterpretation in Book 5 concerns Aristotle's discussion of universal justice. Aristotle begins Book 5 by distinguishing "universal" or "general" or "legal" justice from "particular" justice (*EN* 5.1). Aristotle arrives at this distinction by considering the two fundamental ways in

---

[5] "Our endeavors in philosophy are not for the goal of knowing what people thought, but for knowing what the truth of the matter is" (*Sententia super librum De caelo et mundo* 1.22 n. 8).

which someone can be *unjust*: one can be unmindful of the law, or one can fail to observe equality or fairness in dealing with others.[6] Therefore, there are two corresponding sorts of justice: mindfulness of the law, and equality or fairness. The ambiguity is found in the Greek word "*dikaiosunē*" and also, though to a lesser extent, in the English word "justice," which has been used, though rarely, in the first sense.[7]

Aristotle explains that universal or legal justice is complete virtue toward others (1129b26–7). It is not, in other words, one particular virtue among others, but rather the whole of virtue insofar as it is expressed in one's dealings with others.[8] By contrast, particular justice is a particular virtue, like temperance or courage; it is the virtue that inclines us to fair distributions and exchanges.

Early in his career, Aquinas endorses just this reading of universal justice. In his commentary on the *Sentences*, he identifies four ways in which a virtue can be called general and contends that justice is general on the grounds that it is essentially identical with the whole of virtue. Aquinas writes:

> A virtue is called general in four ways. First, because it is predicated on any virtue whatsoever, such as legal justice, which is convertible with virtue, and is the same in subject, though differing in concept, as the Philosopher says. Thus, legal justice is called general with regard to its essence.
>
> Second, a virtue is called general insofar as other virtues that participate in its activity depend on it. Prudence is called general in this way, since [it is the source] from which all the other moral virtues participate in the rightness of choice; and so its activity is intertwined with the activities of all the other virtues. Nevertheless, in itself it is a specific virtue in that a specific character of object belongs to it, namely, what is choiceworthy with regard to what one undertakes.
>
> Third, a virtue is called general insofar as its functioning concerns the acts of all the virtues, so that [these acts] are all subject to it as its matter. In this class falls magnanimity, which accomplishes great things in the case of all the virtues, as *Ethics* 4 says. Nevertheless, in itself it is a specific virtue, because it concerns a specific character of object in all these [acts], namely, what is worthy of great honor.

---

[6] Because the law prescribes acts pertaining to all the virtues and, at least under the best constitutions, directs them to the common good, when one acts in keeping with the law's spirit one acts virtuously and therefore with universal justice. Aquinas accepts this link between law and virtue at *ST* 2–2.58.5 resp.

[7] This use in English is found generally but not exclusively in Christian texts, such as Isaac Watts's hymn "Not to the Terrors of the Lord": "Behold the spirits of the just / Whose faith is turned to sight."

[8] Contemporary commentators have reached a consensus on this interpretation. See Bostock 2000, 54–8; Gauthier and Jolif 1970, II,1:339–44; Irwin 1988, 424; Pakaluk 2005, 181–6. A rare exception is Aubenque 1995.

Fourth, a virtue is called general in that diverse virtues act together with it precisely because its activity requires the activity of many virtues; in this way, other virtues are once again required for magnanimity, because no one can deem himself worthy of great things unless he is virtuous.

Therefore, the first sort of generality belongs to something on the ground that it is universal; the second on the ground that it is a cause that gives existence; the third on the ground that it moves by its command; and the fourth on the ground that it is an integral whole that contains many things. (*In Sent.* 3.9.1.1 qc. 2 resp.)

Of the four ways in which a virtue can be general, two are important for this discussion: the first and the third. Aquinas here contends that universal justice is general in the first sense: it's really the same as, and only conceptually distinct from, the whole of virtue. So, if one acts courageously in defense of one's state, or if one gives alms generously, one is also thereby acting justly.

Aquinas contrasts this sort of universality with the sort he attributes to magnanimity, which he classifies as a type-3 general virtue. As Aristotle had noted, magnanimity is characterized by what is great in each virtue (*EN* 4.3.1123b30). So, magnanimous people do not simply act courageously and generously, but see to it that their courageous and generous acts have a certain greatness to them, a certain remarkable quality or panache. This is possible, Aquinas theorizes, because magnanimity is an executive virtue: it directs or commands the other virtues so that the distinctive acts of the other virtues take on a further character of greatness and become thereby acts of magnanimity.

By the time he reaches his mature period, in which he writes his commentary on the *Nicomachean Ethics* as well as the Second Part of the *Summa theologiae*, Aquinas has revised his schema of general virtues. He now thinks that there are two type-3 general virtues – charity and universal justice – and he drops magnanimity from the schema entirely.[9] He likewise reads *Aristotle* as holding that universal justice and not magnanimity is a type-3 general virtue. His reasons for moving magnanimity out of this class and for moving justice into it are related, as should become clear. But what I want to stress is that even though in his mature works Aquinas increasingly interprets Aristotle as holding views about moral psychology that are more distinctively Thomistic, Aquinas's intention is to uncover for his readers an authentically Aristotelian ethics.

What, then, led Aquinas to change his mind from what is surely the correct interpretation of universal justice to an incorrect interpretation that

[9] On universal justice, see *ST* 2–2.58.5–6. On charity, see *ST* 2–2.23.7–8 and *QDC* 3.

is arguably more congenial to a Thomistic worldview? He has two reasons. The first is, paradoxically, his concern to interpret Aristotle accurately. The more careful scrutiny to which Aquinas subjects Aristotle's text leads him to think that Aristotle plainly holds that universal justice is a particular virtue. The reason Aquinas is mistaken about this is not that he is partial to seeing his own ideas in other people's works, but rather that he is not a philologist.

Book 5 was undoubtedly not originally written to be part of the *Nicomachean Ethics*. It may have been a free-standing treatise or collection of treatises; more likely, Book 5 (or parts of it) were originally written for the earlier *Eudemian Ethics*. When Aristotle speaks of actualizing the disposition that is virtue in the *Nicomachean Ethics*, he uses the word *energeia*, which Grosseteste renders as *actus*. But in the *Eudemian Ethics*, which Aquinas did not have access to, Aristotle speaks not of the *energeia* of the disposition but rather of its *chrēsis*, which Grosseteste renders as *usus*. Aristotle himself probably meant nothing different by the two terms; in his Greek, there is not much difference between speaking of the actualization of a virtue and the employment of a virtue. However, to the ears of a medieval university professor working in Latin, *actus* and *usus* are hardly interchangeable terms. So, when Aquinas reads that universal justice is complete virtue because it is the *chrēsis* / *usus* of complete virtue (1129b30ff), he naturally thinks of the sense of *usus* that he is familiar with: the will's act of applying something to a task (*ST* 1–2.16.1). Nowhere but in Book 5 does the Latin translation speak of the *usus* of virtue; everywhere else we find *actus*, so Aquinas could not glean the synonymy of these terms from other uses in the text. As far as he could tell, it was universal justice and only universal justice that consisted in the *usus* of virtue. Hence, it was natural for Aquinas to read this claim as asserting that universal justice is complete virtue because it is the application of complete virtue to a task. And that is precisely what characterizes type-3 general virtue.

If we turn to the *Summa theologiae*, we find Aquinas's second reason for denying that universal justice is really the same as the whole of virtue and for asserting that it is instead a virtue that commands all others. In his *Politics*, Aristotle contends that the virtues that make one a good human being do not necessarily make one a good citizen of the state (*Pol.* 3.4 1276b34). As Aquinas understands this claim, to be a good citizen of the state requires a distinct virtue of justice that directs one to the common good of the state (see, e.g., *QDC* 2 resp.). In his mature ethical writings, Aquinas identifies this civic justice with the virtue of universal justice or lawfulness. It is not hard to see why: to be a good citizen of a state is to be oriented to the common good in keeping with the constitution of that state, and it is the lawful person who is just so oriented. With these assumptions as background, Aquinas argues:

> Each virtue, as a result of its distinctive nature, directs its act to that virtue's distinctive end. But for it to be directed to a further end, whether always or sometimes, that is not something it has as a result of its distinctive nature. Rather, there must be a different, higher virtue by which it is directed to that end. And so there must be a single, higher virtue that directs all the virtues to the common good, and that is legal justice, and it is essentially different from every [other] virtue. (*ST* 2–2.58.6 ad 4)

To be oriented to the common good of the state requires that our acts promote that good. However, our non-universal virtues do not accomplish this task unless they have direction from outside themselves. My temperance and my courage, left to themselves, promote my own good; they help me to preserve the good of reason in my own life by moderating my passions. But when I have universal justice, I come to love the state as the guardian of the common good, I come to see my own good as connected with the common good, and as a result direct all my virtues to the common good (*ST* 2–2.58.6; *QDC* 2 resp.). We can now see why Aquinas drops magnanimity from the list of type-3 general virtues. Any virtue that commands others must have as its object a universal end, an end toward which the other virtues can be directed (*QDC* 3). Only charity, whose object is God (the universal end of all creatures), and universal justice have such objects.

What's left is for Aquinas to explain why Aristotle *seems* to be asserting a different thesis – the thesis he really does assert – namely, that universal justice is really identical to the whole of virtue. After all, Aquinas himself had once been convinced that they were really the same. His ingenious solution is that in a sense they *are* really the same. He writes:

> the justice that directs a human being to the common good is general through its command, because it directs all the acts of the virtues to its own end, namely, to the common good. Now, insofar as a virtue is commanded by this sort of justice, it too receives the name "justice." And so, a virtue differs from legal justice only conceptually in the way that a virtue that acts on its own, and [that] virtue acting at another [virtue's] command, differ only conceptually. (*ST* 1–2.60.3 ad 2)

If a politician who is dedicated to the common good acts temperately precisely in order to serve the common good, that is of course an act of temperance, but the very same act is an act of universal justice, so it is an act of temperance and justice. But Aquinas here claims more than that.

He claims that the virtue of temperance in this case *is* the virtue of justice. This might seem an insupportable claim to make. An *act* of temperance might be really the same as an *act* of justice, since the goal of temperance might itself be directed to the further end of justice. But temperance is defined as being a mean in the domain of pleasures of touch, and justice is not. But Aquinas is not arguing here that temperance and justice have the same nature. He is arguing rather that because temperance can be directed by justice – justice is, so to speak, its external form[10] – so that temperance becomes part of a psychological system dedicated to justice, under these conditions we can legitimately call temperance "justice." We can say the same of courage, generosity, magnificence, and all the other virtues. And in this way, we can say that justice is essentially every virtue.

There is no doubt that, in his account of general justice, Aquinas moves from an early correct interpretation to a later incorrect one. But what motivates the later incorrect interpretation is apparently his attempt to articulate the mind of Aristotle more accurately. Given the translation he had, he finds that his later interpretation fits the text better. Once Aquinas comes to see that universal justice is actually a particular virtue and not the whole of virtue, he tries to understand it better by appealing to considerations from the *Politics*, a work that clearly develops ideas articulated in Book 5 of the *Nicomachean Ethics*. And he adopts these views, just as he finds them in Aristotle, for use in the *Summa theologiae*.

9.2 The division of particular justice into species

Aquinas's second misinterpretation is his division of particular justice into the species *distributive* and *commutative*. In this case, there is less scholarly agreement, but Aquinas's interpretation, spelled out in his commentary and propounded in his systematic works, is considerably less plausible than its competitors. Nevertheless, his reason for interpreting the text as he does is not to use his commentary to promote his own thought under the guise of Aristotle, but a genuine concern to understand and articulate the mind of Aristotle. What motivates *this* concern is a question that I'll turn to later.

After Aristotle distinguishes universal from particular justice, he devotes the remainder of Book 5 to particular justice. While universal justice characterizes the lawful person, particular justice is the virtue that makes a person fair or equal. This is the virtue that rectifies our actions vis-à-vis

---

[10] Aquinas argues on similar grounds that charity is the external form of the virtues. See, e.g., *In Sent.* 3.23.3.1 qc. 1, *ST* 2–2.23.8, and *QDC* 3.

other people. Aristotle then tells us that there are two species of particular justice, and in Chapters 3 and 4 he goes on to explain what these two species are. In Chapter 3, he explores distributive justice. This sort of justice concerns the distribution of goods that are not privately owned, but are held in trust by those who administer the state, and are divisible – goods such as honor, riches, and security. The virtuous administrator ensures that there is fairness or equality in this distribution. The criterion of fairness or equality in distributive justice is not arithmetical, but geometrical. For instance, when several candidates are worthy of honors, they are not all honored to the same degree. A person who is doubly deserving of honor will get twice what the others get, just as a person who is doubly deserving of safety will be sent on less dangerous assignments than others, and someone who gives two days' service to the state will be paid twice what a person who gives one day's service is paid. Respecting this geometrical proportion preserves the mean of virtue in distributive justice.

In Chapter 4, Aristotle identifies corrective justice (τὸ διορθωτικὸν δίκαιον), in contrast, as the mean between losing and gaining; it's achieved, he says, "when the parties have neither more nor less but exactly what they had at the start" (1132b14–15), so that the parties "have an equal amount both before and after" (1132b19–20). So, if someone steals my car, and I take that person to court and my car is restored to me, justice is done: I have what's mine, and the thief has nothing. The criterion of fairness or equality here is arithmetical. If I am a worthier citizen, the thief doesn't have to give me more than my car, and if I'm a despicable citizen, the thief doesn't have to give me less than my car. In the case as described, justice is done if I get my car, no matter how worthy or unworthy I am.

Difficulties arise when we proceed to Chapter 5, where Aristotle appears to describe yet another species of justice: proportional justice. Here, Aristotle seems concerned to explain what makes for a fair exchange. He criticizes what he calls the Pythagorean conception of proportional justice, which is a simplistic application of the *lex talionis*. He offers the following sort of example to show the absurdity of this Pythagorean conception: if a police officer bruises criminals who are trying to escape from custody, the officer does not deserve like treatment, but if the criminals bruise the police officer, they deserve a weightier punishment. A simple "eye for an eye" exchange on the basis of arithmetical proportion is absurd. It is the same for commercial exchanges. If a shoemaker and a housebuilder agree to trade five hundred pairs of shoes for an addition to the shoe shop, no one can object that this is unfair because it's a five hundred to one exchange. Aristotle then goes on to offer some remarks on proportional justice that have led commentators to disagree vehemently about what proportional justice is and how it is related to the other species of justice. In fact, there is not even agreement about what it concerns. Some, such as Kraut (2002, 151–3) and Bostock (2000, 63–6), take it to concern only commercial exchanges; while others, such as Gauthier and Jolif (1970, II,1:374), take it to concern punishment as well.

The chief difficulty is seeing where proportional justice fits into Aristotle's taxonomy of justice. After all, Aristotle had said there are two species of justice, and here he seems to introduce a third. As Gauthier and Jolif explain (1970, II,1:369–72), commentators may adopt one of three strategies to resolve the problem.

(1) The first is to reduce proportional justice to one of the other species. Stewart (1892, 1:442–3, 444), for instance, reduces proportional justice to distributive justice; after all, of the two species, only distributive justice consists in a non-arithmetical proportion, and Aristotle begins his discussion of proportional justice by ridiculing the Pythagorean insistence on arithmetical proportion. Nevertheless, Stewart's proposal clearly can't be right, since distributive justice concerns the administration of common goods held in trust and proportional justice doesn't.

Aquinas, following Albert the Great's lead, links proportional justice with corrective justice, categorizing them under the single heading of "commutative" (or "transactional") justice, an expression that Albert apparently coined (*Super Ethica* 5.7 n. 407, Editio Coloniensis 14:346 line 15). This is a more plausible interpretation than Stewart's, but it faces serious problems. The corrective justice of Chapter 4 is found in an arithmetical mean, while Aristotle begins his discussion of proportional justice with a rejection of the arithmetical mean. Moreover, this move may strike contemporary commentators as suspicious precisely because Aristotle's account of corrective justice, taken as an independent species, is likely to strike a thirteenth-century thinker such as Aquinas as thoroughly inadequate. Return to the example of the car theft: Aristotle says that justice is done once the thief returns my car, since the status quo is re-established. But for a thinker for whom violations of justice require not simply re-establishment of the status quo but also punishment, this can't be the whole story. And so, we might think, Aquinas is tempted to interpret Aristotle in ways that support his own preconceptions of justice, both human justice and divine justice as well. Those who think that Aquinas is skewing his commentary to promote his own ideas, or even his own theology, can point to this interpretation of the division of justice as prima facie evidence.

(2) The majority of contemporary commentators, such as Pakaluk (2005), Bostock (2000), Hardie (1980), Irwin (1988), and Kraut (2002), find that proportional justice is a third species. This accords well with

Aristotle's explicit claim at the start of Chapter 5 that proportional justice does not accord with either distributive or corrective justice, and in fact Aristotle does seem to be presenting a third species. The chief barrier to accepting this view is Aristotle's earlier claim that there are two species of justice, distributive and corrective. Commentators generally explain this by contending that these parts of Book 5 were never well integrated by Aristotle in a final redaction.

(3) A third possibility, first proposed by Ritchie (1894) and accepted by Gauthier and Jolif (1970), is that reciprocal justice is not reducible to either species, but it's not itself a third species. It's rather a sort of proto-justice. In other words, it's a statement of the primitive conditions that must hold before a state can formulate a constitution under which there can be distributive and corrective justice.

Most commentators think, and I agree, that the second option is the most plausible view: Aristotle distinguishes three species of justice, and the unredacted state of the text – which is such a mess that editors have been at pains to move multiple passages around in order to make sense of it – explains why he first says there are two species of justice, even though he then introduces a third. The first step in defending Aquinas against charges of skewing his interpretation toward his own preconceptions is to note that he is less likely than a modern editor to accept this reading precisely because he does not follow modern techniques of textual editing, a fact that is especially striking when he deals with repeated sentences, as when a claim Aristotle makes in Chapter 4 at 1132b10 also occurs word for word at 1133a16. Rather than arguing that this is an editor's or a copyist's mistake, Aquinas actually takes pains to justify Aristotle's repetition of the whole sentence, word for word, even though in one context the sentence is obviously out of place.

So, Aristotle's assertion that there are two species of justice, as well as Aquinas's lack of competence as a text editor, explain in part Aquinas's unwillingness to accept the second possibility. But there are other reasons, including the vagueness of the text itself. After treating distributive justice in Chapter 3, Aristotle goes on in Chapter 4 to say that the other sort of justice "is the corrective justice that takes place in transactions, both voluntary and involuntary" (1131b25–6). The Greek "τὸ δὲ λοιπὸν ἓν τὸ διορθωτικόν, ὃ γίνεται ἐν τοῖς συναλλάγμασι καὶ τοῖς ἑκουσίοις καὶ τοῖς ἀκουσίοις" is rendered by Grosseteste as "Reliqua autem una directivum. Quod fit et involuntariis et in commutationibus et in voluntariis" (Aristoteles Latinus 26/1–3:459 lines 19–20). This sentence can be taken in two ways, depending on which word is stressed (Gauthier and Jolif 1970, II,1:370–1). Advocates of the second interpretation take the stressed word to be διορθωτικόν or *directivum*, that is, "corrective"; in other words, the second sort of justice, which takes place in transactions, is corrective. But Aquinas takes the stressed word to be *commutationibus*; in other words, the second sort of justice, which is corrective, has to do with *transactions*. Given the vagueness of the text, together with Aristotle's contention that there are only two species of justice, we may quite reasonably conclude that Aquinas was actually trying as hard as possible to offer a consistent interpretation of Aristotle.

Gauthier and Jolif, however, are unconvinced. Aquinas purports to find in Chapters 4 and 5 a single species of commutative justice; what he cannot explain, they say, is why Aristotle would divide his discussion of commutative justice into two highly distinct units (Gauthier and Jolif 1970, II,1:371). And besides, Aristotle states at the start of Chapter 5 that proportional justice does not fit the other species. One decisive difference is that corrective justice is determined by arithmetical proportion, and proportional justice is not. Therefore, they imply, Aquinas was simply blind to the evidence before him. However, Aquinas can answer these charges: he actually did have reasons – reasons stemming from his attempt to understand Aristotle – for linking Chapters 4 and 5. First, Aristotle's claim that proportional justice does not fit either corrective or distributive justice comes immediately after he has introduced the simpleminded Pythagorean conception (1132b23–8). Aquinas takes Aristotle to be saying that it is this simplistic version of the *lex talionis* that cannot be reduced to the other species of justice. But then Aristotle goes on to offer a more sophisticated version of proportional justice, according to which the parties to a transaction must somehow equalize what's gained and lost on both sides, as when the housebuilder and the shoemaker exchange five hundred pairs of shoes for an addition to the shop. It is this more sophisticated account of proportional justice that Aquinas counts as commutative justice.

Next, Aquinas is himself aware of the potential contradiction in his interpretation, since he himself raises the worry that proportional justice is not an arithmetical equality, while corrective justice is (*SLE* 5.8 lines 102–7). Aquinas then offers a resolution that is as creative as it is complicated. How many shoes must a shoemaker craft in exchange for an addition? With typical economy of expression, Aristotle reports: "As builder is to shoemaker, so the number of shoes must be to a house" (1133a22–4). Aquinas aims to explicate these puzzling remarks in such a way that renders Aristotle's discussion internally consistent (*SLE* 5.8 lines 107–17). In a commutative exchange, there are two persons, two things, two actions, and two undergoings. Aquinas contends that in proportional justice, there must in fact be an arithmetical equivalence of the things exchanged, but in order to achieve this, there may have to be some non-arithmetical equivalence of actions and undergoings. So, Aquinas interprets Aristotle's terse remark as equivalent to this: The value of what the builder does has to be made equivalent to the value of what the shoemaker does, and that will tell us how many shoes it takes to pay for an addition to the house. Let me elaborate. Suppose a housebuilder and a shoemaker are trying to make a fair exchange. If there is arithmetical equivalence between their actions and their undergoings, the result will be unfair, since the shoemaker will perform the action of making one pair of shoes and then undergo their loss, while the housebuilder will perform the action of building one addition and then undergoing its loss. What's fair, Aquinas maintains, is a transaction in which the value of what's exchanged is equivalent. But the housebuilder's single action is simply worth more than the shoemaker's single action (presumably because it takes longer and requires more costly materials to perform it). Therefore, for justice to be served, we must establish some non-arithmetical proportion to determine the relative worth of the housebuilder's action and the shoemaker's action. But once we do that, we are able to establish an arithmetical equivalence, measurable in currency, that will satisfy the demands of commutative justice.

9.3   Un-Aristotelian elements

As I've noted, this solution is as creative as it is complicated. It strives to make Aquinas's reading of Aristotle utterly consistent with the text, and it largely succeeds. But in this very attempt to discover a consistent reading of Aristotle, Aquinas introduces into Aristotle's discussion an element that is anachronistic. Aristotle contends that the sorts of communities we live in – communities that enable exchange for mutual benefit – arise because we find ourselves in need (*EN* 5.5.1133b6–10). In fact, it is need that measures equality in exchanges (*EN* 5.5.1133a26–7). That is because need establishes value, which we measure by money, and once value is established, parties will be able to determine equivalence in exchanges in terms of a common currency.

Aquinas agrees with Aristotle that the practice of exchange originated with and continues to depend on mutual need (*SLE* 5.9). He also agrees that need plays an important role in setting price. However, Aquinas introduces into this discussion the notion of natural worth, that is, the rank a thing holds in the hierarchy of being. He explicitly contrasts natural worth with a thing's monetary value, noting that the two are often at variance (*SLE* 5.9 lines 47–60). After all, we pay more for a pearl than for a field mouse, although as a sentient creature, a field mouse has a greater natural worth than a pearl. Nevertheless, we have no use for field mice, while we prize pearls for their luminous beauty.

However, there are limits to the extent to which need can establish fair price, and to explain this limitation, Aquinas draws not on Aristotle, but, anachronistically, on Albert, who probably drew his ideas from discussions by the Decretists.[11] According to Aquinas, when goods to be exchanged are the products of human effort, the cost of production, such as labor and materials, should play a role in establishing a thing's fair price (*SLE* 5.9 lines 76–100). A farmer who trades a bushel of wheat for a sandal is the victim of unfairness precisely because it takes much more time and effort to grow that wheat than to make that sandal. In introducing these additional factors, Aquinas is not rejecting Aristotle's view that need has a role to play in establishing price. In fact, at *ST* 2-2.77.1, Aquinas explains how need, in some cases, can trump factors such as cost of production in establishing fair price. This happens, for instance, when a seller's livelihood depends on the item for sale, so that the seller's need for the item allows her justly to raise the price so she can find alternative ways to fulfill that need. Ordinarily, however, the cost of production will play the largest role in setting fair price.

In ascribing to Aristotle the view that the cost of production matters for determining fair price, Aquinas is clearly reading the views of later thinkers – including his own – into the *Nicomachean Ethics*. Still, there is a sense in which Aquinas is commenting on Aristotle appropriately, since he is providing a response to an important question Aristotle raises but utterly fails to answer. Aristotle explains how markets in fact determine prices, namely, on the basis of need. His own question, however, is how we determine fair prices in commercial exchanges, and appeal to a need-driven market will not answer that question.[12] Increased need for a certain product might drive market prices up, but we can still reasonably ask whether that high price is a fair one (if, for instance, it costs manufacturers pennies to market something that they are selling for hundreds of dollars). So, even if Aquinas is influenced by considerations that dominated

---

[11] See Baldwin 1959, 76–7. Albert's view can be found in *Ethica* 5.2.10, ed. Borgnet 7:358; cf. *Super Ethica* 5.7 n. 420, Editio Coloniensis 14:357 lines 80–3.

[12] Bostock (2000, 65) makes a similar observation, although he understands "χρῆσις" as demand or something close to it.

the commercial worldview of the thirteenth century, he is nevertheless trying to answer a question that Aristotle raises and never himself provides an
obvious response to, and Aquinas's response is not ad hoc but fits with his
larger attempt to explain Aristotle's views in keeping with what he takes to
be genuinely Aristotelian principles of justice.

9.4   Integration

When he writes the *Summa theologiae*, which includes his most sophisticated treatment of justice, Aquinas adopts nearly all of the Aristotelian
account of this virtue as Aquinas understands it in his commentary. That
adoption includes not simply major contentions, such as the distinction
between universal and particular justice, the division of particular justice
into its two species, and the appeal to psychological conditions such as
ignorance and fear for making accurate judgments about agents' failures
of justice, but also hundreds of smaller details that make up the bulk of
Aristotle's treatment. However, Aquinas also revises features of Aristotle's
account. The most profound changes come as a result of his integrating
Aristotle into his own system of Christian ethics.

Many of Aquinas's changes are subtle. He sometimes develops Aristotle's
thought and sometimes changes emphases to integrate that thought into a
system of Christian values. For instance, unlike Aristotle, Aquinas recognizes that different sorts of cases require the application of different criteria
to discover what distributive justice demands, and he is especially concerned
to identify those improper criteria whose application would result in the
injustice of respect for persons (*ST* 2–2.63). In addition, when he adopts
Aristotle's views (as he interprets them), his own reason for holding them
may differ from Aristotle's. For example, Aristotle and Aquinas have different aims in spelling out the distinction between universal and particular
justice. In acknowledging the exalted nature and sweeping scope of universal justice, Aristotle is making a concession to Plato, whose *Republic*
investigates justice of a similarly grand sort, but Aristotle's focus on
particular justice implies that he thinks Plato has failed to pay sufficient
heed to the notion of justice as equality. Aquinas, in contrast, finds universal justice interesting because of its role in human moral psychology:
Like charity, it is an executive virtue that commands the other virtues and
thereby directs them to its distinctive end.

Other changes Aquinas makes are sweeping, such as his recognition of
the equality of all humans as rational. This equality establishes a community

of all humans not only across socio-economic lines but also across national boundaries. It gives each person the duty to treat all others justly, regardless of differences in rank and citizenship. Although Aquinas did not understand this equality to apply as broadly as most of us would like – he did not advocate the abolition of slavery, for instance – the equality he did advocate has important further implications for widening the scope of self-determination beyond what Aristotle countenanced. For instance, although Aquinas conceived of servants as their masters' tools, he understood this servitude to consist only of labor. Citing Seneca as his authority, he explains that no master has control over the condition of a servant's body or will. So, a master cannot justly order slaves to enjoy their work or to remain virgins (*ST* 2–2.104.5).[13]

The most radical change Aquinas introduces, however, is making the virtue of Aristotelian justice the instrument of divinely infused virtues. In addition to the virtues that Aristotle discussed, the ones we acquire through habituation, there are divinely infused virtues that we need if we are to direct our acts to the ultimate end of otherworldly happiness. The highest of these are the theological virtues of faith, hope, and charity, but there is also a set of moral virtues that people receive as divine gifts, including infused temperance, courage, and justice. While our acquired virtues help direct us to this-worldly flourishing, their infused counterparts regulate our actions and passions so that we can merit otherworldly happiness. Aquinas argues that the virtue of charity, which is the virtue establishing a friendship with God and enabling us to love God for his own sake, directs all the infused moral virtues to serve this love. As a result, when we employ temperance to fast for God's sake, this is an act both of temperance and of charity. Likewise, when we employ infused justice to subject ourselves to God's law, this is simultaneously an act of justice and of charity, since we employ infused justice out of love for God. Acquired virtues have their place in this scheme as well. Performing just acts of the sort that Aristotle pointed to can serve both infused justice and charity. So, an agent can direct her habit of making fair exchanges to her more ultimate ends of upholding God's laws and loving her neighbor for God's sake. In this case, charity and infused justice direct acquired justice to their distinctive goals. Still, even if acquired justice serves the higher infused virtues, it plays an important role in aiding agents to carry out their virtuous activity effectively.[14]

---

[13] See McGrade 1996 for a fuller discussion of this consideration.
[14] See Porter 1992, Hause 2007, and Knobel 2010 for discussions of infused and acquired virtue.

9.5 Conclusion

Aquinas offers a thoughtful, creative interpretation of the *Nicomachean Ethics* that adds to what Aristotle says in useful and innocuous ways, as when he explains the meaning of words, supplies arguments with missing premises to establish their soundness, and introduces cross-references to other Aristotelian texts. He also interprets many passages in obviously correct ways. His misinterpretations and additions, however, raise questions about his purpose in writing a commentary on the *Nicomachean Ethics*. It cannot be, as some scholars have suggested, that this is Aquinas's own philosophical ethics since his systematic works show that he revises, on philosophical grounds, some of the views presented here. He might, despite the un-Aristotelian intrusions, be trying to discover Aristotle's thought; but even if this is so, it cannot be his whole purpose, or even his leading purpose, since Aquinas disavows this sort of scholarship for its own sake.

We may in any case wonder just how concerned Aquinas is to interpret Aristotle accurately. On the one hand, his subtlety and analytical powers often achieve results that are as illuminating as they are accurate, yet on the other, he slips in anachronistic readings that appear to turn Aristotle into a precocious Aquinas. For this reason, Gauthier hypothesizes, "So that Aristotle's ethics, which hardly speaks of anything other than man, could speak of God, Saint Thomas, without wishing it, without his even noticing it, had to transform it profoundly ... Thomas wanted only to compose a work of wisdom" (quoted in Torrell 2005, 228). Gauthier's suggestion faces two serious problems. The first is that it cannot explain why Aquinas makes only the few changes he does. Second, it is hard to believe that so deliberate and cautious a thinker as Aquinas could unwittingly transform Aristotle into a theologian. In any case, the evidence Gauthier points to is compatible with other hypotheses that become more attractive if what I have argued in this chapter is correct.

In my view, Aquinas is genuinely concerned to learn Aristotle's ethical theory, but understanding that theory sometimes requires shoring up what Aristotle writes in principled ways. In particular, Aquinas restricts himself to answering Aristotle's own unanswered questions, to finding readings that make Aristotle's text consistent, and to filling in lacunae that threaten to undermine the entire system. These principled restrictions allow Aquinas a good deal of interpretive leeway while ensuring that any additions must be justified by appeal to Aristotle's own philosophical project, not Aquinas's theological one.

We might well wonder why Aquinas would want to carry out this sort of exercise. It cannot be, as it might be for a contemporary Christian writer, to uncover a philosophical way of life to hedge his bets, just in case Christianity turned out to be incredible after all, or as a way of finding common ethical ground for living in cosmopolitan communities with non-Christians. One reason Aquinas tweaks and "completes" Aristotle as he does is that for him it is a duty of justice. Aquinas contrasts the way we should judge mere things with the way we should judge people: We should always strive to judge mere things the way they really are. In contrast, where there is room for doubt, we should try to judge a person good unless there are evident grounds for judging otherwise, even though this procedure risks false judgment (*ST* 2–2.60.4 ad 2). That is because people's honor is at stake in our judgment of them, and if we deprive people of the honor they deserve, we do them an injustice. On the other hand, if we wrongly judge well of them, what we show is rather our good will. Since Aristotle's honor depends largely on our judgment of his texts, then justice demands that we try to read them as upholding the truth unless there are evident grounds for reading them otherwise. This requirement of justice underlies, for Aquinas, the common medieval practice of *expositio reverentialis*, what we would call "charitable commentary." Of course, Aquinas does not think that Aristotle could have discovered the truths of Christian revelation, but Aquinas would certainly seize on any hint in the text to suggest that Aristotle had uncovered important philosophical truths that would bolster, in Aquinas's eyes, Aristotle's ethical theory.

Nevertheless, this principle of justice cannot by itself explain Aquinas's interest in offering his readers this shored-up Aristotle since it doesn't explain his interest in *Aristotle* in particular. In addition to the *bonum honestum* of serving justice, Aquinas was probably also pursuing the *bonum utile* of ensuring an Aristotle who was safe (if not positively sanitized) for extensive use in Christian theology. But there is one further fine and noble good Aquinas may be pursuing, namely, establishing a fundamental truth of his theological system. As Aquinas reads him, Aristotle, despite a few flaws, lacunae, and putative inconsistencies, succeeded brilliantly in articulating, without the aid of revelation, an ethical system that captured the truth about human ends and how to achieve them, about the sort of person worth becoming, about human action, and about the need for friendship. With some adjustments from the likes of Cicero, Macrobius, and the Stoics, Aquinas finds that Aristotle's ethical system captures important truths about how we should live. When he formulates his own Christian ethics, Aquinas does not repudiate this improved Aristotelian ethics, but adapts it for inclusion in his theological system as an ethics transformed. After all, we still need Aristotelian ethical virtue as long as we live in this world, even if, for Aquinas, it serves the higher infused virtues, and likewise Aquinas does not reject the goods that constitute Aristotelian this-worldly happiness as false ends, even if they are not, for him, the most ultimate goods one can pursue. To demonstrate his transforming embrace of Aristotle's ethics, Aquinas had to write both a philosophical commentary and a theological ethics. The result is a dramatic and powerful illustration of the Thomistic theological thesis that grace does not destroy nature but builds on it. Aristotle's ethics provides Aquinas with what appears to be the best system natural reason has produced, and what Aquinas needs to do is to show that Aristotle's system can be defended against objections of error, inconsistency, and incompleteness. And, as a person of justice and magnanimity, he does this with panache.

CHAPTER TEN

Prudence and practical principles

Tobias Hoffmann

"Virtue makes the goal correct, and prudence makes the things promoting the goal correct" (*EN* 6.12.1144a8–9).[1] I will label this the "goal passage." The first part of this affirmation, that virtue makes the goal correct, has generated a great deal of scholarly debate. As a disposition (ἕξις) in the irrational part of the soul, it seems that moral virtue is incapable of providing knowledge of the correct goal. This passage carries all the heavier weight if one holds that moral virtue alone can make the end right. Deliberation cannot provide the correct end, because we do not deliberate about the end but only about what promotes it (*EN* 3.3.1112b11–16). Some scholars argue that for Aristotle prudence is what discovers the correct end, while others deny this; the question is whether in *EN* 6.9.1142b32–3 Aristotle intends to say that prudence is the correct identification of the end or of that which promotes the end.[2] The issue with the goal passage, then, is whether the end of moral action is determined rationally or rather posited by desire. The former alternative is not straightforwardly affirmed by the texts, while the latter alternative, as has been frequently observed, would turn Aristotle into a proto-Humean, subordinating reason to desire.

It is not my intention in this chapter to settle controversial points about Aristotle's position itself. The aim of this chapter is rather to investigate how the ends of the moral life are known in Aquinas's own mind, and how he understands the goal passage. I intend to show that for Aquinas moral virtue does supply some knowledge of the ends of the moral life, but that outside of a framework provided by self-evident practical principles and moral science such knowledge cannot be adequately articulated. I contend that, according to Aquinas, moral virtue is therefore an insufficient source of the knowledge that is to guide the moral life.

---

[1] Translations from the Greek, with some modifications, are from Aristotle 1999. Translations from the Latin are my own.

[2] The main protagonists of the debate are René-Antoine Gauthier and Pierre Aubenque. For recent discussions, see Moss 2011, 228–41, and Fiasse 2001, who provides an ample bibliography.

In order to fully appreciate the importance of the goal passage in Aristotle's ethics, Section 10.1 examines his Nicomachean account of the role of moral virtue and prudence in acquiring and preserving correct practical knowledge.[3] This brief discussion will raise two main questions: First, how are the ends of the moral life known? Second, how do the moral virtues contribute to our knowledge of right ends? Aquinas's answers to these questions are the subject of Sections 10.2 and 10.3. His solution to the first question is that the general and specific ends of the moral life are known by means of "universal practical principles," which are general standards for how one *should* act. They include self-evident practical propositions as well as more specific conclusions of moral science. His answer to the second question is that the moral virtues provide an affective support for the knowledge of the right end by securing "particular practical principles," which are the ends for which the virtuous individual *does* act. In this context, Aquinas further develops Aristotelian intuitions by way of his theory of the "judgment by connaturality" or "by inclination," which is a non-discursive prudential judgment. Aquinas's theory of universal and particular practical principles provides the proper framework for understanding the place of the goal passage in his ethics. So once that theory is sufficiently clear, we can ask questions about Aquinas's amended Aristotelianism: Is Aquinas only making more explicit what is implicit in Aristotle? Does he improve the Aristotelian account of prudence? Does he fundamentally alter prudence's meaning and scope?[4]

10.1   Aristotle on knowing ends

Aristotle explains prudential reasoning by analogy with technical reasoning. For example, to illustrate that practical deliberation is about means, not

[3] The *Eudemian Ethics* has much to say on this topic as well, but since the relevant portions of the *EE* were not available to Aquinas, I omit its discussion.

[4] I do not intend in this essay to navigate through the vast literature on the relationship between Aristotle's and Aquinas's accounts of prudence. Given the centrality of prudence in both of their ethics, almost every study that compares their ethical theories will have something to say on this issue. I will mention here only the following sample of representative positions. Rhonheimer 1994, and more recently Vaccarezza 2012, defend a fundamental continuity between Aristotle's and Aquinas's theories of prudence. Rhonheimer argues that, where Aquinas goes beyond Aristotle, he complements Aristotle's account in the ways necessary to render it coherent (see especially pp. 434–9; 576–96). Vaccarezza argues against the interpretation of Aristotle as a moral particularist and holds that Aquinas's insistence on universality in ethics is in agreement with Aristotle's position (see especially pp. 207–17). In contrast, Jaffa 1952 claims that, by making prudence depend on self-evident practical principles, he fundamentally alters Aristotle's project (ch. 8). Gauthier advances the same complaint and adds that Aquinas misinterprets Aristotle by denying that prudence grasps the end of the moral life (Gauthier and Jolif 1970, I,1:276–9).

ends, he says that a doctor does not deliberate about whether he should cure, an orator about whether he should persuade, or a politician about whether he should promote good order (3.3.1112b12–14). Sarah Broadie points out that this method obscures a fundamental problem in Aristotle's account of prudential, that is, non-technical reasoning, namely that it leaves unanswered the question of how the end toward which we deliberate is specified. In fact, she argues, the most general end of human life, achieving the best or supreme good, is too general to direct a specific course of practical deliberation that would yield a particular choice (1991, 185; 191–2). Prudential reasoning requires, therefore, that the ends toward which one deliberates be given more specifically. The goal passage, which states that moral virtue rectifies the end, seems to answer to this need of specifying the end.[5]

But how is the goal passage to be understood? More precisely, how does moral virtue make an individual have the correct conception of the end, that is, the correct idea of what is truly worthwhile in life? For Aristotle, this is not the fruit of rational inference. The end is a principle (that is, a starting point) rather than something obtained as a conclusion from a principle, as he states in a famous passage:

> For virtue preserves the principle, whereas vice corrupts it; and in actions the end we act for is the principle, as the assumptions are the principles in mathematics. Reason does not teach the principles either in mathematics or in actions; [with actions] it is virtue, either natural or habituated, that teaches correct belief about the principle.[6] (7.8.1151a14–19)

The point of the analogy is that just as theoretical principles (i.e., assumptions) are had non-inferentially, so also principles in practical matters (i.e., ends) are had non-inferentially.[7] Yet there is also an important difference between the two. Theoretical principles, the starting points for scientific knowledge, are understood thanks to the intellectual virtue of understanding (νοῦς) (6.6.1140b31–5, 6.8.1142a25–6, 6.11.1143a36–b2). Aristotle assigns a role to understanding in the practical domain as well, but here its task is to grasp not general principles but rather the particular contingent fact that is perceived as relevant in the given situation. Practical understanding thus allows one to form the minor premise that completes a practical

---

[5] For in-depth discussions, see Broadie 1991, ch. 4, Moss 2011, Price 2011, and the ample literature considered by Moss and Price.

[6] Here and in the Aristotle-quotations below, the additions in brackets are Irwin's (Aristotle 1999), except for a few instances where I add a Greek term.

[7] For a detailed analysis of the analogy Aristotle draws between theoretical and practical principles, see Irwin 1978.

syllogism, and that hence sets the individual in motion (6.11.1143a35–b5).[8] But practical understanding is not the source of general knowledge about which ends are worth pursuing, statements which could be used as a major premise in practical syllogisms. For Aristotle, it is theoretical understanding that is concerned with universals, such as definitions, while practical understanding is concerned with the particular (6.8.1142a25–6).

A further comment about the previous quotation from *EN* 7.8 is in order. As was suggested at the beginning of this chapter, it is unlikely that we should take Aristotle to mean literally that virtue "teaches" correct belief about the principle, that is, the end. But the result of virtue's activity is certainly a correct belief, that is, a cognitive state. In this respect Anthony Price pointedly asks, "Yet how can the possession of a right practical starting point be a cognitive state if there is no *sullogismos* or *logos* by which it might be derived?" (2011, 142).

An answer has been suggested by Jessica Moss, who argues that virtuous habituation of the non-rational part of the soul, though itself non-rational, can yield cognitive content, because "being pleased and pained in the right ways, or admiring and being disgusted by the right things . . . is an operation of non-rational cognition" (2011, 254). The capacity for having the correct evaluative dispositions results from our character, which in turn is the fruit of our upbringing (p. 250). Whatever the merits of this interpretation, it begs the question of how the criteria for good upbringing themselves are grasped.

Aristotle dedicates *EN* 10.9, as well as *Pol.* 8, to moral education. Good laws are responsible for the correct molding of character. Again we must ask, however, from what source the lawgiver obtains the right view of what counts as a good character and good education. Presumably, the lawgiver can look to people who are virtuous, for they embody the criteria for what is truly good and hence for what constitutes good upbringing. For Aristotle, the excellent person (σπουδαῖος) possesses correct judgment of the good and serves as a standard for goodness (I call this the "*spoudaios*-doctrine"):

> For the excellent person [σπουδαίῳ], then, what is wished will be what is [wished] in reality, while for the base person what is wished is whatever it turns out to be [that appears good to him]. Similarly in the case of bodies, really healthy things are healthy to people in good condition, while other

---

[8] For example, practical understanding allows me to see that this is light meat, and, since I know that light meat is healthy, I can now conclude that I should eat this meat. Cf. *EN* 6.7.1141b18–21.

things are healthy to sickly people, and the same is true of what is bitter, sweet, hot, heavy, and so on. For the excellent person judges each sort of thing correctly, and in each case what is true appears to him . . . Presumably, then, the excellent person is far superior because he sees what is true in each case, being himself a sort of standard and measure. (3.4.1113a25–33)

Elsewhere, Aristotle makes an analogous point: "Virtue, i.e., the good person insofar as he is good, is the measure of each thing" (10.5.1176a17–18). For example, he is the measure of what true pleasures, that is, decent pleasures, are: "What appear pleasures to him will also really be pleasures" (1176a18–19). The problem is, however, how the virtuous person can be recognized as virtuous if there are no external, agent-independent standards.

The question, then, of how a correct assessment of the ends of human actions is to be obtained is problematic in Aristotle. Less problematic is his view of how such a correct assessment is preserved by virtue and corrupted by vice, as is best expressed in these two passages:

This is also how we come to give temperance [σωφροσύνην] its name, because we think that it preserves [σώζουσαν] prudence. It preserves the [right] sort of supposition. For the sort of supposition that is corrupted and perverted by the pleasant and painful is not every sort – not, for instance, the supposition that the triangle does or does not have two right angles – but suppositions about matters of action. For the principles of matters of action [ἀρχαὶ τῶν πρακτῶν] are their end, but if someone is corrupted because of pleasure and pain, no [appropriate] principle can appear to him, and it cannot appear that this is the right end and cause of all his choice and action; for vice corrupts the principle. (6.5.1140b11–20)

[Prudence,] this eye of the soul, requires virtue in order to reach its fully developed state . . . For inferences about actions have a principle, "since the end and the best good is this sort of thing" (whatever it actually is – let it be any old thing for the sake of argument). And this [best good] is apparent only to the good person; for vice perverts us and produces false views about the practical principles [πρακτικὰς ἀρχάς]. Evidently, then, we cannot be prudent without being good. (6.12.1144a31–b1)

Virtue preserves, and vice corrupts, not only what individuals actually pursue as an end, but also their beliefs about the end. Since prudence is by definition the disposition of deliberating about what promotes good ends, when the belief about what counts as a worthwhile end is corrupted, prudence is corrupted as well. For this reason, Aristotle argues, prudence presupposes the moral virtues that preserve the correct assessment of what is good and bad.

Aristotle makes a general claim about correct desire as a necessary condition for successful practical thinking in a statement that reaches beyond the immediate context of prudence. In it he presents the notion of "practical truth," which involves both correct desire and right reason:

> As assertion and denial are to thought, so pursuit and avoidance are to desire. Now virtue of character is a state that decides; and decision is deliberative desire. If, then, the decision is excellent, the reason must be true and the desire correct, so that what reason asserts is what desire pursues. This, then, is thought and truth concerned with action [ἀλήθεια πρακτική]. The thought concerned with study, not with action or production, has its good or bad state in being true or false; for truth is the function of whatever thinks. But the good state of what thinks about action is truth agreeing with correct desire. (6.2.1139a21–31)

This passage echoes the problem implied in the goal passage: if correct desire is what measures practical thinking, what is it that provides the criterion for correct desire, other than correct practical thinking?

This brief sketch of Aristotle's view about the connection between desire and thought in practical knowledge gives rise to the two questions mentioned earlier: How are the ends of the moral life known? How do the moral virtues contribute to this knowledge? The next two sections will present Aquinas's answers to these.

10.2   Aquinas on universal practical principles

Aristotle's account of practical truth gives a good illustration of the general problem of making right desire constitutive of correct knowledge. If all correct practical knowledge is measured by right desire, and if at the same time all right desire is measured by correct practical knowledge, then the relation between correct desire and correct knowledge is circular. The connection between the moral virtues and prudence poses the same problem: the moral virtues presuppose prudence (2.6.1106b36–1107a2; 6.13.1144b1–17), and at the same time, as we have seen, prudence presupposes the moral virtues. In this section, we shall first look at Aquinas's interpretation of Aristotle's account of practical truth and then at his explanation of how the ends of the moral virtues are known. A trait common to Aquinas's treatment of both these issues is his concern to anchor whatever has the appearance of being self-referential or relativistic in Aristotle's ethics to a naturally given ground.

10.2.1 *Practical truth and the naturally given end*

While much of the *SLE* limits itself to exposition and paraphrasing explanation of the text, Aquinas occasionally inserts little discussions that address particular issues that emerge in the text. One such discussion is dedicated to the threat of circularity in Aristotle's account of practical truth in 6.2.1139a21–31, and proposes a solution:

> There seems to be a problem here. For if the truth of the practical intellect is determined by comparison with right desire, while the rightness of desire is determined by the fact that it agrees with true reason, as was said before, then there will be a certain circular relationship in these determinations. And therefore it must be said that desire concerns the end and that which promotes the end. The end, however, is determined for the human being by nature, as was said above in Book 3; in contrast, that which promotes the end is not determined for us by nature, but rather needs to be investigated by reason. Thus it is clear that the rectitude of desire with respect to the end is the measure of the truth in practical reason, and in this regard, the truth of practical reason is determined according to its agreement with right desire. But the truth of practical reason is the criterion [*regula*] for rightness of desire concerning that which promotes the end, and, therefore, in this regard the desire is called right which pursues that which true reason dictates. (*SLE* 6.2 lines 109–27)

Aquinas indicates the Archimedean point upon which all standards for rightness depend: the first criterion for rightness is the end that is determined by nature.[9] That this end is naturally given implies, for Aquinas, that it is naturally desired; it does not imply, however, that it is rightly identified and hence rightly desired. Only "*rectitude* of desire for the end" gives the standard for truth in practical reason. In his *Sentences* commentary, Aquinas identifies this naturally given end with happiness (*In Sent.* 3.33.1.1 qc. 2 resp.). In the *Prima Secundae*, he concisely explains the assertion that practical truth agrees with right desires as follows. The correct knowledge of the end is the work of reason; this correctly assessed end Aquinas calls the "due end" (*finis debitus*). Reason judges correctly about that which promotes this end (*ea quae sunt ad finem*) when its judgment conforms to correct desire for the due end (*ST* 1–2.19.3 ad 2). The upshot of these passages seems to be this: happiness is by nature the ultimate end;

---

[9] He refers to an earlier discussion in Book 3 from which the reader might expect further light, but neither Aristotle nor Aquinas's commentary contain any passage that would make the statement about the naturally given end any clearer. The passage indicated by the Leonine Edition (47:337) is not to the point.

the correct judgment about what happiness consists in is the work of reason; desire is correct when it conforms to this judgment, that is, when it aims at happiness rightly understood; and the practical intellect is truthful when it correctly discovers what agrees with correct desire, that is, what is conducive to happiness rightly conceived.

10.2.2   Prudence and universal practical principles

The way Aquinas explains the relation between right reason, right desire, and naturally given ends in his gloss on Aristotle's account of practical truth is almost identical to the way he conceives of the relation between prudence, moral virtue, and the naturally given ends of moral virtue. He seems to think of the latter relation as an instance of the former.

The key text for this is *ST* 2–2.47.6. The question asked in this article is whether prudence determines (*praestituat*) the end for the moral virtues. In the *sed contra* he cites the goal passage: "The Philosopher says that moral virtue rectifies the intention of the end, while prudence rectifies what promotes the end." Aquinas uses this authority only to deny that prudence makes the goal right, without saying anything about the role of the moral virtues in making it right; he continues, "Therefore, the task of prudence is not to determine the end for the moral virtues, but only to establish that which promotes the end" (*ST* 2–2.47.6 s.c.). In the body of the article, Aquinas argues that what determines the end for the moral virtues is not prudence, nor the moral virtues themselves, but "naturally known principles" (*principia naturaliter nota*) of practical reason:

> The end of the moral virtues is the human good. But the good of the human soul is to live according to reason, as is clear from Dionysius. Hence it is necessary that the ends of the moral virtues pre-exist in reason. Now in theoretical reason there are certain naturally known things, with which understanding is concerned, and certain things that are made known by means of these, namely the conclusions, with which science is concerned. In the same manner, in practical reason there pre-exist certain things as naturally known principles, and these are the ends of the moral virtues. In fact, the end in practical matters acts like the principle in theoretical matters, as was said above. Also, in practical reason there exist certain other things as conclusions, and these are the things that promote the end, at which we arrive from our knowledge of the ends themselves. Prudence is about the latter, applying universal principles to particular conclusions about matters of action. And for this reason, the role of prudence is not to determine the end for the moral virtues, but only to govern those things that promote the end. (*ST* 2–2.47.6 resp.)

In order properly to grasp this text, we must clarify what Aquinas means by naturally known principles in practical reason. He explains them by analogy with the principles of theoretical reason.[10] But the analogy does not sufficiently define the nature of the practical principles. Do they state what everyone should pursue as an end or simply what all people do in fact pursue as an end?

A discussion of the connection between moral virtues and prudence in *ST* 1–2.58.5 sheds further light on this. While Aristotle speaks simply of practical principles without distinction (πρακτικαὶ ἀρχαί, e.g., 6.13.1144a35–6), Aquinas distinguishes explicitly between universal and particular practical principles. The first part of the *responsio* concerns the universal principles:

> I answer that the other intellectual virtues can exist without moral virtue, but prudence cannot exist without moral virtue. This is so because prudence is right reason in matters of action – not only in the universal, but also in the particular, which is where actions happen. For right reason presupposes principles from which reasoning may proceed.
>
> Concerning particulars, reason must proceed not only from universal principles but also from particular ones. Concerning universal principles of action [*principia universalia agibilium*], an individual is rightly disposed by means of his natural understanding [*per naturalem intellectum*] of principles, by which he knows that no evil is to be done; and also by means of some practical science. (*ST* 1–2.58.5 resp.)

The universal practical principles, says Aquinas, are grasped by means of our "natural understanding of principles," and his example is that "no evil is to be done." This example indicates that Aquinas understands these principles to be universally valid normative statements. Elsewhere, in discussing the first principles of natural law, Aquinas pushes the analogy between theoretical and universal practical principles even further. He not only ascribes universal validity to both but also claims that both are "*principia per se nota*," that is, self-evident statements, provided one has a proper grasp of the terms of which they are composed. The most fundamental one, which is also the primary precept of the natural law, is that "good is to be done and pursued and evil to be avoided" (*ST* 1–2.94.2).[11]

---

[10] Aquinas's favorite example of a theoretical principle is "every whole is greater than its part," without which the science of geometry would be impossible; see, e.g., *ST* 1–2.65.1 ad 4.

[11] Although in *ST* 1–2.94.2 Aquinas does not call them practical principles but "praecepta legis naturae," he clearly identifies the two because he explains them equally by analogy with theoretical principles. See also *ST* 1–2.94.1 ad 2.

With these clarifications in mind, we can go back to *ST* 2–2.47.6, Aquinas's treatment of the origin of the ends of the moral virtues. In this article, Aquinas seems to have universal rather than particular practical principles in mind, and he seems to consider them to be self-evident. This is confirmed by his response to the first objection, which had argued that prudence determines the end for the moral virtues just as reason in general determines the end for the appetitive power. In reply, Aquinas reiterates the point he had made in the body of the article, that it is not prudence but rather natural reason that determines the end for the moral virtues. He then goes on to identify this natural reason with the notion of *synderesis* (*ST* 2–2.47.6 ad 1). Aquinas understands *synderesis* as an infallible fundamental moral awareness that derives its correctness from insight into self-evident principles (*ST* 1.79.12; cf. *QDV* 16.2). Two of the examples he gives of dictates of *synderesis* are "God is to be obeyed" and "one must live according to reason" (*QDV* 16.1 ad 9).

By way of conclusion to *ST* 2–2.47.6, Aquinas summarizes the relationship between natural reason (*synderesis*), prudence, and the moral virtues: prudence, governing what promotes the virtuous end, realizes the moral virtues, while *synderesis* moves prudence in the same way as understanding of (theoretical) principles moves science (*ST* 2–2.47.6 ad 3). So by anchoring prudence in natural reason rather than in the moral virtues, Aquinas avoids a circular causal relationship of desire and reason.

What does it mean, then, to say that the universal practical principles determine the end for the moral virtues? These self-evident practical principles determine general ends, such as the promotion of what is good, the avoidance of evil, and obedience to God. It would seem that these ends do not necessarily enter directly into practical deliberations; rather, virtuous individuals seem to take them for granted and deliberate instead about more particular ways of promoting the good, avoiding evil, and obeying God. But they may also be targeted directly, in which case they can form the major premise of a practical syllogism: "Evil is to be avoided"; "This act of adultery is evil"; "Therefore I should avoid this act of adultery" (*In Sent.* 2.24.2.4 resp.).

Universal principles also serve to determine more specific ends. While the principle to do good is itself too general to determine concretely which acts ought to be done to promote the good, for Aquinas it serves as the basis for a further specification of the ends of the moral life. According to this principle, everything that practical reason identifies as a human good is to be pursued. For Aquinas, "reason naturally understands as good, and therefore to be actively pursued, all that to which man has a natural inclination, and their contraries it understands as evil and to be avoided." For instance, from the fact that man has a natural inclination to live in society, Aquinas derives that one must not offend others (*ST* 1–2.94.2 resp.). This is an example of how Aquinas thinks that the more specific end of the virtue of justice can be known, but unfortunately his explanation of how this works is all too condensed. But even a further specification of the ends leaves us at a level of generality that does not close the gap between moral considerations and concrete actions.

10.2.3 Aquinas on particular practical principles

What is difficult in the moral life is often to know what is right and wrong not in general, but in the concrete. I easily understand that I should live healthily, but I don't easily acknowledge that now I should watch what I eat. Nor is the difficulty merely at the cognitive level, for it is easy to suggest to others what to do, but hard to admit this in one's own case if it is contrary to one's preference. This shows that a general understanding of right and wrong is not enough to guide concrete actions. To allow the general understanding of right and wrong to become operative in the concrete, Aquinas argues in *ST* 1–2.58.5 that in addition to the universal principles one needs "particular practical principles." Here is the remainder of the *responsio* that was quoted above:

> But that is not enough to reason correctly concerning particulars. For it sometimes happens that such a universal principle, known by understanding or science, is corrupted in the particular by some passion. For example, to someone who lusts – when lust prevails – that for which he lusts seems good, even though it is against the universal judgment of reason.
>
> Therefore, just as by natural understanding or by the disposition [*habitum*] of science an individual is put into the position of being rightly disposed concerning universals, in like manner, in order to make him rightly disposed with respect to particular principles of action [*principia particularia agibilium*], which are the ends, it is necessary that he be perfected by some dispositions that make it somehow connatural [*connaturale*] to him to judge correctly about the end.
>
> And this is done by moral virtue, for the virtuous individual judges correctly about the end of virtue, for "such as a person is, so the end appears to him," as it is said in Book 3 of the *Ethics* [3.5.1114a32–b1]. And hence right reason in matters of action, which is prudence, requires that one have moral virtue. (*ST* 1–2.58.5 resp.)

Aquinas here identifies particular practical principles with the ends pursued in action. For this, he depends on Aristotle (*EN* 7.8.1151a16; 6.5.1140b16–17). The end is a principle in that it is the final cause for one's actions (*Phys.* 2.9.200a19–24; *ST* 1–2.13.3 resp.). The above quotation obscures the fact, however, that it is not unique to particular principles to be identified with ends; this is true of universal principles as well, as we have seen in Section 10.2. Aquinas makes this particularly clear in *QDV* 5.1, an earlier treatment of prudence that closely corresponds to *ST* 1–2.58.5:

> The end in matters of action pre-exists in us in two ways: [in one way,] by our natural knowledge of man's end. According to the Philosopher in Book 6 of the *Ethics*, this natural knowledge pertains to understanding [*intellectum*], which concerns the principles of practical and theoretical matters; and the principles in practical matters are the ends, as is said in the same book. In another way, [the end pre-exists in us] affectively [*quantum ad affectionem*], and in this way the ends in matters of action are in us by means of the moral virtues, by which man is brought to live justly or courageously or temperately, which is as it were the proximate end in matters of action. (*QDV* 5.1 lines 136–47)

What Aquinas calls a "proximate end" here is what he calls a "particular practical principle" in *ST* 1–2.58.5. It is the end a person pursues here and now, not one that he should, but might fail, to pursue. It is not "proximate" in contrast to some "remote," that is, further or more general end, but in contrast to an end that might be intellectually grasped as good but still lacks an affective grip on the person. For this reason, Aquinas says the proximate end pre-exists in us "affectively." Its "pre-existence" does not seem to mean, however, that the end is also cognitively self-explanatory. It is true that the particular principles, like the universal principles, can be articulated in propositions that can be used as major premises of practical syllogisms, for example "one must avoid fornication" or "whatever is pleasurable must be enjoyed" (*QDM* 3.9 ad 7; see also *SLE* 6.10 lines 232–47). But unlike Aquinas's "universal principles," which are either self-evident or demonstratively deduced from self-evident principles, the particular principles are neither. Thus, while universal principles guarantee their own rightness, particular principles do not.

What is the source, then, for a correct judgment about particular principles? Aquinas tells us that the disposition of moral virtue allows for correct judgment by means of some connaturality. That moral virtue guarantees knowledge of the end is precisely the claim of the goal passage. The theoretical difficulties we have encountered in Aristotle also apply to Aquinas's adaptation of it: how can a disposition of an appetitive power provide any knowledge? Clarifying Aquinas's understanding of connaturality will help us assess what cognitive role he attributes to moral virtues. In what follows I want to show that, for Aquinas, virtuous dispositions provide the right sense of what is good in the concrete, but they do not suffice to articulate what the good of each virtue in general consists in.[12]

Aquinas finds the term "connaturality" in verb form in Robert Grosseteste's translation of *EN* 7.3, where Aristotle explains how incontinence is possible. The general idea is that one can have knowledge superficially without having appropriated it. Aristotle illustrates this with those who have just learned something but do not yet know it, because the knowledge must "grow into them" (*oportet enim connasci*, δεῖ γὰρ συμφυῆναι) (1147a22; Editio Leonina 47:389). Aquinas comments:

> The second example is about children when they first learn something. They connect words that they utter with their mouth, but they do not know them yet in such a way as to understand them with their mind. That, in fact, requires that what someone hears become as it were connatural [*connaturalia*] to him through a perfect impression of what was heard upon the intellect; and this requires time, since the intellect must think it over again and again in order to be made firm in what it has taken in. This is also the case with the incontinent man, for although he says, "It is not good for me to pursue this pleasurable thing now," he does not feel that way in his heart. (*SLE* 7.3 lines 206–18)

According to this passage, the terms of the relation of connaturality are the known object and the knower. There is connaturality when the known object is perfectly impressed upon the knower's mind. When this happens, the individual "feels it in his heart"; the knowledge becomes congenial to his or her character, that is, fully internalized. Why is it important to "feel" a judgment about an end of action "in one's heart"? For Aquinas, the will is inclined to what is apprehended as good and suitable (*bonum et conveniens*), that is, as good for the individual, here and now (*ST* 1–2.9.2; *QDM* 6 lines 420–2). When a judgment about a good becomes connatural, I apprehend a good not only as good in general, but also as good for me.

---

[12] My analysis and discussion of knowledge by connaturality has greatly profited from Caldera 1980. In an important respect my interpretation differs from his, for he makes the much stronger claim that virtuous dispositions are a source of practical knowledge; see especially pp. 101–4. See also Suto 2004.

Although Aquinas only occasionally discusses knowledge by connaturality, he attributes great importance to it in his ethics and theology. The relevant texts – three of which we will consider below – are concerned with the mode of mystical knowledge that is not acquired through study but obtained through a "gift of the Holy Spirit," namely the gift of wisdom, which is a divinely infused disposition allowing one to "judge and order everything according to divine criteria" (*ST* 2–2.45.1). As we shall see, for Aquinas, the working of mystical knowledge is closely analogous to prudential knowledge; hence these texts, although stemming from a theological context, shed precious light on the dynamic of connaturality in practical judgments.

In *ST* 1.1.6, Aquinas asks whether theology (*sacra doctrina*) is wisdom. The third objection denies that theology is wisdom because theology is acquired by study, whereas wisdom, since it is a gift of the Holy Spirit, is received by infusion. In his reply, Aquinas distinguishes between two kinds of wisdom, namely as a gift of the Holy Spirit versus as acquired knowledge. He illustrates this by means of an analogy with two kinds of practical judgments:

> On the one hand, one can judge by inclination: thus, one who has the disposition of virtue judges rightly about that which is to be done according to virtue insofar as he is inclined to do those deeds. Hence it is said in Book 10 of the *Ethics* that the virtuous individual is the measure and rule of human actions [10.5.1176a15–19; cf. 3.4.1113a25–33]. In another way, one can judge by knowledge: thus someone who has learned moral science can make judgments about the acts of a virtue, even if he does not have the virtue. (*ST* 1.1.6 ad 3)

Aquinas makes the same comparison in a question that is directly concerned with the gift of wisdom. What he called "judgment by inclination" in the above quote he now calls "judgment by connaturality":

> Rectitude of judgment can come about in two ways: on the one hand, by the impeccable [*perfectum*] use of reason; on the other, because of some connaturality with that which one is about to judge. Thus in matters of chastity, one who has learned moral science judges correctly through the investigation of reason, but one who has the disposition of chastity judges correctly by some connaturality to these matters. (*ST* 2–2.45.2 resp.)

In his commentary on the *Divine Names*, Aquinas makes the relation between judgment by connaturality and desire clearer. Pseudo-Dionysius maintains that an individual who is divinely inspired attains knowledge not only by learning but also by *"patiens divina"* (παθὼν τὰ θεῖα), that is, thanks to a loving union with God (*De divinis nominibus* 2.9, ed. Suchla, 134).[13] Aquinas appropriates this idea and elaborates it further. To gain knowledge of divine things *"patiens divina"* means to do so

> not merely by acquiring scientific knowledge about divine things in the intellect, but also by love [*diligendo*], being united to the divine things by loving will [*per affectum*]. In fact, undergoing [*passio*] something seems to belong more to desire than to knowledge, because the known is in the knower according to the mode of the knower and not according to the mode of the known things, but desire stretches out to the things desired according to the mode in which they are in themselves, and thus enters somehow into an intimate relation to them [*ad ipsas res quodammodo afficitur*]. Just as the virtuous individual achieves right judgment about that which pertains to his virtue from the disposition of virtue that is in his appetitive power [*in affectu*], so he who intimately relates [*afficitur*] to divine things receives right judgment regarding divine things by divine influence. (*In De divinis nominibus* 2.4 nn. 190–2)

What this text adds to the two passages considered above is an explanation of the role of desire in the judgment by connaturality. When an object becomes connatural to us, it engages not only our intellect but also our affective powers. Intellect and will have different relations to the object of their operation: the intellect relates to an object in that the notion (*ratio*) of the understood thing is in the knower, whereas the will relates to it by an inclination to the thing itself, in its concrete existence (see also *ST* 1.82.3). Because of its affective component, knowledge by connaturality allows one to experience the good present before one in an immediate way, while discursive knowledge only provides a conceptual grasp of the object's goodness. Since the intellect apprehends the movements of the will (*ST* 1.87.4 ad 1), one can perceive an object as valuable by means of a judgment by connaturality because of the intellect's apprehension of the affective reaction to the experienced good (see Caldera 1980, 66–8).

Are virtuous dispositions, then, a source for practical judgments? In some sense, Aquinas seems to think so. In all three of the above quotations he states that the virtuous individual acquires right judgment about virtue from the disposition of virtue itself. Elsewhere he even compares the judgment of the virtuous person with assent to self-evident principles, thus suggesting that this judgment is intuitive (*ST* 2–2.2.3 ad 2). The source of this judgment is an experience of congruence or fittingness (*convenientia*) between the good presented and one's disposition of

---

[13] Elsewhere, Aquinas explains the Dionysian expression of *"pati divina"* as follows: "passio divinorum ibi dicitur affectio ad divina, et coniunctio ad ipsa per amorem" (*ST* 1–2.22.3 ad 1).

virtue, as Aquinas expresses elegantly when commenting on the Aristotelian *spoudaios*-doctrine of *EN* 3.4.1113a25–33:

> He says that the virtuous individual judges correctly about particular things pertaining to human actions; in these particular things, what appears good to him is indeed truly good. This is so because every disposition perceives that which is proper to it, that is, that which is in agreement with it [*quae ei conveniunt*], as good and pleasurable. But that which is in agreement with the disposition of virtue is truly good, because a disposition of moral virtue is defined by its being in accord with right reason. Therefore that which is according to reason, which is unqualifiedly good, appears to him as good. And in this regard, the excellent person [*studiosus*, translating σπουδαῖος] differs greatly from the others, for in particular matters of action he sees what is truly good, as though he were the living standard and measure of all matters of action; for, in these matters, things are to be judged good or bad according to how they appear to him. (*SLE* 3.10 lines 76–91)

Yet although virtuous dispositions allow for a judgment by inclination that provides some knowledge of the goods pertaining to that virtue, this is insufficient to articulate an account of those goods. The judgment by inclination relies on the fact that the virtuous individual is in the presence of some good pertaining to virtue. But this experience discloses only *that* the present good is good, not *why* it is so. There is also a second, more fatal impediment against virtuous dispositions providing an account of the goods of virtue. In order to rightly claim that something is good because one experiences it as in agreement with one's virtue, one would have to know that one actually is a virtuous individual. This knowledge cannot come from connaturality in its own turn. In fact, according to Aquinas, one may perceive that one's acts stem from a certain disposition, but in order to know that this is a virtuous disposition, one needs to have some definitional knowledge of what that disposition is: "I cannot know that I have chastity unless I know what chastity is" (*QDV* 10.9 lines 157–61). Accordingly, although the virtuous objectively have correct knowledge of the ends of the moral virtues, nonetheless, since one cannot know by connaturality whether one is virtuous, without moral science they cannot be subjectively certain that they do indeed have the right moral perception. Therefore, possession of the moral virtues does not by itself provide the resources to determine what the good of the virtues consists in. Indeed, Aquinas states explicitly that it is not the moral virtues that determine the end but rather natural reason, that is, *synderesis* (*ST* 2–2.47.6 ad 1 and ad 3). Because of the affective support they provide, particular practical principles are crucial to avoid the corruption of universal practical principles in the concrete (*ST* 1–2.58.5). But they cannot articulate what the good of virtue consists in and why it is a good. For this, universal practical principles (that is, self-evident principles and moral science) are indispensable, although probably not by themselves sufficient.

Accordingly, Aquinas holds that prudence depends on both universal and particular practical principles (*ST* 1–2.58.5). In fact, prudence applies universal principles to the concrete situation (e.g., *ST* 2–2.47.3, 47.6, 47.15). How might Aquinas think this happens concretely? Let us consider the case of chastity, one of his own favorite examples. In the *Secunda Secundae*, he uses rational considerations (that is, moral science) to argue for the value of chastity, incidentally by tacitly using considerations from *EN* 3.12.1119b8–10 about intemperance: consenting to sexual pleasure makes the desire grow (rather than appeasing it) and obstructs the use of reason (*ST* 2–2.151.3 ad 2). These considerations from moral science reveal why chastity is a worthwhile end, but they still have limited motivational power. Moral science is not necessarily sustained by the appetitive power; only prudence requires an appetitive foundation (*SLE* 6.7 lines 87–95; *ST* 2–2.47.4). The prudential judgment therefore has a motivational force that moral science lacks, and this force results from connaturality, by which the good of virtue is apprehended as *conveniens*, that is, correspondent, agreeable, good for me in the here and now. Therefore, as long as the prudential judgment lasts, one cannot act against it (*QDVCom* 6 ad 1).

How, then, does Aquinas understand the goal passage? In the *SLE* he glosses that moral virtue secures a right intention for the end by inclining the appetitive power to the due end (*SLE* 6.10 lines 152–5). Expressed differently, the moral virtues secure the "particular principles" (*ST* 1–2.58.5) or the "proximate ends" (*QDV* 5.1). But an articulate account of the end that would determine why something is indeed a right end can only be had by means of universal principles.

An important misunderstanding must be avoided, however: Aquinas does not hold that the particular dictate of prudence is deduced from universal principles (see Hibbs 2001, 88–98). Only to a small degree can necessary conclusions be deduced from the first practical principles. Thus, for example, from the principle that one must not do harm to anyone, one can conclude that one must not kill (*ST* 1–2.95.2); the principle that no one is to be unjustly injured entails that one must not steal (*SLE* 5.12 lines 110–14). Prudence, however, relies on the cognition of particular facts, in which it is aided by qualities such as memory, docility, foresight, and the like. Aquinas calls these "integral parts" (that is, indispensable constituents) of prudence and discusses them in great detail in *ST* 2–2.49. Rather than deducing a particular decree from universal principles, prudence applies a universal principle to a concrete situation. This means that in a given situation, the prudent person is aware of which universal principle is relevant. As the case of conflicting obligations shows, deliberation about a concrete decision is done in light of universal principles, but not as a straightforward deduction from them.

10.3   Conclusion

Aquinas wholeheartedly subscribes to the goal passage's claim that the moral virtues rectify the goal. What they rectify is the "proximate goal" or the "particular practical principle," e.g., that it is good for me to live temperately right now. As I have argued, the moral virtues do not provide any articulate knowledge of what this goal consists in and why it is worthwhile. This seems to motivate Aquinas to integrate the goal passage into a larger framework, with universal self-evident practical principles and demonstrative conclusions from them as the warrants for correct orientation in the moral life. Prudence now depends not only on the moral virtues, as it did for Aristotle, but also on the intellectual virtue of understanding as that which allows for knowledge of universal practical principles (ST 1–2.58.4 resp.; ST 2–2.47.6 ad 3). By means of these universal practical principles Aquinas anchors all moral knowledge in fixed foundations that are given with human nature. For Aquinas, the universal practical principles are naturally knowable by everyone and hence they are the foundation for a universally valid ethic.

The extent to which this insistence upon universal practical principles as a precondition for prudence is a departure from Aristotle depends upon one's interpretation of Aristotle himself. I think at least this much can be safely said: Aristotle acknowledges universal practical principles, such as that one ought to live according to reason, to seek happiness, to avoid cowardice, and the like.[14] But Aristotle does not have any explicit treatment of universal principles. More importantly, he does not ground ethics in self-evident practical principles but rather in principles that are commonly accepted by society and that are communicated by way of moral upbringing. Therefore, Aristotle's universal principles have a certain flexibility to them (Owens 1996, ch. 9).

---

[14] Irwin 2000; see also Reeve 2012, 147–50 and 191–4. Accordingly, Aquinas's insistence that prudence applies universal principles to concrete cases does not seem to contradict Aristotle's account, pace Deman 2006, 426–43 and Gauthier and Jolif 1970, I,1:278–9.

To what degree Aquinas is self-conscious about his departure from Aristotle is not clear. In his *Ethics* commentary, he frequently refers to self-evident propositions to explain Aristotelian doctrines. He grounds the possibility of virtue acquisition in them (*SLE* 2.4 lines 97–106); he uses them to explain Aristotle's notion of the "just by nature" and mentions as examples "evil is to be avoided," "no one is to be unjustly harmed," and "one must not steal."[15] Likewise, in his commentary on the *De anima*, Aquinas explains Aristotle's statement that the understanding is always right while desire and imagination are sometimes right and sometimes wrong (*An.* 3.10.433a26–7) by pointing out that there is no error in the grasp of first practical principles such as "No one is to be harmed" and "Injustice is not to be done to anyone" (*SLA* 3.9 lines 104–10).

To make prudence depend upon one's understanding of self-evident universal practical principles is not Aquinas's invention; Albert the Great had made this move before him in his first *Ethics* commentary (Payer 1979, 66; Celano 1995, 236). From the perspective of a Christian medieval thinker, this theory fits nicely with the traditional teaching of *synderesis* as the infallible underpinning for the judgments of conscience, as well as with the doctrine of the natural law.

While Aquinas's theory of universal practical principles differs in important respects from Aristotle's teaching, his account of particular practical principles seems instead to be an elaboration of it. Whether for Aristotle the moral virtues have a cognitive role or not is controversial (e.g., for Moss 2011 they do, while for Price 2011 they do not). What is uncontroversial is that, according to Aristotle and Aquinas, the moral virtues put a person into the right position to judge about the principles, that is, the ends, while vice corrupts such judgments. Like Aristotle, Aquinas emphasizes therefore that prudence presupposes the ordering of the affections by the moral virtues, which prevent us from losing sight of the virtuous ends. With his theory of connatural knowledge, Aquinas can give a more elaborate account than Aristotle of how this is the case.

---

[15] *SLE* 5.12 lines 49–64. Cf. Melina 1987, 78–84; Perkams 2008a, 143–5.

CHAPTER ELEVEN

Aquinas on incontinence and psychological weakness

Martin Pickavé

We often experience that our beliefs are utterly inefficacious when it comes to setting ourselves up to undertake a particular course of action. Even worse: sometimes it seems that we entertain a belief and act against it at the very same moment. But how is this possible? Philosophers of all ages have wondered how an agent can fail to set herself up to undertake an action that she knows is in accordance with what would be best to do. The great interest this question enjoys among philosophers no doubt has to do with the fact that it touches on core issues in the philosophy of action. How can we fail to do what we know would be best to do, if it is characteristic of human agents to act on account of reasons? And isn't a belief regarding what we ought to do a reason for action? What exactly is the relationship between reasons and action? And what kind of knowledge does the agent really have in the first place if she is unable to bring herself to act on it? It should come as no surprise that Thomas Aquinas too was intrigued by these issues.

In this contribution I would like to reexamine Aquinas's account of this phenomenon of acting contrary to our own best knowledge. The topic has received growing attention in recent scholarly literature on Aquinas, so it may not be immediately obvious why we would need yet another study of it. However, it is my contention that most of the recent literature does not pay enough attention to the fact that Aquinas's thinking on this issue is closely tied to his interpretation of the relevant passages in Aristotle's *Nicomachean Ethics*. All interpreters are of course aware that Aquinas's *Ethics* commentary is one of the main texts where he deals with the issue in question, but I believe that a close look at his reading of Aristotle can still provide us with some new and important insights.

Contemporary philosophers use the expression "weakness of will" when they discuss the inability to act on one's knowledge, yet Aquinas speaks primarily about *incontinentia* ('incontinence'), which in turn is the common Latin translation of Aristotle's *akrasia*. As will become clear below, incontinence is a rather specific condition. But in order not to jump directly to the conclusion I shall proceed in the following way. First I shall deal with various aspects of Aquinas's account of incontinence in his commentary on the *Nicomachean Ethics* (Sections 11.1–11.3), before I move on to Aquinas's other works (Section 11.4). Like Aristotle, Aquinas frequently contrasts incontinence with temperance and its opposite vice, intemperance. I shall follow him in this, since it will tell us more about the scope of incontinence (Section 11.5). Finally, I will draw some conclusions regarding the philosophical lessons one can draw from Aquinas's understanding of incontinence.[1]

11.1 Incontinence and knowledge in the *Sententia libri Ethicorum*

The centerpiece of Aristotle's discussion of incontinence (ἀκρασία) in Book 7 of the *Nicomachean Ethics* is chapter 3, where he discusses the knowledge of the incontinent agent. Aquinas explains the fact that Aristotle chooses to solve this problem first by reminding the reader of Socrates's denial of this sort of moral weakness. According to Socrates, no one is capable of acting against what one knows one ought to do. For Socrates, an incontinent person who, under the influence of her emotions, abandons what she thinks is best to do, simply does not know what it is best to do; for if she really knew, she would act in accordance with her knowledge. So before we proceed to examine what exactly incontinence is, we first have to face the Socratic challenge and show that the condition actually exists. And insofar as this question of whether or not incontinence exists at all will involve an exploration into the knowledge of the incontinent agent, Aquinas considers it appropriate that Aristotle addresses the epistemological question first (*SLE* 7.3 lines 11–20).

Of course, to understand how it is possible to act against one's knowledge we have to be more precise about what we mean by "knowledge," and distinguish different ways of knowing. Aquinas highlights three relevant distinctions. The first is the distinction between merely habitual knowledge and habitual knowledge that has been actualized, i.e., is being "used." For "it makes a great difference whether someone who is doing what she ought not has habitual knowledge but does not use it, or has the habit

---

[1] The correct translation of terms such as *incontinentia* or *temperantia* (and cognate forms) is a matter of debate. I use the transliterations despite their strange connotations because, as will become clear later, incontinence and temperance are for Aquinas much more specific states than those we usually associate with expressions such as "lack of self-control," "moral weakness," and "moderation," terms that are sometimes employed as translations of *incontinentia* and *temperantia*.

and does use it in thinking" (*SLE* 7.3 lines 136–9; see *EN* 7.3.1146b31–4).[2] The second important distinction is between knowing a particular proposition and knowing a universal one (*SLE* 7.3 lines 144–53; see *EN* 1146b35–1147a4). Both kinds of propositions are employed in practical reasoning (*ratio practica*), for the goal of practical reasoning is to apply general considerations to particular situations. This is impossible without employing general beliefs (such as "theft is bad") and beliefs about this or that particular object or circumstance (such as "taking this bill from that person's wallet is theft"). Consequently, it should make a difference whether one is said to act against the knowledge of a particular proposition or against knowledge of a universal one. These two distinctions lead Aquinas to a first response to Socrates's challenge:

> Therefore what appeared impossible to Socrates differs so much according to these various modes of knowing that it does not seem problematic for a human being who acts incontinently [*incontinenter*] to have one kind of knowledge, i.e., universal knowledge alone, or even particular knowledge, if it is habitual but not actual. But it would seem inconvenient for the human being who acts incontinently to have another kind of knowledge, i.e., actual particular knowledge. (*SLE* 7.3 lines 163–70)

As we can see, the distinctions between actual and habitual knowledge, on the one hand, and between particular and universal knowledge, on the other, form for Aquinas the core of Aristotle's account of how incontinence is possible. Although the quoted passage is loosely based on Aristotle's own words (see *EN* 1147a8–10), Aquinas here draws a much more decisive conclusion by inserting an explicit reference to the Socratic challenge, a feature that goes beyond Aristotle's text. Notice also that Aristotle does not mention incontinence (ἀκρασία) when he himself introduces the two distinctions, leaving it open in what sense exactly the distinctions are relevant to the explanation of incontinence. By explicitly mentioning incontinent action, Aquinas makes clear what role he thinks these distinctions play in delineating the incontinent person's knowledge.

From what we can see, Aquinas and "his" Aristotle agree with Socrates that it is impossible to act against knowledge, but the Socratic claim requires a clarification, namely that it is impossible to act against *actual particular* knowledge. Socrates was right insofar as it is impossible to have actual particular knowledge that, say, this particular action is bad, and at the

---

[2] Here and in the following I use, with modifications, C. J. Litzinger's translation of the *SLE*. Translations from Aquinas's other works are my own.

same time to act in a way that is contrary to this knowledge.[3] Yet it does not follow that we cannot act against other forms of knowledge, and experience teaches us clearly that many people exhibit incontinent behavior.

But why it is impossible for someone to have an actual *particular* belief while simultaneously acting against it? The reason seems obvious: since human action is always accompanied by and grounded in a belief (directing that action), it would follow that the agent not only entertains but also affirms two contradictory beliefs at the same time. There is, however, no such problem when a habitual particular belief exists in the mind at the same time as a contradictorily opposed actual particular belief (directing the action), for, as Aquinas says elsewhere, acts and habitual dispositions are of different kinds (*QDM* 3.10 ad 5; *ST* 1–2.77.2 ad 3). And why is there no logical inconsistency in having an actual *universal* belief and acting against it? As he explains again elsewhere, acting against universal knowledge does not involve my holding that, say, fornication is evil and to be shunned, while at the same time consciously pursuing an act of fornication in the belief that this act of fornication should be pursued. For this would entail having two mutually exclusive beliefs at the same time, namely that "all fornication is evil" and "this fornication is good."[4] Rather, acting against active universal knowledge somehow involves the action guiding particular belief being "de facto" opposed to universal knowledge, but not in the way in which the belief conceptualizes the action.[5]

So far so good. Nonetheless, Aquinas's Aristotelian response – namely that acting against knowledge is possible so long as the knowledge at issue is not active particular knowledge – leads to two further questions. First, how is it possible for one to have active "*universal* knowledge alone," i.e., without the correlative active particular knowledge? Suppose I am a botanist. Isn't the activation of my universal knowledge, for instance, my knowledge about roses, always tied to my relevant active particular knowledge ("this is a rose")? But if so, how can I have active universal knowledge regarding, say, fornication if I do not think about some particular act as an instance

---

[3] However, it is possible, broadly speaking, to act against actual particular knowledge, since, as Aristotle and Aquinas emphasize later (*EN* 7.3.1147b15–17; *SLE* 7.3 lines 324–7), it is this knowledge (but not universal knowledge) that can be affected by the passions; thus at any given moment I can act against the active particular knowledge I had at a *previous* moment.

[4] In Aquinas's words: "It is impossible that someone at the same time have knowledge or true belief regarding an affirmative universal proposition and a false belief about a negative particular one, or vice versa" (*QDM* 3.9 ad 5; see also *ST* 1–2.77.2 ad 3).

[5] In this sense the particular belief "this sexual pleasure is to be pursued" and the ensuing action are opposed to (but compatible with) the active universal belief "all fornication is evil."

of fornication? The second question is how it could be possible to have *habitual* particular knowledge without it also being actual.

Let's start with the second question, since that's the one Aquinas's Aristotle takes up explicitly. How is it that certain pieces of knowledge can remain habitual in situations that normally call for their activation? Take a mathematician: faced with a blackboard and a mathematical formula written on it, the mathematician normally will activate the relevant bits of his knowledge. Granted, the mathematician's habitual knowledge is merely universal. But if it is hard to understand how habitual universal knowledge can remain habitual in circumstances calling for its activation, it is even harder to understand how habitual *particular* knowledge can remain merely habitual, for instance, the habitual knowledge that I am a diabetic or that this is chocolate. At this point, the reader is presented with the third main distinction between ways of knowing, a distinction between two types of habitual knowledge. Some habitual knowledge is indeed such that it can be activated at will under the right kind of circumstances; in this case the knowledge is present in the knower as a "free habitual disposition" (*habitus solutus*). There is, however, another kind of habitual knowledge that cannot be so activated because it exists in the knower only as a "bound habitual disposition" (*habitus ligatus*). It would, for instance, be strange to say that a sleeping mathematician does not have habitual knowledge of math, even though she is not able to exercise her mathematical skills at will during sleep. So her knowledge must be habitual in the "bound" sense. Something similar happens in the conditions of drunkenness and frenzy (*SLE* 7.3 lines 171–83; see *EN* 1147a10–14).

How does pointing to "bound habitual dispositions" help us understand incontinence? Well, in some important respects the physiological conditions of the sleeper, the drunk, and the person in a frenzy are very similar to those of the incontinent person, who owes her state to the influence of emotions (*passiones*).[6] In all these cases physiological processes in the body interfere with cognitive capacities and render the full activation of knowledge impossible. Moreover, as the mathematician's knowledge is neither destroyed by her falling asleep or becoming drunk nor newly acquired upon her awaking or sobering up, so the incontinent person's beliefs seem

---

[6] Here and in the following I translate "*passio*" (*animae*) as "emotion." Some deny that passions are emotions, but I have argued elsewhere that we should consider Aquinas's views on passions as his account of emotions (Pickavé 2008). That Aquinas's *passiones* cover phenomena that we now would not classify as emotions is no argument against my identification. We shouldn't rule out the possibility that Aquinas has an understanding of emotions that is different from ours.

not to undergo change when the agent is exposed to strong desires; what changes is rather the way in which they are available to the agent. But since physiological processes can only interfere with cognitive capacities that use corporeal organs, namely the sensory capacities, and since the senses deal with singular objects (as opposed to the intellect, which is concerned with universals), the incontinent agent has a "bound habitual disposition of practical knowledge" only "with respect to particulars" (*SLE* 7.3 lines 183–93; see *EN* 1147a14–18).

At this point we can see that the idea of "bound habitual dispositions" offers answers to both of the two questions raised earlier. It explains how an agent's particular knowledge can sometimes be merely habitual, for the actualization of such knowledge can be blocked by physiological factors, and it also seems to explain how an agent can have active universal knowledge without any corresponding active particular knowledge. It might be true that universal knowledge can never become active without this active particular knowledge; but once the universal knowledge has been actualized, the agent's particular knowledge might become "bound" under the influence of emotions and strong desires, leaving the universal knowledge active but unconnected to a particular object or circumstance. That some incontinent agents pay lip service to what they ought not do, even in the situation where they are exhibiting their incontinent behavior, is no indication that actual particular knowledge is present in them. Aristotle illustrates the point with two examples where verbal expression is obviously not directly linked to the corresponding active mental state: the case of a drunk reciting verses of Empedocles, and that of learners who merely repeat the teacher's words without already possessing an actual understanding of what the verses and words are about. Aquinas dedicates a great deal of attention to explaining Aristotle's reply to this objection (*SLE* 7.3 lines 194–220; see *EN* 1147a18–22).

Aquinas's Aristotelian account of incontinence might appear puzzling. On the one hand, Aquinas considers it impossible to act against actual particular knowledge; on the other hand, he maintains that it is precisely particular knowledge that desires and bodily pleasures can tamper with. This puzzle, however, is easily dispelled. By the first claim he means simply that we cannot have actual particular knowledge forbidding an action and at the same time intentionally carry out that very same action; for in that case we would be in two contradictory mental states at the same time. But because of its dependence on the senses and their bodily organs, particular knowledge can be impeded from being actualized or, if it is already actual, it can be disabled ("bound"); thus our desires and pleasures can put us in a new state of mind without causing us to simultaneously possess two conflicting items of actual particular knowledge.

11.2 The syllogism of the incontinent agent

In his commentary on the *Nicomachean Ethics*, Aquinas makes it look as if the answer to the Socratic challenge, and thus to the question regarding the knowledge of incontinent people, is sufficiently settled by means of the three distinctions between different ways of knowing. This is also confirmed by the way he describes the structure of Aristotle's text.[7] Yet, Aristotle's chapter and Aquinas's *lectio* are not finished, for there remains a lengthy passage in which Aristotle puts particular emphasis on the incontinent agent's reasoning. According to Aquinas, this passage contains a further attempt to answer the question of how someone can act against one's own better knowledge. Before we move on to this last part, it is necessary to stress that Aquinas's way of reading Aristotle's solution (i.e., as articulated in three major distinctions followed by a further solution) shows us Aquinas's take on one of the central interpretative puzzles posed by Aristotle's text. In *EN* 7.3, the four pieces of text containing, respectively, the three distinctions and the final passage are separated from each other by the adverb "further" (ἔτι, Lat. *adhuc*; see *EN* 1146b35, 1147a10, a24). According to some modern commentators, these four passages each present somewhat different solutions to the problem of how the akratic agent can act against knowledge. For some, Aristotle's answer is already fully present in the passage detailing the distinction between actual and habitual knowledge; others see Aristotle as engaging in a gradual approach culminating in the fourth and last passage; still others see Aristotle as addressing different forms of weakness in the different passages.[8] With this background in mind, we will be better able to appreciate Aquinas's interpretive moves.

In Aquinas's own words, the last part of Aristotle's chapter deals with doubts regarding the possibility of incontinence "according to the natural process of practical knowledge" (*secundum naturalem processum practicae scientiae*; *SLE* 7.3 lines 222–3). It is in this part that Aristotle describes, in the words of Aquinas and his medieval contemporaries, the "syllogism of

---

[7] In his outline of the last two thirds of the *lectio* Aquinas writes (*SLE* 7.3 lines 126–30): "Deinde cum dicit: *Sed quia dupliciter* etc., ponit veram solutionem. Et primo solvit dubitationem per quasdam distinctiones; secundo per naturam ipsius operativae scientiae, ibi: *Adhuc autem, et si naturaliter* etc." This indicates that the three distinctions were meant to have already solved the issue in question.

[8] For a discussion of these different approaches, see Pickavé and Whiting 2008, 332–3.

the incontinent." Aquinas's way of rendering the syllogism of the incontinent has received much attention, in part because he presents different versions of the syllogism throughout his works. These differences seem even more significant given that many modern commentators consider Aquinas's account of the syllogism of the incontinent to be the core of his account of incontinence.[9] However, in light of the textual observations just discussed, the modern obsession with the incontinent agent's syllogism is somewhat surprising. Notice also that, in the discussion of incontinence in both the *Disputed Questions on Evil* (*QDM* 3.9) and the *Prima Secundae* of the *Summa theologiae* (*ST* 1–2.77.2), Aquinas separates his description of the incontinent agent's syllogism from his main response to the question and places it instead among the replies to the objections. Not that the responses to the objections are not to be taken seriously, but the peculiar place in which the syllogism of the incontinent is discussed indicates in my view that Aquinas considers references to the syllogism as somewhat secondary to the main answers he gives in all three texts.

All this does not mean, however, that it is not worth looking at how the three aforementioned distinctions between ways of knowing apply to the "natural process of practical knowledge." Remember that since actions have to do with particular objects and circumstances, two sorts of beliefs are crucial in practical knowledge: beliefs regarding universal propositions and beliefs regarding particular ones. Just as, in the sphere of theoretical knowledge, two adequately related beliefs will lead to a third one, namely a conclusion resulting from the previous ones, so in the sphere of practical knowledge two adequately related beliefs will lead to a conclusion – with the difference, however, that under normal circumstances an action will also follow upon this conclusion. Aquinas explains this point by expanding on Aristotle's examples, but one of them should suffice to illustrate the issue: if the agent believes that "everything sweet must be tasted" and she also believes that this particular object in front of her is sweet, then the belief that this thing should be tasted arises in her naturally and she will act accordingly, if nothing prevents her (*SLE* 7.3 lines 230–45; see *EN* 1147a25–31).

This account of "the natural process of practical knowledge" allows us now to see where incontinence can creep in. For unlike temperate or intemperate agents who view an individual action or object in a certain light and decide in light of their general beliefs whether to pursue the action

---

[9] Examples of this tendency are Bradley 2008 and Barnwell 2010.

or object,[10] the mindset of the incontinent agent is more complicated. Insofar as the incontinent agent knows, for instance, that "sweets should not be tasted outside a certain time," she has the right universal belief. Yet because of the desire aroused by the perception of something sweet, her sensitive appetite suggests a new universal belief to her, namely that "all sweet things are pleasant." The desire has a further effect insofar as it blocks the particular belief "now is not the right time for sweets" from entering into the agent's consideration and being connected with the prohibiting general belief. Instead, desire makes the particular belief "this is sweet" be joined to the new (permissive) general belief. So unlike in the case of temperate or intemperate agents, the incontinent agent actually entertains four propositions: two universal ones, the particular belief "this is sweet," and the conclusion (*SLE* 7.3 lines 258–72).

Aquinas's paraphrase of Aristotle's text raises questions. Is it significant that the permissive general belief is a descriptive belief ("all sweets are pleasant") and not an imperative belief, such as "sweets should be tasted"? How significant is it that elsewhere Aquinas presents different accounts of the incontinent person's reasoning?[11] The main problem, however, is how the explanation "according to the natural process of practical knowledge" fits with Aquinas's earlier analysis of the incontinent person's knowledge. What exactly does it mean to examine incontinence "according to the natural process of practical knowledge" in the first place? We might point to Aristotle's text, which at this point speaks, equally mysteriously, of exploring *akrasia* "in a natural way" (φυσικῶς, *EN* 1147a24), but this doesn't really promise more insight, since the meaning of Aristotle's remark is highly contested.[12] Of greater help are the parallel passages in the *QDM* and the *Prima Secundae*. In both works, the incontinent person's syllogism is introduced in response to the objection that it seems impossible to have active universal knowledge (e.g., that fornication is bad) and at the same time to lack the corresponding particular knowledge (e.g., that this action here would be fornication) (*QDM* 3.9 arg. 7; *ST* 1–2.77.2 arg. 4). The objections and responses in both texts seem to vary only in length,

---

[10] For the practical syllogism of the intemperate agent, see the previous example about tasting something sweet. For the temperate person's practical knowledge, Aquinas gives the following example: "Everything unethical [*inhonestum*] should be avoided"; "This action is unethical"; "Therefore this action should be avoided" (*SLE* 7.3 lines 234–7).

[11] For a detailed analysis of the various incontinent syllogisms in Aquinas's works, see Barnwell 2010. I agree with Barnwell and Kent (1989, 211–13 and 1995, 165–71) that the different versions of the incontinent person's syllogism do not indicate a real change in Aquinas's account, but I do not have space to argue for this in detail.

[12] See Pickavé and Whiting 2008, 346–8.

yet Aquinas's longer response in the *QDM* is a bit more helpful. He starts his response by emphasizing the choice (*electio*) of the temperate and the intemperate agents and then draws a connection from choice to deliberation (*consilium*) and finally to syllogizing. This move makes clear that for Aquinas the incontinent person's syllogism is meant to explain how the incontinent fail in their deliberation. They fail because desire interferes by blocking a particular belief that would lead them to make the morally correct inference and so to do the right thing; instead, desire gives rise to other beliefs, which move them to go astray.

If this reading of the incontinent person's syllogism is correct, it would help to explain why the syllogism is not so central in Aquinas's account of incontinence. For as Aristotle explains later in Book 7, there are two types of incontinent agents: the impetuous and the weak.[13] Whereas the former do not deliberate at all but instantly abandon previously held beliefs when tempted by desires and pleasures, the weak are said to deliberate but fail to abide by the results of their deliberation. The incontinent person's syllogism thus appears relevant only in the description of weak incontinence and not for an account of incontinence as such.

11.3 What exactly is incontinence?

Human beings seem to succumb to incontinence because of that part of their nature which they share with animals, for it is in the lower-level appetitive powers that the relevant emotions (*passiones*) and desires arise. And although non-rational animals are incapable of incontinent behavior in the sense described here, insofar as they lack the sort of knowledge we are capable of acting against (*SLE* 7.3 lines 291–5), the emotions that lead us to abandon our better judgment appear to be triggered in us by external objects (such as sweets). Hence it looks as if we aren't really responsible for what we are doing when we act incontinently. Aquinas, however, rejects this line of reasoning. Incontinent behavior is voluntary – and we are thus responsible for it – not only because it proceeds from within us, i.e., from our emotions, but also because it is done with knowledge. The incontinent agent knows what she does, she knows the circumstances of her action, and she even knows that the action is bad (*SLE* 7.10 lines 67–9); she therefore cannot invoke any sort of responsibility-cancelling ignorance. Furthermore, it would be a mistake to believe that we cannot be responsible

---

[13] See *EN* 7.7.1150b19–28. Aquinas comments on this distinction in *SLE* 7.7. That Aquinas refers to "weakness" (*debilitas*; lines 202–36) as a particular species of lack of control provides an additional reason why "weakness" is a problematic translation for *incontinentia*.

for our emotions and for what follows from them. Aquinas discusses the responsibility we have for our emotions in various works. The key idea is always that emotions can be moderated and controlled through our reason and will. Even if that control is sometimes only indirect, it is robust enough to establish that we are responsible for them.[14]

One might wonder what kind of psychological condition incontinence is. It is obviously not a habitual disposition like temperance or intemperance, i.e., a disposition acquired through repeated acts of a similar kind, for these dispositions are said to remain in the agent and to continue to incline her to make certain choices even when she doesn't use them. Someone who always acts against her better judgment because she has a stable disposition inclining her to do what is opposed to her better judgment is not incontinent, but rather someone with a very peculiar vice. Nevertheless, incontinence looks like a disposition insofar as it describes the condition of an agent, a condition that is not expressed by a single uncontrolled act. For this reason, Aquinas has no problems with referring to incontinence as a *habitus*. An example that Aquinas borrows from Aristotle is meant to illustrate the peculiar dispositional character of incontinence: the incontinent are like epileptics. Someone prone to epileptic fits possesses a certain disposition, but epilepsy is not like a normal disease insofar as it only manifests itself episodically, whereas other diseases manifest themselves over a longer period of time. Similarly, incontinence does not persist in the agent and is only active at the moment in which she is overcome by emotions (*SLE* 7.8 lines 33–43).

Since incontinence is voluntary and involves non-conformity to the dictates of right reason, it fulfills the conditions for moral badness (*SLE* 7.8 lines 165–70). And because of its transitory character, Aquinas terms it a "transitory vice" (*malitia non continua*; *SLE* 7.8 lines 43 and 85). Aquinas locates virtues and vices, such as courage, intemperance, justice, and injustice, in various psychological powers.[15] Hence the question arises where incontinence should be located. The answer seems obvious: isn't the sensitive appetite, the power responsible for our emotions (*passiones*), the "seat" or the "subject" of incontinence, since emotions are the immediate causes for the condition? However, Aquinas rejects this conclusion:

> We cannot say that the subject of each [i.e., continence and incontinence] is the concupiscible appetite since the continent and the incontinent do not differ with respect to their desires, both having evil ones; nor is reason the

[14] See, e.g., *ST* 1–2.17.7 and 1–2.74.3. For a detailed treatment, see Murphy 1999.
[15] See, e.g., *ST* 1–2.61.2; *QDVCard* 1.

subject of each since both have right reason. It remains then that the subject of each is the will because the incontinent agent willingly sins, as was just pointed out; the continent agent willingly keeps to reason. (*SLE* 7.10 lines 89–97)

The main difference between incontinent and continent agents consists in their respective wills.[16] Needless to say, the will, understood here as a psychological power, does not appear in Aristotle's text; the remark is thus Aquinas's own addition. That Aquinas alludes to the will is instructive. First, it indicates that, for him, incontinence is in some sense a weakness of the will, for it is ultimately the incontinent agent's will that allows the emotions to take over. Yet this should not lead us to the conclusion that incontinence really is a *weakness* of the will. A weakness of the will, whatever this might be, has no place in Aquinas's explanation of incontinent behavior.[17] He points to our emotions (*passiones*) wherever he is concerned with explaining how instances of incontinence occur. Second, if the will should be deemed the subject of incontinence insofar as the agent sins willingly (*volens*) in incontinent action, then we must ask in what sense the will is involved in these actions. Following Aristotle, Aquinas stresses that the incontinent person does not act from choice (*ex electione*).[18] For unlike temperate and intemperate agents, who shun or pursue bodily pleasures because they consider them good or bad beyond a certain measure, the incontinent agent does not properly choose what she ends up doing, i.e., indulging in sweets or sexual intercourse. She indulges in these things despite what she herself considers good and choiceworthy. Incontinence occurs notwithstanding the fact that the agent's choice (*electio*) is a good one and resembles that of the temperate and the prudent agent (*SLE* 7.10 lines 54–6 and 69–70; see *EN* 7.10.1152a17).[19] This explains why we consider the failure of the incontinent person to be less blameworthy than the failure of the intemperate person, whose choice is bad (*SLE* 7.4 lines 118–29 and 7.8).[20]

The will's involvement in incontinent action leads to two further questions that point beyond the *Ethics* commentary. First, if the will is indeed involved in such behavior (and it would seem that it must be, given that

---

[16] See also *ST* 2–2.155.3.

[17] Kent 2007 argues forcefully and, in my view, convincingly for this point.

[18] See *SLE* 7.7 lines 76–107 and 119–21, 7.8 lines 18–24 and 103–11, 7.9 lines 241–5. These passages render Aristotle's line that the akratic agent does not act from *prohairesis* (*EN* 7.4.1148a13–17, 7.7.1150a19–31, and 7.8.1151a1–14).

[19] In *SLE* 7.8 lines 158–9, Aquinas adds – somewhat misinterpreting Aristotle (*EN* 7.8.1151a24) – that the incontinent retain the "best principle" (*optimum principium*). On this point, see Chapter 2, Section 2.1, in this volume.

[20] See also *ST* 1–2.78.4; 2–2.156.3; *QDM* 3.13.

there is no human action outside of the will's control), doesn't this mean that the will in some sense chooses uncontrolled behavior? And second, Aquinas seems to be committed to the idea that the will can choose only what appears to the agent as good. Yet doesn't this entail that, despite what Aquinas says to the contrary, the uncontrolled agent possesses a wrong conception of what is good?

11.4   Incontinence in Aquinas's other works

As we have already seen, the *Ethics* commentary is not the only work in which Aquinas deals with the phenomenon of incontinence. The topic receives further attention in his *Disputed Questions on Evil* and the *Summa theologiae* (both in the *Prima Secundae* and the *Secunda Secundae*).[21] Although all these works date from roughly the same time,[22] interpreters have wondered whether there are significant differences between the commentary and Aquinas's theological works, and whether as a result the theological works would not be a better guide to Aquinas's own thoughts on incontinence.[23] Yet one thing emerges from all of Aquinas's texts on the issue: incontinence is due to the fact that strong emotions (*passiones*) either prevent an item of particular knowledge from linking up with a prohibiting general belief, thus leaving the agent only with active universal knowledge, or else make it the case that an item of particular knowledge is reduced to a "bound habitual disposition." The incontinent agent's knowledge of what one ought not do thus remains only general or habitual: she does not possess active particular knowledge of the right kind at the moment when she acts.

The most natural way to read the account of incontinence in Aquinas's theological works is as adding to the account we find in his *Ethics* commentary. Good examples are the two questions with which I closed the previous section. In his theological works Aquinas is more explicit about the fact that if the will is involved in incontinent action, then the agent must also in some way be choosing, as a result he is not reluctant to speak of the

---

[21]   Some commentators are also drawn to Aquinas's commentary on Paul's letter to the Romans, and in particular to his comments on Romans 7:14–25, as a further text for Aquinas's understanding of incontinence. However, I agree with Kretzmann 1988 that incontinence is not an issue in the relevant passages of this commentary.

[22]   The relevant part of the *QDM* was published in 1270, and Aquinas worked on the *Prima Secundae* between early 1269 and late 1270; the *Ethics* commentary and the *Secunda Secundae* date from 1271–72. For the chronology of Aquinas's works, see Torrell 2005, 333–43.

[23]   See, for instance, Saarinen 1994, 119.

incontinent person as someone who is choosing.[24] However, as Bonnie Kent has pointed out, Aquinas draws a crucial distinction between doing something *eligens* ('while choosing') and doing it *ex electione* ('from choice'). Aquinas explains this distinction as follows:

> It is one thing to sin while choosing and another to sin from choice. For the one who sins from passion sins while choosing, but does not sin from choice, because in this person choice is not the first principle of the sin. Rather, the person is moved by passion to choose that which she would not choose in the absence of passion. But the person who sins from deliberate malice [*ex certa malitia*] chooses evil of her own accord . . . And therefore the choice that is in her is the first principle of her sin, and because of this she is said to sin from choice. (*ST* 1–2.78.4 ad 3)[25]

Since this distinction builds on the difference between acting *ex passione* and *ex electione* (from *SLE* 7.7), it is unclear why it should indicate a change of mind rather than a mere clarification of his account. In any case, his theological works offer Aquinas more opportunities to develop what exactly the incontinent agent's choosing amounts to, an endeavor that requires a more thorough examination of the acts of the will. In this respect, many scholars have rightly remarked on the importance that the act of consent turns out to have in Aquinas's understanding of incontinence.[26]

This leads us to the second question left over from the *Ethics* commentary. Whatever Aquinas has in mind exactly when he says that the incontinent choose, the will can choose only what is either a real good or an apparent one. But how can the incontinent then not have a mistaken (and indeed corrupted) judgment about what is good, since they at the same time have to consider incontinent actions as good so as to be able to choose them? Aquinas raises this question himself. In his response he mentions two ways in which something bad can appear good to the will. On the one hand, it might appear so because the agent has a perverted judgment about what is good and thus thinks that objects of a certain kind

---

[24] The best illustration of this move can be found in *ST* 2–2.155.3, where Aquinas deals with the "seat" of incontinence. Aquinas reaffirms that the will is the seat of incontinence and continence alike, because the "first difference" between the incontinent and the continent lies in their choices. The former choose (*eligit*) to follow the emotions, whereas the latter choose not to.

[25] See also *QDM* 3.12 ad 5 and *QDV* 17.1 ad 4. Passages in which Aquinas says that the incontinent choose (*eligit*) also include *In Sent.* 2.28.3.3; *ST* 2–2.155.3; 2–2.156.3 ad 1; *QDM* 3.12 ad 11. See also Kent 1989, 207–9 and 1995, 160–2.

[26] For consent as an act of the will, see *ST* 1–2.15.1. The role of consent in Aquinas's account of incontinence is discussed by Irwin 2006, 50–8. I agree, however, with Kent 2007, 84, that we should not think of consent as a specific particular mental act of the will. For that would make the will the cause of incontinence, something that goes against Aquinas's contention that incontinence is caused by emotions. Consent can also consist just in the will abstaining from any further interference.

are good, although they are not. On the other hand, the agent might consider something as good not because of a mistaken belief, but because of the influence of emotions (*passiones*) (*QDM* 3.9 ad 4; *ST* 1–2.77.2 ad 2).[27] With this distinction in mind it is easy to see what happens to the moral judgment of the incontinent. For unlike in the case of the intemperate, the reason why fornication and the like appear good to the incontinent is not because they believe these sorts of things to be good; on the contrary, this is the sense in which they aren't mistaken about what is good and bad. That they nevertheless in certain instances consider a particular bad act as good is due to the influence of the emotions. For Aquinas, the emotions belong to the sensitive appetite, and strong movements of this lower appetite can resonate in the higher appetite, i.e., the will; it is not surprising that they also induce a corresponding judgment about what is good.[28] However, since the influence of the emotions is only momentary and since they do not destroy (but rather merely disable) the moral judgment of the incontinent agent, the judgment remains good. Here again Aquinas seems more to be clarifying the Aristotelian account of incontinence than proposing a modification.[29]

Despite his efforts to integrate the will into his account of incontinence, Aquinas leaves intact the role the emotions have as the "prime mover" (*primum movens*) in incontinent action (*ST* 2–2.155.3 ad 2). In one important respect, however, Aquinas's account of incontinence in the *Ethics* commentary does differ from that in his theological works. We shouldn't overlook the fact that in the often-quoted passages in the *QDM* and the *Prima Secundae* incontinence (*incontinentia*) is not, strictly speaking, the issue. Aquinas's attention there is rather devoted to what he calls "weakness" (*infirmitas*), which he considers, together with ignorance (*ignorantia*) and malice (*malitia*), to be one of the three causes of sin (see *ST* 1–2.76 pr.). It would be foolish to identify weakness with incontinence. In the *Summa*, Aquinas does not abandon Aristotle's fairly narrow understanding of incontinence as a condition involving pleasures and desires related to touch, as we can gather from his explicit treatment of incontinence in the *Secunda Secundae* (*ST* 2–2.156). Rather, the texts in the theological works

[27] See also Kent 1989, 205–6.
[28] For this sort of influence, see *QDV* 24.2 and 26.10; *ST* 1–2.9.2, 1–2.10.3, 1–2.77.1, and 1–2.77.7. There is, however, a further question as to what exactly it means to say that the incontinent momentarily consider their bad action as good. Does this also entail that they momentarily think that bodily pleasures are good *simpliciter*? See Kent 1989, 214–16, and 1995, 168–70.
[29] As B. Kent points out (1989, 213; 1995, 165–7), Aquinas in fact says elsewhere in his *Ethics* commentary that passions can lead us to consider something as good *prout nunc* but not *simpliciter* and *secundum se* (*SLE* 3.13 lines 63–73). So the substance of the replies in *QDM* and *ST* is also present there.

indicate that, for Aquinas, Aristotle's account of how one can act against one's better knowledge is not limited to incontinence in the strict sense but rather describes a somewhat more general condition, which he calls "weakness." For our practical knowledge is subject to the interference not only of the pleasures and desires associated with touch but also of any emotion (*passio*) of the sensitive appetite, or so it seems.

In line with this shift of focus, Aquinas attempts in his theological works as well to give a more fine-grained answer to what exactly the emotions do when they interfere with our knowledge. Whereas influence through physiological change is the only mechanism that Aristotle alludes to (*EN* 7.3.1147a14–18 and b6–9), Aquinas distinguishes three ways in which emotions might interfere. First, they might do so simply by distracting the mind from focusing on a specific thought. For example, my perception of a piece of chocolate and the desire arising from that perception may simply distract me from thinking that I had decided to stay off chocolate. Or, second, an emotion may impede knowledge insofar as it blocks opposing beliefs from arising. The desire for this piece of chocolate comes with a belief that this piece of chocolate is good for me now. But the presence of that belief is incompatible with the simultaneous presence of other beliefs, for instance, the belief that this piece of chocolate should be avoided. Contrary beliefs are thus kept at bay. And third, due to its psychosomatic nature, an emotion always involves a bodily change. But through bodily changes emotions are capable of affecting our sensory capacities, including our higher-level sensory capacities, and hence they manage to affect our rational capacities, which rely on input from the senses (*QDM* 3.9; *ST* 1–2.77.2). Aquinas leaves unclear whether these three mechanisms are complementary insofar as they pick out partial aspects of weakness or whether, somewhat more plausibly, they stand for three potentially independent ways in which weakness occurs.[30]

11.5 Incontinence and temperance

In contrast to "weakness" (*infirmitas*), incontinence is a specific "transitory vice" related to pleasures and desires associated with touch. To conclude this examination of incontinence, it is now time to look briefly at its corresponding virtue. It might be natural to think that, since incontinence is opposed

---

[30] For the first interpretation, see Müller 2009b, 521n; for the second, see Saarinen 1994, 121–2. Müller (522–5) offers a thorough analysis of the three processes.

to continence (*continentia*), the latter must be the moral virtue we are looking for, but this is not so. An agent is continent if she resists immoderate
pleasures and desires of touch and abides by her judgment of what is best to
do. But insofar as the continent are still subject to disordered emotions, continence falls short of the bar set for being a moral perfection (*ST* 2–2.155.1).
The perfect condition is one through which we abide by our judgment and
are not troubled by our emotions. This condition is temperance, which is
a disposition of the very psychological power responsible for the relevant
pleasures and desires. In other words, the "seat" or "subject" of temperance
is not the will, as is the case with incontinence, but the sensitive appetite.
Or to be more precise, temperance is a habitual disposition of the so-called
concupiscible appetite, one of the two sensitive appetites in charge of our
emotions (*ST* 1–2.56.4). Reason and emotions are no longer antagonists in
the temperate agent because temperance is nothing other than a "habitual conformity" (*habitualis conformitas*) of the relevant sensory appetite to
reason. Temperate people will thus have a rational response to pleasures of
touch, such as the pleasures of food, drink, and sex, meaning that they enjoy
them as is fitting: "in the right things, in the right way, and at the right time –
as reason directs" (*SLE* 3.22 lines 180–2; see also *SLE* 3.21 lines 101–22).[31]

It is typical of Aquinas's approach to the virtues and vices that he
embraces Aristotle's fine-grained phenomenology. It may not be a surprise
that he follows Aristotle's extremely narrow definition of temperance as a
virtue concerned with certain pleasures of touch, or more precisely with
those pleasures of touch that arise from food, drink, and sex, in his *Ethics*
commentary (*SLE* 3.20).[32] Yet he adopts the same narrow conception in his
theological works (*ST* 2–2.141.4). For Aquinas, as for Aristotle, temperance
and intemperance have to do with pleasures we share with even the basest
of animals – for all animals possess at least the sense of touch and can thus
experience pleasures related to this sense. This explains why temperance
is such an important virtue and why the "greatest degree of shamefulness"
(*maxima turpitudo*) is associated with intemperance; through the former
we start distinguishing ourselves from animals and through the latter we
again become like them (*SLE* 3.20 lines 50–2). We can, of course, also be
immoderate with respect to other pleasures, say, the pleasures of reading
or the pleasures of listening to classical music. But if these forms of

---

[31] See Butera 2006 on the role of reason in temperance, and Cates 2001 for a general overview of
Aquinas's account of temperance.

[32] Strictly speaking, temperance is also concerned with sorrow (*tristitia*), the opposite of pleasure, but
only secondarily, insofar as the relevant sorrows follow from the absence of the pleasures of food,
drink, and sex (*SLE* 3.21 lines 28–32).

immoderation turn out to be vices, they are clearly not instances of intemperance, with which they share only a vague resemblance. Yet, as Aquinas would point out, we should be careful not to be led astray by resemblance and pay attention to the details. The same lesson applies to incontinence. For Aristotle and Aquinas, temperance and incontinence are about exactly the same subject matter. If temperance is strictly speaking concerned only with the pleasures of food, drink, and sex, incontinence is likewise not about just any pleasure of touch but precisely about these pleasures (*ST* 2–2.155.2). Aquinas acknowledges that there are other psychological conditions similar to incontinence. He distinguishes incontinence proper from qualified forms of incontinence and other similar conditions, such as "incontinence with respect to anger" (*incontinentia irae*), "softness" (*mollitia*), and the like (*SLE* 7.4; see also *ST* 2–2.156.2). There may be good reasons to classify many of them as instances of weakness (*infirmitas*), as Aquinas seems to do in his theological works, for they all appear to involve emotions interfering with our beliefs. But we should also be careful not to lose sight of the differences.[33]

11.6 Conclusion

Aquinas's account of incontinence is a subtle attempt to develop Aristotle's teachings. In going beyond Aristotle, Aquinas not only tries to clarify the moral psychology behind the phenomenon of incontinence and to situate it with respect to wider psychological views, he also makes efforts to connect Aristotle with a somewhat different philosophical tradition. The best examples for both moves are his attempts to find a place for the will in the account of incontinence. There is, in my view, no reason to believe Aquinas made these two aspects of his approach his explicit goals, indeed quite the opposite. We should bear in mind that the Latin Aristotle is not like the Greek one; the Latin term for "will," *voluntas*, and its cognates make appearances in the Latin translations.[34] And we should not forget that Aquinas was not the first to write a commentary on the *Nicomachean Ethics* in the thirteenth century.

Aquinas has been praised for his account of incontinence because he "alters and expands Aristotle's account in ways that allow a better analysis

[33] To mention two examples: First, the qualified forms of incontinence are not as bad as unqualified incontinence (*SLE* 7.6; *ST* 2–2.156.4). Second, in *ST* 1–2.6.7 ad 2, Aquinas contrasts someone acting against knowledge from fear and someone acting against knowledge from concupiscence. There it looks as if the cognitive processes in the two cases are very different. For discussion of this passage, see also Kent 1989, 221–2.

[34] Kent 1989, 218–19 and Kent 1995, 172. See also Chapter 2, Section 2.6, in this volume.

of the incontinent person's choice."[35] I am not sure everyone would agree with this positive assessment. Whatever Aquinas's merits as a commentator and/or mender of Aristotle, his treatment of incontinence offers some important philosophical guidelines, especially to his contemporaries. The first is that good moral psychology has to take into account the complexities of the human psyche. It might be true that human responsibility – and morality with it – is grounded in a power such as the will, but this should not lead the moral psychologist to disregard other aspects of the human person. The second guideline is that good philosophy, and especially good moral philosophy, has to be attentive to details. In approaching the objects of our study we have to be as specific as is appropriate. Too much generality will bar us from real philosophical progress and will most likely lead us astray. Some modern readers reject Aquinas's narrow conception of incontinence as too wedded to a particular historical point of view and think we can easily replace it with wider accounts that would also apply today. I think this misses Aquinas's point. He might be happy to accept that his descriptions are sometimes wrong, but they should then be replaced by more precise ones, not by more general ones. Aquinas might not be the only one to offer these counsels, but that he exemplifies them in his works is part of what makes his writings so interesting and worth studying, even today.

[35] Irwin 2006, 54.

CHAPTER TWELVE

Philia *and* Caritas
Some aspects of Aquinas's reception of Aristotle's theory of friendship

Marko Fuchs

It is generally agreed today that Aquinas was deeply influenced by Aristotle's *Nicomachean Ethics* on the one hand[1] and that at the same time he transformed many of Aristotle's concepts in order to integrate them into Christian moral and religious thought on the other.[2] This is also true for the Aristotelian theory of friendship (φιλία), which Aquinas uses to interpret the central features of his genuine conception of Christian love (*caritas*), namely love of God (*dilectio Dei*) and of neighbor (*dilectio proximi*), as friendship in the highest sense (*maxime amicitia*). However, some scholars such as Harry Jaffa and Lorraine Smith Pangle seem to suggest that the Greek concept of *philia* is inherently opposed to Christian *caritas* in that the latter implicitly or explicitly excludes the former.[3] Thus, the question arises whether Aquinas's reception of Aristotle's thought on friendship can be characterized as a successful integration of the Greek theory into medieval Christian theology, or rather whether Aquinas, willingly or unwillingly, is forced by his integrative account to exclude some essential aspects of the former.

In this chapter, I shall discuss this question by comparing both theories of friendship, focusing on some of their basic features.[4] In the first section, I will give a short sketch of some of the central aspects of Aristotle's conception of *philia* in the *EN*, which Aquinas generally adopts in his *SLE* and elsewhere. In the second section, I will start working out some differences between Aristotle's *philia* and Aquinas's *amicitia*. In order to do so, I will first discuss the two theories' different concepts of friendship toward oneself as basis of friendship toward the other. Second,

---

[1] See for instance McEvoy 1996, 297. See also McEvoy 1993.
[2] Jaffa 1952 provides a still prominent defense of this thesis.
[3] See Pangle 2003, 2, and Jaffa 1952, 123–34.
[4] In other words, I will concentrate on some basic aspects of Aristotle's and Aquinas's discussions of friendship and will not investigate their philosophy or theology as a whole. For a more exhaustive discussion of Aquinas's reflection on friendship, see Schwartz 2007.

I will scrutinize Aquinas's idea that *caritas* as love of God (*dilectio Dei*) can be understood as friendship (*amicitia*) with God. Third, I will discuss the concept of charitable love as friendship toward our neighbor (*dilectio proximi*), which is based on the love of God and can extend to all mankind. The main result of this discussion will be that, though this was probably not intended by Aquinas, the concept of *caritas* as *dilectio proximi* does not seem to fully integrate Aristotelian perfect *philia* into itself, and indeed even shows a certain tendency to exclude it. I will show this with regard to a basic feature of perfect *philia*, viz., the wishing the other person well *for his or her own sake*. In the conclusion I shall summarize these results and plead for the ethical independence of perfect *philia* from theological charity.[5] I shall concentrate on the *Nicomachean Ethics*, the *Sententia libri Ethicorum*, the *Summa theologiae*, and the *Quaestio disputata De caritate*.

12.1 Basic features of Aristotle's theory of friendship

The virtue of friendship (φιλία) in its various forms is one of the most important virtues in Aristotle's ethics. Similar to justice, it is a virtue that relates the acting person toward another and not only toward him- or herself. *Philia*, however, is more basic than justice.[6] The reason is not only because, according to Aristotle, the legislators are more interested in making the citizens "friends" to each other, that is, in supporting the concord (ὁμόνοια) of a *polis*, than in implementing justice (*EN* 8.1.1155a22–6), but also because Aristotle uses the term *philia* to describe almost every conceivable kind of successful human sociality. Thus, *philia* can mean the particular friendship between individual persons as well as the just-mentioned concord among the citizens of a *polis*; it can designate relations between the members of the family as well as between lovers or business partners. This widespread range of possible meanings of *philia* is based, on the one hand, on a set of fundamental distinctions between the different species of *philiai* and, on the other, on genuine relations between them, which shall briefly be developed in what follows.

The first basic distinction is that there are three general kinds of *philia*. This distinction results from a difference between the possible "loved" objects (τὰ φιλητά) or, more precisely, from the focuses under which

---

[5] This is not meant to criticize the idea of Christian charity as such, as illustrated, e.g., in the parable of the Good Samaritan in Lk 10:25–37. The present chapter pursues no theological interests, only philosophical ones.

[6] See Sokolowski 2001, 355.

somebody can be the object of love (φίλησις), namely the good or virtuous (ἀγαθόν), the useful (χρήσιμον), and the pleasant (ἡδύ) (*EN* 8.2.1155b17–19). This tripartite structure can be reduced to a twofold one, since only the first kind, i.e., the friendship that one has for another because he or she is virtuous, is *philia* in a proper sense. Only here is the friend loved for his or her own sake; in the other two kinds of *philia* the friend is loved by the *philos* because he or she causes the latter pleasure or benefit (*EN* 8.3.1156a14–17). The second basic distinction applies to all three kinds of *philia* and refers to the status of the partners or *philoi*, i.e., the question of whether or not they are equal (*EN* 8.8.1158b1–5). Even unequal friendship is based on some proportion (ἀνάλογον) between the unequal partners (*EN* 8.8.1158b23). In the family, for instance, the unequal friendship between parent and child can be described in terms of the parent's giving life and education to the child and the child's reciprocal care for the old parent (*EN* 8.8.1158b20–3).

   All the kinds of friendship, equal and unequal, have common constitutive features. *Philiai* are based on benevolence (εὔνοια), which must be mutual (ἀντιφίλησις) (*EN* 8.2.1155b28) and known to the *philoi* (*EN* 8.2.1156a3–5). Nevertheless, the three kinds of *philia* are not species of a common genus. Only the friendship between equally virtuous persons is *philia* in the proper sense; the other two kinds are called *philiai* because they are similar (ὅμοιος) to the first one (*EN* 8.6.1157b4–5).[7] This relation of similarity (ὁμοιότης) is an important element in Aristotle's theory of friendship in *EN*, because it allows Aristotle to discuss the different kinds of human interrelation as forms of *philia* without his being forced to reduce them to one of them, namely perfect friendship. Furthermore, the concept of similarity is also important for describing the *philoi* in perfect friendship. If perfect friends are equally virtuous, it means that they are similar to each other. This aspect of his theory enables Aristotle, unlike many other philosophers of friendship, to develop a philosophy of friendship that can focus on the friend as a *particular person*, i.e., a "friend with a name."[8] This particularity of the perfect friend becomes manifest in the aspect, mentioned above, of our wishing our friend well for his or her own sake, i.e., insofar as he or she is this particular, special person; whereas in the other forms of friendship the friend is loved only because of the usefulness

---

[7] This emphasis on the similarity (ὁμοιότης) between the three kinds of *philia* distinguishes Aristotle's approach to the phenomenon of friendship in the *EN* from that in the *EE*, where he describes this relation as a πρὸς ἕν structure. See Fuchs 2011.

[8] The importance of this aspect of the friend's particularity for Aristotle's conception of perfect *philia* is emphasized by Price 1989, 103.

or pleasantness he or she affords to us. This is the reason why friends in the improper sense are replaceable. It is also the reason why Aristotle says that we cannot have many perfect friends (*EN* 8.7.1158a10–11), while surely we could have, for instance, many fellow citizens, who by Aristotle's approach would be friends in an improper sense. Another effect of Aristotle's use of the concept of similarity is a definition of the boundaries of the Aristotelian concept of friendship. Aristotle thinks that too high a degree of inequality can destroy friendship and that there can be no friendship between highly unequal partners. That is why there can be no friendship between men and gods according to Aristotle (*EN* 8.9.1159a4–5).

By mentioning these last two points, viz., the particularity of the perfect friend and the small number of perfect friends resulting from it, on the one hand, and the impossibility of being befriended to a (or the) god, on the other, we already see two major deviations of Aquinas's approach from Aristotle's. Regarding the first point, some interpreters have seen Aristotle's theory as an aristocratic and exclusive conception that Aquinas significantly broadened by transforming the concept of perfect friendship into the theological virtue of *caritas* as love of neighbor (*dilectio proximi*) – a virtue that is, as Maarten J. F. M. Hoenen (2002, 136) puts it, "cosmologically" related to all mankind. Second, Aquinas explicitly claims that charitable love of God is friendship in the highest degree (*ST* 2–2.23.1 resp.), i.e., that the primary and proper object of perfect friendship is God and not man.

Before discussing these transformations, we should observe some of the general similarities between both theories of friendship. I shall confine myself to the *SLE*, where these similarities become especially obvious since Aquinas is to a large extent simply following Aristotle there. He agrees with him that there are three kinds of friendship, which are defined by the way their object is loved: in Aquinas's terminology they are called *amicitia propter honestum, amicitia propter delectabile*, and *amicitia propter utile* (*SLE* 8.3 lines 33–5). "*Amicitia propter honestum*" means that the friend is loved because of her or his virtuous goodness (*propter bonum virtutis*; *SLE* 8.3 lines 163–4), while the friend is loved with *amicitia propter delectabile* because of the pleasant passions she or he currently incites in us (*SLE* 8.3. lines 126–35), and with *amicitia propter utile* when she or he is useful for us (*propter utilitatem*; *SLE* 8.3 lines 62–4). The first one is described as *amicitia per se* or friendship in a proper sense, while the second and third are *amicitiae per accidens* (*SLE* 8.3 lines 76–9). Furthermore, Aquinas follows Aristotle's suggestion of a possible reduction of these three kinds of *philia* – or *amicitia* – to a twofold dichotomy according to the *propter quid* (the "wherefore") underlying the goodwill. Only in the *amicitia propter honestum* or *amicitia honesti* do the friends wish each other well for each other's sakes, while in the other two forms the friend is loved not for his own but for the lover's sake (*SLE* 8.3 lines 76–9). In accordance with this characterization of *amicitia propter honestum* as *amicitia per se*, Aquinas agrees with Aristotle that within the boundaries of a non-theological ethics this kind of friendship is friendship in the highest degree (*maxima amicitia*), and that the friends connected to each other by this bond are friends in the highest degree (*maxime amici*; *SLE* 8.3 lines 183–9).

While Aquinas follows Aristotle in these basic outlines in both his *SLE* and his theological works, he tends to reinterpret their specific meaning or structural foundation in the latter. This allows him to transpose them into the theological context of the *ST*, but it also causes some difficulties. To make this clear I shall analyze three important aspects of Aristotle's theory of friendship and Aquinas's interpretation of it, namely the interconnection between friendship or love toward oneself and friendship or love toward the other (2.1), the friendship of man toward God (2.2), and man's friendship toward the other (2.3).

12.2   Differences between Aristotle's and Aquinas's theories

12.2.1   Friendship toward oneself as basis for friendship toward the other

Aristotle argues that one precondition of friendship is that the friend love himself (*EN* 9.8), or, more precisely: be a friend to himself (*EN* 9.4.1166b28–9). In order to be somebody's friend in the Aristotelian "perfect" sense, two conditions have to be met: (1) we must wish him, on account of his virtuous qualities, all the good that we wish for ourselves, and (2) we must have a well-ordered relation toward ourselves. Aristotle does not mean that our goodwill, that is, the fact that we wish the friend well for his own sake, is *derived* in a strict sense from our self-love. His idea is that we cannot be someone's friend if we are torn apart by our emotions and inclinations, for these would not only prevent us from loving the other in an orderly way but also would mean that we ourselves were not lovable persons and, one might add, could not be relied upon.[9] Neither does Aristotle want

---

[9] See the long passage *EN* 9.4.1166b5–29: The wicked (φαῦλοι, b6–7), who are not friends towards themselves, are divided within themselves (διαφέρονται... ἑαυτοῖς, b7); they flee from themselves (ἑαυτοὺς... φεύγουσιν, b14); their souls are in an uproar, as if they were being torn apart (ὥσπερ διασπῶντα, b21–2); thus, they do not possess the quality of being lovable (μηδὲν ἔχειν φιλητόν, b26).

to render natural self-love a natural condition for friendship; rather, he focuses on the achieved moral virtue of a good relation toward oneself.[10]

I will follow David Gallagher's excellent analysis to guide my examination of how Aquinas's approach deals with this important structural feature of Aristotle's theory in order to elaborate the important differences of the former from the latter.[11] Gallagher tries to show how Aquinas explains the following three things: "1) how ... all love for others is based on a natural love for oneself, 2) how self-love leads to love of others, and 3) how there are different kinds of self-love that appear in Thomas's works and which of these serves as the basis of love of others."[12] In order to do so, he shows that Aquinas "considers self-love to be natural to the will and to be the source of all other acts of willing" because this self-love is nothing else than the natural inclination of the will to *felicitas* or *beatitudo* (Gallagher 1999, 25). It is not the result of an act of deliberation but rather precedes deliberation. Because of its fundamental nature, natural self-love is also the principle and basis for "the loves one has for other persons" (ibid.). On the rational level, this inclination to self-love has the character of dilection (*dilectio*) and is a fundamental component of the structural interconnection between *amor amicitiae* and *amor concupiscentiae*.[13] With *amor amicitiae* we love someone for whom we want some good, while with *amor concupiscentiae* we love the good that we want for that person, be it someone else or ourselves. On the level of natural self-love, this means that (1) we love ourselves naturally with an *amor amicitiae* as the person for whom we wish beatitude, while (2) at the same time and in the same act we naturally love this beatitude that "contains in its very notion every possible good for a person" for ourselves with an *amor concupiscentiae* (Gallagher 1999, 27–8). This first step of his analysis of Aquinas's theory leaves Gallagher with a problem: for, though according to him the *amor amicitiae* for another person has to be derived from this basic *amor amicitiae* toward oneself, it is not clear how exactly the generation of this second kind of love from the first one can be explained in Aquinas's approach.

[10] See Fuchs 2011.   [11] Gallagher 1999; see also Gallagher 1996.

[12] Gallagher 1999, 25. The question of how Aquinas conceives of the connection between self-love and the love of others has been the topic of intense discussion among scholars. Most interpreters share the opinion that self-love cannot be the basis of love of the other but disagree about whether Aquinas shared this opinion himself. Some scholars blame Aquinas for having tried to found love for others on self-love (Nygren 1953); others, if they intend to defend Aquinas, deny he made any such attempt at all (Wohlman 1981). See Gallagher 1999, 24–5. Since Mansini gives a very instructive synopsis of the development of these two kinds of love before Aquinas, I can leave this topic out of the present chapter. See Mansini 1995, especially 138–51.

[13] See Gallagher 1999, 26. Gallagher quotes a passage from *ST* 1–2.26.4 resp., where Aquinas refers to *Rhet.* 2.4.1380b35 ("to love is to will the good for someone").

The solution Gallagher provides for this problem is based on Aquinas's concept of the "union of love" (*unio amoris*) (Gallagher 1999, 29–35; see also *ST* 2–2.17.3 resp). For Aquinas "it does not seem possible for a person to love another person – seek that person's good – without the good of the person loved being in one way or another the good of the lover" (Gallagher 1999, 29–30). Thus, the lover has to be united with the beloved in such a way that he would be "taking as his own good a good that inheres or belongs to another person" and loving it with an *amor concupiscentiae* – but, as Gallagher emphasizes, "precisely *as belonging to that other person*" (ibid., 31; emphasis in original). This means that "Thomas presupposes the possibility of a relationship between persons of such a sort that one person takes the other to be one with himself (another self) and consequently the other's good (well-being) to be his own," which at the same time is nothing other than Aquinas's understanding of *amor amicitiae* toward the other. This kind of union is not an ontological one in the sense that lover and beloved would cease to have their own existence (ibid., 31–2). Rather, it is a union of affection or an "affective union" that causes the lover to seek "*effectively* . . . the good of the beloved (i.e., beneficence)" (ibid., 32; emphasis in original).

The question remains, however, how this kind of affective union can emerge from self-love. Gallagher names two possible principles that Aquinas thinks could constitute the basis for an "affective extension of one's self to include another person such that the other person is treated as another self": unity (*unitas*) in general and similitude (*similitudo*) as a special kind of unity (ibid., 32–3). Unity serves as the basis for any affective extension of the self, since in "some mode the other person must be taken as one with the lover" (ibid., 32). One mode of unity can be described in mereological terms insofar as the beloved belongs to the lover in the way a part belongs to the whole; an example of unity playing this role is the friendship between parents and children (*ST* 2–2.26.9 resp.). Similitude as a second mode of unity derives from a "formal sameness" in the sense of some "formal perfection" which, according to Gallagher's interpretation of Aquinas, "constitutes a kind of unity which, when perceived, is the basis for benevolence and even beneficence" (Gallagher 1999, 33). This unity or "formal sameness" is the foundation for the unity of affection and the various kinds of friendships that arise from it (ibid.).[14] Finally, there is the

---

[14] Here we do indeed find an ontological foundation for friendship: this was pointed out by Yamamoto, who emphasizes that Aquinas's theory of friendship differs from that of Aristotle due to the influence of Neoplatonic ontology. See Yamamoto 2008, 251. Aristotle, however, explicitly rejects an ontological or metaphysical ('natural') interpretation of friendship in *EN* 8.2.1155b8–9.

unity that serves as basis for the love of God: this too consists in a relation of part to whole, but here the lover is not the whole but rather the part, which loves its principle and desires to participate therein (ibid., 36).[15] However, all three kinds of affective unions, each based on its own kind of ontological unity, emerge primarily from self-love, since in all three unities the good of the other is loved as a good for oneself.

Gallagher's reconstructions of Aquinas's thought, though insightful, do not seem to show that Aquinas convincingly derives love of others from self-love. It seems, on the contrary, that Aquinas's attempt to found the phenomenon of friendship in self-love is ultimately unsuccessful. "Good" self-love,[16] which is supposed to lead directly into love of the other, is characterized as an *amor amicitiae* toward oneself that involves an *amor concupiscentiae* for "what is best for oneself (beatitude)" (Gallagher 1999, 44). It may indeed be true that, by virtue of this kind of self-love, one can extend one's love to the good of the other person and love it as one's own insofar as one is in a "union of love" with the other (ibid., 30–1). Given this description, however, it still remains unclear how there can be a "process of generation" from an "extended" *self-love* of this sort to another love of quite a different type, namely the love of the other for *his or her own sake* and not for ours. The structure of extended self-love, as presented by Aquinas and lucidly reconstructed by Gallagher, works quite well as an explanation of the imperfect kinds of Aristotelian friendship, since these simply require that we wish someone some good, which we very well can do for *our own sakes*,[17] but it gives no explanation of how wishing the other well for his own sake, not for ours, as the specific feature of perfect friendship would be possible. One reason why Aquinas apparently passed over this problem may have been his desire to unify the principles of friendship into one basic structure or to reduce them to a single principle, whereas Aristotle tends to give such systematizing tendencies a back seat in favor of a more descriptive approach to the phenomena. As we shall see below, this tendency toward unification also characterizes Aquinas's further analysis of the structure of charity. In Aquinas's theory, *caritas* as friendship with God is closely connected to *caritas* as a specific kind of friendship with neighbor. In the following I shall consider these two aspects of *caritas* separately, beginning with the love of God.

---

[15] This kind of friendship is discussed in the next subsection.

[16] See Gallagher 1999, 39–44. "Bad" self-love would be simply seeking goods for oneself egoistically, i.e., seeking goods that cannot be shared with others.

[17] For instance, we can wish our business partner well not because we love him for his own sake but because his doing badly could cause us financial loss. This kind of well-wishing would still fit Aquinas's definition of loving someone with *amor amicitiae*.

12.2.2 Caritas *as* dilectio / amicitia Dei

Aquinas's most obvious transformation of Aristotle's theory of friendship is the way he applies the Aristotelian category of friendship between unequal persons to the charitable relation between man and God, and yet at the same time declares this relation to be the perfect form of friendship – a combination impossible for Aristotle. This clear deviation from the Greek philosopher, for whom, as we have seen, too great a difference makes friendship impossible and who therefore rejects the idea of a friendship between men and gods, is at the same time "the heart of Thomas's ethics" (Gallagher 1999, 36) or, more precisely, of his moral theology. In *SLE* 8.7, Aquinas concedes that some equality (*aequalitas*) between friends is necessary because it is the first basis (*primum*) of friendship (lines 115–16). When this equality is no longer present, the friendship between the persons vanishes (lines 122–5). In this context he has to discuss Aristotle's thesis that we cannot befriend the gods because their superiority renders them too distant from us. Aquinas comments on this in two ways: In the first place, he identifies Aristotle's gods with the separated substances (*substantiae separatae*; *SLE* 8.7 line 131), i.e., as we must conclude from *De ente et essentia* 4, with the angels or intelligences (*intelligentiae*) and with God as the first cause (*causa prima*). Second, he concedes Aristotle's argument about the impossibility of having friendship with God by restricting this concession to the kinds of unequal friendship Aristotle investigates in the *EN*.[18] This is to say, that there is no *ethical* friendship with God, i.e., a friendship that is based solely on the *natural* grounds of the *conditio humana*. *Caritas* as friendship with God and neighbor consequently is no ethical acquired virtue, but a supernatural infused one (*ST* 2–2.23.2 resp.), which allows human beings to pursue their ultimate end, i.e., the vision of the divine essence, which is described as a union with God (*unio*; *ST* 1–2.3.8 resp.).[19] This end cannot be achieved in our mortal life (*ST* 2–2.27.2 resp. and *ST* 1–2.3.8 resp.).

When he turns to his moral theology, Aquinas does not deny that God is absolutely other and completely different from human beings. He nevertheless believes that the concept of friendship still properly describes the charitable relation between men and God, because, in spite of all the vast

---

[18] *SLE* 8.7 lines 141–5: "hoc in generali sufficit scire quod multis ablatis ab uno quae insunt alii adhuc remanet amicitia, et si multum distent, puta sicut homines a Deo, non adhuc remanet talis amicitia de qua loquimur."

[19] I shall confine myself to the basic structure that Aquinas develops for charity as it exists here on earth, and set aside the question of what, according to him, happens in the beatific vision of God in the afterlife.

difference that separates them, there is a "communication" (*communicatio*) (*ST* 2–2.23.1 resp.) between them, i.e., the bestowing of God's beatitude on us, which serves as the foundation of mutual benevolence and thus as a common basis for friendship between man and God.[20] According to Aquinas, we love God with a charitable love of friendship because, as we have mentioned above, our beatitude consists in the vision of the divine essence (*ST* 1–2.3.8 resp.). At the same time, we love God for his own sake, which means that we love Him as the ultimate end, an end not subordinated to any higher aim (*ST* 2–2.26.1 resp.). Thus God is the proper and primary object of *caritas* because of this communication of beatitude (*ST* 2–2.25.12 resp.). The mutuality of this love, which is another essential constituent of friendship, is also guaranteed for Aquinas, since God's communication of beatitude to us is an expression of the love with which he loves us (*In Rom* 5.1 nn. 392–3).

Since God is the highest principle of our beatitude and thus the most lovable object we can charitably love, he is also the basis and principle of the complex "order of charity" (*ordo caritatis*; *ST* 2–2.26.1). This order emerges from the fact that *caritas* as love of God is perfect friendship to the highest degree (*maxime amicitia honesti*) (*ST* 2–2.23.1 ad 3) and thus the highest form of friendship as such; however, it does not only extend to God himself but also includes others, specifically ourselves and our neighbors, as lovers of God. Within this order of charity, God, as mentioned above, is to be loved as "principle of beatitude" (*ST* 2–2.26.1 resp.); second, we are to love ourselves insofar as we belong to God (*ST* 2–2.25.4 resp.), i.e., insofar as we are capable of achieving beatitude;[21] third, we are to love our neighbors (*ST* 2–2.25.1 resp.). The lover himself and the neighbor are not to be loved to the same degree, because "out of charity we ought to love more that which has more fully the reason for being loved out of charity" (*ST* 2–2.26.5 resp.), i.e., those persons or things which are closer to God as the principle of beatitude (*ST* 2–2.26.6 resp.). This is the reason why "*ex caritate*" we ought to love God more than ourselves and anyone else (*ST* 2–2.26.2 resp. and 3 resp.), and again ourselves more than our neighbor (*ST* 2–2.26.4 resp.).

God as the principle of our beatitude is to be charitably loved "on account of himself" (*propter seipsum*; *ST* 2–2.27.3 resp.). For Aquinas, this "*propter*" denotes at least one of the four genera of causes, i.e., the *causa finalis, formalis, efficiens*, and *materialis*. In fact Aquinas holds that God can

---

[20] This focus on *communicatio* clearly shows Aquinas's implicit reference to Aristotle, which becomes manifest in *ST* 2–2.25.5 resp. (with reference to *EN* 8.12.1161b11).

[21] This was discussed in the previous section.

be loved "*propter seipsum*" in the first, second, and third meaning of cause: He is loved not as something ordered to another end, but as himself being the ultimate end (*causa finalis*). He is loved as being in himself the formal cause of every goodness, since his goodness is his very substance, while all other good things owe their goodness to him as to their exemplar. Finally, he is loved "*propter seipsum*" in the line of efficient causality, since he does not receive his goodness from another thing, but all good things receive their goodness from him. However, God can be loved "*propter aliud*" in the fourth sense of cause, i.e., in the sense of *causa materialis* or disposition, because we can be disposed to grow in our love for him by things other than God, such as received benefits, anticipated rewards, or punishments we want to avoid.

The non-Aristotelian aspects and features of Aquinas's conception of *caritas* as friendship with God can be summarized as follows: unlike Aristotle's, Aquinas's highest form of perfect friendship is not a relation between equals but one between highly unequal partners. Its prime object is not a particular human person but God, while other human beings are loved in the light of this dilection of God. Our neighbor is loved with charity inasmuch as he shares with us the common feature of being capable of achieving beatitude (*ST* 2–2.25.12 resp.).

In order to determine whether Aquinas's application of the structure of *philia* to the relation between man and God does in fact result in a genuinely new form of perfect friendship, we have to examine the constitutive features of friendship put forward by Aristotle, which are: (a) mutual benevolence; (b) not being hidden from either of the friends; and (c) being founded in the goodness, pleasantness, or usefulness that each finds in the other.[22] In the case of Aquinas's perfect charitable friendship, the *propter quid* of the mutual, mutually known benevolence is the goodness of the beloved. Concerning our friendship with God we can certainly maintain (b), namely the non-hiddenness of God's benevolence to us, since Aquinas suggests that Christian faith reveals God's love to the beloved (see *ST* 2–2.23.1 resp.). We can also maintain (c), since this friendship is obviously founded on the goodness of the beloved, i.e., God, who is *bonum ipsum*. However, one might wonder whether (a), mutual *benevolence*, is still a constitutive feature of Aquinas's perfect friendship. Admittedly, God does demonstrate benevolence toward us when he offers us divine love for our own sakes. We can ask, however, whether we indeed are able

---

[22] See *SLE* 8.2 lines 111–16: "oportet ad rationem amicitiae quod per eam aliqui sibi bene velint ad invicem et quod hoc non lateat eos et quod hoc sit propter unum aliquod praedictorum, scilicet propter bonum vel delectabile vel utile."

to love him back with benevolence, in the sense of wishing him some good for *his own sake*. This becomes clear in Aquinas's discussion of the question whether we can benefit God (*beneficentia*) or not.[23] In *ST* 2–2.31.1 ad 1, Aquinas quotes a passage from Pseudo-Dionysius before admitting that it is not our task to benefit God, but simply to honor him by obeying him (*nostrum non est Deo benefacere, sed eum honorare, nos ei subiiciendo*). As we have seen above, Aristotle had attributed this kind of mutuality to *unequal* and hence *imperfect* friendship, one which is not a friendship in the proper sense; Aquinas uses it to characterize his idea of *perfect* friendship instead. For an Aristotelian philosopher on the one hand, this interpretation of what the mutuality of benevolence means in Aquinas's perfect friendship may seem odd. The Thomistic theologian, on the other hand, may argue that at this point we are dealing not with natural but supernatural relations, which are mediated not primarily by natural knowledge but by faith.[24]

Either way, however, it seems that Aquinas has difficulty integrating the Aristotelian aspect of wishing someone well for his own sake into his transformed theory of perfect friendship. To put this another way, "wishing the other well for his or her own sake" means something different for Aristotle than it does for Aquinas. As we will see below, this is also true for his description of friendship toward the other as *caritas* or *dilectio proximi*.

12.2.3   *Perfect* philia *and* caritas *as* dilectio / amicitia proximi

A passage that is very important for the problem of whether Aquinas can integrate Aristotelian perfect friendship into his conception of *caritas* as *dilectio proximi* can be found in the *Quaestio disputata De caritate*. Article 4 discusses the question of whether charity is a single virtue (*una virtus*). The response can be read as a more detailed version of an argument Aquinas develops in *ST* 2–2.25.1 resp. The question of the habitual status of charity arises since there seem to be two kinds of *caritas*, i.e., one by which we love God and another one by which we love our neighbor. To show that there is only one virtue of *caritas*, Aquinas starts by asserting that the unity of each faculty (*potentia*) and each habit (*habitus*) is specified by its object (*obiectum*). There are, however, two sides or aspects one can distinguish in the object, viz., its formal side and its material side. It is only the formal side which defines the faculty. For instance, the faculty of sight is specifically

---

[23] For the concept of *beneficentia* see also *ST* 2–2.31.4 resp.
[24] For the relation of charity and faith see Sherwin 2005, ch. 5.

and *per se* related to color itself (the object's formal side), not to the body (*corpus*), which is the substance in which the color inheres (the object's material side) and to which sight is related only accidentally (*per accidens*). This structure also applies to the virtue of charity. But here again there is another distinction to be made, since even when we consider only the formal side we can still love (*diligere*) somebody in two different ways. First, we can love that person because of him- or herself (*ratione sui ipsius*) as long as we love him or her because of a good proper to him or her (*ratione boni proprii*), i.e., because he or she is morally good (*in se honestus*) or pleasant or useful for us (*nobis delectabilis, aut utilis*).[25] Second, we can love someone because of another (*ratione alterius*), i.e., because he or she belongs to or is related to someone we love because of him- or herself. For instance, we love *ratione alterius* all the family members or friends of someone whom we love *ratione sui ipsius*. Both kinds of love, however, have the same formal object, namely the good of the person whom we love *ratione sui ipsius*, since it is also this good that we love in those whom we love *ratione alterius*. Thus, when we love God out of charity, we do so *ratione sui ipsius*, whereas we charitably love our neighbors *ratione alterius*, i.e., because of God.[26] What we love in our neighbors when we love them out of charity is, broadly speaking, God: we love our neighbor "because God is in him or desiring that God may be in him."[27] In other words, our love is a love of charity only insofar as it is referred to this divine indwelling, in which our neighbor's beatitude consists. Thus, we can also say that we love our neighbor out of charity on account of the common nature he possesses, since it is this that enables every human being to achieve beatitude (*ST* 2–2.25.6 resp.). This *caritas proximi*, however, clearly cannot be one of the kinds of friendship Aristotle describes in his *EN*, since in these the friend is not loved *ratione alterius*, but *ratione sui ipsius*.[28]

This passage, and most of all the statement cited in the previous sentence, seems to indicate that Aristotelian perfect friendship and Aquinas's charitable love of neighbor are somehow mutually exclusive. When we love someone with charitable *dilectio proximi*, we do so not because of her- or

[25] As we can see from this, loving someone *ratione sui ipsius* does not per se mean loving her or him for her or his own sake.

[26] This difference is equivalent to the difference described above between loving someone *propter seipsum* and *propter aliud*.

[27] *QDC* 4 resp.: "Sic igitur dicendum, quod caritas diligit Deum ratione sui ipsius; et ratione eius diligit omnes alios inquantum ordinantur ad Deum; unde quodammodo Deum diligit in omnibus proximis; sic enim proximus caritate diligitur, quia in eo est Deus, vel ut in eo sit Deus."

[28] Ibid.: "Sed si diligeremus proximum ratione sui ipsius, et non ratione Dei, hoc ad aliam dilectionem pertinet: puta ad dilectionem naturalem, vel politicam, vel ad aliquam aliarum quas Philosophus tangit in VIII Ethic."

himself (*ratione sui ipsius*), but because of God (*ratione Dei*), while in any Aristotelian friendship we love our friend *ratione sui ipsius*. Furthermore, the focus of our charitable love is not primarily the particularity of our friend but rather his common nature. Nonetheless, Aquinas is undeterred in his attempt to integrate Aristotelian friendship into his concept of charitable love. I shall concentrate on a combination of two passages and show that this attempt of Aquinas's does not really solve the problems we have mentioned.

In *ST* 2–2.26.6 resp., Aquinas tries to explain why we are allowed to love our neighbors with different levels of affective intensity in charity. Aquinas says that the affection of charity, which is an inclination of grace, is not structured in less orderly fashion than the natural appetite, which is an inclination of nature, since both proceed from divine wisdom. Natural inclinations are proportionate to the act or movement that is fitting for the nature of the inclined being. Analogously, the inclination of grace is proportionate to the outward acts that are to be done out of charity, such that we will have a more intense charitable affection toward those to whom we owe a higher degree of beneficence.[29] Aquinas defines the measure of this debt of beneficence to be our neighbor's nearness to either of the two principles of charity, i.e., God or the lover. When we consider Aquinas's reply to the second objection in this article, we see that he means that we have a greater affection for those who are closer to God. Although God is the one and identical reason to charitably love every neighbor, we need not love all of them with the same affection of dilection (*affectio dilectionis*), since not all of them have the same relation to God: some, due to their higher degree of goodness, are closer to him, and thus are to be loved in charity more than others who are not so close to him.[30]

As we can see from this consideration, Aquinas tries to integrate different levels of affection for the other into a single love of charity; this could

---

[29] "Videmus autem in naturalibus quod inclinatio naturalis proportionatur actui vel motui qui convenit naturae uniuscuiusque...Oportet igitur quod etiam inclinatio gratiae, quae est affectus caritatis, proportionetur his quae sunt exterius agenda: ita scilicet ut ad eos intensiorem caritatis affectum habeamus quibus convenit nos magis beneficos esse" (*ST* 2–2.26.6 resp.).

[30] *ST* 2–2.26.6 arg. 2: "Praeterea, ubi una et eadem est ratio diligendi diversos, non debet esse inaequalis dilectio. Sed una est ratio diligendi omnes proximos, scilicet Deus, ut patet per Augustinum in I De doctr. christ. Ergo omnes proximos aequaliter diligere debemus." Ibid. ad 2: "Ad secundum dicendum quod non omnes proximi aequaliter se habent ad Deum, sed quidam sunt ei propinquiores, propter maiorem bonitatem. Qui sunt magis diligendi ex caritate quam alii, qui sunt ei minus propinqui." This "magis diligendi ex caritate" refers to the extent of our affection toward our neighbor, as Aquinas makes clear in *ST* 2–2.26.7 resp.: "cum principium dilectionis sit Deus et ipse diligens, necesse est quod secundum propinquitatem maiorem ad alterum istorum principiorum maior sit dilectionis affectus."

perhaps then be the basis for including Aristotelian perfect friendship into charity as well. These affective differences, however, are obviously still located on the level of loving our neighbor *ratione Dei*. Thus, they may allow us to integrate the imperfect and improper kinds of Aristotelian friendship into charity, but it seems doubtful that they could do the same for the perfect one. This may be the reason why, in the quite complex *ST* 2–2.26.7 resp., Aquinas introduces a further differentiation between the different kinds of friends we can love out of charity, and why in the course of so doing he introduces Aristotelian perfect friendship itself. The question is whether we ought to love those who are better more than those who are more closely united to us. Aquinas begins his answer with the statement that every act has to be proportionate to its object and to its agent. The object defines the species of the act, while the relation of agent to patient determines its intensity. If we apply this principle to charitable love (*dilectio secundum caritatem*), the act's specific object will be God, while its agent will be man. The specific diversity of charitable love in relation to our various neighbors therefore depends on each neighbor's relation to God in such a way that we want a greater good for that neighbor who is closer to Him. Although the *bonum* that charity wants for everyone, i.e., eternal beatitude, is only one and the same, there are still diverse possible degrees of participation in this good, and divine justice demands that better neighbors be granted a higher degree of participation.

This specific difference in the degree of love stands in contrast to the variation on the level of intensity, which is determined not by the object but by the loving subject. Aquinas states that we desire those who are closer to us to receive the lesser *bonum* specifically proper to them more than we desire the better ones to receive the greater good they deserve. This difference in intensity depends not on the beloved's virtuous goodness, i.e., his propinquity to God, but only on that person's natural closeness to us. While the latter is fixed and unchanging, the former is mutable. From this Aquinas concludes that we can charitably wish for someone who is naturally closer to us to become better than we wish for someone not naturally related to us.

Still, even these reflections and differentiations do not seem to satisfy Aquinas in his attempt to prove his point, viz., that we can *ex caritate* have a greater love for those close to us than to those who are better. Because of the inconclusiveness of the previous argument, Aquinas adduces another reason to prove his thesis, namely that while we love those close to us in many ways, i.e., with all the other Aristotelian friendships, for those who are not close to us we have only charitable love. Thus, this seems to be the point where Aquinas succeeds in integrating perfect *philia* into charity. Aquinas concludes, however, that every other kind of friendship has to be referred to God to become compatible with charity, which commands them inasmuch as it orders them toward God as their last end. Finally, Aquinas states that even Aristotelian perfect friendship (*amicitia honesta*) is to be ordered toward the *bonum* that is the foundation of charity.[31]

We can conclude from Aquinas's quite complex considerations here that there is a twofold difference between the kinds of friends whom for Aquinas we can love out of charity. The first difference again refers to our friend's closeness to God and can be called an "objective" quality of his, while the second concerns his closeness to us and is more "subjective," inasmuch as it signifies the intensity with which we love him. While from the perspective of the first measure we again charitably love our neighbor not because of himself but because of God, in the second the case appears to be otherwise. It seems clear that it cannot limit itself to encompassing merely imperfect (in the Aristotelian sense) relations of friendship like those based upon natural unities such as family origin (*consanguineus*), but that it ought to be able to integrate even perfect *philia*. However, the last passage of *ST* 2–2.26.7 resp. (see n. 31) shows that loving those close to us with *charitable* love still requires us to refer our neighbor's intrinsic goodness, which is the basis for our other kinds of friendship, to God as the ultimate end. When we combine this consideration with Aquinas's beginning of the same *responsio*, where he says that those closer to God are loved more by charitable love, we seem to have come full circle. Loving or being befriended with someone in charity, then, means ultimately loving them because of God, not because of themselves. To summarize: When we *charitably* love our neighbor, no matter how close he is to us, we do not love him because of him- or herself, but because of God. Thus, Aquinas's conception of perfect friendship as charitable love of neighbor does not seem able to truly integrate the Aristotelian focus on wishing the friend well for her or his own sake in perfect *philia*.[32]

---

[31] *ST* 2–2.26.7 resp.: "Cum autem bonum super quod fundatur quaelibet alia amicitia honesta ordinetur sicut ad finem ad bonum super quod fundatur caritas, consequens est ut caritas imperet actui cuiuslibet alterius amicitiae, sicut ars quae est circa finem imperat arti quae est circa ea quae sunt ad finem. Et sic hoc ipsum quod est diligere aliquem quia consanguineus vel quia coniunctus est vel concivis, vel propter quodcumque huiusmodi aliud licitum ordinabile in finem caritatis, potest a caritate imperari. Et ita ex caritate eliciente cum imperante pluribus modis diligimus magis nobis coniunctos." This change in perspective is not considered by Schwartz, who uses this passage to criticize Pangle for not having seen that Aquinas indeed integrates differences of personal affection into his theory of charity. See Schwartz 2007, 6.

[32] This does not mean that we love our neighbor as an instrument for achieving eternal beatitude. It only means that the focus of our charitable *dilectio proximi* is not the neighbor insofar as she or he

12.3 Conclusion

I have tried to elaborate some problems that Aquinas has to face when he attempts to transform the Aristotelian theory of friendship and to integrate it into his moral theology. These problems occur on different levels: in friendship toward oneself, in charity as friendship toward God, and finally in charity as friendship toward neighbor. On all three levels, Aquinas seems to have difficulty integrating the Aristotelian element of wishing somebody well for his or her own sake in perfect *philia*.[33] It seems, thus, that perhaps Aristotelian perfect friendship is a *sui generis* ethical phenomenon that cannot be subsumed into Aquinas's theological synthesis without losing some of its central aspects. Aristotelian perfect *philia* asserts a certain independence from charity. A theory that attempted to take this into account would probably have to describe the relation between perfect friendship and charity not as integration but rather as coexistence.

is this particular person, but insofar as he or she is a child of God. This also provides the answer to a possible objection to our considerations. One could try to argue that loving our neighbor out of charity *ratione Dei* or *propter Deum* does not exclude loving him *ratione sui ipsius* or *propter se*, insofar as the structural relation of these two modes of loving might seem analogous to the relation between virtue and beatitude: virtue, after all, is loved or desired for its own sake (*ratione sui ipsius / propter se*), and yet also at the same time because of the beatitude it allows us to achieve (*ratione Dei / propter aliud*). Nonetheless, although this analogy shows that to love one's neighbor *ratione Dei* does not necessarily turn him into a pure instrument for achieving the desired union with God, it still does not seem to show that the neighbor is loved *only* because of himself. It seems that in the case of charity the root of the *ratione sui ipsius* again lies in a *propter aliud*.

[33] One could of course say that Aquinas actually shows no explicit interest in the problem posed by such an integration, and that this is because the focus of his considerations lies on another, theological level, namely the loving union of the Christian community and God. Then the problems mentioned would appear only when we begin to ask questions that Aquinas himself does not discuss in his theory, which could seem to be an unjust approach. The present chapter's main interest, however, is not in criticizing Aquinas simply for the sake of criticism, but rather in reflecting on how changes in the underlying theoretical premises will affect our discourse about friendship.

CHAPTER THIRTEEN

Pleasure, a supervenient end

Kevin White

The *Nicomachean Ethics* contains two treatises on what might be called pleasure, enjoyment, or delight (ἡδονή, *delectatio*). One, at the end of Book 7, is a sequel to the discussion of continence and incontinence; the other, at the beginning of Book 10, is a prelude to the concluding discussion of happiness. Both treatises present and respond to opinions about the goodness or badness of pleasure. Both argue that pleasure is not a movement or change (κίνησις, *motus*), or a process (γένεσις, *generatio*). Both say what pleasure is by describing it in terms of action (ἐνέργεια, *operatio*), but in different ways: the first treatise says that pleasure is unimpeded action of a habit that is according to nature (7.12.1153a14–15); the second says that pleasure perfects or completes (τελειοῖ, *perficit*)[1] action, as a supervenient end, as beauty supervenes on the young (οἷον τοῖς ἀκμαίοις ἡ ὥρα, *velut iuvenibus pulcritudo*) (10.4.1174b23, b33). Both treatises close with considerations of human nature, the first arguing that change is pleasant to us because our nature is not simple (7.14.1154b20–31), the second that the properly human pleasures are those of the perfect and blessed man (10.5.1176a15–29).

Aristotle's treatises on pleasure should be seen in the context of symmetrical, framing passages near the beginning and near the end of the *Ethics*, in which he argues that his account of happiness agrees with the common view that happiness must include pleasure. In Book 1, he says that the human good is action of soul in accordance with virtue, and, if

---

For their helpful comments on a draft of this chapter, I am grateful to Sean Cunningham, Tobias Hoffmann, and Robert Sokolowski.

[1] Aristotelian scholars hesitate whether to translate τελειοῖ as *perfects* or *completes* (see Strohl 2011, 259n5). Likewise, I hesitate whether to translate *perficit* as *perfects* or *completes*, for the Latin term, as used by Aquinas, includes both the notion of perfection and that of completion (see Blanchette 1994, 107–16). To complicate matters, Aquinas sometimes speaks as if *perficere* is interchangeable with *complere* (e.g., in *In Sent.* 2.26.1.5 resp.), and *perfectio* with *complementum* (e.g., in *SCG* 3.8). It is worth noting that *perfect* and *complete* seem to have entered the English language directly from scholastic Latin, in the thirteenth and fourteenth centuries, respectively (see Franklin 1983, 181 and 183).

there is more than one virtue, in accordance with the best and most perfect. The pleasures that the many seek conflict with one another, because they are not pleasurable by nature. Virtuous action is pleasurable by nature, and the life of those who love such action has no need of pleasure as an addition; it is pleasurable in itself (1.7.1098a16–18; 1.8.1099a11–15). The uncertainty here – Is there more than one virtue? If so, which is best and most perfect? – anticipates the discussion of moral and intellectual virtues in Books 2–6. The uncertainty is alluded to again in both treatises on pleasure (7.13.1153b10–11; 10.5.1176a26–7). It is finally resolved in Chapter 7 of Book 10, when happiness is identified as contemplative action of intellect in accordance with the intellectual virtue of wisdom. This, Aristotle says, is the most pleasurable of acts, for philosophy, the pursuit of wisdom, has pleasures to be wondered at for their purity and solidity, and it stands to reason that life should be even more enjoyable for those who know than for those who inquire (10.7.1177a12–18, a22–7).

Aristotle evidently thinks that the many, in maintaining that happiness must include pleasure, speak better than they know (cf. *EN* 7.13.1153b14–15). Aquinas, in turn, evidently thinks that Aristotle speaks better than he himself knows in Chapter 7 of Book 10, for he, Aristotle, is unaware that what he says there about the happiness of contemplation can serve to describe a happiness that will belong to the blessed in an afterlife, in a contemplative vision of God that will be accompanied by a sublime delight (see Pegis 1963, 5). To borrow from the vocabulary of phenomenology, happiness, for both Aristotle and Aquinas, is an intentional act; and for Aquinas, it is a filled intention, that is, an awareness of something in its presence – or rather, of someone in his presence (see Sokolowski 2000, 33–41). It is thus analogous to an act of seeing, and the accompanying delight is analogous to the pleasure of seeing. This sublime delight is, for Aquinas, the standard and the focal reference for all considerations of pleasure. As I will suggest in what follows, it was his need of a philosophical language in which to speak of this delight that first roused his interest in the treatises on pleasure in the *Ethics*.

In order to establish an appropriate setting in which to consider Aquinas's reading of these treatises of Aristotle, I will begin, in Section 13.1, by describing two discussions of pleasure that he himself composed, one in his commentary on the *Sentences*, the other in the *Summa theologiae*. This will allow us to start from Aquinas's own approach to the subject, and also to see some important uses he makes of Aristotle's treatises. Then, in Section 13.2, I will discuss Aquinas's interpretation of a series of remarks concerning the distinction between bodily and non-bodily pleasure in the latter part of Aristotle's first treatise. Finally, in Section 13.3, I will discuss a passage explaining how pleasure is perfective of action in Aristotle's second treatise. In both Section 13.2 and Section 13.3, I will discuss the relevant parts of Aquinas's commentary on the *Ethics* and a thematically related article in the *Summa theologiae*. In both cases, as I hope to show, the two perspectives on what Aristotle says – that of the commentary and that of the *Summa* – complement one another, providing a broader basis for understanding the Aristotelian dimension of Aquinas's view of pleasure than would either perspective by itself.

13.1 Aquinas's two texts on pleasure (*In Sent.* 4.49.3 and *ST* 1–2.31–34)

Like Aristotle's *Ethics*, Peter Lombard's *Sentences* is a work in which the theme of happiness, blessedness, or beatitude is associated with the theme of pleasure, enjoyment, or delight, both near the beginning and again near the end. The first distinction of Book 1 introduces the Augustinian contrast between enjoyment (*frui*) and use (*uti*). Augustine is quoted as saying that what we enjoy are things known by us, in which, and because of which, our will, having been delighted, comes to rest (*conquiescit*) (*Sententiae* 1.1, c. 2, n. 5; Augustine, *De Trinitate* 10.10.13). This quotation is the source of Aquinas's frequent descriptions of pleasure as repose (*quies*) of appetite (see Editio Leonina 1*.2:156, note to lines 349–50). The second to last distinction of the *Sentences*, distinction 49 of Book 4, is on the vision of God that the blessed will enjoy. Here Augustine is quoted as saying that he lives blessedly who lives as he wills, and who does not will anything wrongly (*Sententiae* 4.49.1 n. 8; Augustine *De Trinitate* 13.5.8). In the exposition of the text of distinction 49 that he presents in his commentary on the *Sentences*, Aquinas says that this opinion (*sententia*) of Augustine's agrees with an opinion of Aristotle's, if we take *living* to refer to an *action* of life, and *not willing anything wrongly* to mean that the action is *connatural*, inasmuch as what is wrong is against nature. Augustine, according to Aquinas, thus says in other words what Aristotle says when, in his first treatise on pleasure, he describes pleasure as unimpeded action of a habit that is according to nature. Like the quotation from Augustine in Book 1 on the delighted will coming to rest, however, this Augustinian quotation about living as one wills introduces the un-Aristotelian notion of *will* into Aquinas's thinking about pleasure.

In *In Sent.* 1.1.1.1, Aquinas asks whether the enjoyment (*fruitio*) accompanying the beatific vision is an act of intellect or of will. He describes the beatific vision in Aristotelian terms, as an act of man's highest power, namely, intellect, in relation to its noblest object, namely, God. In this vision, he says, God unites us to himself in an intimate union of love. We are thereby united with what is *maxime conveniens*, congenial in the greatest degree, from which there follows the highest pleasure, a pleasure in which our happiness is perfected. The characterization of the object of pleasure as *conveniens* alludes to a scholastic maxim that derives from Avicenna.[2] As Aquinas states it, with reference to Avicenna, in *In Sent.* 4.49.3.2. arg. 1, pleasure arises from perception of something congenial that has been joined to us.

The argument of *In Sent.* 1.1.1.1 resp. continues as follows: because it includes pleasure, our happiness is called enjoyment from the point of view of its completion (*ex parte sui complementi*), not from the point of view of its beginning (*ex parte principii*). The vision is an act of intellect, the enjoyment an act of will. The vision is happiness in the full sense (*habet perfectam rationem felicitatis*) only as an action that is perfected by what follows on it (*per ea quae sequuntur*); for pleasure perfects action, as beauty perfects youth, as is said in *Ethics* 10. Here, then, at the outset of his *Sentences* commentary, and the outset of his career, Aquinas applies the description of pleasure as perfective of action in Aristotle's second treatise to the case of the beatific vision and the pleasure that follows on and completes it. Similarly, in *Quodl.* 8.9.1 [19], he says that beatitude consists *originally and substantially* in an act of intellect, *formally and by way of completion* (*completive*) in an act of will; its *origin* is in vision, its *completion* in enjoyment (see Editio Leonina 25:81, note to lines 62–76). And in his commentary on *Sent.* 4.49, he discusses the vision of God, in which beatitude *principally* consists (q. 2), and pleasure, which *formally completes* beatitude (q. 3) (see 4.49 pr.). As these contrasts suggest, adverbs (and adverbial phrases, as well) play an important role in Aquinas's account of pleasure.

The discussion of pleasure in *In Sent.* 4.49.3 addresses the following topics: what pleasure is, its cause, the comparison of pleasure to pain, the goodness and badness of pleasure, and the comparison of spiritual to bodily pleasure. Fifteen questions are asked, only the last of which explicitly concerns the pleasure of the blessed. By and large, it is a philosophical treatment of pleasure in general, worked out with a vividness and a freshness that are characteristic of Aquinas's *Sentences* commentary (Owens 1990, 239).

---

[2] Avicenna, *Liber de philosophia prima sive scientia divina* 8.7, ed. S. Van Riet, 2:432 lines 67–8 and 2:433 lines 93–4.

The most important philosophical sources are the two treatises on pleasure in the *Ethics*.

Some fifteen years after finishing the *Sentences* commentary, Aquinas returned to the subject of pleasure in the *Summa theologiae*. In keeping with his rethinking of questions of order in the *Summa*, he relocated pleasure in the sequence of theological topics, moving it from the end to the middle, and from the context of the beatific vision to that of the passions of the soul. *Summa theologiae* 1–2 begins by discussing beatitude (qq. 1–5), acts of will (qq. 6–21), and the passions (qq. 22–48). Eleven kinds of passion are distinguished: six are actuations of the concupiscible power, namely, love and hatred, desire and aversion, and pleasure and pain; five are actuations of the irascible power, namely, hope and despair, fear and daring, and anger (*ST* 1–2.23.4). Among these eleven, pleasure is first in the order of intention, and last in the order of execution (*ST* 1–2.25.2).

The discussion of pleasure in the *Summa* is a revision of the discussion in the *Sentences* commentary. The revised version is divided into four *quaestiones*, in which 24 questions are raised. The principal divisions of the two versions line up as follows.

In Sent. 4.49.3.1–5 (15 questions)	*ST* 1–2.31–34 (24 questions)
1 what pleasure is (4 quaestiunculae)	31 pleasure in itself (8 articles)
2 the cause of pleasure (1 qc.)	32 causes of pleasure (8 aa.)
3 comparison of pleasure to pain (3 qcc.)	33 effects of pleasure (4 aa.)
4 goodness and badness of pleasure (3 qcc.)	34 goodness and badness of pleasure
5 comparison of spiritual to bodily pleasure (4 qcc.)	(4 aa.)

Comparison of pleasure to pain is now part of a separate treatise on pain that parallels and complements the treatise on pleasure (*ST* 1–2.35.3–6). Comparison of spiritual to bodily pleasure is now part of the consideration of pleasure in itself (*ST* 1–2.31.5). Consideration of a single cause of pleasure (namely, unimpeded action) now extends to several causes (*ST* 1–2.32). And there is a new topic, the effects of pleasure (*ST* 1–2.33). The result is a simpler, four-part structure, in which the two descriptions of pleasure in the *Ethics* have important roles at strategic points. The description of pleasure as unimpeded action in *EN* 7.12.1153a14–15 is the basis of the first article of the *quaestio* on the causes of pleasure (*ST* 1–2.32.1); the description of pleasure as perfective of action in *EN* 10.4.1174b23 and b33 is the basis of the last article of the *quaestio* on the effects of pleasure (*ST* 1–2.33.4).[3]

---

[3] In addition to its relocation in the order of theological topics, and its revised ordering of the topic of pleasure itself, *ST* 1–2.31–34 is distinguished from *In Sent.* 4.49.3 by its references to a new

Both of Aquinas's discussions of pleasure begin with the un-Aristotelian claim that pleasure is a passion (*In Sent.* 4.49.3.1 qc. 1; *ST* 1–2.31.1); in doing so, both make reference to Augustine's Stoic account of the passions in the *City of God* (9.5, 14.8). In both texts, Aquinas goes on to make the further claim that there is a pleasure that is not a passion, namely, joy (*gaudium*), which follows on rational awareness, not sense perception. Joy is a simple motion of will, involving no bodily change (*In Sent.* 4.49.3.1 qc. 4; *ST* 1–2.31.3). The distinction between the two kinds of pleasure recurs throughout both of Aquinas's discussions of pleasure, and, in the *Summa theologiae*, far beyond (*ST* 1–2.35.5; 2–2.180.7). There is a community of analogy linking the sensual pleasures of brute animals and the joys of pure spirits (*In Sent.* 4.49.3.1 qc. 2 ad 3; cf. *ST* 1–2.31.4 ad 3). That human beings enjoy both bodily and non-bodily pleasure is a central consideration in Aquinas's moral thought, as it is in Aristotle's.

13.2 Aquinas on Aristotle's first treatise: Bodily pleasure and intellectual pleasure

> The moderns, obeying inveterate habits of mind, have often unknowingly modified the doctrines of Plato and Aristotle, that is to say the purest expression of Greek thought, by forgetting that pleasure . . . is by right a part of the definition of the sovereign good. Aristotle, going further than Plato on this point, does not hesitate to attribute pleasure to God himself. (Brochard 2009, 60)

I turn now to Aquinas's commentary on the *Ethics*, which he wrote at about the same time as the second part of the *Summa theologiae*. In this section, I will focus on his commentary on a series of five suggestive remarks in the latter part of Aristotle's first treatise on pleasure. In all of these remarks, Aristotle is concerned with the difference between bodily and non-bodily pleasures; in none of them, however, does he say what the non-bodily pleasures are. Aquinas the commentator makes explicit what he takes the remarks to imply, namely, that the non-bodily pleasures are pleasures of intellect; in doing so, he introduces reflections of his own on the pleasures of contemplation, consideration, and reason. The last of the remarks occurs in a contrast Aristotle draws between human beings and God with respect to pleasure. At the end of the section, I will also discuss an article of the *Summa theologiae* in which Aquinas presents his own version of this contrast.

authoritative text, namely, the chapter on pleasure in Aristotle's *Rhetoric* (1.11), a work Aquinas seems to have read carefully for the first time just before writing *ST* 1–2 (see Gauthier 1993, 80).

13.2.1   *"All things by nature have in them something divine"*
(EN 7.13.1153b32–3)

In *EN* 7.13, Aristotle begins by arguing that, since pain, the contrary of pleasure, is admittedly something bad, pleasure must be a good. That some pleasures are shameful is no hindrance to *a* pleasure being the greatest good, he says; in fact, this must be so, if, as was said earlier, pleasure is unimpeded activity (7.12.1153a14–15), and unimpeded activity of all or one of our good habits is what is most choiceworthy (1.7.1098a16–18). Aristotle takes the fact that all human beings and brute animals pursue pleasure to be a sign that it is somehow the greatest good; what many people say cannot be completely wrong, he says, quoting Hesiod (7.3.1153b1–4, b7–14, b25–8). At this point in his commentary, Aquinas explains why the many cannot be completely wrong. Nature fails only rarely, not always or usually. What is always or usually the case, then, would seem to be from an inclination of nature; and nature does not incline to what is bad or false. Pleasure, on which the desires of all agree, would seem therefore to be some greatest good (*SLE* 7.13 lines 133–9).

Aristotle says that not everyone pursues the same pleasure, but everyone pursues pleasure. Then he reverses himself: perhaps everyone pursues, not the pleasure they each think or say they do, but the same pleasure, for all things by nature have in them something divine. But the bodily pleasures have taken over the inheritance of the name of pleasure, because they are chosen most often, and everyone participates in them. Since they are the only ones that are known, they are thought to be the only ones (1153b29–1154a1).

Aquinas explains Aristotle's cryptic reference to something divine as follows. All human beings desire the same pleasure according to natural appetite, but not according to their own judgments. That is, not everyone thinks or says that the same pleasure is best, but nature inclines everyone to the same pleasure, the one greatest pleasure, namely, pleasure in contemplation of intelligible truth, inasmuch as all human beings by nature desire to know. This is so because human beings, like all things, naturally have in themselves *something divine*, a term that Aquinas interprets as referring to one of two things: an inclination of nature, nature depending on the (divine) first principle; or ("divine") form itself, which is the principle of the inclination (*SLE* 7.13 lines 155–68). That all human beings by nature desire to know is the opening statement of Aristotle's *Metaphysics*; that form is something divine is a remark in Aristotle's *Physics* (1.9.192a17–19; see Dewan 2007). Aquinas thus explains *Aristoteles ex Aristotele*: the inclination of nature ultimately depends on the divine first principle; form, the proximate principle of such an inclination, is itself something divine; the inclination of which the human form is the proximate principle is desire to know; and so all human beings, knowingly or unknowingly, desire to know in contemplation of intelligible truth, an activity that contains the greatest human pleasure.

Aquinas here uses the term *contemplation* in the broad sense of any consideration of truth (*ST* 1–2.35.5 ad 3). By *consideration*, a term we will come across shortly, he means the act of an intellect "looking at" (*intuens*) the truth about something (*ST* 2–2.53.4). Both *contemplation* and *consideration*, in his usage, suggest insight and understanding, as distinct from inference and inquiry.

Aquinas's explanation of the term *something divine* is certainly in keeping with what Aristotle will say later, at the great resolution of the argument of the *Ethics* in Chapter 7 of Book 10, about the pleasure of contemplation (1177a12–18); but it goes beyond what Aristotle says in *EN* 7.13. Aquinas does not wish to keep the reader in suspense on the question of what is the greatest pleasure, namely, the pleasure of contemplating intelligible truth.

13.2.2 *"If the habits and motions have no excess, neither does the pleasure" (EN 7.14.1154a13–14)*

In *EN* 7.11–13, according to Aquinas's division of the text, Aristotle discusses pleasure and pain in general; in *EN* 7.14, he discusses bodily pleasures in particular (*SLE* 7.14 lines 1–4). Aristotle begins in *EN* 7.14, as he began in the previous chapter, with the generally conceded point that pain is bad. Why, he asks, if there are noble pleasures that are more choiceworthy than the bodily pleasures that the intemperate enjoy, are the pains contrary to the latter pleasures bad? The contrary of what is bad would seem to be a good. His answer is that bodily pleasures *are* good, inasmuch as they are necessary; that is, they are good, but not absolutely, only up to a point. If the habits and motions have no excess, he says, neither does the pleasure. But there can be excess in bodily goods, and it is by pursuit of excess that a vicious person is vicious, not by pursuit of the necessary pleasures as such, which everyone enjoys, although not everyone enjoys them rightly (1154a8–18).

Aquinas takes *motion* to mean *action* here, and he explains the remark about habits and motions without excess by again referring to contemplation. He says that there can be no excess beyond what is good in the action that is contemplation of truth. The more one contemplates truth, the better, so that the pleasure that follows is also good absolutely, not just in a certain measure (*SLE* 11.14 lines 40–50).

13.2.3   "Remedies are intense" (EN 7.14.1154a29–30)

We should state not only the truth, Aristotle says, but also the cause of falsehood, because this contributes to confidence in the truth; one is all the more sure of what is true when one sees why what is untrue seems true. We must, then, say why bodily pleasures – being merely necessary, good only up to a point, liable to excess, and less choiceworthy than the noble pleasures – nevertheless seem more choiceworthy than the latter (7.14.1154a22–6). Aristotle suggests two reasons for this.

One is that bodily pleasure drives off pain. It is because of excessive pain that people pursue excessive pleasure, and bodily pleasure in general, as a remedy (ὡς οὔσης ἰατρείας, *ut existente medicina*). Remedies are intense (σφοδραί, *vehementes*), because they show up against their contrary; this is why they are sought (1154a26–31).

Here again Aquinas brings up intellect. He comments that there is no pain contrary to intellectual pleasure, for instance, the pleasure there is in considering something, because this consists, not in a process, but a finished state (*non est in fieri, sed in facto esse*). He also says that bodily pleasures seem intense by the very fact that they are remedies for pain, because they are thereby measured not only by their own nature, but also by the contrary that they drive off; hence the custom of those who eat salty things, the better to enjoy their drink (*SLE* 7.14 lines 111–14). Intellectual pleasures, Aquinas implies, *are* "measured only by their own nature." They are not remedial, and they have no natural temporal terminus.

In the *Topics*, Aristotle discusses a number of ways of detecting ambiguity (see Owens 1978, 107–18), one of which is to see whether there is a contrary to one sense of a word but not another. His example is that the pain of thirst is contrary to the pleasure of drinking, but nothing is contrary to the pleasure of seeing that the diameter is incommensurable with the side. Pleasure, he concludes, is spoken of in more than one sense (πλεοναχῶς, *multipliciter*) (*Top.* 1.15.106a36–b2; cf. *EN* 7.12.1153a1). In this respect, pleasure is like being, which is spoken of in many senses (πολλαχῶς, *multis modis*), but always with reference to a primary instance (*Met.* 4.2.1003a33–4 and b16; cf. *EN* 10.5.1176a26–9). Nemesius echoes Aristotle when he says that the pain of thirst is opposed to the pleasure (ἡδονή, *voluptas*) of drink, but nothing is opposed to the pleasure (*voluptas*) of contemplation (*De natura hominis* 17, p. 96 lines 84–6).[4] Aquinas echoes Nemesius (whom he calls Gregory of Nyssa) when he says that there is no pain contrary to the pleasure of contemplation (*In Sent.* 4.49.3.5 qc. 1; *ST* 1–2.35.5), or, as he puts it here in his commentary on the *Ethics*, to the pleasure of consideration.

Aristotle's second reason why bodily pleasures seem more choiceworthy is that they are pursued for their intensity by those who cannot enjoy other pleasures. He mentions three cases of this incapacity: that of animal nature, which is always toiling; that of the young, who, because their growing bodies are in flux, are like persons who are drunk; and that of the melancholy, whose nature it is always to need a remedy, because their body is constantly in pain, and they always feel strong desire. Pain is driven off by contrary pleasure, but any pleasure, if it is strong, will do; this is why the melancholy become intemperate and vicious (1154b2–3, b6–15). Aquinas comments that Aristotle's discussion of these three cases is his explanation of something he has presupposed, namely, that all human beings need to be restored or refreshed – literally "recreated" (*recreari*) – by *some* pleasure (*SLE* 7.14 lines 175–8; cf. *ST* 1–2.34.1 resp.). This sense of *recreari*, which is distantly related to the modern notion of *recreation*, is unusual in Aquinas.

In his own discussions of pleasure, Aquinas explains how it is that, although spiritual pleasure is greater than bodily pleasure, the latter is more intensely felt by us. In doing so, he adopts Aristotle's characterization of bodily pleasure as a remedy (*In Sent.* 4.49.3.5 qc. 1; *ST* 1–2.31.5).

13.2.4 *"What is pleasurable by nature causes action proper to a nature of a certain kind" (EN 7.14.1154b19–20)*

Pleasures that do not involve pain, Aristotle says, have no excess. Their objects are not pleasant accidentally, that is, merely as remedies. Rather, they are pleasant by nature, in the sense that they cause action proper to a nature of a certain kind (7.14.1154b15–20). Aquinas comments that the proper action of a nature is pleasurable to it because it is the nature's completion (*perfectio*), and this is why an act of reason is pleasurable to a human being (*SLE* 7.14 lines 239–41).

---

[4] For evidence of the importance of Nemesius's chapter on pleasure (*De natura hominis* 17, "*De voluptatibus*") in scholastic discussions of pleasure just prior to the appearance of Grosseteste's translation of the *Ethics*, see the discussion of the definition of pleasure in Albert the Great's *De bono* 5.1.3, Editio Coloniensis 28:206–9, "Quid sit diffinitione et substantia voluptas sive delectatio."

13.2.5 *"Our nature is not simple" (EN 7.14.1154b21–2)*

Aristotle closes *EN* 7.14 by comparing human nature and divine nature with respect to pleasure. He says that no one thing is always pleasant to us, because our nature is not simple. There is something *other* in us, insofar as we are perishable. The action of one part of us is beyond the nature of the other part; and if the two parts balance out, action is neither painful nor pleasurable. From this, Aristotle draws what Aquinas calls a corollary (*SLE* 7.14 line 265). If the nature of a thing were simple, Aristotle says, the same action would always be most pleasurable to it. This is why God always enjoys one simple pleasure: for there is not only the action that is change, but also action without change, and pleasure consists more in repose than in change. But change in all things is sweet, as "the poet," i.e., Euripides, says, and this because of a certain badness (πονηρία, *malitia*). Just as a bad man is changeable, so a nature that needs change is bad; it is neither simple nor good (1154b20–31).

In his comment on this passage, Aquinas once more introduces the theme of the pleasure of contemplation. He says that contemplation is natural to us by reason of our intellect, but beyond our nature by reason of our organs of imagination, which "labor" in the act of contemplation; this is why contemplation cannot be continually pleasurable to us (*SLE* 7.14 lines 252–9). Elaborating on Aristotle's corollary, he says that if we were pure intellect, we would always delight in contemplating; it is because God is simple – and immutable, Aquinas adds – that he always enjoys one simple pleasure, which is the pleasure he has in contemplation of himself. Intellectual activity, Aquinas notes, makes it clear that pleasure-causing action consists not only in change, but also in stillness (*in immobilitate*). Pleasure in activity without change is greater than pleasure in activity that is change, because, as was said earlier, the latter consists in a becoming, the former in a finished state. It is a bad man who is changeable, not having his mind fixed on one thing; likewise, a nature that needs change is not simple or completely good; for change is actuality of the imperfect, as Aristotle says in the *Physics* (3.3.201b31–2; *SLE* 7.14 lines 268–89).

Commentary on the concluding passage of *EN* 7.14 is thus an occasion for Aquinas to touch briefly on some points of agreement between Aristotle and Christian theology, namely, the divine simplicity, immutability, and self-knowledge (cf. *ST* 1.3, 1.9, 1.14.2–3). Conversely, in his major theological works, Aquinas subsumes into Christian theology Aristotle's remark that God always enjoys one simple pleasure (*In Sent.* 1.45.1.1; *SCG* 1.91; *ST* 1.20.1 ad 1).

13.2.6 "Our nature is changeable" (ST 1–2.32.2 resp.)

In his chapter on pleasure in the *Rhetoric*, Aristotle explains how it is that both doing the same thing repeatedly and doing something different are pleasurable. He says that what we do often, we do with pleasure, because what is customary is pleasurable. But it is also pleasurable to make a change, because this is to return to what is natural, when too much repetition becomes excessive in relation to one's normal state (ὑπερβολὴν ποιεῖ τῆς καθεστώσης ἕξεως, *excessum facit constituti habitus*). Here again he quotes the line from Euripides: "Change in all things is sweet." He adds that this is why people or things we see from time to time are pleasurable: because they are a change from what is present (*Rhet.* 1.11.1371a26–31).

Aquinas discusses change as a cause of pleasure in *ST* 1–2.32.2, with reference to *EN* 7.14 and *Rhet.* 1.11, as well as Augustine's *Confessions*. He analyzes the pleasure of change according to the three elements of the Avicennian maxim concerning pleasure: someone pleased by a good, conjunction of the pleasing thing, and awareness of the conjunction. (1) From the point of view of ourselves, the ones who are pleased, change is made pleasurable because our nature is changeable (cf. *EN* 7.14.1154b20–2), so that what is congenial to us now will not be so later (it is congenial to warm ourselves at a fire in winter, but not in summer). (2) From the point of view of the pleasing good that is conjoined to us, change becomes pleasurable because the continued action of an agent increases its effect (the longer one stays by a fire, the more it heats and dries), but our natural state consists in a certain measure, and when the continued presence of a pleasant object goes beyond the measure of our natural state (*superexcedit mensuram naturalis habitudinis*; cf. *Rhet.* 1.11.1371a27–8), removal of the object becomes pleasurable. (3) From the point of view of our awareness of the conjunction, change is pleasurable because we desire to know things in their wholeness and completeness, but some things cannot be apprehended all at once. In such cases, it is pleasurable to us to have one part pass away and another succeed, so that eventually we are able to perceive the whole. To illustrate, Aquinas quotes a passage from Augustine's *Confessions* in which, characteristically, Augustine presents something spoken as an example of a whole that unfolds in time. "You do not want the syllables to stand steady; you want them to fly away, so that others may succeed to them and you may hear the whole statement. So it is always with all things out of which some one being is constituted and the parts out of which it is fashioned do not all exist at once" (4.11.17; trans. Ryan).

The argument of *ST* 1–2.32.2 concludes with a corollary, parallel to Aristotle's corollary at the end of *EN* 7.14. If there is some thing (1) whose nature is unchangeable; (2) in which there is no possibility of excess beyond a natural condition by continued presence of the object of its pleasure; and (3) that is able to intuit the object of its pleasure all at once – to such a thing, change will not be pleasurable. And the closer other pleasures approach to this condition, the more continuous they can be.

Aristotle's contrast in *EN* 7.14.1154b20–31 is between our non-simplicity and the divine simplicity. Aquinas, in *ST* 1–2.32.2, emphasizes rather the difference between our changeable nature and a hypothetical unchangeable nature. His unusually oblique supposition of "a thing whose nature is unchangeable" (cf. *EN* 7.14.1154b25) is evidently a reference to God, whose immutability he has discussed in *ST* 1.9. What are the pleasures that he says "approach" the unchanging, continuous pleasure of God? Perhaps they are those of the angels, who are clearly the "things" (*quaedam*) mentioned in another quotation from the *Confessions* in the article; the quotation describes them as eternally rejoicing in God (*ST* 1–2.32.2 s.c.). Or perhaps Aquinas is anticipating the other causes of human pleasure he is about to discuss in the rest of *ST* 1–2.32, culminating in the intellectual pleasures of wonder, inquiry, and discovery. In itself, he says, the contemplation of what is already known is more pleasurable, because more perfect, than inquiry into what is unknown. Accidentally, however, investigation and discovery can sometimes be more pleasurable than contemplation, inasmuch as they proceed from greater desire (*ST* 1–2.32.8 ad 2).

13.3 Aquinas on Aristotle's second treatise: "Pleasure perfects action"

> End, as *telos*, signifies a continuing state of perfectedness; it is akin to the meaning of "finish," where we are speaking about what the cabinet maker does last in making a piece of furniture: he puts the finish on it, that is, brings it to perfection in completion. (Slade 1997, 83)

At the beginning of his commentary on Book 10 of the *Ethics*, where the second treatise on pleasure starts, Aquinas naturally notes that this is a second treatise on the same subject in the same work. Like pre-modern commentators in general, he takes the *Nicomachean Ethics* to be a well-composed unity.[5] He explains the difference between the treatises as follows.

---

[5] A number of modern scholars question this unity, in part because Books 5–7 of the *Nicomachean Ethics*, which include the first treatise on pleasure, are identical to Books 4–6 of the *Eudemian*

In Book 7, Aristotle discusses pleasure as "the matter of continence," and therefore mainly considers sensible and bodily pleasures; in Book 10, he discusses pleasure as it attaches to happiness and therefore mainly considers intelligible and spiritual pleasure (*SLE* 10.1 lines 21–7). In remarks on pleasure outside of his *Ethics* commentary, on the other hand, Aquinas usually quotes from the two treatises without distinction, as if they both belonged to a single treatise on pleasure.

At one point, however, in a reply to an objection in *ST* 1–2.33.4, he does compare the two treatises with respect to their most striking difference, that between the description of pleasure as unimpeded action in the first treatise (7.12.1153a14–15) and the description of it as perfective of action in the second treatise (10.4.1174b23, b33). Aquinas's argument in the article is that pleasure perfects action, to which the following objection is made. Nothing can be perfective either of itself or of its own cause, but in the first treatise Aristotle says pleasure *is* action, and this must be understood in either an essential or a causal sense; therefore, pleasure cannot *perfect* action. Aquinas's answer begins with a quotation from *Physics* 2.3.195a8: two things can be causes of each other in such a way that the first is an efficient cause of the second, and the second a final cause of the first. (He does not mention the example Aristotle gives, that exercise is an efficient cause of health, and health the final cause of exercise.) In this manner (*per hunc modum*), he says, action causes pleasure as an efficient cause,[6] and pleasure perfects action in the manner of an end (*per modum finis*), "as was said." This backward reference is to an explanation in the body of the article of the precise sense in which pleasure perfects action in the manner of an *end*.

In striking contrast to this statement that pleasure perfects action in the manner of an end, Aquinas says in his commentary on the *Ethics* that pleasure perfects action in the manner of a *form*. How can he say both that pleasure perfects action in the manner of a form, and that it does so in the manner of an end?

Ethics. Some argue that the two treatises on pleasure represent different stages in the development of Aristotle's thinking about pleasure. Festugière (1960, xxiv) and Gauthier and Jolif (1970, II,2:778–81) argue that the treatise in Book 7 is earlier than that in Book 10, Gosling and Taylor (1982, 285–300) that the treatise in Book 10 may have been composed first. According to Van Riel (2000, 43n37), "it seems to be clear that . . . both accounts cannot belong to the same work (because of the absolute absence of cross-references, which would hardly be possible if the same subject were treated twice within one and the same work)."

On the other hand, some recent scholarship is favorable to the view that the *Nicomachean Ethics* constitutes a well-ordered whole, one in which both treatises on pleasure have a function. See Burger 2008, 154, and Pakaluk 2011, 41–3.

[6] In *In Sent.* 4.49.3.2, Aquinas presents action as the *formal* cause of pleasure.

13.3.1 "In the manner of a form" (SLE 10.6 line 76)

The statement that pleasure perfects action occurs in *EN* 10.4. Aristotle begins this chapter by comparing pleasure to vision. Like an act of vision, he says, a pleasure is at any moment perfect, a whole, not a gradual process toward completion, such as the construction of a building or a walk to a destination (1174a14–b14). Then, in a subtle shift, he turns to the pleasure *of* vision, as a paradigm of pleasure in general (an auspicious paradigm for a Christian theologian). All pleasure, Aristotle says, occurs in an act of awareness, whether of sense perception, thought, or contemplation. The best, most perfect, most pleasurable act of vision is an act of a power of sight that is in good condition, and that is directed to its most beautiful, most powerful, most important object. In short, there is pleasure when patient and agent are both at their best (1174b14–23, b26–31), and the pleasure perfects the action (1174b23, b24, b31–2; 1175a15–16, a21). To indicate how the pleasure perfects the action, Aristotle makes two comparisons whose correct interpretation has been much disputed by scholars. (1) Pleasure does not perfect action in the manner that a sense power and a sense object do; likewise, health and a doctor are not in the same manner causes of being healthy (1174b23–6). (2) Pleasure perfects action, not as an indwelling state (οὐχ ὡς ἡ ἕξις ἐνυπάρχουσα, *non sicut habitus qui inest*), but as a supervening end (ἀλλ᾽ ὡς ἐπιγινόμενόν τι τέλος, *ut superveniens quidam finis*), as beauty supervenes on the young (1174b31–3).

In his commentary on the *Ethics*, Aquinas explains the first comparison as follows. The manner (*modus*) in which pleasure perfects, say, an act of sense perception, is not the same as the manner in which the object of the act (the sensible thing) and the active principle (the sense of power) do, although all of these – pleasure, object, active principle – are good, and all contribute goodness to the act.[7] Health and a doctor are both causes of being healthy, but in different ways: health is a cause in the manner of a form (*per modum formae*), a doctor in the manner of an agent (*per modum agentis*). Likewise, pleasure, the perfection of action, perfects action in the manner of a form; a sense-power in good condition and a congenial object perfect the action of sense perception in the manner of agents, the sense power as a moved mover, the object as an unmoved mover (*SLE* 10.6 lines 68–80).

---

[7] In translating *modus* as *manner*, I am taking Aquinas to be using the Latin word in its "ordinary," as distinct from its properly metaphysical, sense, in the passages I discuss (see Tomarchio 2001, 585–6 and 591). At the same time, I take him to be using the word *modus* with great philosophical deliberateness in these passages.

At this point in his own commentary on the *Ethics*, R. A. Gauthier accuses Aquinas of entangling his interpretation in a contradiction here (Gauthier and Jolif 1970, II,2:839).[8] He charges that, following the lead of Michael of Ephesus, Aquinas takes health, and correspondingly pleasure, to be meant by Aristotle as instances of formal causality, when Aristotle is about to affirm, in his second comparison, that pleasure perfects action as a *final* cause. What Aquinas has just said, however, is not quite that pleasure perfects action as a *formal cause*, but that it does so *in the manner of a form*, and what Aristotle is about to say is not quite that pleasure is *a final cause*, but that it is "τι τέλος" (*quidam finis*) – *a certain, a sort of, end*. Both Aristotle and Aquinas, it seems, are using language in a more exploratory and tentative way than is allowed for by the terms *formal cause* and *final cause*, when these are used in a sharply delineated, mutually exclusive way.

Aquinas introduces Aristotle's second comparison as a clarification of the manner in which pleasure perfects action. Then he says that "it has been said" that pleasure perfects action, not efficiently (*efficienter*), but formally (*formaliter*). This is rather ambiguous. He is not referring to the Aristotelian text, but to the distinction he himself has just made between perfecting action in the manner of an agent and doing so in the manner of a form; he is restating his adverbial phrases (*in the manner of an agent, in the manner of a form*) as adverbs (*efficiently, formally*). Then, as a preliminary to a paraphrase of the second comparison, he says that there are two kinds of *formal perfection*: one is intrinsic and constitutes the essence of a thing; the other supervenes on a thing already constituted in its essence. Therefore (*ergo*), Aristotle says that pleasure perfects action, *not as an indwelling state*, not, that is, as a form that enters into the essence of a thing, but *as a certain end*, that is, as a certain perfection, one that *supervenes, as beauty supervenes on the young* (1174b33). G. E. M. Anscombe (1958, 3) famously described this simile as "sheer babble," but Aquinas finds it quite meaningful. He says that beauty is not of the essence of youth, but something that follows, as it were, from the good disposition of the causes of youth; likewise, pleasure follows from the good disposition of the causes of action, that is, of the object and the active principle of action (*SLE* 10.6 line 100–16; cf. lines 69–70). With this distinction between what is *of the essence* and what *follows from* the good disposition of causes, Aquinas evokes the language of the predicables, in which a property is defined as what is not *of the essence* of a thing, but is *caused by* the thing's essential principles (*ST* 1.77.1 ad 5). The beauty of the

---

[8] The commentary on Book 10 of the *Ethics* in Gauthier and Jolif 1970 is the work of Gauthier alone; see n. 7 in Chapter 8 in this volume.

young and the pleasure taken in an action, he thus suggests, are *properties* following from the good disposition of the causes of the *essences* of youth and of the action, respectively. Pleasure, in short, is a property of an act of awareness in which a cognitive power and a congenial object to which it is directed are both excellent. The suggestion is reinforced by Aquinas's assertion in *ST* I–2.2.6 that pleasure is not *of the essence* of beatitude, but *a proper and per se accident* that follows on it.

In 1982, J. C. B. Gosling and C. C. W. Taylor distinguished three lines of interpretation of Aristotle's statement that pleasure is a supervening end: the majority view (shared by Gosling and Taylor, and attributed by Gauthier to Aquinas) that pleasure is "the formal cause of actualization"; the view that it is "some subtle extra perfection" that may or may not be added to the perfection of actualization; and the view of Gauthier that it is "the final cause of (perfect) actualization" (Gosling and Taylor 1982, 241–2). A recent discussion of Aristotle's statement by Matthew S. Strohl proposes to go beyond this set of interpretations.

> The three types of interpretations of Aristotle's account of pleasure that past commentators have favoured are unattractive, and none of them, it seems, is supported by conclusive evidence. My own view is that, for Aristotle, pleasure is simply the perfection of a perfect activity of awareness, the very perfection that is brought about by the good condition of the capacity activated and the fine object it is active in relation to. That is to say, it is the character that such an activity has in virtue of the good condition of the capacity and the fineness of the object. (Strohl 2011, 277–8)

Aquinas, I think, would be more sympathetic to this view than to any of the interpretations described by Gosling and Taylor. He might, however, ask for clarification of Strohl's use of the term "character," and of his description of pleasure as *an essential aspect* of perfect activity of awareness (ibid., 273). Pleasure, on Aquinas's interpretation, is not *of the essence* of the activity; it completes the activity as a *property* that flows or follows from the activity's essential causes.

13.3.2 *"In the manner of an end" (ST 1–2.33.4 resp.)*

I come back, finally, to *ST* I–2.33.4, in which Aquinas says not that pleasure perfects action in the manner of a form, but that it does so in the manner of an end. Distinguishing two senses of *end*, he says that pleasure does not perfect action in the manner of an end in the sense in which "end" means that for the sake of which something is (*id propter quod aliquid est*), but rather in the sense in which every good that supervenes by way of completion (*omne bonum completive superveniens*) can be called an end. Accordingly (*secundum hoc*), Aristotle says that pleasure perfects action *as a supervening end*, inasmuch as, over and above the good that an action itself is, there supervenes another good, pleasure, which implies repose of appetite in the presupposed good of action. Aquinas's qualification here of pleasure's supervenience by the adverb *completive* ('by way of completion') resonates with remarks on pleasure as completion toward the beginning and toward the end of his *Sentences* commentary: happiness is called pleasure from the point of view of its completion, rather than the point of view of its beginning (*ex parte sui complementi, magis quam ex parte principii*; *In Sent.* 1.1.1.1); pleasure is required for beatitude as a sort of form, as it were, that completes it (*quasi forma completiva beatitudinis*), as the beauty that adorns youth may be said to supervene on the young (*In Sent.* 4.49.1.1 qc. 2 ad 2).

According to the *Ethics* commentary, then, pleasure perfects action in the manner of a form, formally, as a *formal perfection*, in a secondary sense of that term. It supervenes on an action as an end or perfection that follows from the good disposition of the act's causes, namely, the capacity of which it is the act, and the object to which it is directed.

According to the *Summa theologiae*, on the other hand, pleasure perfects action in the manner of an *end*, in a secondary sense of *that* term, the sense in which every good that supervenes by way of completion can be called an end. It supervenes on an action as a further good, the good of repose of appetite.

There seems to be no reason to think that these two accounts are not compatible with one another, with the Aristotelian text, and with the nature of pleasure. The beauty that supervenes on the young is a sort of *finish*, to use a word that suggests a union of both formality and finality, and of both perfection and completion. The finish that a cabinet-maker puts on a piece of work is neither the cabinet's essence-constituting formal cause nor that for the sake of which the cabinet exists, yet it is the cabinet's formal perfection and final completion. Analogously, pleasure is neither the formal cause nor the final cause of an act of awareness. It is rather the finish on an act of awareness in which in which agent and patient are both at their best, the finish that is repose of appetite. Pleasure is the calm of completion that supervenes on energetic awareness of an object worthy of awareness.

13.4 Conclusion

I have twice compared a passage in Aquinas's *Ethics* commentary and an article of the *Summa theologiae*. Both articles introduce an Augustinian element that is not present in the *Ethics* commentary. *ST* 1–2.32.2 argues that change is pleasurable to us, not just on the Aristotelian grounds that our nature is changeable, and that an object of our pleasure may become excessive in relation to our natural state and therefore painful, but also on the Augustinian ground that it is sometimes our pleasure to know a whole, such as a composition of words, whose parts must give way to one another in time, in order for us to come to know the whole. *ST* 1–2.33.4 completes the Aristotelian thought that pleasure perfects action as a supervenient end by adding the Augustinian thought that this further good that is pleasure is a repose of appetite. On the subject of pleasure, as on many others, Aquinas the Aristotelian is finally inseparable from Aquinas the Augustinian.

CHAPTER FOURTEEN

Aristotle, Aquinas, Anscombe, and the new virtue ethics

Candace Vogler

Analytic philosophy divides itself into theoretical and practical regions, the boundaries of which are rooted in Immanuel Kant's critical philosophy. Traditionally, analytic philosophy analyzes thought rather than being, where thought is distinguished from actual psychological states or processes, and analysis of thought is accomplished through abstract analysis of language. Although almost no philosophical work that calls itself "analytic" adheres to these strictures nowadays, in this chapter I will focus on one strand that sometimes *does*: analytic virtue ethics.[1]

Contemporary analytic work on virtue covers a wide range of views, relying upon divergent historical sources, and has spawned several regions of lively disputation. I will concentrate on work that understands itself as responsive to Elizabeth Anscombe's call for a return to Aristotle, using both Aristotle and Aquinas, with no express explicit commitment to a body of revealed doctrine.[2] I will use Anscombe's writings as anchor points throughout.

[1] A note on terminology: "practical philosophy" covers ethics, action theory, value theory, work on practical reason, and some political philosophy. The contrast term is "theoretical philosophy," which includes metaphysics and epistemology, philosophy of language, logic, and philosophy of science, as well as some kinds of work in philosophy of mind. Virtue ethics is one of three large areas in analytic practical philosophy. The other two are neo-Humean practical philosophy and neo-Kantian practical philosophy. Philosophers used to use "deontology" and "consequentialism" to denote different approaches to work in ethics. Newer work does not fit these categories. Most neo-Humeans are not consequentialists: they do not focus on outcomes (expected, unexpected; foreseeable, unforeseeable) of actions or policies. What unites them is the view that foundational questions in ethics are best answered with reference to moral psychology or custom. Most neo-Kantians are not deontologists: their work is not centered on questions about which acts are morally required, which are morally permitted, and which are morally impermissible. What unites them is the view that foundational questions in ethics are best answered with reference to reason and standards of rationality. Neo-Aristotelian virtue ethics, instead, holds that foundational questions in ethics are best answered in terms of an account of human nature. In all three cases the "neo" marks a retreat from the metaphysics associated with the historical source.

[2] Accordingly, I will not consider Martha Nussbaum's path-breaking work *The Fragility of Goodness* (1986) as she neither draws directly from Aquinas nor is indebted to Anscombe. I will not address work that expressly parts company with Aristotle and ignores Aquinas (e.g., Slote 2003), and I will leave to the side many other writings in contemporary virtue ethics that are not expressly indebted

Anscombean neo-Aristotelians draw from Aquinas. I will begin by laying out Anscombe's challenge and then discuss the kind of engagement with Aquinas that came in its wake. Analytic practical philosophers distinguish work in ethics from work on action and practical reason, and I will discuss the sense in which analytic neo-Aristotelians think that thought about good and bad is nevertheless crucial to work on action and practical reason. I will then focus on the centerpiece of Anscombe's challenge: the claim that mainstream Anglophone moral philosophy no longer understood moral prohibitions, and that this prevented philosophers from making progress in ethics. Finally, I will consider some ways that analytic neo-Aristotelianism might treat moral prohibitions.

14.1 Anscombe's call

In her 1958 essay, "Modern Moral Philosophy," Anscombe argued that analytic philosophers in search of an account of morality had reached a dead end. She suggested that philosophers interested in morality might start fresh by returning to Aristotle's work on action, practical reason, and virtue, with special emphasis on individual justice. Nothing happened for a long time. But the youth took notice, started reading Aristotle, and eventually launched analytic virtue ethics.

Anscombe was a Thomist. It is very hard to say what kind of Thomist she was. Mary Geach recalls:

> Anscombe drew upon [Aquinas] to an unknowable extent: she said to me that it aroused prejudice in people to tell them that a thought came from him: to my sister she said that to ascribe a thought to him made people boringly ignore the interest of it, whether they were for Aquinas or against him. (Mary Geach 2011, xix)

Although Peter Geach is more likely than Anscombe to name Aquinas as a source, work with Aquinas informs Anscombe's writings in practical philosophy. And work with Aquinas began to inform analytic Aristotelian virtue ethics as well. Partly through Anscombe's influence and Geach's, Philippa Foot, Rosalind Hursthouse, and their students, intent on developing the called-for neo-Aristotelian practical philosophy, began reading some Aquinas. (Anthony Kenny, Alasdair MacIntyre, and Anselm Müller have a deeper relation to Aquinas.)

to Anscombe, Aristotle, and Aquinas. There are many ways of being neo-Aristotelian. The analytic neo-Aristotelians who draw from Aquinas work under Anscombe's influence, which is why some adhere to traditional strictures in analytic philosophy as well.

Almost all of the philosophers who turn to Aquinas as part of their work developing new Aristotelian practical philosophy focus on *Summa theologiae* 1–2 qq. 1–21 and 49–62. They are especially interested in Aquinas's discussions of acquired virtues. In Aquinas they find a more detailed, more focused, and in some ways more systematic treatment of acquired virtue than they find in Aristotle. In this spirit, Foot writes:

> By and large Aquinas followed Aristotle – sometimes even heroically – where Aristotle gave an opinion, and where St. Thomas is on his own, as in developing the doctrine of the theological virtues of faith, hope, and charity, and in his theocentric doctrine of happiness, he still uses an Aristotelian framework where he can: as for instance in speaking of happiness as man's last end. However there are different emphases and new elements in Aquinas's ethics: often he works things out in far more detail than Aristotle did, and it is possible to learn a great deal from Aquinas that one could not have got from Aristotle. It is my opinion that the *Summa Theologica* is one of the best sources we have for moral philosophy, and moreover that St. Thomas's ethical writings are as useful to the atheist as to the Catholic or other Christian believer. (Foot 1978, 1–2)

In short, looking to Aristotle for guidance came to include looking to Aquinas.

It is not immediately obvious why philosophers turning to Aristotle would turn to Aquinas at the same time. On the face of it, there are profound differences between the two. Although both Aquinas and Aristotle understand contemplation of the divine as the highest good for human beings, Aristotle's god is not the almighty creator of Aquinas's theology, Aristotle certainly did not hold that this highest good was best identified with beatific union with God in a resurrected life, and Aristotle did not think that the virtues were best understood as giving more specific direction to a human reason bound by natural law, understood in the broader context of divine or eternal law. Whatever one makes of the place of law in Aristotle's ethics, Aristotle does not have a divine law approach to ethics in any ordinary sense, whereas thought about law and a divine legislator provides the framework for discussion of ethics in Aquinas.[3] Virtuous action *cannot* be the ultimate end for human beings in Aquinas's understanding of practical reason. On some readings, virtuous action *might* have this status for Aristotle, if happiness as the ultimate end is understood as essentially

---

[3] Much ink has been spilled over this question, partly because, in "Modern moral philosophy," Anscombe insisted that Aristotle had no concept corresponding to the divine law understanding of moral obligation. For a balanced and thoughtful treatment of the controversy that partly vindicates Anscombe, see O'Brien 2011, ch. 2.

connected with virtue. On standard readings of Aristotle, the fully rational, fully virtuous, practically wise person will rarely have occasion to regret his actions, passions, or judgment. Practical wisdom and virtue do not obviate the frequent need to go to confession in Aquinas. For these and other reasons, there are questions about the extent to which Aquinas's practical philosophy is Aristotelian.[4]

Lively, scholarly debate on these matters has had very little impact on analytic virtue ethics. For the most part analytic neo-Aristotelians are neither scholars of medieval philosophy nor Latinists, do not identify themselves as Christians, and are more concerned with moving contemporary moral philosophy forward than they are with the history of their subject. Many follow Foot in finding part of the *Summa theologiae* useful.[5] If they read more widely in Aquinas, this is not marked in footnotes or bibliographic materials. It is easiest to think of my target group as a band of contemporary analytic neo-Aristotelians inspired by Anscombe who conduct periodic raids on portions of the *Summa theologiae* in search of wisdom.

They share the view that right action is action from and for the sake of virtue and that right practical reasoning is virtuous practical reasoning. Relatedly, all hold that practical reason is the defining mark of the human being,[6] and that virtue and practical wisdom are the highest expression of practical reason.[7] Virtues pattern right choice, right action, appropriate emotions, and developed sensitivities to ethical salience. Further, the virtues make the adult good *qua* human being. Philosophers in my target group find significant common ground between what they take from Aquinas and Aristotle on these points.

In practice, Anscombean virtue ethics often seems to operate with the sensibility expressed in *Summa theologiae* 1.1.1 arg. 1:

> It seems that, besides philosophical science, we have no need of any further knowledge. For man should not seek to know what is above reason . . . But whatever is not above reason is fully treated of in philosophical science. Therefore any other knowledge besides philosophical science is superfluous.[8]

---

[4] See, for example, Kluxen 1998 and Bradley 1997.

[5] Foot moves easily between Aristotle and Aquinas. In Foot 2003, see: "Moral relativism," pp. 20–36; "Von Wright on virtue," pp. 105–16; "Nietzsche's immoralism," pp. 144–58; and "Moral dilemmas revisited," pp. 175–88.

[6] The best discussion of the relevant stress on rationality is in Matthew Boyle's "Additive theories of rationality" and "Essentially rational animals." Both are manuscripts that are in wide circulation.

[7] Foot takes her conviction on this matter from Warren S. Quinn's work; see Quinn 1993, 228–57 ("Putting rationality in its place") and pp. 210–27 ("Rationality and the human good"). His expressed debt to Aquinas is to be found in his discussion of double effect; see Quinn 1989.

[8] All quotations from the *ST* are from Aquinas 1947–48.

Aquinas responds that although philosophy would seem entirely adequate in its methods (disciplined, systematic reasoning) and its subject matter (being), it cannot provide adequate understanding of the nature of human happiness. For this, we need knowledge about God. Very talented philosophers, given adequate time for reflection, might develop some cognition of God, but the philosophical view will be slow in coming and come mixed with error. We need God's self-revelation to understand our ultimate end, and we need a true account of our ultimate end if we are to orient our lives appropriately.

Does it matter that my target ethicists seem to have never read the beginning of the *Summa theologiae*? Not necessarily. Just as there are many places where Aquinas and Aristotle seem to diverge, there are many places where new Aristotelian virtue ethics diverges from both Aquinas and Aristotle. For example, Aristotle and Aquinas took it that ethics required a general understanding of human good but was ultimately aimed at guiding conduct. Analytic practical philosophy does not purport to guide conduct. Then too, Aristotle and Aquinas took it that not every human being could be expected to be virtuous and practically wise – practical wisdom is more rare than practical knowledge. Both seem to have held that practical wisdom required uncommon intellectual capacities, and that acquiring virtue was a daunting task.[9] Aquinas, however, held that human nature as we know it is postlapsarian human nature in which the intellect is not necessarily subjected to God, the lower powers are not necessarily subjected to the higher powers, and the will is accordingly disordered; the loss to our nature is at once a loss of governance and a loss of the appropriate directedness of natural inclinations toward the highest good possible for us.[10] Virtues are meant to help to reintegrate – or at least foster appropriate relations among – our appetitive and intellectual powers. In this sense, acquired virtue helps to reorder human nature and so dispose us for the grace that fits intellectual creatures for their ultimate end. The human as such, however muddled, is so directed, even though almost no one will have all the benefits of acquired virtue. All varieties of analytic virtue ethics, on the other hand, are more egalitarian than Aristotle, and most are more egalitarian than Aquinas as well. Finally, analytic virtue ethics distances itself from the thought that there *is* a single ultimate end in human life – a thought crucial to both Aristotle and Aquinas.

---

[9] For an account of the kind of intellectual achievement at issue, see Porter 1992.

[10] For discussion of the effects of original sin, see De Letter 1954.

Aquinas's picture of why we need sacred doctrine is based on an account of ethics as fundamentally practical, of practical wisdom as an extraordinary achievement, of human life as having a single ultimate end (an end that is beyond our reach unless we are given gratuitous divine assistance), and of acquired, cultivated virtue as at best a partial means to that end. Aquinas's ambitions do not intersect with the ambitions of analytic virtue ethics at *any* of these points. Accordingly, we should not expect seamlessly to weave Aquinas's work on virtue and practical reason into the fabric of analytic virtue ethics. Of course, *Aristotle's* work on virtue and practical reason fails to be of a piece with analytic virtue ethics as well.[11]

I have mentioned various junctures where Aquinas apparently parts company with Aristotle, and various points at which both Aristotle and Aquinas seem to be at odds with the ambitions of analytic virtue ethics. In the remainder of this chapter, I will look at one place in which Aristotle and Aquinas seem to share a view crucial to Anscombe's call for new research that has been largely ignored by those who have taken up her challenge.

14.2 Anscombe's Complaint

My target neo-Aristotelians understand themselves as, in part, responding to Anscombe's 1958 call for a return to Aristotle. In her essay, Anscombe claims that the landscape in Anglophone moral philosophy went perfectly flat in the twentieth century because English philosophers – like Englishmen and North Americans more generally – no longer understood moral prohibitions.

Both Aristotle and Aquinas hold that there are moral prohibitions. According to Aristotle, envy, spite and shamelessness are always bad passions and must be dealt with in whatever way one deals with bad passions; murder, theft, and adultery are always bad acts and must not be done; he tells us that the names of such actions and passions imply badness (*EN* 2.6.1107a8–17). It is, however, possible to hold that there are no such things as moral prohibitions. MacIntyre (2009, 8–9) treats dispute over whether there are any as one of five varieties of apparently intractable moral disagreement, which he understands as a dispute over means to an ultimate end. If those who think that there are moral prohibitions are on the side of truth in the dispute, then prohibition attaches to things that it is in one's power to do simply in virtue of the fact that the action, or action-in-prospect, is of a determinate kind.

---

[11] For a summary of this point, see Hursthouse 1999, 8–16.

Anscombe's work on practical reason always concerned determinate *kinds* of intentional action – what analytic philosophers came to call "act-types." The closest equivalent to act-types in Aquinas is the *obiectum* – the object or objective of the act (*Summa theologiae* 1–2.18.2). The *obiectum* establishes the species of the act for Aquinas. It seems likely that Anscombe had Aquinas's *obiectum* in mind when introducing act-types into analytic philosophy.[12] The analytic philosophical act-type, however, is distinct from Aquinas's *obiectum*. An act-type is just any isolable, determinately describable aspect of an exterior act done on purpose, such that the agent can answer a question about what he's doing couched in terms of that description.[13] In Donald Davidson's example, "writing the letter *a*" counts as an act-type, as does "writing the word *action*," and "writing an essay about actions," even though one is writing out the word *action* in the course of writing the essay.[14] In Anscombe's famous example, "moving one's arm up and down," "pumping," "replenishing the house water-supply," and "poisoning the inhabitants of the house" all count as act-types (Anscombe 2000, § 23). Analytic philosophical practice designates act-types with capital letters drawn from the beginning of the alphabet. Anscombe's act-types take their sense from the proximate end of the action in question (as do the act-types at issue in subsequent analytic philosophical action theory). This is part of the way in which she appears to be drawing from Aquinas.

Although Anscombe gives us many benign examples of act-types (doodling, heading off to market to buy cattle), she also gives extended treatment of examples involving morally prohibited act-types: murdering the inhabitants of a house (the example that she uses to introduce the means-end structure of intentional action and practical reason), murdering Jewish children (ibid., § 38), and suicide (Anscombe 1995, 7).

When addressing her fellow Catholics, Anscombe followed Aquinas in holding that no particular act is morally indifferent, and that an act is good just in case it is not bad in its species, its circumstances, or its end.[15]

---

12 In *Intention* (and elsewhere), she uses the phrase "under a description" to mark this feature of practical reason, intention, and action. See Anscombe 2000, §§ 4–6, 16–18, 21–6; see also Anscombe 1979.

13 The closest that analytic neo-Aristotelianism comes to giving an account of an act-type is to be found in Michael Thompson's account of actions unfolding over time (2008, 85–148: "Naïve action theory"). For Thompson, an intentional action is an actual token of an act-type that might be deployed in a larger intentional action. At the limit, this analysis can lead to the conclusion that crossing the street involves tokens of continuum-many act-types, since one can produce an account of moving halfway across, and halve that again, and again, and again, and so on until one has a Zeno-paradoxical description of crossing the street.

14 Davidson 1980, 88. Davidson read both Aristotle and Aquinas.

15 Particular acts with indifferent act-descriptions will be good or bad in light of their circumstances and end. See Anscombe, 1982.

"Chewing on a piece of straw," like "stroking one's beard," is an intentional act-type with an indifferent description. A token of such a type need not count as an *actus humanus*. Aquinas distinguishes acts that count from those that don't in terms of the combined acts of intellect and will at issue in an *actus humanus*. Analytic philosophy is inherently unfriendly to acts of intellect or acts of will: it is predicated upon distancing itself from focus on actual psychological processes and would require a suitably de-psychologized account of intellect and will in order to figure out how to make use of Aquinas on this point. Anscombe's treatment of Aristotle's practical syllogism provides a kind of model: she treats the syllogism as articulating the rational anatomy, as it were, of the action-in-prospect rather than as an argument one rehearses to oneself in advance of acting (Anscombe 2000, §§ 33–5).

The challenge for analytic philosophers will be to offer a similar account of Aquinas's more elaborate characterization of the paired work of reason and will in the human act.[16] In spite of the distance between analytic philosophy and Aquinas over the analysis of particular human acts, the two will intersect at this point: moral prohibition attaches to a type or species of intentional action that will count as a specifically bad *actus humanus* that is bad in its species.[17] Anscombe's colleagues had lost the ability to comprehend prohibited kinds of act as such. Complaining about this, she remarks:

> It is noticeable that none of these philosophers displays any consciousness that there is such an ethic, which he is contradicting: it is pretty well taken for obvious among them all that a prohibition such as that on murder does not operate in face of some consequences. But of course the strictness of the prohibition has as its point that *you are not to be tempted by fear or hope of consequences*. (Anscombe 1958, 10)

That is the doctrine. It comes into play whenever we are inclined to calculate the likelihood that doing something specifically bad (bad in its kind, bad because of the kind of action that it is) will result in getting something good, or in preventing something worse.

In coining the term "consequentialism," Anscombe highlighted the philosophical source of the loss of an ability to comprehend moral prohibitions. Anscombe's term drew attention to accounts of good, bad, right,

---

[16] For interpretation and discussion of scholarly controversy over Aquinas's account of human action, see Westberg 1994a, 119–35.

[17] For discussion of *obiectum* in Aquinas, see Westberg 2002. For discussion of the determinacy and objectivity of morally prohibited species of acts in Aquinas, see Porter 1989.

and wrong that focused on expected outcomes of actions (the part that became the standard definition of "consequentialism") and obliterated the distinction between intended and merely foreseen expected outcomes of an action (the part that was ignored by most of her followers). Consequentialists did *both*, she thought, and the latter was the more serious issue. Only a subset of the outcomes I expect are intended, and we need to be able to track intention in action in order to so much as *pick out* the particular act I do (in the sense of "particular act" at issue for Aquinas and Aristotle). For analytic philosophers, an intentional action is a kind of event describable in indefinitely many ways. Some of those descriptions will be descriptions under which the act is intentional. Others will not. For example, suppose that I walk to campus to hold office hours. In doing so, I do many things: I alter the traffic pattern by hitting the signal at the crosswalk and crossing the street, I startle a cat that was stalking a bird in the yard, I wear down the soles of my shoes, I think about my students, my family, and the day ahead, I nod to my neighbors, and so on. Many of these consequences are foreseen (startling the cat is not foreseen when I leave home, but becomes a foreseen consequence when I notice the cat and what it is up to and how it responds to me). The foreseen consequences are also events that will have consequences of their own. Suppose that a consequentialist joins me on my walk. Since my companion cannot register the distinction between foreseen and intended consequences of my act, "impeding the progress of drivers" and "startling a cat" are, for him, accounts of what I am doing that are of the *same sort* as the account that focuses on walking to school in order to hold office hours. Accordingly, my companion's assessment of my act could just as well focus on the cat's future, or the drivers', as on my office hours. Unlike me, *he* has no reason to prefer focus on analysis of the consequences of holding office hours to focus on analysis of the consequences of disrupting drivers. The consequentialist thinks of me as a sort of causal force moving through the world initiating many chains of events each time I do anything on purpose, and so will have to see walking to school as rather like knocking down the first domino in the indefinitely many different stacks of dominos that have their points of efficient causal origin along my path through the neighborhood. A cat's future and the future of its targeted prey lie along one subsequently branching causal chain. Each driver's future might take off from the single point of stopping at the pedestrian light that I triggered by pressing a button. Of course scaring a cat and impeding some drivers do not belong to the calculative order of my act: walking to school is not my (tremendously inefficient) means to the end of interfering with traffic and cats. And so the consequentialist cannot accurately say *what* my intentional action *was* – what I intentionally did, and to what end. In this sense, the consequentialist cannot correctly isolate and describe those aspects of what happened that belonged to my intentional action from the aspects that were merely the act's foreseen consequences. Obviously, if analytic philosophy has lost the capacity correctly to isolate and describe – in this sense, to *apprehend* – particular acts because it has embraced consequentialism, it cannot possibly give appropriate consideration to the consequences of particular acts.

Much of Anscombe's work in her monograph on intention is devoted to providing the analytic philosophical equipment needed to identify particular acts, as part of the work required before analytic philosophy can turn to ethics (Anscombe 2000). Reaching a point where analytic philosophy can cope with moral prohibitions was crucial for Anscombe and figures as the basis for the puzzle about justice that Michael Thompson traces in a recent essay.[18] A genuine rejection of consequentialism in Anscombe's sense of the term is bound up with recognition of moral prohibitions. This makes it especially surprising that analytic virtue ethics inspired by her call has devoted so little attention to the topic.

14.3   Good is to be pursued and bad is to be avoided

Although most analytic philosophers of action treat Anscombe's *Intention* as the first work in analytic action theory, almost all of them think that we can develop a philosophically sound account of action without drawing in thought about good and bad. My target ethicists take from Aquinas and Aristotle the thought that the first principle of practical reason tells us that good is to be pursued and bad avoided. Since this is a controversial claim in analytic action theory, they have had to argue that the intelligibility of intentional action as such is bound up with thought about good and bad.[19] In being asked questions like "Why are you doing that?" or "What's the point?" or "What are you up to?" we are being asked to address the sense in which *A*-ing, say, seems like a good sort of thing to do. There is a lot of work by analytic neo-Aristotelians arguing that we cannot so much as apprehend intentional actions without seeing them as undertaken *sub specie boni*. However, since they take themselves to be following Anscombe in supposing that concern over ethical good and bad need not belong to action theory or work on practical reason, they have worked to come up

18 Thompson 2004; Anscombe 1958 and 2008.
19 See, e.g., Boyle and Lavin 2010.

with an account of practical good and bad remote from ethics.[20] Rather than argue that thought about ethical good and bad are required for apprehending action and understanding practical reason, my target virtue ethicists have pursued the study of virtue as a distinctive enterprise that draws from Anscombean action theory, but is not a part of basic work on action or practical reason. Perhaps because of this, moral evaluation of kinds of acts – the sort at issue in moral prohibition – is not a part of most work in analytic virtue ethics. In this section, I will explain how my target philosophers understand the sort of good and bad at issue in apprehending intentional action, and why this seems separate from work in ethics.

Analytic virtue theorists draw from Anscombe in urging that the most basic orientation to good involved in intentional action attaches to the means–end structure of the act and establishes what is *supposed to* happen next. This "supposed to" has normative force in two directions: understanding what is supposed to happen next allows us to see what is being done and to what end (this is the sense in which it is crucial for understanding particular acts), and by exactly the same token, it shows what the agent has in mind in doing what she is doing (the immediate point or sense or good of her action), and so opens the possibility of rational criticism of what she does. I do *A* in order to do *B*, *B* in order to do *C*, and so on.[21] Intentional action, that is, has a calculative, means–end structure. That structure makes it possible to identify success, failure, obstacles, and interruptions. Without some way of identifying these, we don't have a concept of intentional action at all. We lose track of the kind of process at issue when people do things on purpose. Call this the "low form" of orientation to good and bad in action.

The things ruled out by this feature of intentional action – the things that will signal some sort of intellectual or appetitive problem – are such things as attempting to do things that it is manifestly not in your power to do (for instance, leap across a highway in a single bound), attempting to combine pursuits that cannot be combined (like read a newspaper while swimming), failing to stop doing what you are doing in order to attain some end when you already have successfully attained your end (having already edited, revised, and submitted the page proofs, you keep pulling up the file with some thought about working on the page proofs), continuing to deploy means to an end having ascertained that the means will not

---

[20] See, e.g., Vogler 2002, 26–52, Thompson 2008, 24–84, and Ford 2011.
[21] See Anscombe 2000, §§ 17–26, 38–40. For work drawing on Anscombe, see Vogler 2002, 126–46.

work (you already have emptied your bag completely in search of lost keys and keep returning to look for the keys in your bag) – these kinds of problems can be identified *as problems* in light of the low, calculative form of orientation to good and bad in action.

We are as yet at some distance from ethics. You can see that ethical orientation appears to be at a distance when you notice that egregiously bad actions can be undertaken as effective means to various ends.

In an undated typescript published in 2008 and addressed to an audience of her fellow Catholics, Anscombe begins to address specifically ethical practical reason by way of considering how a practical orientation takes shape (Anscombe 2008). Pre-ethical practical orientations concern how to move about and get along in a human society and normally include "raw material" for the ethical, she thinks:

> Moral action descriptions are not natural event descriptions. But it is part of the natural history of mankind that the human young acquire concepts corresponding to them, or in some cases, at least concepts in which they are rooted, as adultery is in that of marriage, or stealing in that of property. Some notion of property will be picked up by anyone in the course of his upbringing, and almost certainly some notion of stealing in its train. Quite generally: to grow up as a child of normal intelligence in a human society is *eo ipso* to be equipped with a range of concepts which form the raw material for moral action descriptions, and in many cases to acquire these as well, at least in a rough inchoate form. (Anscombe 2008, 225)

Given this sort of rough-and-ready cognitive basis for an ethical practical orientation, it is possible to make some distinctions. There is, on the one side, volition, appetite, and emotion (Anscombe 2008, 226). On the other, there is justification, judgment of right and wrong, accusation, excuse, condemnation, and the like. Anscombe thinks that it is possible to separate these because it is possible to have one without the other. She writes:

> I am imagining someone who does not seek to be justified or ask others to justify themselves. He is not defective in his grasp of language. He functions mentally as a juryman, who can say what has been done: never as a judge, who condemns or discharges the accused person. (Anscombe 2008, 226)

Such a person can correctly understand a moral code and deploy the relevant action-descriptions. He never seeks to condemn or to exonerate, to accuse or to excuse, on this basis. He never seeks this from others. He never asks it of himself. The relevant region of ethics involves *seeking* ethical justification, and standing prepared to accuse, excuse, condemn, or exonerate on ethical grounds.[22]

Notice that, with respect to the plainest calculative form of orientation to good and bad in action, it is hard to conceive the position of Anscombe's juryman – the fellow who understands and can correctly track the calculative relation in action but does not hold himself or anyone else accountable to basic standards of calculative practical reason. He knows that he must put one foot in front of the other in order to walk across the street but does not ask this of himself when setting out to walk across the street. He knows that the mechanic must do various things in order to change the oil in his car, but he would not dream of accusing her of some error, or demanding that she explain herself, if she failed to do those things when he left his car with her, having asked that she change the oil. In this sense it seems that, in the operation of plain calculative practical reason, it is *not* possible to separate appetite and emotion from the apparatuses of justification. Nevertheless, where nothing but accountability to standards of calculative practical reason is at issue, the apparatus of justification is stripped of some of its force. It would be odd to conceive a strictly calculative sense of duty, for example, and embarrassment – more than guilt – would appear the appropriate response to failures of pre-ethical calculative practical reason.

Prima facie, in advancing to the ethical, then, the sense in which intentional action has the intelligibility of good shifts. (The going metaphor for this shift is always one of rising, perhaps because the calculative order is a kind of lowest common denominator in understanding what people are up to and why.) The formal constraint – one should pursue good and avoid bad – remains constant when we shift from the bland calculative concern to ethics; the practical specification of good and of bad changes. It's no longer enough to seek adequate means to intelligible ends, as I might in settling upon using blackmail to increase my wealth. Substantive questions of right and wrong enter into the framework for assessing what's done.

The first thing to say about what one gets when one has an ethically sensitive practical orientation is this: a person with a practical orientation alive to the ethical is prepared to accuse, excuse, justify, or condemn what's done on ethical grounds, and this stance informs such a person's self-understanding and relations with others.

The second thing to say is that tendencies to seek justification establish a strong theme of right and wrong, obligation and guilt, accusation and

[22] Some philosophers have held that I cannot understand a moral code without holding myself accountable to it. Anscombe here attempts to urge that the view is false.

justification, at the core of a practical orientation. They involve a particularly high form of orientation to good and bad.

The third thing to say is that the *substance* of an ethically alert practical orientation comes from the *content* of the ethical system at issue, and there is no guarantee that it will be sound. Anscombe writes:

> a sense of duty must of course be accompanied by *some* way of conceiving something as your duty. Thus it can be filled out with a notion of party loyalty, military obligation to obedience, or of acting for the best consequences, and in all these cases leads to very evil actions. Only if it is combined with truth in the moral code can it be trusted to lead to good actions. Similarly, someone who "always tries to do what is right," but has not got such truth, will not succeed in acting well. (Anscombe 2008, 230)

In the absence of a sound ethical framework, any exercise of reason – speculative thought about ethics, moral theory, general philosophical reflection, or action on the basis of practical deliberation – will misconstrue the whole apparatus of ethically directed practical justification that forms the core of an ethically alert practical orientation.

14.4   Negative moral precepts; positive moral precepts

Although Aristotle and Aquinas share the view that some species of acts are never right and always wrong, neither seems to hold that some species of acts are always right and never wrong. This is, I take it, the actual insight that underlies analytic virtue ethicists' excitement over the claim that virtue is uncodifiable.[23] You cannot produce a complete, comprehensive, and exhaustive code (or manual or what have you) that will tell you what, under any conceivable circumstance, will count as a right thing to do.

There are familiar Wittgensteinian routes to this conclusion having to do with the impossibility of setting out the rules that will determine in advance how to apply existing rules. Commenting on Aristotle, Denis J. M. Bradley describes the traditional position this way:

> A fixed moral principle is one that is universally true or exceptionless, it covers every member of a class of actions. Aristotle means to distinguish (though not always unhesitatingly) between fixed negative and fixed positive principles. His treatment of universal negative precepts rests on generic considerations of actions. There are exceptionless universal *prohibitions* that

---

[23] John McDowell was the first contemporary neo-Aristotelian writing about virtue to stress this point. See the essays reprinted in McDowell 1998, especially "Virtue and reason," 50–73, "Values and secondary qualities," 131–50, and "Non-cognitivism and rule-following," 198–218.

fixedly forbid, even at the price of terrible death, certain action-types, no matter what the extenuating circumstances of their action-tokens. (Bradley 1997, 190)

Bradley continues with the contrast:

a general [positive] moral principle is too inexact to be applied truthfully to those actions that are exceptions to the principle. A particular action as particular is contingently determinate. Of course, both universal and general moral principles can be given further and further specification. But the process of specifying narrower and narrower moral principles, by making morally relevant subdivisions among the members of a larger class of actions, is endless... Since general positive moral principles, however usually correct, cannot secure the knowledge of the moral character of singular actions, ethics, which above all is a practical science aimed at enabling agents to act, can best be put in outline form. (Bradley 1997, 192–3)

In short, the *only universal moral principles geared to kinds/species of act* are the negative ones that tell us *never to do* acts of such-and-such a kind.[24]

Anscombe might put the point this way: we are always in the ethical; the only way to ensure that a kind of act will be good to do here and now will be to screen out the world in such a way that it cannot obtrude and make what is ordinarily good bad; it is not in our power to stop the world from interfering in this way.[25] For example, it is usually good to fix breakfast for one's children before they leave home in the morning, but not if the house is on fire. Philosophers err when they extend the idea that some kinds of act that are usually wrong (e.g., pulling one's children out of their beds and rushing them into the street in their nightclothes) can be right *under the circumstances* (e.g., the house is on fire) to specifically wrong acts.

There are various things to be said about the importance of recognizing specifically wrong acts. First, it is clear that these are among the moral act descriptions that are part and parcel of ordinary ethical life and conduct. Anscombe's juryman needs to understand moral prohibitions in order correctly to deploy moral action descriptions and to understand the special weight of some kinds of accusation.

Second, it is hard to see how anyone could receive a moral education without acquiring a rough and ready understanding that some kinds of acts are specifically bad. Children come into accountability for their acts

---

[24] For discussion of Aristotle's understanding of the kind of generality we can expect from ethics, see Anagnostopoulos 1994.

[25] Aquinas makes this point in his discussion of sins of omission: praising God is usually good, but if I am praising God when I ought instead to be honoring my father and mother, then I sin (*QDM* 2.1 ad 7).

by being told what not to do – the usual starting points involve a mixture
of prohibitions that belong to etiquette (e.g., injunctions not to stare or
shout), to concern over safety (e.g., injunctions not to run into the street,
climb some things, jump off other things), and to ethics (e.g., injunctions
not to hit, lie, or take what doesn't belong to them).

Third, it is very hard to see how there could be such a thing as an
ethically alert practical orientation without an understanding that some
acts are specifically wrong. Framing someone for a capital criminal offense,
rape, vivisecting the children in the local daycare center – *none* of these are
ruled out as such in advance if there are no moral prohibitions. It is one
thing to argue that some acts that have been regarded as specifically wrong
are not, actually, specifically wrong. It is quite another to hold that there
are no such things as specifically wrong acts – as though the sphere of kinds
of act that it might be good to do here and now were entirely unbounded.

14.5   Moral prohibition and analytic virtue ethics

Most analytic virtue ethicists do not discuss moral prohibition. Peter Geach
urged that virtue ethics pursued in the absence of a theological framework
could not adequately ground moral prohibitions. Imagining the contemporary Aristotelian faced with a question about the status of moral prohibitions, Geach writes:

> [Somebody] might very well admit that not only is there something bad
> about certain acts, but also it is desirable to become the sort of person who
> needs to act in the contrary way; and yet *not* admit that such acts are to be
> avoided in all circumstances and at any price. To be sure, a virtuous person
> cannot be ready in advance to do such acts; and if he does do them they
> will damage his virtuous habits and perhaps irreparably wreck his hard-won
> integrity of soul. But at this point someone may protest "Are you the only
> person to be considered? Suppose the price of your precious integrity is a
> most fearful disaster! Haven't you got a hand to burn for your country (or
> mankind) and your friends?". This sort of appeal has not, I think, been
> adequately answered on Aristotelian lines, either by Aristotle or by Mrs.
> Foot. (Peter Geach 1978, 123)

It is fairly clear from the context that Geach means to point to the kind
of example ordinarily given in support of doing a bad sort of thing for
the sake of securing great good or avoiding catastrophe. In such examples
we normally are invited to imagine an agent who is very nearly uniquely
positioned to do the bad act in question and are being asked to consider

the particular bad act in isolation from that agent's ordinary practical orientation.

It is helpful in this connection to consider Thomas More facing a choice between falsely swearing an oath and going to prison. The example has various things to recommend it. Unlike examples in which we are asked to imagine a virtuous person being asked to do a kind of act that it would be very difficult for a virtuous person even to know how to do – like torture a prisoner – few things are easier for a lawyer, a judge, and a former holder of high political office than signing his name to an official document. The kind of act at issue requires no addition to the agent's established practical repertoire. Then too, More was sensitive to the reversals of fortune that his family suffered because of his dispute with Henry VIII. Finally, it is reasonable to think that the King was going to do what he was going to do anyway; More could not compel a change in circumstances. In short, in this example things in fact appear to net down to a question about the hard-won integrity of a man being asked to perform an act that only he can perform under the circumstances.

In conversation, Hursthouse urges that analytic neo-Aristotelians ought to treat the More example as of a piece with examples in which the courageous person faces death in battle: More stands to the Church as Aristotle's soldier stands to the City. The two may seem to come apart because More was isolated in martyrdom, whereas soldiers are engaged in joint defense, but More had to understand himself in relation to the larger community of the Church in order to make the choice that he made. There was a question of a common good at issue. In general, Hursthouse accepts that some kinds of acts, as such, are avoidance-worthy: she takes seriously Aristotle's suggestion that some kinds of acts are such that the very description of the act-type – the name of the kind of act in question – "connotes depravity," and she is willing to urge that such acts are appropriate subjects of moral prohibition.[26] It is unclear how this view is to be grounded apart from general consideration of character – which is the line of defense Geach imagines for analytic Aristotelians.

Analytic Aristotelians also could appeal to the *telos* of More's act. More hoped for beatific union with God; although this end is not attainable by human means, a life lived in obedience to Church authority *is* the available means for directing one's life to God. Officially endorsing the King's claim required defying the Church. More was prepared neither to embrace the

---

[26] Hursthouse 1999, 83–7; see also Hursthouse 1984.

new church the King had made, nor to swear an oath that he recognized the King's authority to remake the Church.[27]

Geach will find appeal to More's end as suspicious as appeal to his character. Geach takes it that the believer has two things to say that are closed to non-theist virtue ethics. First, the believer understands that he will need to account for his acts before God, and signing was, for More, tantamount to defying God. Second, faith provides assurance that, ultimately, no good can come of wrongdoing. God makes it such that we are always in error if we think that we can secure great good, or avoid great evil, through wrongdoing.[28]

There has been scholarly controversy over Aquinas's work on moral prohibition.[29] The prohibition at issue for More was the prohibition on lying and, in this case, on an act of lying that would count as a mortal sin.[30] It is a lie about God and the authority of the Church, invited by a King who was actively turning away from God in order to secure temporal advantage, and can be contrasted with a lie about contingent matters that harms no neighbor. As such, it is a lie directed at More's relation to God and at More's right relation to the King, packaged as perjury. There is no sense in which such a lie can be other than a mortal sin. Refusing to sign is not merely a matter of preserving personal integrity or pursuing one of any private ends. It is a matter of siding with knowledge of one's nature, one's right relations with others, and the relation between humans and God. Whether or not Geach has fastened upon the right aspects of the relevant order – fear of judgment, faith in the understanding that no good can come of mortal sin – the appropriate context for understanding More's refusal is theological understanding of relations between humans and between humans and God.

I think that it is hard to avoid the sense that attention to theological context provides the more satisfying account of the prohibition. The analytic neo-Aristotelian could respond that being unable to face oneself, or being unable to face fellow members of one's community, or one's children, is a very serious matter, adding that, without the fixed points provided by moral prohibition, we cannot give an adequate account of virtue. Then too, the analytic philosopher could suggest that centuries of Christian influence

---

[27] I am grateful to Gabriel Lear for this suggestion.
[28] O'Brien 2011 considers Geach's view in detail. See chapter 3: "The authority of morality."
[29] For a good survey of the scholarship, see Dedek 1979.
[30] For discussion of these matters, see Dewan 1997.

in practical philosophy inspires the expectation that there is more to be said on behalf of respecting moral prohibitions than non-theists can say.[31]

14.6 Conclusion

I have canvassed various aspects of analytic virtue ethics produced in response to Anscombe's call – work that draws from both Aristotle and Aquinas. In so doing, I have pointed to a number of places where Aquinas seems to be at odds with Aristotle, and where both Aquinas and Aristotle seem to be at odds with analytic Aristotelianism. I gave special attention to questions about moral prohibitions, stressing that moral prohibitions provide the few specific fixed points for ethical deliberation for both Aquinas and Aristotle.

Although moral prohibitions offer genuine fixed points for ethical practical deliberation and may in fact be indispensable for ethics, having a sound system of moral prohibitions in place does not exhaust ethics. Anscombe makes the point this way:

> A morality which consisted solely of absolute prohibitions on fairly definitely described actions would leave you free to do anything else whatsoever. Such in fact is not our morality; we have absolute prohibitions indeed, but you would not be guaranteed to do no wrong purely by abstaining from what they positively prohibited. Take lying. If you are not to lie, that doesn't tell you what you are to do in a particular situation: tell the truth? Mislead in some other way? Turn the subject? Make a joke? Say nothing? Lose your temper? Or whatever else might be a good course of action. Nor is it always clear what committing the offending action is. (Anscombe 2008, 231)

Still, Anscombe took it that developing an account of moral prohibition was crucial for analytic ethics, and it seems that much of the work is yet to be done.

---

[31] Hursthouse and I considered this possibility in conversation.

Bibliography

PRIMARY SOURCES

Albert the Great (1890–99). *B. Alberti Magni Ratisbonensis episcopi, Ordinis Praedicatorum, Opera omnia*, ed. A. Borgnet. 38 vols. Paris: Vivès.

(1951–). *Alberti Magni Opera omnia*, ed. B. Geyer *et al.* Münster: Aschendorff (Editio Coloniensis).

Aquinas (1852–73). *Sancti Thomae Aquinatis, Doctoris Angelici, Ordinis Praedicatorum Opera omnia, ad fidem optimarum editionum accurate recognita.* 25 vols. Parma: Typis Petri Fiaccadori. Repr. New York: Musurgia, 1948–50.

(1882–). *Opera omnia, iussu Leonis XIII edita cura et studio Fratrum Praedicatorum.* Rome.

(1929–47). *Scriptum super libros Sententiarum magistri Petri Lombardi Episcopi Parisiensis*, ed. P. F. Mandonnet (vols. 1–2) and M. F. Moos (vols. 3–4). Paris: Lethielleux.

(1941). *Summa theologiae, cura et studio Instituti Studiorum Medievalium Ottaviensis.* Ottawa: Garden City Press.

(1947–48). *Summa theologica.* Translated by the Fathers of the English Dominican Province. New York: Benziger Bros. Repr. Scotts Valley, CA: NovAntiqua, 2008–.

(1950). *In librum Beati Dionysii De divinis nominibus expositio*, ed. C. Pera, P. Caramello, and C. Mazzantini. Rome and Turin: Marietti.

(1953). *Super Epistolas S. Pauli lectura*, vol. I, *Super Epistolam ad Romanos lectura*, ed. R. Cai. 8th edn. Turin and Rome: Marietti.

(1964–80). *Summa theologiae.* Latin and English. Translated by the Fathers of the English Dominican Province. 61 vols. New York: McGraw-Hill.

(1965). *Quaestiones disputatae*, ed. P. Bazzi, M. Calcaterra, T. S. Centi, E. Odetto, and P. M. Pession. 2 vols. 10th edn. Turin and Rome: Marietti.

(1981). *Summa Theologica.* Translated by Fathers of the English Dominican Province. Westminster, MD: Christian Classics.

(1993). *Commentary on Aristotle's Nicomachean Ethics.* Translated by C. J. Litzinger. Notre Dame, IN: Dumb Ox Books.

(1999). *Disputed Questions on Virtue.* Translated by R. McInerny. South Bend, IN: St. Augustine's Press.

Aristoteles Latinus (1972–74). *Ethica Nicomachea*, ed. R. A. Gauthier. 5 vols. Aristoteles Latinus 26/1–3. Leiden: Brill; Brussels: Desclée de Brouwer.

(1976). *Metaphysica. Translatio Anonyma sive "Media,"* ed. G. Vuillemin-Diem. Aristoteles Latinus 25/2. Leiden: Brill.

(1995). *Metaphysica. Recensio et Translatio Guillelmi de Moerbeka*, ed. G. Vuillemin-Diem. Aristoteles Latinus 25/3.2. Leiden, New York, and Cologne: Brill.

Aristotle (1967). *Nikomachische Ethik.* Übersetzt und kommentiert von Franz Dirlmeier. Berlin: Akademie Verlag.

(1980). *Nicomachean Ethics.* Translated by D. Ross, revised by J. L. Ackrill and J. O. Urmson. Oxford: Oxford University Press.

(1999). *Nicomachean Ethics.* Translated, with introduction, notes, and glossary, by T. H. Irwin. 2nd edn. Indianapolis, IN and Cambridge: Hackett.

(2002). *Nicomachean Ethics.* Translation (with historical introduction) by C. Rowe; philosophical introduction and commentary by S. Broadie. Oxford and New York: Oxford University Press.

Aspasius (1889). *Aspasii in Ethica Nicomachea quae supersunt commentaria*, ed. G. Heylbut. Commentaria in Aristotelem Graeca 19,1. Berlin: G. Reimer.

Augustine (1900). *De mendacio*, ed. J. Zycha, 411–66. Corpus Scriptorum Ecclesiasticorum Latinorum 41. Prague and Vienna: F. Tempsky; Leipzig: G. Freytag.

(1955). *De ciuitate Dei libri* xx, ed. B. Dombart and A. Kalb. 2 vols. Corpus Christianorum Series Latina 47–48. Turnhout: Brepols.

(1960). *The Confessions of St. Augustine.* Translated with an introduction and notes by J. K. Ryan. Garden City, N.Y.: Image Books.

(1962). *De doctrina christiana, libri* IV, ed. J. Martin. Corpus Christianorum Series Latina 32. Turnhout: Brepols.

(1969). *Enchiridion ad Laurentium de fide et spe et caritate*, ed. E. Evans, 21–114. Corpus Christianorum Series Latina 46. Turnhout: Brepols.

(1970). *De libro arbitrio*, ed. William Green. Corpus Christianorum Series Latina 29. Turnhout: Brepols.

(1984). *Retractationes*, ed. A. Mutzenbecher. Corpus Christianorum Series Latina 57. Turnhout: Brepols.

(1998). *De civitate dei.* Translated by R. W. Dyson. Cambridge: Cambridge University Press.

Averroes (1953). *Commentarium magnum in Aristotelis De anima libros*, ed. F. Stuart Crawford. Cambridge, MA: The Mediaeval Academy of America.

Avicenna (1977–80). *Liber de philosophia prima sive scientia divina*, ed. S. Van Riet. 2 vols. Avicenna Latinus 3–4. Leuven: Peeters; Leiden: Brill.

Cicero, Marcus Tullius (1977). *Rhetorici libri duo qui vocantur de inventione*, ed. E. Strobel. Stuttgart: Teubner. Repr. of the 1905 edn.

Eustratius (1892). *Eustratii et Michaelis et anonyma in Ethica Nicomachea commentaria*, ed. G. Heylbut, 1–121 and 256–406. Commentaria in Aristotelem Graeca 20. Berlin: G. Reimer.

Heliodorus (1889). *Heliodori in Ethica Nicomachea Paraphrasis*, ed. G. Heylbut. Commentaria in Aristotelem Graeca 19,2. Berlin: G. Reimer.

John Duns Scotus (1950–). *Doctoris subtilis et mariani Ioannis Duns Scoti Ordinis Fratrum Minorum Opera omnia*, ed. C. Balić *et al.* Rome: Typis Vaticanis. (Editio Vaticana).
  (1997–2006). *Opera Philosophica*, ed. G. J. Etzkorn, T. B. Noone, *et al.* 5 vols. St. Bonaventure, N.Y.: Franciscan Institute; Washington, DC: The Catholic University of America Press.
Nemesius (1975). *De natura hominis: Traduction de Burgundio de Pise*, ed. G. Verbeke and J. R. Moncho. Leiden: Brill.
Peter Lombard (1971–81). *Sententiae in IV libris distinctae.* 2 vols. 3rd edn. Spicilegium Bonaventurianum 4–5. Grottaferrata, Rome: Editiones Collegii S. Bonaventurae Ad Claras Aquas.
Philip the Chancellor (1985). *Philippi Cancellarii Parisiensis Summa de bono*, ed. N. Wicki. 2 vols. Bern: Editiones Francke.
Plato (1967). *Platonis Opera*, ed. J. Burnet. 5 vols. Oxford: Clarendon Press.
Pseudo-Dionysius (1990). *De divinis nominibus*, ed. B. R. Suchla. Berlin and New York: Walter de Gruyter.

SECONDARY SOURCES

Adams, D. (1991). Aquinas on Aristotle on happiness. *Medieval Philosophy and Theology*, 1: 98–118.
Adams, R. M. (2006). *A Theory of Virtue: Excellence in Being for the Good.* Oxford: Oxford University Press.
Anagnostopoulos, G. (1994). *Aristotle on the Goals and Exactness of Ethics.* Berkeley, CA: University of California Press.
Anscombe, G. E. M. (1958). Modern moral philosophy. *Philosophy*, 33: 1–19. Repr. in *The Collected Philosophical Papers of G. E. M. Anscombe*, vol. 3, *Ethics, Religion and Politics*, 26–42. Minneapolis, MN: University of Minnesota Press, 1981.
  (1979). Under a description. *Nous*, 13: 219–33.
  (1982). Action, intention, and "double effect." *Proceedings of the American Catholic Philosophical Association*, 56: 12–25. Repr. in *Human Life, Action, and Ethics: Essays by G. E. M. Anscombe*, ed. M. Geach and L. Gormally, 207–26. Exeter, UK; Charlottesville, VA: Imprint Academic, 2005.
  (1995). Practical inference. In *Virtues and Reasons: Philippa Foot and Moral Theory*, ed. R. Hursthouse, G. Lawrence, and W. Quinn, 1–34. Oxford: Clarendon Press.
  (2000). *Intention.* Cambridge, MA: Harvard University Press.
  (2008). The moral environment of the child. In *Faith in a Hard Ground: Essays on Religion, Philosophy and Ethics by G. E. M. Anscombe*, ed. M. Geach and L. Gormally, 224–33. Exeter, UK; Charlottesville, VA: Imprint Academic.
Aubenque, P. (1995). The twofold natural foundation of justice according to Aristotle. In *Aristotle and Moral Realism*, ed. R. Heinaman, 35–47. Boulder, CO: Westview Press.

Baldwin, J. W. (1959). *Medieval Theories of the Just Price: Romanists, Canonists and Theologians in the Twelfth and Thirteenth Centuries.* Philadelphia, PA: Transactions of the American Philosophical Society.

Barnes, J. (1981). Aristotle and the methods of ethics. *Revue Internationale de la Philosophie,* 34: 490–511.

Barnwell, M. (2010). Aquinas's two different accounts of *akrasia. American Catholic Philosophical Quarterly,* 84: 49–67.

Bejczy, I., ed. (2008). *Virtue Ethics in the Middle Ages: Commentaries on Aristotle's* Nicomachean Ethics, *1200–1500.* Leiden and Boston, MA: Brill.

Bennett, J. (1974). *Kant's Dialectic.* Cambridge: Cambridge University Press.

Blanchette, O. (1994). The logic of perfection in Aquinas. In *Thomas Aquinas and His Legacy,* ed. D. M. Gallagher, 107–30. Washington, DC: The Catholic University of America Press.

Bossi de Kirchner, B. (1986). Aquinas as an interpreter of Aristotle on the end of human life. *The Review of Metaphysics,* 40: 41–54.

Bostock, D. (1994). *Aristotle, Metaphysics: Books Z and H.* Translated with a commentary. Oxford: Clarendon Press.

(2000). *Aristotle's Ethics.* Oxford: Oxford University Press.

Bourke, V. J. (1974). The *Nicomachean Ethics* and Thomas Aquinas. In *St. Thomas Aquinas 1274–1974 Commemorative Studies,* ed. A. Maurer, I: 239–59. Toronto: Pontifical Institute of Mediaeval Studies.

Bowlin, J. (1999). *Contingency and Fortune in Aquinas's Ethics.* Cambridge: Cambridge University Press.

Boyle, M. *Additive theories of rationality.* Manuscript.
Essentially rational animals. Manuscript.

Boyle, M. and Lavin, D. (2010). Goodness and desire. In *Desire, Practical Reason, and the Good,* ed. S. Tennenbaum, 161–201. Oxford: Oxford University Press.

Bradley, D. J. M. (1997). *Aquinas on the Twofold Human Good: Reason and Human Happiness in Aquinas's Moral Science.* Washington, DC: The Catholic University of America Press.

(2008). Thomas Aquinas on weakness of the will. In *Weakness of Will from Plato to the Present,* ed. T. Hoffmann, 82–114. Washington, DC: The Catholic University of America Press.

Broadie, S. (1991). *Ethics with Aristotle.* New York and Oxford: Oxford University Press.

Brochard, V. (2009). The theory of pleasure according to Epicurus. *Interpretation,* 37: 47–83.

Brock, S. L. (1998). *Action and Conduct: Thomas Aquinas and the Theory of Action.* Edinburgh: T&T Clark.

Burger, R. (2008). *Aristotle's Dialogue with Socrates: On the* Nicomachean Ethics. Chicago and London: The University of Chicago Press.

Burnet, J. (1900). *The Ethics of Aristotle.* London: Methuen.

Butera, G. (2006). On reason's control of the passions in Aquinas's theory of temperance. *Mediaeval Studies,* 68: 133–60.

Caldera, R. T. (1980). *Le jugement par inclination chez saint Thomas d'Aquin*. Paris: Vrin.

Cates, D. F. (2002). The virtue of temperance (IIa IIae, qq. 141–70). In *The Ethics of Aquinas*, ed. S. J. Pope, 321–39. Washington, DC: Georgetown University Press.

Celano, A. J. (1986). The understanding of the concept of *felicitas* in the pre-1250 commentaries on the *Ethica Nicomachea*. *Medioevo*, 12: 29–53.

(1987). The concept of worldly beatitude in the writings of Thomas Aquinas. *Journal of the History of Philosophy*, 25: 215–26.

(1995). The end of practical wisdom: Ethics as a science in the thirteenth century. *Journal of the History of Philosophy*, 33: 224–43.

Chenu, M.-D. (1950). *Introduction à l'étude de St. Thomas d'Aquin*. Paris: Vrin.

(1964). *Toward Understanding Saint Thomas*, translated with authorized corrections and bibliographical additions by A. M. Landry and D. Hughes. Chicago: Regnery.

Cooper, J. M. (1997). *Plato: Complete Works*. Indianapolis, IN and Cambridge: Hackett.

Crisp, R. C. (1994). Aristotle's inclusivism. *Oxford Studies in Ancient Philosophy*, 12: 111–36.

Cunningham, S. B. (2008). *Reclaiming Moral Agency: The Moral Philosophy of Albert the Great*. Washington, DC: The Catholic University of America Press.

Davidson, D. (1980). Intending. In *Essays on Actions and Events*, 82–102. Oxford: Clarendon Press.

De Letter, P. (1954). Original sin, privation of original justice. *The Thomist*, 17: 484–5.

De Young, R. K. (2003). Power made perfect in weakness: Aquinas's transformation of the virtue of courage. *Medieval Philosophy and Theology*, 11: 147–80.

Dedek, J. F. (1979). Intrinsically evil acts: An historical study of the mind of St. Thomas. *The Thomist*, 43: 386–413.

Deman, T. (2006). Appendice II: renseignements techniques. In *Saint Thomas d'Aquin, Somme théologique: La prudence 2a–2æ, Questions 47–56*, translated, with notes and appendices, by T. Deman. 3rd edn, revised by J.-P. Torrell. Paris: Les Éditions du Cerf.

Destrée, P. (2011). Aristotle on responsibility for one's character. In *Moral Psychology and Human Action in Aristotle*, ed. M. Pakaluk and G. Pearson, 285–318. Oxford: Oxford University Press.

Dewan, L. (1997). St. Thomas, lying, and venial sin. *The Thomist*, 61: 279–300.

(2007). *St. Thomas and Form as Something Divine in Things*. Milwaukee, WI: Marquette University Press.

Di Muzio, G. (2000). Aristotle on improving one's character. *Phronesis*, 45: 205–19.

Dihle, A. (1982). *The Theory of Will in Classical Antiquity*. Berkeley, CA: University of California Press.

Doig, J. C. (1993). Aquinas and Jaffa on courage as the ultimate of potency. *Tradition and Renewal: Philosophical Essays Commemorating the Centennial of*

Louvain's Institute of Philosophy, ed. D. Boileau and J. Dick, 2: 13–21. Leuven: Leuven University Press.

(2001). *Aquinas's Philosophical Commentary on the* Ethics: *A Historical Perspective*. The New Synthese Historical Library 50. Dordrecht, Boston, MA, and London: Kluwer.

Doris, J. M. (2002). *Lack of Character: Personality and Moral Behavior*. Cambridge: Cambridge University Press.

Durantel, J. (1919). *Saint Thomas et le Pseudo-Denis*. Paris: Librairie Félix Alcan.

Eardley, P. S. (2003). Thomas Aquinas and Giles of Rome on the will. *The Review of Metaphysics*, 56: 835–62.

Elders, L. J. (1987). *Autour de saint Thomas d'Aquin: recueil d'études sur sa pensée philosophique et théologique*, vol. 1, *Les commentaires sur les œuvres d'Aristote*. Paris: FAC-éditions; Bruges: Tabor.

(2009). The Aristotelian commentaries of St. Thomas Aquinas. *The Review of Metaphysics*, 63: 29–53.

Feingold, L. (2010). *The Natural Desire to See God according to St. Thomas Aquinas and His Interpreters*. 2nd edn. Faith and Reason: Studies in Catholic Theology and Philosophy. Ave Maria, FL: Sapientia Press of Ave Maria University.

Festugière, A. J. (1936). *Aristote, Le Plaisir (Eth. Nic.* VII *11–14,* X *1–5)*. Paris: Vrin. Repr. 1960.

Fiasse, G. (2001). Aristotle's φρόνησις: A true grasp of ends as well as means? *The Review of Metaphysics*, 55: 323–37.

Flannery, K. L. (2008). Anscombe and Aristotle on corrupt minds. *Christian Bioethics*, 14: 151–64.

Foot, P. (1978). Virtues and vices. In *Virtues and Vices and Other Essays in Moral Philosophy*, 1–18. Berkeley, CA: University of California Press.

(2003). *Moral Dilemmas and Other Topics in Moral Philosophy*. Oxford: Clarendon Press.

Ford, A. (2011). Action and generality. In *Essays on Anscombe's Intention*, ed. A. Ford, J. Hornsby, and F. Stoutland, 76–104. Cambridge, MA: Harvard University Press.

Franceschini, E. (1933). *Roberto Grossatesta, vescovo di Lincoln, e le sue traduzioni latine*. Venice: C. Ferrari.

Franklin, J. (1983). Mental furniture from the philosophers. *Et cetera*, 40: 177–91.

Fuchs, M. J. (2011). Die Identität des Freundes: Derrida, Spinoza, Aristoteles. In *Memoria – Intellectus – Voluntas. Festschrift für Erwin Schadel*, ed. C. Schäfer and U. Voigt, 51–66. Frankfurt am Main: Peter Lang.

Gallagher, D. M. (1996). Desire for beatitude and love of friendship in Thomas Aquinas. *Mediaeval Studies*, 58: 1–47.

(1999). Thomas Aquinas on self-love as the basis for love of others. *Acta Philosophica*, 8: 23–44.

Gauthier, R. A. (1951). *Magnanimité: L'idéal de la grandeur dans la philosophie païenne et dans la théologie chrétienne*. Bibliothèque thomiste, 28. Paris: Vrin.

(1954–56). Review of *Thomism and Aristotelianism*, by H. Jaffa. *Bulletin Thomiste*, 9: 157–59.

(1969). Praefatio. In *Sancti Thomae de Aquino Opera Omnia*, vol. 47, *Sententia libri Ethicorum*, 1*–275*. Rome.

(1971). Appendix: Saint Thomas et l'éthique à Nicomaque. In *Sancti Thomae de Aquino Opera Omnia*, vol. 48, *Sententia libri Politicorum / Tabula libri Ethicorum*, v–xxv. Rome.

(1993). *Somme contre les gentils: Introduction.* Paris: Éditions Universitaires.

Gauthier, R. A. and Jolif, J. Y. (1970). *L'éthique à Nicomaque.* 4 vols. 2nd edn. Leuven: Publications universitaires; Paris: Béatrice-Nauwelaerts. Repr. Leuven: Peeters (2002).

Geach, M. (2011). Introduction. In *From Plato to Wittgenstein: Essays by G. E. M. Anscombe*, ed. M. Geach and L. Gormally, xiii–xx. Exeter, UK; Charlottesville, VA: Imprint Academic.

Geach, P. (1978). *God and the Soul.* London: Routledge & Kegan Paul.

Gosling, J. C. B. and Taylor, C. C. W. (1982). *The Greeks on Pleasure.* Oxford: Clarendon Press.

Grabmann, M. (1926). Die Aristoteleskommentare des heiligen Thomas von Aquin. In *Mittelalterliches Geistesleben: Abhandlungen zur Geschichte der Scholastik und Mystik*, 266–313. Munich: Max Hueber Verlag.

Grant, A. (1885). *The Ethics of Aristotle: Illustrated with Notes and Essays.* London: Longmans, Green, & Co.

Gründel, J. (1963). *Die Lehre von den Umständen der menschlichen Handlung im Mittelalter.* Münster: Aschendorff.

Guindon, R. (1956). *Béatitude et théologie morale chez saint Thomas d'Aquin. Origines – Interprétation.* Ottawa: Éditions de l'université d'Ottawa.

Hardie, W. F. R. (1965). The final good in Aristotle's ethics. *Philosophy*, 40: 277–95.

(1980). *Aristotle's Ethical Theory.* 2nd edn. Oxford: Clarendon Press.

Hause, J. (1997). Thomas Aquinas and the voluntarists. *Medieval Philosophy and Theology*, 6: 167–82.

(2007). Aquinas on the function of moral virtue. *American Catholic Philosophical Quarterly*, 81: 1–20.

Heinaman, R. E. (1986). Eudaimonia and self-sufficiency. *Phronesis*, 33: 31–53.

Herdt, J. A. (2008). *Putting On Virtue: The Legacy of the Splendid Vices.* Chicago: University of Chicago Press.

Hibbs, T. S. (2001). *Virtue's Splendor: Wisdom, Prudence and the Human Good.* New York: Fordham University Press.

Hoenen, M. J. F. M. (2002). Transzendenz der Einheit: Thomas von Aquin über Liebe und Freundschaft. In *Ars und scientia im Mittelalter und in der frühen Neuzeit: Ergebnisse interdisziplinärer Forschung. Georg Wieland zum 65. Geburtstag*, ed. Cora Dietl, 125–37. Tübingen: Francke.

Hoffmann, T. (2006). Voluntariness, choice, and will in the *Ethics* commentaries of Albert the Great and Thomas Aquinas. *Documenti e studi sulla tradizione filosofica medievale*, 17: 71–92.

(2007). Aquinas and intellectual determinism: The test case of angelic sin. *Archiv für Geschichte der Philosophie*, 89: 122–56.

(2008). Albert the Great and Thomas Aquinas on magnanimity. In *Virtue Ethics in the Middle Ages: Commentaries on Aristotle's* Nicomachean Ethics, *1200–1500*, ed. I. Bejczy, 101–29. Leiden and Boston, MA: Brill.

(2011). Eutrapelia: The right attitude toward amusement. In *Mots médiévaux offerts à Ruedi Imbach*, ed. I. Atucha, D. Calma, C. König-Pralong, and I. Zavattero, 267–77. F.I.D.E.M. Textes et études du moyen âge 57. Turnhout: Brepols.

Houser, R. E. (2004). *The Cardinal Virtues: Aquinas, Albert, and Philip the Chancellor*. Toronto: Pontifical Institute of Medieval Studies.

Hursthouse, R. (1984). Acting and feeling in character: *Nicomachean Ethics* 3.i. *Phronesis*, 29: 252–66.

(1999). *On Virtue Ethics*. Oxford: Oxford University Press.

Imelmann, J. (1864). *Observationes criticae in Aristotelis Ethica Nicomachea: Dissertatio inauguralis philologica*. Halle: Bernstein.

Irwin, T. H. (1978). First principles in Aristotle's ethics. *Midwest Studies in Philosophy*, 3: 252–72.

(1988). *Aristotle's First Principles*. Oxford: Clarendon Press.

(1992). Who discovered the will? *Philosophical Perspectives*, 6: 453–73.

(2000). Ethics as an inexact science: Aristotle's ambitions for moral theory. In *Moral Particularism*, ed. B. Hooker and M. O. Little, 100–29. Oxford: Clarendon Press.

(2006). Will, responsibility, and ignorance: Aristotelian accounts of incontinence. In *The Problem of Weakness of Will in Medieval Philosophy*, ed. T. Hoffmann, J. Müller, and M. Perkams. Leuven: Peeters, 39–58.

(2007). *The Development of Ethics: A Historical and Critical Study*, vol. 1: *From Socrates to the Reformation*. Oxford and New York: Oxford University Press.

(2012). Conceptions of happiness in the *Nicomachean Ethics*. In *The Oxford Handbook of Aristotle*, ed. C. Shields, 495–528. Oxford: Oxford University Press.

Jaffa, H. V. (1952). *Thomism and Aristotelianism: A Study of the Commentary by Thomas Aquinas on the* Nicomachean Ethics. Chicago: The University of Chicago Press.

Jedan, C. (2000). *Willensfreiheit bei Aristoteles?* Göttingen: Vandenhoeck & Rupprecht.

Jenkins, J. (1996). Expositions of the text: Aquinas's Aristotelian commentaries. *Medieval Philosophy and Theology*, 5: 39–62.

Jordan, M. D. (1991). Thomas Aquinas's disclaimers in the Aristotelian commentaries. In *Philosophy and the God of Abraham: Essays in Memory of James A. Weisheipl, OP*, ed. J. R. Long, 99–112. Papers in Medieval Studies 12. Toronto: Pontifical Institute of Medieval Studies.

(1992). Aquinas reading Aristotle's *Ethics*. In *Ad Litteram: Authoritative Texts and Their Medieval Readers*, ed. M. D. Jordan and K. Emery, Jr., 229–49. Notre Dame, IN: University of Notre Dame Press.

(2004). Thomas as commentator in some programs of neo-Thomism: A reply to Kaczor. *American Catholic Philosophical Quarterly*, 78: 379–86.

(2006). *Rewritten Theology: Aquinas after His Readers*. Oxford: Blackwell Publishing.

Kaczor, C. (2004). Thomas Aquinas's *Commentary on the Ethics*: Merely an interpretation of Aristotle? *American Catholic Philosophical Quarterly*, 78: 353–78.

Kenny, A. (1992). *Aristotle on the Perfect Life*. Oxford: Clarendon Press.

(1999). Aquinas on Aristotelian happiness. In *Aquinas's Moral Theory*, ed. S. MacDonald and E. Stump, 15–27. Ithaca, NY and London: Cornell University Press. Repr. in A. Kenny, *Essays on the Aristotelian Tradition*, 32–46. Cambridge: Cambridge University Press (2000).

Kent, B. (1989). Transitory vice: Thomas Aquinas on incontinence. *Journal of the History of Philosophy*, 27: 199–223.

(1995). *Virtues of the Will: The Transformation of Ethics in the Late Thirteenth Century*. Washington, DC: The Catholic University of America Press.

(2007). Aquinas and weakness of will. *Philosophy and Phenomenological Research*, 75: 70–91.

Keys, M. M. (2003). Aquinas and the challenge of Aristotelian magnanimity. *History of Political Thought*, 24: 37–65.

Kleber, H. (1988). *Glück als Lebensziel: Untersuchungen zur Philosophie des Glücks bei Thomas von Aquin*. Beiträge zur Geschichte der Philosophie und Theologie des Mittelalters – Neue Folge 31. Münster: Aschendorff.

Kluxen, W. (1998). *Philosophische Ethik bei Thomas von Aquin*. 3rd edn. Hamburg: Felix Meiner.

Knobel, A. M. (2004). The infused and acquired virtues in Aquinas' moral philosophy. Ph.D. dissertation, University of Notre Dame.

(2010). Can Aquinas's infused and acquired virtues coexist in the Christian life? *Studies in Christian Ethics*, 23: 381–96.

Kraut, R. (1989). *Aristotle on the Human Good*. Princeton, NJ: Princeton University Press.

(2002). *Aristotle: Political Philosophy*. Oxford: Oxford University Press.

(2012). Aristotle's ethics. *The Stanford Encyclopedia of Philosophy* (Spring 2012 edn), ed. E. N. Zalta. Stanford, CA: Stanford University.

Kretzmann, N. (1988). Warring against the law of my mind: Aquinas on Romans 7. In *Philosophy and Christian Faith*, ed. T. V. Morris, 172–95. Notre Dame, IN: Notre Dame University Press.

Lear, G. R. (2004). *Happy Lives and the Highest Good*. Princeton, NJ: Princeton University Press.

Leonhardt, R. (1998). *Glück als Vollendung des Menschseins: Die beatitudo-Lehre des Thomas von Aquin im Horizont des Eudämonismus-Problems*. Berlin and New York: de Gruyter.

Lottin, O. (1957). Libre arbitre et liberté depuis saint Anselme jusqu'à la fin du XIIIe siècle. In *Psychologie et morale aux XIIᵉ et XIIIᵉ siècles*, 1: 11–389. 2nd edn. Gembloux: J. Duculot.

MacDonald, S. (1998). Aquinas's libertarian account of free choice. *Revue internationale de philosophie*, 52: 309–28.

MacIntyre, A. (1988). *Whose Justice? Which Rationality?* London: Duckworth.

(1990). *Three Rival Versions of Moral Inquiry: Encyclopaedia, Genealogy, and Tradition.* London: Duckworth.

(2007). *After Virtue: A Study in Moral Theory.* 3rd edn. Notre Dame, IN: University of Notre Dame Press.

(2009). Intractable moral disagreements. In *Intractable Disputes about the Natural Law: Alasdair MacIntyre and Critics*, ed. Lawrence S. Cunningham, 1–52. Notre Dame, IN: University of Notre Dame Press.

Mansini, G. (1995). *Duplex amor* and the structure of love in Aquinas. In *Thomistica*, ed. E. Manning, 137–96. Recherches de théologie ancienne et médiévale, Supplementa 1. Leuven: Peeters.

McCluskey, C. (2002). Intellective appetite and the freedom of human action. *The Thomist*, 66: 421–56.

McDowell, J. (1998). *Mind, Value, and Reality.* Cambridge, MA: Harvard University Press.

McEvoy, J. (1993). Amitié, attirance et amour chez S. Thomas d'Aquin. *Revue philosophique de Louvain*, 91: 383–408.

(1996). Zur Rezeption des Aristotelischen Freundschaftsbegriffs in der Scholastik. *Freiburger Zeitschrift für Philosophie und Theologie*, 43: 287–303.

McGrade, A. S. (1996). Aristotle's place in the history of natural rights. *The Review of Metaphysics*, 49: 803–29.

McInerny, R. (1993). Foreword. In *St. Thomas Aquinas: Commentary on Aristotle's Nicomachean Ethics*, translated by C. I. Litzinger. Notre Dame, IN: Dumb Ox Books.

Melina, L. (1987). *La conoscenza morale: Linee di riflessione sul commento di san Tommaso all'Etica Nicomachea.* Rome: Città Nuova Editrice.

Moss, J. (2011). "Virtue makes the goal right": Virtue and *phronesis* in Aristotle's ethics. *Phronesis*, 56: 204–61.

Müller, J. (2001). *Natürliche Moral und philosophische Ethik bei Albertus Magnus.* Beiträge zur Geschichte der Philosophie und Theologie des Mittelalters – Neue Folge 59. Münster: Aschendorff.

(2006). Der Einfluss der arabischen Intellektspekulation auf die Ethik des Albertus Magnus. In *Wissen über Grenzen: Arabisches Wissen und lateinisches Mittelalter*, ed. A. Speer and L. Wegener, 545–68. Miscellanea Mediaevalia 33. Berlin and New York: de Gruyter.

(2008). In war and peace: The virtue of courage in the writings of Albert the Great and Thomas Aquinas. In *Virtue Ethics in the Middle Ages: Commentaries on Aristotle's Nicomachean Ethics, 1200–1500*, ed. I. Bejczy, 77–99. Leiden and Boston, MA: Brill.

(2009a). La vie humaine comme un tout hiérarchique – Félicité contemplative et vie active chez Albert le Grand. In *Vie active et vie contemplative au Moyen Age et au seuil de la Renaissance*, ed. C. Trottmann, 241–63. Rome: Ecole française de Rome.

(2009b). *Willensschwäche in Antike und Mittelalter: Eine Problemgeschichte von Sokrates bis Johannes Duns Scotus.* Leuven: Leuven University Press.

Murphy, C. E. (1999). Aquinas on our responsibility for our emotions. *Medieval Philosophy and Theology*, 8: 163–205.

Nussbaum, M. (1986). *The Fragility of Goodness: Luck and Ethics in Greek Tragedy and Philosophy*. Cambridge: Cambridge University Press.

Nygren, A. (1953). *Agape and Eros*. Philadelphia, PA: Westminster Press.

O'Brien, M. (2011). Practical necessity: A study in ethics, law, and human action. Ph.D. dissertation, University of Texas at Austin.

Owen, G. E. L. (1971–72). Aristotelian pleasures. *Proceedings of the Aristotelian Society*, 72: 135–52.

Owens, J. (1974). Aquinas as an Aristotelian commentator. In *St. Thomas Aquinas 1274–1974 Commemorative Studies*, ed. A. Maurer, 1: 213–38. Toronto: Pontifical Institute of Mediaeval Studies.

(1978). *The Doctrine of Being in the Aristotelian Metaphysics: A Study in the Greek Background of Mediaeval Thought*. 3rd edn. Toronto: Pontifical Institute of Mediaeval Studies.

(1990). *Towards a Christian Philosophy*. Washington, DC: The Catholic University of America Press.

(1996). *Some Philosophical Issues in Moral Matters: The Collected Ethical Writings of Joseph Owens*, ed. D. J. Billy and T. Kennedy. Rome: Editiones Academiae Alphonsianae.

Pakaluk, M. (2005). *Aristotle's Nicomachean Ethics: An Introduction*. Cambridge: Cambridge University Press.

(2011). On the unity of the *Nicomachean Ethics*. In *Aristotle's* Nicomachean Ethics*: A Critical Guide*, ed. J. Miller, 23–44. Cambridge: Cambridge University Press.

Pangle, L. S. (2003). *Aristotle and the Philosophy of Friendship*. Cambridge: Cambridge University Press.

Papadis, D. (1980). *Die Rezeption der Nikomachischen Ethik des Aristoteles bei Thomas von Aquin: Eine vergleichende Untersuchung*. Frankfurt am Main: R. G. Fischer.

Pasnau, R. (2002). *Thomas Aquinas on Human Nature: A Philosophical Study of Summa theologiae Ia 75–89*. Cambridge: Cambridge University Press.

Payer, P. J. (1979). Prudence and the principles of natural law: A medieval development. *Speculum*, 54: 55–70.

Pears, D. (1980). Courage as a mean. In *Essays on Aristotle's Ethics*, ed. A. O. Rorty, 171–88. Berkeley, CA: University of California Press.

Pegis, A. C. (1963). St. Thomas and the *Nicomachean Ethics*: Some reflections on *Summa contra gentiles* III, 44, § 5. *Mediaeval Studies*, 25: 1–25.

Pelzer, A. (1964). Les versions latines des ouvrages de morale conservés sous le nom d'Aristote en usage au XIIIe siècle. In *Etudes d'histoire littéraire sur la scolastique médiévale*, ed. A. Pattin and E. van de Vyver, 120–87. Leuven: Publications Universitaires.

Perkams, M. (2005). Gewissensirrtum und Gewissensfreiheit: Überlegungen im Anschluß an Thomas von Aquin und Albertus Magnus. *Philosophisches Jahrbuch*, 112: 31–50.

(2008a). Aquinas's interpretation of the Aristotelian virtue of justice and his doctrine of natural law. In *Virtue Ethics in the Middle Ages: Commentaries on Aristotle's Nicomachean Ethics, 1200–1500*, ed. I. Bejczy, 131–50. Leiden and Boston, MA: Brill.

(2008b). Naturgesetz, Selbstbestimmung und Moralität: Thomas von Aquin und die Begründung einer zeitgemäßen Ethik. *Studia Neoaristotelica*, 5: 109–31.

(2008c). Augustinus' Auseinandersetzung mit der stoischen Schicksalslehre in *De civitate Dei* 5. *Gymnasium*, 115: 347–59.

Piché, D. (1999). *La condamnation Parisienne de 1277*. Texte latin, traduction et introduction. Paris: Vrin.

Pickavé, M. (2008). Thomas von Aquin: Emotionen als Leidenschaften der Seele. In *Klassische Emotionstheorien: Von Platon bis Wittgenstein*, ed. H. Landweer and U. Renz, 187–204. Berlin: De Gruyter.

Pickavé, M. and Whiting, J. (2008). *Nicomachean Ethics* 7.3 on akratic ignorance. *Oxford Studies in Ancient Philosophy*, 34: 323–71.

Porter, J. (1989). Moral rules and moral actions: A comparison of Aquinas and modern moral theology. *The Journal of Religious Ethics*, 17: 123–49.

(1992). The subversion of virtue: Acquired and infused virtues in the *Summa theologiae*. *The Annual of the Society of Christian Ethics*: 19–41.

Price, A. W. (1980). Aristotle's ethical holism. *Mind*, 89: 338–52.

(1989). *Love and Friendship in Plato and Aristotle*. Oxford: Clarendon Press.

(2011). Aristotle on the ends of deliberation. In *Moral Psychology and Human Action in Aristotle*, ed. M. Pakaluk and G. Pearson, 135–58. Oxford and New York: Oxford University Press.

Quinn, W. S. (1989). Actions, intentions, and consequences: The doctrine of double effect. *Philosophy and Public Affairs*, 18: 334–51.

(1993). *Morality and Action*, ed. P. Foot. Cambridge: Cambridge University Press.

Reeve, C. D. C. (2012). *Action, Contemplation, and Happiness: An Essay on Aristotle*. Cambridge, MA and London: Harvard University Press.

Reichberg, G. (2010). Aquinas on battlefield courage. *The Thomist*, 74: 337–68.

Rhonheimer, M. (1994). *Praktische Vernunft und Vernünftigkeit der Praxis: Handlungstheorie bei Thomas von Aquin in ihrer Entstehung aus dem Problemkontext der aristotelischen Ethik*. Berlin: Akademie Verlag.

Ritchie, D. G. (1894). Aristotle's subdivisions of particular justice. *Classical Review*, 8 (5): 185–92.

Ross, W. D. (1923). *Aristotle*. London: Methuen.

Saarinen, R. (1994). *Weakness of the Will in Medieval Thought: From Augustine to Buridan*. Studien und Texte zur Geistesgeschichte des Mittelalters 44. Leiden, New York, and Cologne: Brill.

Schwartz, D. (2007). *Aquinas on Friendship*. Oxford: Clarendon Press.

Shanley, B. (2008). Aquinas's exemplar ethics. *The Thomist*, 72: 345–69.

Sherwin, M. S. (2005). *By Knowledge and By Love: Charity and Knowledge in the Moral Theology of St. Thomas Aquinas*. Washington, DC: The Catholic University of America Press.

(2009). Infused virtue and the effects of acquired vice: A test case for the Thomistic theory of infused cardinal virtues. *The Thomist*, 73: 29–52.

Shorey, P. (1938). *Platonism Ancient and Modern*. Berkeley, CA: University of California Press.

Sidgwick, H. (1886). *Outlines of the History of Ethics for English Readers*. London and New York: Macmillan.

Slade, F. (1997). Ends and purposes. In *Final Causality in Nature and Human Affairs*, ed. R. F. Hassing, 83–5. Washington, DC: The Catholic University of America Press.

Slote, M. (2003). *Morals from Motives*. Oxford and New York: Oxford University Press.

Sokolowski, R. (2000). *Introduction to Phenomenology*. New York: Cambridge University Press.

  (2001). Friendship and moral action in Aristotle. *The Journal of Value Inquiry*, 35: 355–69.

Sorabji, R. (1980). *Necessity, Cause and Blame: Perspectives on Aristotle's Theory*. London: Duckworth.

Steel, C. (2001). *Der Adler und die Nachteule: Thomas und Albert über die Möglichkeit der Metaphysik*. Lectio Albertina 9. Münster: Aschendorff.

Stewart, J. A. (1892). *Notes on the* Nicomachean Ethics *of Aristotle*. 2 vols. Oxford: Clarendon Press.

Strohl, M. S. (2011). Pleasure as perfection: *Nicomachean Ethics* 10.4–5. *Oxford Studies in Ancient Philosophy*, 41: 257–87.

Stump, E. (2003). *Aquinas*. London and New York: Routledge.

  (2011). The non-Aristotelian character of Aquinas's ethics: Aquinas on the passions. *Faith and Philosophy*, 28: 29–43.

Susemihl, F., and Apelt, O., eds. (1912). *Aristotelis Ethica Nicomachea*. Teubner: Leipzig.

Suto, T. (2004). Virtue and knowledge: Connatural knowledge according to Thomas Aquinas. *The Review of Metaphysics*, 58: 61–79.

Thompson, M. (2004). What is it to wrong someone? A puzzle about justice. In *Reason and Value: Themes from the Moral Philosophy of Joseph Raz*, ed. R. J. Wallace, P. Pettit, S. Scheffler, and M. Smith, 333–84. Oxford: Clarendon Press.

  (2008). *Life and Action: Elementary Structures of Practice and Practical Thought*. Cambridge, MA: Harvard University Press.

Tomarchio, J. (2001). Aquinas's division of being according to modes of existing. *The Review of Metaphysics*, 54: 585–613.

Torrell, J.-P. (2005). *Saint Thomas Aquinas*, vol. 1, *The Person and His Work*. Translated by R. Royal. Revised edn. Washington, DC: The Catholic University of America Press.

Urmson, J. O. (1980). Aristotle's doctrine of the mean. In *Essays on Aristotle's Ethics*, ed. A. O. Rorty, 157–10. Berkeley, CA: University of California Press.

Vaccarezza, M. S. (2012). *Le ragioni del contingente: La saggezza pratica tra Aristotele e Tommaso d'Aquino*. Naples: Orthotes.

Van Riel, G. (2000). *Pleasure and the Good Life: Plato, Aristotle, and the Neoplatonists*. Leiden, Boston, MA, and Cologne: Brill.

Vogler, C. (2002). *Reasonably Vicious*. Cambridge, MA: Harvard University Press.

Weisheipl, J. A. (1983). *Friar Thomas d'Aquino: His Life, Thought, and Works*. Washington, DC: The Catholic University of America Press.

Westberg, D. (1994a). *Right Practical Reason: Aristotle, Action, and Prudence in Aquinas*. Oxford: Clarendon.

(1994b). Did Aquinas change his mind about the will? *The Thomist*, 58: 41–60.

(2002). Good and evil in human acts (Ia IIae, qq. 18–21). In *The Ethics of Aquinas*, ed. S. J. Pope, 90–102. Washington, DC: Georgetown University Press.

White, K. (1993). The virtues of man the *animal sociale*: *affabilitas* and *veritas* in Aquinas. *The Thomist*, 57: 641–53.

(2011). Friendship degree zero: Aquinas on good will. *Nova et Vetera*, English edn 9: 479–518.

Wieland, G. (1981). *Ethica – Scientia practica: Die Anfänge der philosophischen Ethik im 13. Jahrhundert*. Beiträge zur Geschichte der Philosophie und Theologie des Mittelalters – Neue Folge 21. Münster: Aschendorff.

(1982). The reception and interpretation of Aristotle's *Ethics*. In *The Cambridge History of Later Medieval Philosophy: From the Rediscovery of Aristotle to the Disintegration of Scholasticism, 1100–1600*, ed. N. Kretzmann, A. Kenny, and J. Pinborg, 657–72. Cambridge: Cambridge University Press.

Wohlman, A. (1981). Amour du bien propre et amour de soi dans la doctrine thomiste de l'amour. *Revue Thomiste*, 81: 204–34.

Wolter, A. B. (1990). Duns Scotus on the will as a rational potency. In *The Philosophical Theology of John Duns Scotus*, ed. M. M. Adams, 181–206. Ithaca, NY: Cornell University Press.

Yamamoto, Y. (2008). Thomas Aquinas on the ontology of *Amicitia*: *Unio* and *Communicatio*. *Proceedings of the American Catholic Philosophical Association*, 81: 251–62.

Young, C. (2009). Courage. In *A Companion to Aristotle*, ed. G. Anagnostopoulus, 442–56. Oxford: Wiley-Blackwell.

Zanatta, M. (1986). *Aristotele, Etica Nicomachea: introduzione, traduzione e commento*. Milan: Biblioteca Universale Rizzoli.

Zembaty, J. S. (1993). Aristotle on lying. *Journal of the History of Philosophy* 31: 7–29.

Index of names

For EU product safety concerns, contact us at Calle de José Abascal, 56–1°, 28003 Madrid, Spain or eugpsr@cambridge.org.

www.ingramcontent.com/pod-product-compliance
Ingram Content Group UK Ltd.
Pitfield, Milton Keynes, MK11 3LW, UK
UKHW020335140625

459647UK00018B/2160

* 9 7 8 1 1 0 7 5 7 6 4 0 7 *